PUBLIC PLUNDER

David Loth

PUBLIC PLUNDER

A History of Graft in America

GREENWOOD PRESS, PUBLISHERS
WESTPORT, CONNECTICUT

First Greenwood Reprinting 1970

Library of Congress Catalogue Card Number 71-109295

SBN 8371-3838-8

Printed in the United States of America

"There is no kind of dishonesty into which otherwise good people more easily and frequently fall than that of defrauding the government."—*Benjamin Franklin.*

CONTENTS

PUBLIC PLUNDER

I

F. F. V.

1

CAPTAIN SAMUEL ARGALL brought the good ship *George* to anchor off Point Comfort on a calm May morning in 1617, and saw Opportunity lurking in the mists that lent the Virginia coastline a pleasant vagueness. Other men who had passed that way—Raleigh, Lord de la Warr, Captain John Smith and their like—had also seen the vision. But to them it had appeared in a golden haze shot through with precious stones.

Captain Argall's dreams were of a more practical nature. He proposed as Governor of Virginia to achieve riches by prosaic administration of that post in the English manner. He had not been privileged to acquire experience in civil service, but he was an observant man. He had watched the King's servants rise from poverty to wealth in positions that ostensibly offered no more than a living wage, and he had longed for the chance to put the lesson into practice.

Thirty-odd years of an adventurous life had fitted him, he flattered himself, to make the most of his opportunities. Fifth son of a country squire, he had grown to manhood in the last years of Elizabeth's reign, absorbing the spirit of businesslike adventure that so distinguished the Virgin Queen's sailors. Navigating unknown seas, exploring uncharted shores, fighting or negotiating with savage tribes, he had kept constantly before him the goal of all his efforts— increased trade for England and a share of the spoil for Captain Argall.

So now, perspiring gently inside his breastplate, he impatiently hastened preparations for going ashore to wrest a fortune from the wilderness. In the process, and quite unconsciously, he established upon a new continent the principle of personal gain in public office, which was in his day as firmly fixed an element of British government as the English tradition of liberty. Both bloomed luxuriantly in the fertile soil of the New World, reacting so persistently upon each other that their development was inseparable.

Corruption, stemming from the early English model, but modified and amplified to meet the changing problems of exploiting so vast a territory, made possible some of the more generally admired features of our civilization. Its contributions to progress and reaction rather than its expositions of individual greed are the factors that demand serious consideration of the system in any study of the country's rise to greatness. Argall was the first of a long line of men who turned American politics to the service of personal interest. Without an understanding of their activities, the history of the United States is a meaningless tale.

Later generations have applied the term "graft" to the wages paid by the entrepreneur (whether streetwalker or wizard of finance) to the servants of the state (from the policeman on the beat to the elder statesman in the Cabinet). We have scorned the grafter while offering profound homage to the triumphs of industrial and financial giantism which his graft protected and nourished. Corrupt politicians betrayed the noble sentiments which the people claimed as their ideals, but the betrayal was a necessary help in rearing that network of private enterprise to which they attributed their material progress. Whatever the popular slogan of the moment, the grafters and the "rugged individualists" have always moved hand in hand to create the massive, complex machinery of modern capitalism by which the world lives.

It was, therefore, more than a mere historical oddity that the first of the Thirteen Colonies, the first English settlement overseas, should have been the creation of a joint stock company organized for profit. English civilization in America was rooted in the commercial character of the Virginia Company of London and nurtured in the conflicts that made up the inglorious reign of James I.

Merchants, emerging from the status of medieval guildsmen, were introducing a progressive force into the static society to which conservative courtiers clung. Trading vessels fared forth in ever larger numbers from the mouth of the Thames, carrying the products of a stimulated English industrial life. They returned freighted with the riches of the world, putting into the hands of their owners an economic influence which the merchants themselves were slow to realize. As yet the City men were content to exercise power indirectly, glad to depend upon the good will of titled gentlemen who had the ear of the King or the King's Ministers.

Ever since monarchs first surrounded themselves with cabinets and courts, the influence of these officials had been for sale. In England they reckoned their places as worth so much a year in gifts and fees. Many jobs were in the open market, passing from hand to hand like shares in a trading company. The price was fixed by the graft that went with the post, the salaries being negligible, and the politicians considered their offices as a form of private property. In prosecuting claims through the agency of these persons, merchants trod a path worn smooth by generations of landed gentry before them. No one questioned the propriety of offering a purse of gold, a share in a profitable voyage, a pipe of wine or a service of plate to the public man who could facilitate deals between business and the state.

Success in these fields led the wealthier commercial figures to recognize their dominant role in making their country a world power. And, such is the ingratitude of man, as soon as they felt their strength they became resentful of limitations upon it. The familiar arguments about an English-

man's freedom were suddenly applied to his business as well
as to his land or his person. A new conception of property
rights rose to confront the vested interests of autocracy.
Within a generation it was to sweep Britain into civil war.
Meanwhile it found expression in graft.

The Virginia Company of London, chartered in the first
decade of the seventeenth century, was an outgrowth of this
movement's early phases—and of the lamentable ignorance
of its incorporators. America to them meant the treasures of
Mexico and Peru. Many of the shareholders were old enough
to remember that a single one of Drake's voyages had paid a
dividend of 4,700 per cent. to the lucky persons who
financed it. Visions of an annual Virginia plate fleet
freighted with gold and silver, pearls and diamonds, floated
enchantingly before the bemused merchants of London as
they threaded the narrow streets from 'Change to counting
house.

King James was brought to share the pleasant delusion.
He freely bestowed upon the new venture his blessing,
prayers of the Church of England and the North American
continent between North Carolina and Maine. The promoters of the Virginia Company were not the men to be-
little the princely gift in the telling. As they poured forth
their eloquence to prospective buyers of stock, the carved
wooden housefronts of the City seemed to become magically
gilded with a precious American veneer. Shares were
snatched at £12 10s. The salesmen, by no means novices,
had already organized in similar fashion that model of corporate power, the East India Company. Samuel Insull and
Jay Gould could have taught them nothing in the way of
"conserving assets for the investing public." They were the
authors of England's commercial supremacy, inheritors of
the traditions of Italian and Hanseatic merchant princes,
realists whose heirs would be able to smile at a Sun King's
juvenile boast, "L'état, c'est moi!"

The earliest effective administration in what was to be

the United States was conditioned by the conception of public service which the bourgeois pioneers would have applied in London had they dared. Their dawning belief that government should be in the interest of trade met no opposition in the wilderness, as it did at home, for government and trade were vested in one body—the Virginia Company.

2

The sort of rule that Samuel Argall would apply to the young colony was one he had learned from his employers, and they were a mixed lot. Solid guildsmen of the City made up the majority, but there was a leavening of noblemen, gentlemen and politicians. Most of the noblemen and gentlemen were there as ornamental appendages to attract their inferiors. Most of the politicians were expected to supply influence at court or in Parliament. But these supposed figureheads were sometimes inclined to complicate matters by using the company to further their own aims.

At first all differences were submerged in the difficulty of planting a permanent settlement in Virginia, and the several hundred stockholders deferred eagerly to the judgment of one man. This was trim-bearded, elderly Sir Thomas Smith, the most considerable international merchant of his generation. One of the first Englishmen to see the possibilities of profit in corporate dealings with "backward" nations, he was a founder of the Turkey Company, a leader in the Russia Company, first Governor of the East India Company. The Virginia stockholders thought themselves honored to have as Treasurer (equivalent of chairman and general manager) a man of such experience. Besides, Sir Thomas was the wealthiest tradesman in the country with a fortune estimated at the then colossal figure of £100,000. His great wealth was supposed to raise him above temptation, an odd impression often entertained regarding rich men.

Another guiding spirit in the company was young Robert Rich, soon to become Earl of Warwick. A genuine pirate king in the grand manner, he inherited from his father a fleet of privateers that had been preying on commerce in far places (mostly Spanish) since the days of Drake and Hawkins. Representative of the older nobility was Lord de la Warr, titular Governor of Virginia, largest individual stockholder in the company. He was an ardent imperialist, one of many in that age whose imagination had been captured by readings in Roman history. The ideal of vast barbarian provinces subject to a London purged of the vices of Rome commanded his purse and his energies.

These men brought to the task of founding a British empire the very realistic, almost sordid spirit of their time. The parochial narrowness of the Middle Ages had given way to the beginnings of a world outlook. Expansive economic forces had been released, and common folk were no longer quite so much preoccupied with the problems of their own neighborhoods or the universal aspects of religion. Even in philosophy the practical curiosity and materialism of Francis Bacon had succeeded the dreams of Thomas More. Yet Bacon himself was not immune to influences exerted by the traditions and customs of his race.

A few months before Argall landed at Point Comfort, the philosopher had been elevated to the posts of Lord Chancellor and Lord Keeper of the Great Seal, imposing and remunerative offices. He was, he admitted, "the justest chancellor that hath been in the five changes since Sir Nicholas Bacon" (his father). Nevertheless, the thinker, so far ahead of his time in science and learning, accepted with worldly alacrity bribes of which, in theory, he disapproved.

3

Argall could share Bacon's methods if not his scruples or his scholastic attainments, for he was quite as eager to get rich. Known in his twenties as an "ingenious, forward and active young gentleman," he had been hired by the Virginia Company in 1609 to discover a "short passage" to Jamestown. Hitherto the route had been by way of the Canaries and Puerto Rico, a three months' voyage at best. Argall, defying navigators who decreed the North Atlantic unsafe, set a course due west and amazed the world by crossing in a month. For four years more he gave loyal, industrious, unnoticed service as a ship commander. Then, in the summer of 1613, two exploits raised him above the ranks of unhonored workers whose labors are so gracefully taken for granted by the powerful.

One was the first kidnaping in the annals of civilized America. On a trading voyage up the James, he learned that Pocahontas, the girl about whom Captain John Smith a few years later wove a prettier tale, was staying with relatives near the river. The English still had exaggerated notions of the wealth of an Indian chief, and Argall had read in historical chronicles of ransoms paid for a king's daughter. The child he had in mind wore deerskins and ornaments of bone instead of velvet and rubies, but the Captain determined to capture her for the benefit of the suffering colony. It was done, he wrote to a friend, by threatening one of her kinsmen "that if he did not betray Pocohuntis into my hands, wee would be no longer brothers nor friends."

The guns of his ship were an added argument, and the Indian Princess was invited to visit the winged paleface canoe. As soon as she was on board, marveling at the wonders of the cabin, a rude affair of some bunks, a table and a few rough chairs, the vessel cast off. It was easy and friendly, for the prisoner was delighted to be in captivity. She wanted to see Jamestown. Her father, Powhatan, surrendered seven Englishmen and a quantity of corn as ransom, but like so many kidnapers the Virginians overreached themselves. They raised their demands, and Powhatan told them to keep the child; his tepee was plentifully supplied with other offspring.

Argall took no part in the negotiations. With a well-armed privateer, the *Treasurer,* owned by Warwick, he was on his way to "drive foreigners from Virginia," in this case a French Jesuit colony at Mt. Desert on the Maine coast. He destroyed every building in the place, and on his way back stopped to force a few Dutch fur traders on the island of the Manahattas to acknowledge that they were intruders on English soil. No one, least of all the Dutch, paid a great deal of attention to the incident at the time, but it was useful half a century later as the one reed on which Charles II could prop his claim that New Amsterdam "did belong to England heeretofore."

The summer's successes commended the Captain to the favorable notice of two powerful patrons, Smith and Warwick, and led to his appointment as governor, deputizing for de la Warr, who was prevented by illness from playing a proconsular role in America.

Only a man of the seaman's ingenuity could have seen that he had entered on the road to wealth. Before him lay a continent of forest, mountain and swamp. For a thousand miles there was nothing but undefiled Indian hunting ground, with only the mysterious rivers and faint native trails leading through impassable woods to the unexplored interior. Eleven years old, Jamestown was an ill-built, unattractive village, low, damp, misty and with a water supply feelingly described by one who had suffered from it as "brackish, ill sented, penurious and not gratefull to the stumack."

Sensibly abandoning hopes of sudden riches, the fever- and dysentery-ridden people had reconciled themselves to wringing a livelihood from the soil and the fur trade. Tobacco and sassafras were the money crops, cultivated by bondsmen working out their passage to the land of promise or, as humble builders of empire, expiating crimes committed in England. It remained for the new Governor to introduce outright slavery.

Eleven years of misery and hope, toil and death—a great deal of death—had left fewer than 1,000 British subjects firmly established on the edge of the wilderness. In England stockholders were beginning to think there might some day be a dividend more valuable than uncleared forest. The company's own plantation, well stocked with the cattle and hogs that stood the sea voyage so badly, was producing £300 a year from the labor of 135 tenants and servants. Private planters were getting an even better return.

These signs of the earliest American boom had not escaped the discerning Argall. His right to apply it to his own account did not seem to be covered by his commission, but no Elizabethan sailor was diverted from plunder by sensible words on a paper drawn up 3,000 miles away. The Captain proceeded to assemble the first political machine in the land from among the men who were later to be acclaimed as founders of liberty, democracy and opportunity in the New World, but were known to him only as agents, employees, stockholders, dupes or serfs of the Virginia Company of London. The machine was formed to advance the thesis that, although early hardships and scanty food had been shared equally, profits should be divided more nicely.

The new Governor therefore selected planters like John Rolfe, husband of Pocahontas, as the chief props of his administration. The partnership thus begun set the tone for American officialdom and helped to shape the course of colonial life for generations. The easy, gracious society of an agricultural aristocracy that could produce Washingtons, Jeffersons, Madisons and Randolphs got its start when a sailor-governor learned just what influences could bid highest for his favor.

The system he worked out anticipated in miniature nearly all the graft of the next 300 years. The tobacco and sassafras trade centered in Argall's hands and paid tribute in passing. Lesser crops were discouraged as not immediately profitable to him, and ceased to be an item in the colony's economy.

Supplies at the company store, essential to life and work, were obtainable only at his pleasure and at his price. Bondsmen, whose terms of service expired were unable to secure their freedom unless they paid in cash or kind to the Governor. Planters seeking title to land they had cleared or wanted were charged a larger fee than formerly. A bit extra and Argall would add a zero to the number of acres stipulated in the deed.

Argall sympathized easily with the larger planters in their quest for more and richer tobacco lands, for he had promptly entered their ranks. His estate—"obtained by slight and cunning," the company later complained—lay a mile from Jamestown and was appropriately named "Argall's Guifte." It throve apace, so much so that when the first American representative assembly, the father of Congresses and free institutions, was called two years later, Argall's Guifte was big enough to send two delegates.

Its growth was in exact ratio to the decline of the "Common Garden." By the time the Guifte achieved the dignity of two burgesses, the company's plantation had disappeared, "ther beinge not lefte either the land aforesaid or Any Tennant, Servant, Rent, or Trybute Corne, Cowe, or Saltworke w^thoutt one penny yeilded to the Company for their so great losse." Of the flourishing stock only six goats remained. Their former stablemates fattened at Argall's Guifte; the improved land had been given away to men who made suitable presents in return; the servants were bound out to new masters.

One of the Governor's major sources of illicit revenue was a partnership with Warwick. Protection extended by government to organized lawbreakers whose crimes were condoned by public opinion had long been an element of British politics and was naturally introduced into the colonies. Warwick wanted an American base for his pirate fleet, and Argall had agreed that it might be Virginia, although he had been ordered to avoid offending Spain. An expedition from the

West Indies might wipe out Jamestown as thoroughly as Argall had destroyed Mt. Desert. Therefore the apprehensive Virginians developed an almost Spanish aversion to buccaneering.

Not until the famous *Treasurer* came to Jamestown to refit for a cruise to the Spanish Main were suspicions aroused. Then they were promptly expressed, together with some vigorous comments on Argall's rapacity. This was surprising, for state officials in that day were not accustomed to outspoken criticism from those they ruled. In England far greater exactions than anything Argall had attempted were borne with exemplary patience by a liberty-loving race. The first families of Virginia, however, had faced more than their share of insecurity and hardship. That fact altered their habits of thought in more ways than one, but in nothing so markedly as their determination to keep what they had wrung from a hostile environment. They had braved the ocean in leaky ships with the scantiest of provisions. They had survived illness and hunger and a detestable warfare of skirmishes with elusive natives. They had labored through unaccustomed heat for a bare subsistence. They were not prepared to submit meekly while a governor bled them of the first fruits of their suffering.

Their attitude was one that became familiar to a succession of American officials who overstepped the bonds of tolerated corruption. Argall's favors were not widely distributed, so his graft was attacked as bad for business. Bribery becomes offensive when it is opposed to prevailing trade interests instead of being employed in their behalf.

The Governor, his official dignity reinforced by quarter-deck ideas of discipline, dealt sternly with the first manifestations of discontent. He had Captain Edward Brewster court-martialed and sentenced to death for daring to question his superior's practices "in matter of pryvate varience." There was such an instant outcry that he was forced to spare Brewster's life and send the facts to England for review.

With them went a bundle of complaints and depositions that could hardly have reached home at a more unfortunate time.

4

Among the stockholders Argall was already suspect. Their hopes of dividends had been disappointed, and they were inclined to blame the administration. The reports from Virginia were so alarming that Sir Thomas Smith had been constrained to write a strong letter to his erring protégé.

"It is laid vnto yor charge that you appropriate the Indian Trade to yor selfe," he remonstrated. "It is also iustified that you take the auncient planters of the Colony wch ought to be free and likewise those from the comon garden to set them vpon yor owne imployments and that you spend vp our store Corne to feede yor owne men as if ye Plantacon were onely intended to serue yor turne."

Sir Thomas's indignation was intensified by a quarrel with Warwick, the one man who found Argall still useful. Smith's son had married Warwick's sister, but none of the bridegroom's family had been invited to the wedding. The outraged father's wrath rose higher when some of the noble Earl's privateers turned up in the Orient where the East India Company claimed and enforced a monopoly. Warwick's ships were confiscated by superior force and Warwick's friends were attacked with fury. In August, 1618, Smith was writing to Lord de la Warr, who had at last set out for Virginia for the purpose of reviving the glories of the Roman Empire:

"Wee pray y^r Lordp y^t you will cause him [Argall] to be shipped home . . . and for y^t wee suppose there will bee found many misdemeanours of his, wee pray your Lordp to ceaze uppon such goods of his as Tobacko and Furrs wherof it is reported he hath gotten together a greate stoare to the Collonies preiudice."

But De la Warr had died as he neared the American coast,

and before Smith could pursue the issue of Argall a greater storm was upon him. His fight with Warwick had set the stage for a reform movement, and a reformer was not wanting. Sir Edwin Sandys, son of an Archbishop of York, was looked up to by many merchants as their Parliamentary chief. He was a leader of the forces that wished to whittle away some of the Crown's powers. He was also one of the stockholders who thought he had waited overlong for a return on his Virginia investment. Nor was he unmindful of the political advantages to be derived from control of a great commercial enterprise.

In the battle of the Titans, Warwick and Smith, Sir Edwin saw his chance. Armed with a list of Argall's misdeeds, he raised a cry for a complete change. Cunningly he argued that corruption in Virginia, matched by corruption in London, kept the golden dreams of the stockholders from coming true. He was so uncouth as to ask an accounting of expenditures. Smith spurned the idea as unbecoming a Treasurer, an attitude which failed to allay suspicion that he had diverted company funds to personal ends. For twelve years he had been unquestioned master of the corporation, but hardly on the strength of his stake in it. At this time the paid-up capital was £36,624. Sir Thomas, the richest merchant in the city, had invested £165. Sandys held £287 10s. and Warwick £75. There was, however, no complaint that one-half of one per cent. ownership should exercise complete control. Battle was joined over the more congenial issues of corruption and mismanagement. At the annual meeting early in 1619 Sandys replaced Smith at the head of the company's affairs.

An immediate turning out of officers followed. Warwick, whose support had enabled Sir Edwin to carry the election, argued in vain for Argall; Sandys named George Yeardley, a veteran of Virginia hardships, to the post. Knighted as a token of the confidence reposed in him, the new Governor sailed for Jamestown with a set of instructions calculated to

bring the colony back to prosperity and Argall home in
chains. But Sir Edwin was not the last reformer to discover
that a policy which appears fair and reasonable in the struggle
for power is not so easy to execute. Warwick, loyal to his
accomplice, sent one of the swiftest of his fleet, the pinnace
Eleanor, to warn the menaced grafter.

All through that winter Virginians had been in ignorance
of events in London. Argall continued to put money in his
purse, winning over some of the colonists, Yeardley later declared, "with the love of his good Licour and fayre protestations." The arrival of the *Eleanor* on April 16, 1619, put an
abrupt end to many pleasant transactions between him and
some of the leading planters. The commander of the pinnace made that clear in a few words, and added that time
was short. Argall wasted none of it.

Within four days the *Eleanor* put to sea with His Excel-
lency the Governor in the best cabin and his goods nearly
filling the hold. And not only his. Lady de la Warr never
was able to get an accounting or an explanation for £1,500
of her late husband's property taken by Argall out of Virginia. When Yeardley turned up to carry out his orders a
few days later, the intended prisoner was well on his way
to England, his strong box plentifully stocked with all that
was necessary to circumvent or conciliate his accusers.

5

Argall reached London without undue publicity to find
the company indulging in the bitter recriminations that
sprout in the decay of failing corporations. Warwick and
Smith had been drawn together by their hatred of reform,
and Sandys had driven Alderman Robert Johnson, a leader
of the rich Grocers Company, into their camp. Johnson had
been in charge of the magazine that supplied goods to the
colonists and marketed their produce. He was no more willing than Smith to submit to the indignity of an audit, de-

manded by the new Treasurer. To this faction was added a Privy Councillor rejoicing in the name of Sir Julius Caesar. His brother-in-law, John Martin, held a grant from Argall on such generous terms that his plantation was an independent principality. Martin not only had five times as much land as he had paid for but was exempted from all service to the colony or obedience to its laws. Sandys wanted to force him to exchange his deed for one drawn more in accordance with the company's charter. He only added to those who complained that reform was too expensive, a feeling that was to confound later generations of reformers.

Argall promptly aligned himself with his former patrons. He adopted an attitude toward the accounting of funds that Smith might have envied. Not until December, more than six months after his arrival, would he even listen to charges preferred against him in open meeting. He was establishing his position in society. He bought a commission in the navy, the taste for public service having grown upon him, and when the company pressed for a hearing, Captain Argall, in command of His Majesty's man o' war *Golden Phoenix,* was winning honor in the Mediterranean. On his return the prosecution, already "intollerable trouble some" to Sandys, had become still more difficult. The company had now to deal with Sir Samuel Argall, knight.

Doggedly it clung to the offensive, and minutes of stockholders' meetings abound with entries threatening "to proceed in a legall course against him." That was not seriously meant. Sandys was painfully aware that he had fallen into the error of adopting some of the enemy's tactics, although his motives had always been of the best. Nevertheless, he and other new officers of the company, to tide their affairs over a trying time, had awarded themselves certain lands and revenues without noticeable authority. They were afraid the judicial mind might not be able to distinguish between such meritorious practices and Argall's system.

For four years the struggle continued in the same fashion.

Lady de la Warr vainly clamored for her £1,500; the widow Smalley testified that she had been robbed of her all by the Governor; the company calculated that his wealth was "the ffruite of ffoureskore Thousande pounds."

It may be that in this period the culprit learned something from the case of Bacon. The Chancellor, despite or perhaps because of his abilities, had lost his friends. That blunder made his acceptance of bribes a crime, and the greatest mind in Europe spent several days in the Tower while his foes stripped him of offices and honors. Argall clung to his allies, and they saved him from danger.

He could have pointed out that his graft did less harm than that of his accusers. The officers of the company drew salaries to fit out proper expeditions, but whole ship loads of emigrants were dispatched with only enough food for the voyage and insufficient tools. Of one party of thirty-eight only seven survived—not an unusual proportion. The Spanish Ambassador reported gleefully to his master that criminals begged to be hanged rather than transported to Virginia.

The colonists, encouraged by Argall to concentrate on tobacco, had no supplies for the newcomers except a strange beverage. George Thorpe, a planter of an inventive turn of mind, had discovered corn whisky while seeking a substitute for water. The result was so "gratefull to the stumack" that the pioneer of Bourbon wrote to a friend at home:

"I have found a waie to make so good drinke of Indian corne as I protest I have divers times refused to drinke good stronge English beere and chosen to drinke that."

So many followed his example that when the Indians rose against their white neighbors, killing nearly 400 in a day, London pamphleteers declared the massacre was God's punishment for "those two enormous excesses of apparel and drinking."

Beset by troubles on all sides, Sandys had one more card to play. He obtained a Crown monopoly on tobacco for his company, but the King's negotiators drove such a hard bargain that it would be impossible to meet the guaranteed annuity. Sir Edwin, however, allowed himself £500 a year for managing the monopoly, six times what the East India Company paid Smith for a greater task, and for a few months his reports were optimistic. Then he was obliged to confess a default, and his regime was doomed. The insolvent company, hopelessly split by the bitterest of enmities, went down to ruin too.

For some time the minority had been insisting on a Parliamentary investigation. But King James, who knew Sandys was a leader of the people's representatives, did not care to leave it to the House of Commons. Perhaps he was aware that at least forty-nine members of that body had been taken into the company without going through the formality of paying for their stock. This sort of thing was one of the advantages of a Parliamentary seat and would not for many years be considered ground for expulsion. Most of the members had received their stock from Sandys.

It did not avail him. His Majesty decided on a royal inquiry, and on May 9, 1623, he set up a body known as the Jones Commission, under which homely title the first of innumerable American "probes" was undertaken. This one was to conduct a searching examination of the company's affairs from the day of incorporation. Sir William Jones, Justice of the Court of Common Pleas and talented in discovering the truth, presided. His report, made after five months of hearings, revealed the whole extent of the corruption and mismanagement. On May 24, 1624, the Court of Kings Bench ruled that officials of the company had usurped powers never intended for them and that their charter and all privileges previously granted should therefore "be now taken and seized into the hands of our Lord the King."

Government by joint stock company had been tried and condemned for its own corruption, but the verdict was due to the King's dislike of Sandys rather than any objection of graft. This was plain when in July James appointed Sir Samuel Argall, Sir Thomas Smith, Sir Julius Caesar and Alderman Johnson as the leading members of a commission to devise a royal government for Virginia.

II

PIRATE GOLD

1

WHAT, IF ANYTHING, EIGHT-
een years had taught the commissioners is not apparent in
the form of government they drafted for Virginia. The new
system was so like the old that Argall promptly applied for
the post of governor. He did not get it, but his record could
not have stood in his way, for a little later, promoted to
Admiral, he commanded a combined English and Dutch
fleet that attacked Cadiz and took seven prizes worth £100,-
000. His share enabled him to retire to Essex and out of the
pages of history.

The system of government he had introduced into Virginia was not so easily dismissed. Graft had become an economic necessity in the colony because it alone bridged the
gulf between the law and establishment of the large plantations on which the prosperity of the province already depended. The tobacco market was expanding rapidly, but the
theory of small farms operated by an independent yeomanry
remained the ideal toward which the rulers thought they
ought to strive. Unfortunately it was not compatible with
the facts of Virginia agriculture. Nor did it square with the
desire of men to make the most profit possible whether han-
dling colonial produce in London or raising it in America.
In both places corruption enabled the contradictory forces
of conservatism and progress to exist in outward harmony.

Successful tobacco culture called for ever larger holdings
and a steady labor supply to keep pace with them. These

were obtainable from the King's appointees as readily as
from Argall, but the price of evading the law rose in proportion to the discontent with what the law allowed. The graft,
then as later, served a genuinely desirable end. It prevented
a violent clash between popular ideals and profitable colonial expansion.

The solid benefits of corruption were soon apparent elsewhere on the American coast. The English never again attempted to exploit their claims in what was to become the
United States by such corporations as the Virginia Company.
Rather they sought, perhaps unconsciously, to prove by trial
and error the best method of settlement.

Massachusetts, from which England hoped for little profit,
although a few discerning souls saw a future in naval stores
and land speculation, was allowed to develop her theocratic
government and work out her salvation in prayer and town
meeting. Virginia was an experiment in a crown colony.
Maryland and Pennsylvania were grants to single proprietors.
Although both were owned by idealists planning perfect
commonwealths as well as havens for persecuted sects, they
attracted settlers interested in neither philosophy nor faith,
but only in land and security. Lord Baltimore and William
Penn, different as they were in other respects, seemed to offer
these blessings.

Carolina was a partnership affair, less attractive to the immigrant, granted in 1663 to eight of Charles II's chief ministers and favorites because, their patent recited, they were
"excited with a laudable and pious zeal for the propagation
of the Christian faith and the enlargement of our empire
and dominions." By this time the corruption of British
officialdom was so well advanced that even these powerful
lords proprietors had to disburse a considerable sum in petty
graft to clerks, doormen and the like before their patent
could pass the Great Seal.

Connecticut and Rhode Island were, for practical purposes, autonomous republics, while New Hampshire was a

battleground of conflicting interests. Massachusetts claimed it of course. Several old deeds to early explorers were interpreted as conferring the proprietorship of the province. The most daring of the claimants, Samuel Allen of London, had bought an old, generally discredited charter for £260. On the strength of this document and judicious bribery he modestly hoped to levy a rent roll of £22,500 a year, an income any Duke in England would have envied. For many years men in charge of colonial affairs were on Allen's salary list, and he came so near success that only the unlikely accident of an incorruptible governor defeated him at last. This unique executive, Lord Bellomont, rejected an offer of £10,000 for his signature to a paper acknowledging Allen's title.

In all the governments set up and amended from time to time, only one factor was constant. The granting of land and trade privileges by responsible officials to themselves or to others for payments that never found their way into the public treasury was carried on with equal success and scope in Puritan New England, in honest Quaker Pennsylvania, in free tolerant Maryland, in cavalier Virginia, in imperalist Carolina.

Immigrants brought into every colony the standard of official conduct to which they had been accustomed at home. Even those who came to America chiefly because they hoped to found a better society were more largely preoccupied with religious than with secular reforms. They had learned their politics in the same school as Argall, and that deteriorated throughout the century in which the colonies were established and during which they were most susceptible to English example. Political life took its tone from the top. The handsome, talented but astonishingly weak Charles I, the grim class conscious merchants and squires who ruled the Commonwealth, the polished but cynical Charles II—these were the men English and colonial public servants imitated.

Civil war and the even more significant struggle of commercial interests to break the dominance of a conservative landed gentry produced their own standards among job-holders. The rivals threatened, but they also resorted to bribes. Roundhead and cavalier, tradesman and farmer, court party and country party, offered substantial induce-ments to men in office, who were generally swayed in almost equal parts by avarice and fear—and somewhat less by con-science. When Charles II introduced the systematic corrup-tion of Parliament while himself accepting ill-concealed bribes from the King of France, the last effective remnant of moral opposition to graft vanished.

The highest type of public man was then represented by Samuel Pepys, properly regarded today as one of the fathers of England's imposing civil service tradition. The diary of this admiralty clerk expresses better than the report of a commission of inquiry the frankness of seventeenth century corruption. With even greater zest than he chronicled his loves, his dinners, his domestic troubles or his opinions, Pepys noted the growth of his estate. The increasing size of "presents" made to him as he gained in importance delighted his soul. Terror lest he lose his job was as keenly felt, yet through his whole career Pepys remained rarely efficient and honest. Acceptance of bribes was condoned by his entire generation; it was only fair that there should be this com-pensation for the insecurity, not to say danger of office. The Tower, a crushing fine, impeachment and disgrace were perils every Minister faced if he fell from favor. Similar men-aces hung over the heads of minor appointees. In America the greater safety of distance worked, in time, for greater honesty. But in the seventeenth century Americans were content with English models.

2

It might have been expected that the righteous, tenacious, industrious folk of Massachusetts would have used their town meetings and independent spirit to curb graft, or that the godly heads of their administration would have been above such earthly temptations as pasture, garden and wood. But the men who referred to themselves as "unspottyd lambs of the Lord" were at least as shrewd as their descendants.

One hundred acres in the close village settlements of New England formed a tidy competence and as much as one family could work profitably. Yet Governor Winthrop had already acquired 1,800 acres; Dudley, 1,700; Saltonstall, 1,600, when in 1634 Boston held an election for commissioners to divide additional town land. For the first time in America a secret ballot was used, and the electorate chose men of small estates, described by the disgruntled Governor as "the inferior sort," with the naïve notion of making the division equal. The leaders of the community thereupon appealed, not in vain, to the church, for the, Rev. John Cotton, then rising to spiritual deanship in the colony, was of the opinion:

"Democracy I do not conceive that ever God did ordeyne as a fit government eyther for church or commonwealth. If the people be governors, who shall be governed?"

Boston was unable to answer the question. When Master Cotton admonished the electors of 1634 that in Israel (ideal of good New England Christians) it had always been the custom to entrust such business as division of land to the elders, the people meekly took another vote. That poll enabled Winthrop and his friends to distribute town sites more in accordance with their reading of Old Testament precepts.

A generation later the Puritans found their vocation and a graft to go with it. They built their own ships, showing a fine spirit of independence in ignoring laws designed to reserve for the royal navy those tracts of virgin forest known as "the King's woods." They made themselves carriers for the southern colonies, treating navigation and revenue acts to the same contempt displayed for the broad arrow on His Majesty's trees.

The first Americans to engage in commerce on a scale larger than village barter, they were laying the foundations of a great industry. A too nice adherence to the King's regulations, drawn up in the exclusive interest of English shipping, would have made their business unprofitable and therefore impossible. The colonials adopted the expedient that naturally occurred to Englishmen. They hired customs and other officials to forget the navigation acts.

By 1677 the traffic had grown to such proportions that Londoners complained of lost business. Their government obligingly decided to enforce customs decrees, but the very attempt led to insurrection in Carolina. Robert Holden, dispatched to America to investigate, found that the rioters were protecting a popular graft. Six Boston merchants, said Holden, controlled both the Carolina trade and the Carolina customs officials. Cavalier wrath was stirred by researches among the pious New Englanders and, surprised that respectable tradesmen should be even more corrupt than a civil servant, he cried:

"They have made their adoration [of God] their prime best commodity of merchandise & their Zeale their cheef broaker, as their occasions and affares in the world shall require, that these two may now pass for the grand Cheates of the world."

This was a common reproach, for the unconverted always failed to appreciate the distinction that "unspottyd lambs" drew between the concerns of the spirit and the prosaic business of the counting house.

3

The Puritans were not, however, the only canny folk in America, and they knew it. They were frankly envious of Dutch trade at the mouth of the Hudson and covetous of Dutch territory. The West India Company, which operated New Netherlands, was a joint stock enterprise similar in form to that once dominated by Smith and Sandys. But the wealthy burghers on the canals had more understanding and experience of those things for which a commercial organization is fitted. Devoting themselves to the sound business project of furs, the directors made an ample return for their stockholders.

Instead of trying to twist their trading machine to the unaccustomed task of disposing of land or financing settlers, the Dutch adopted feudal ideas for colonization. Baronial tracts, larger than anything the timid English dared confer upon an actual settler, were freely given without graft. The patroon, unlike the English proprietor, did not hold his grant for resale at a profit. He was also sufficiently independent of colonial authority that he could gain nothing by corrupting a governor, who in turn was powerless to practice extortion against him.

It did not prove the best way to attract population—New Netherlands grew more slowly than less favored sections—but it was honest and profitable, for government existed frankly for the promotion of trade and did not need to be bribed to that end. This was in accordance with custom in the Dutch commonwealth, which was ruled by merchants in the interests of business. In England and other less mercantile lands, the privileges necessary to profitable enterprise could only be acquired from the dominant aristocracy by bribery or civil war. Graft was better for everyone than fighting.

For a short time after the English took New Netherlands in 1664 the substitution of the name New York was almost the only change. But the new proprietor—King Charles gave the province to his brother James, Duke of York—could hardly be expected to operate the fur trade. This soon fell into private hands, while the owner's agents turned to the more congenial tasks of land granting and politics. New York's only graft-free period was at an end.

The peculiarly orderly upheaval of 1688 that brought

William and Mary of Orange to the throne of England was echoed in New York. Jacob Leisler led the provincial idealists. A German merchant of philosophical tendencies, he made the mistake of trying to carry the principles of liberty to their logical conclusion. He proposed to break the oligarchy of patroons and wealthy traders in favor of what came to be known as Jeffersonian democracy.

In part his movement was a protest against the corruption of James's emissaries. Under their patronage the colony's trade had been increasingly centralized in the hands of a few men. Leisler's followers were animated by a desire for a more equitable division, which they expected to achieve by putting the rich out of business and conducting the government in an honest manner themselves, an admirable plan recurrent in American politics ever after.

During Leisler's brief rule the colonial magnates lived in fear, in jail or in hiding, while Nicholas Bayard, who had experienced all three, rent the air with lamentations and complaints because in the turmoil of a revolution he lost six silver spoons. Bayard, after dodging about the woods near Albany, spent a year in confinement, chained by the leg to a post. But the loss of his spoons took up at least as much space in his correspondence as his other sufferings.

Leisler, however, made the error of leaving to men like Bayard more substantial arguments than spoons with which to buy the new royal officials sent from England. The "Glorious Revolution" was made in the sacred name of property, and the adventurers risen to power in those times would have been foolish not to rally round the Van Cortlandts and Van Rensselaers who had the property to share. They obligingly hanged Leisler as a traitor who had usurped authority, but bitter feeling persisted, and in the summer of 1692 New Yorkers were waiting impatiently for a new governor. All were able to cheer him with hopeful fervor, for no one in America had ever heard of Benjamin Fletcher.

He was not much better known at home. A professional

soldier, such as he were suspect in Stuart England where the phrase recalled unpleasant memories of Cromwell's "Ironsides." However, King William was a respecter of military talent and had remarked Colonel Fletcher's gallantry in action. The modest post of Governor of New York seemed a fitting reward for a "necessitous man," for thus alone was the Colonel known to London gossipers.

In March, 1692, he was furnished with instructions full of wise and thoughtful advice on good government. His commission, sealed ten days later, interested the new civil servant more. Here he read that his salary was £600 a year; that he was empowered to appoint admiralty judges, that he could dispose of royal lands "under such moderate Quitt Rents as you shall think fitt," and that his lawful perquisites were to consist of a share in ships confiscated for smuggling or piracy, the sum of legal fines and forfeitures he imposed and fees for marriage licenses and the probate of wills. These were to be his "honest graft." Anything further must be on his conscience.

Some men later remarked as an ominous sign that Fletcher arrived on a ship named the *Wolf*. She dropped anchor off the Battery on the evening of Aug. 29th and the next morning at 8 o'clock the Colonel and his lady came ashore to inaugurate a typical English colonial administration. They were dressed in their best—not very fine at that—and were most dignified and solemn. The attitude was not altogether assumed, for to the Governor's military eye New York appeared in a parlous state. The fort was in bad repair, the artillery useless, the troops poorly equipped—and in time of war with France, too! The Colonel noticed not at all the neat Dutch houses and gardens, the wooded river banks, the typical midsummer Manhattan odor, described by a more cultivated soul as "such a sweet smell in the air that we stood still, because we did not know what it was we were meeting."

Fletcher thought New Yorkers an "impoverished people,"

but he changed his mind as he learned more about their commerce. The fur trade and naval stores hardly accounted for the volume of shipping that sometimes made the harbor as crowded as the Thames. The more agreeable source of this activity was the pirates, who had moved from the Spanish Main to the Indian Ocean. They still called themselves privateers, but the pretense was wearing thin. It had been lightly accepted in northern Europe when Spain was the only victim. Now that all commerce was attacked, all western nations adopted Castilian morality and made war on freebooters.

New York, however, was as tolerant of piracy as the London partners of Drake and Hawkins a century before; a thieves' market is a profitable market for honest men. By Fletcher's time traffic with buccaneers had assumed respectable proportions and even an air of respectability, for merchants made a double profit buying pirate loot cheap and selling pirate outfits dear. The only drawback was that even more respectable, wealthier merchants in England and the Netherlands were clamoring for suppression of the business. Since the new King of England was also a Dutchman, Fletcher's instructions were more than usually pointed. But the Stadtholder King was very far away, and the Colonel faced the realities of commerce.

New Yorkers were at first alarmed lest he take his orders seriously. His normal manner was so sternly military as to be disconcerting to simple burghers. When he did doff his soldierly strictness, it was to reveal an ostentatious piety that would have been more appropriate in Boston. It would also have been more accurately interpreted. The lengthy sessions twice a day in which the Governor wrestled with himself in prayer, his audible approval of long sermons, the godly references that interlarded his conversation would not have disturbed Bostonians.

Within a few months the worldly fellows of New York also understood. Colonel Fletcher's Council, composed of prosperous merchants and landowners recommended by the Lords of Trade in London, found it easy to teach him that although public report and the English authorities might brand men as pirates, it was a Christian's duty to give them the benefit of the doubt, especially if they were prepared to make suitable presents. They were, and Fletcher was far too conservative a fellow to interfere in established custom. Ships that had been hovering along the coast for news of the administration's attitude now drew up before the fort, which had not been repaired, and the city hummed with profitable activity.

4

Prosperity is pleasing to the head of any government; it redounds to his credit no matter how little he is responsible. But Fletcher could justly claim some part in bringing wealth to New York, and no one thought it strange he should share the profits. He and his lady were now seen of all men garbed in imported splendor with rather more lace than the current fashions prescribed. The executive mansion was hung with some of the finest silks in America, nor had they paid duty. The Fletcher collection of gold and silver snuff boxes took on museum proportions. The once "necessitous man's" table was set with massive plate. And when Mrs. Fletcher went calling she reclined luxuriously in a coach drawn by six horses, the first such equipage any American governor had yet sported.

She and her husband dispensed the most magnificent hospitality ever seen by the sober Dutchmen of New York. At their festive board Philipses, Nicollses and Schuylers dined familiarly with the notorious Captain Tew and lesser pirate chiefs. At these gatherings the Governor's pious demeanor relaxed. When he and his prime favorite, Tew, drove abroad in the famous coach, the buccaneer was always telling stories and the soldier always laughing.

Despite an outward show of harmony, a dissatisfied element remained. For a long time letters denouncing Fletcher were filed away in London and forgotten. In them his superiors might have read that their Governor was forcing his military subordinates "to pimp to his frauds upon the public," taking part of each man's subsistence pay and collecting for full regiments, although the ranks were half empty. This was a common practice which he had not needed to come to New York to learn. Fletcher had also issued protections to the crew of the *Jacob,* a suspicious ship just returned from the East, and accepted the vessel herself as a gift from her commander, Captain Coats. Fletcher sold the *Jacob* next day for £800, and Coats later swore that his own personal protection cost him £1,300 more.

Others than pirates and merchants concerned in illegal trade were finding the Colonel a source of wealth, for he was catering to the American dream of land. The size of the continent, all the more impressive for being unknown, tempted the imagination or the cupidity of a people steeped in the European tradition that land is power and security, the only real form of wealth. In America no free man was so poor that he could not hope to own a farm as large as his family could till. The first great tide of immigration from war-ravaged Europe was setting in; whole communities, particularly from Germany, were translating themselves to the wilderness. Fortunes were to be won by pre-empting desirable, accessible tracts and waiting for increasing population to boost the value.

Title, however, was only to be obtained from the King or the King's representative. In every colony the Governor was besieged by eager speculators. The pressure was irresistible. It was the duty of public men to distribute the public domain, and although it is obvious now that it should have been reserved for actual settlers, few men understood the problem less than Fletcher. None, however, was so willing to take advice. His only concern was that New York should be settled by gentlemen, and he judged a citizen's breeding solely by the value of the present bestowed upon the Governor. Plenty of men, including most of his Council, were prepared to prove their gentility.

Captain John Evans of the Navy, diligent in keeping his frigate out of the way of the pirates he was supposed to catch, gave his friend Fletcher £100 for an estate so ill-defined it was impossible to say whether it contained 600,000 acres or only 350,000. The King's interests were protected by an annual rental of twenty shillings.

Henry Beekman, although not of the ruling caste, offered the Governor £25 and found himself the owner of a tract he valued at £5,000. Godfrey Dellius, a clergyman as well as a gentleman, had a patent for a strip seventy miles by twelve. Bayard, convalescent from the loss of his spoons, contracted to give the Crown of England one otter skin or ten shillings every year in return for a valley thirty miles long and of unknown width. Caleb Heathcote, preparing to acquire most of Westchester County, accepted as "makeweight" a deed to a city lot twenty-seven by fifty feet, "part of Our Garden." The beneficiaries of these and dozens of other grants formed a close corporation. The Governor was so free with his signature that it was estimated he had disposed of three-quarters of the province. But only thirty men got any of it.

Revenue did not keep pace with the Colonel's generosity. It had been hoped that some day the "moderate Quitt Rents" would be a sizable addition to the King's income. The year before Fletcher's arrival, New York's receipts from this source had totaled £306 10s. Three years later, with three times as much land in private hands, quit rents amounted to £36 17s. 6d.

Unfortunately colonial and English economies were destined to clash, and New York was first to experience the unpleasant truth that in an empire the mother country's interests are paramount. The volume of New York trade with the pirate base at Madagascar was the subject of angry talk in the City of London, and the day had gone by when an English sovereign could ignore the emotions of the 'Change. Repeatedly Fletcher was commanded to act vigorously against pirates "since your Govern^t is named as a place of protection for such like villains and your favour to Captn Tue given as an instance of it." Fletcher blandly replied that he knew nothing of pirates, but in one of his last reports he displayed a better knowledge than he pretended. He wrote:

"One Captn Kid lately arrived here and produced a Commission under the great seal of England for suppressing of Piracy. When he was here many flockt to him from all parts, men of desperate fortunes and necessitous, in expectation of getting vast treasure. He sailed from hence with 150 men as I am informed great part of them from this province; It is generally believed here they will have money p^r fas aut nefas, that if he misse of his design intended for which he has commission, 'twill not be in Kidd's power to govern such a hord of men under no pay."

5

When Fletcher dispatched this prophecy he was no longer governor, although he did not know it. His successor, Richard Coote, Earl of Bellomont, Kidd's patron, was commissioned on June 16, 1697. The London merchants had exhausted their patience with the Colonel.

Lord Bellomont, an elderly, sincere, active Whig who believed Utopia had been embodied in the "Glorious Revolution," was the ostensible head of the syndicate that backed Kidd, but even greater men stood behind the Earl. The most important members of William's cabinet had shares in the enterprise that was to exterminate buccaneers and make a tidy profit out of the recovered loot. It was natural that the prime mover in this scheme should carry on the work in New York. Perhaps his rank, higher than that of any man yet sent to rule an American colony, would overawe the provincials.

Bellomont was set apart from previous royal appointees in the New World by something more fundamental than his earldom. He was a reformer, a type not unlike the un-unfortunate Leisler, but far more disinterested—the first in a succession of American heroes who were to go down fighting corruption. He was, however, no cloistered theorist but very much a man of his world. He could remember Cromwell's protectorate and had seen the whole panorama of Restoration and Revolution. He had learned from it a philosophy which most of his peers were content to keep in the library. He believed in the possibility of good men ruling by honest principles in the joint interests of King and country. His story is the story of American reform, persistent through repeated defeats, so that the changes its leaders were reviled for seeking came to be accepted without a struggle by later statesmen.

His lordship did not reach New York until April 2, 1698, and it was nearly a week more before he grasped the real nature of his task. New Yorkers were gratifyingly flattered to have an Earl, even an Irish Earl, for their Governor, but they lost no time in making it abundantly clear that they regarded him as entirely ornamental.

Within a few days of his arrival, the *Fortune* put into port. Inquiry brought the frank information that she was from the East, quite innocent of any open relation with customs officials. But, said the pleased New Yorkers, obviously expecting the Governor to share their pleasure, her cargo was worth £20,000. Bellomont ordered ship and cargo seized, whereupon to his amazement "the Merchants were almost ready to mutiny." His Collector of Customs delayed four days while the freight was removed. Partners in the *Fortune's* venture intimidated possible witnesses, and a mob of angry tradesmen locked the royal customs officers in a garret when Bellomont finally persuaded the agents to act.

The Governor had to send soldiers to release them, and then his Council protested against the "tyranny" of using troops to invade a citizen's home.

"I shall have but small assistance from the Gentlemⁿ of His Maj^{tys} Councill," wrote Bellomont five weeks after his arrival, "because they are most of them Merchants and several of themselves the persons concerned in the breach of these laws."

His report to the Lords of Trade showed at once his discouragement and his resolution. He declared that if it were at all possible he would rid the province of corrupt officials, and he began with his Council. The cleansing process reduced the membership from thirteen to five, and those expelled were of first influence in the community.

Graft in the collection of the revenue also attracted Bellomont's notice. In 1697 there were ten times as many public houses in the province as in 1687, but the excise had actually shrunk. In 1687 before Heathcote, the first commuter, began to develop Westchester, taxes there netted the Crown £20. Ten years later, thanks to the promoter's activity, the population had increased many fold. But the County excise had been farmed to Heathcote, a member of the Council, for £7. Bellomont was sure the Collector of Customs "went snips in so cheap a Bargain." The revenue from all Long Island's liquor traffic was let to "Samuel Burt and Company" for £72, the lessees making a net profit of £500 a year. The "Company" was Sheriff Ebenezer Wilson.

The Earl reorganized the customs service, but his new agents proved either timid or corrupt, and soon the ships from Madagascar appeared in the harbor as openly as in Fletcher's time. The Governor made an extra effort in 1699 to bar Captain Giles Shelley, who came from the East to retire. Bellomont thought his presence an insult to honest men, but the old pirate "so flushed them with Arabian Gold and East India goods that they set the Government at defiance." Captain Shelley, as a matter of fact, fitted very smoothly into New York society. His mansion, his fine brass hearth, his elegant gaming table, his forty-five beer glasses and seventy chairs were much admired by the better sort of New Yorker. He was genially hospitable and did not mind if his guests were a little unappreciative of his aesthetic side. He had a really pretty taste, and his home was adorned with seventy-four pictures, for some of which he had paid.

Captain Kidd was less fortunate in his reception. The same year that saw the retirement of Shelley witnessed the arrest of the fugitive pirate-catcher, who had sought refuge in America after accurately fulfilling Fletcher's prediction in the East. Not the weakest of the evidence in support of his protestations of innocence was the fact that he found no defenders among the men who welcomed Shelley. Nor did it assuage the Governor's bitterness that his own protégé was the sole captive in the crusade against buccaneering.

Bellomont's attack on land steals proved the easier task. He convoked an Assembly, and won an electoral victory on the issues of clean government and cancellation of the worst Fletcher grants. Sixteen of the twenty-one Assemblymen were committed to reform. Their first bill annulled a number of land acts, but clean government was more difficult to achieve. After a year of vain efforts, the Governor dejectedly reported:

"In plaine termes I must tell your Lordships that I can have nobody prosecuted here that hath ten pieces of eight."

He added in a mood of profound discouragement that there was not an honest man among the English in all New York, and that the only honest Dutchmen were utterly ignorant. He was, he mourned, reduced to appointing a convicted clipper of the coin as clerk to the Assembly. The rogue was as nearly a man of probity as any who could perform the duties of the office.

For three years Bellomont maintained the struggle, which killed him in the end. Worn out at sixty-five, he refused to rest, even when he was ill, and as the last late snows of March, 1701, were melting in the fields above Wall Street, his disobedient subjects buried him most respectfully in the chapel of the fort.

He had not learned that the wisest and best-intentioned governors can give no better administration than the governed are willing to receive. New York had supported his anger against corrupt land grants and he had been able to annul them. He succeeded, too, in keeping his own land policy pure, giving only small tracts to actual settlers. His failure to suppress piracy was also caused by the majority of his subjects. Illicit traffic harmed no one in New York and benefited many, so it had many friends, who naturally preferred a grafting regime to an honest one.

Unfortunately for the grafters, the path of least resistance in America was apt to become a rocky road in England. While Bellomont was exhausting his strength in fruitless assaults upon "vested interests," the Board of Trade, goaded by the City, was acting with unnatural vigor to bring Fletcher to justice. Charges were delivered to the culprit in November, 1698, and a mere four weeks allowed for an answer. On the day before Christmas the Colonel faced the Board to read as lame a defense as any official ever offered.

He dwelt at some length on his military services, his sufferings, the loss of his Irish patrimony during the ascendancy of the Catholics, his devotion to Church and State and an imaginary promise by the King to give him another job. Descending finally to matters alleged against him, he asserted that he had never prosecuted pirates because no one ever told him there were pirates in New York. He had, he confessed, taken the *Jacob* as a gift, but he explained that it "fell so by accident and without fraud, prospect or contrivance for it."

He admitted drawing full pay and subsistence for half companies, for only so "in that dear place" could he keep troops on the border. He passed over his land steals with the remark that they had all been made with the advice of his Council, whose members gained most from the grants. As for his association with Tew, that was purely evangelical, designed solely "to make him a sober man, and in particular reclaime him from a vile habit of swearing." In conclusion Colonel Fletcher begged their lordships to believe that he came home with no more than £3,000. The Board, unimpressed, recommended a criminal prosecution on charges of neglect of duty and encouraging pirates. There was little law to cover the situation, and everyone concerned was mortally afraid of creating precedents. It was common gossip in the coffee houses that far greater men than any provincial governor had been guilty of far greater frauds. Fletcher's admissions and most of Bellomont's evidence were declared legally inadmissible. The Colonel was acquitted, but it does not appear that he ever enjoyed civil or military employment again, for forty years later another colonial executive, poring over the records of the Fletcher administration in search of guiding principles of conduct, noted:

"He was a generous man . . . but the King was not pleased with him, as I am told."

III

SEEDS OF REVOLUTION

1

LORD BELLOMONT WAS THE last colonial executive to make a successful stand against land grabbers. Most of his successors did not try. Modestly they allowed themselves to drift with the prevailing current of imperial policy, heedless of the danger that rebellion might be waiting at the end of the course. Not least of the causes of the final revolt was the graft that permeated the American administration. Originally corrupted in the interest of colonial development, dishonest officialdom was encouraged until the very rottenness of the system became a drag on further progress. Only then were bribery, favoritism and privilege suddenly recognized as intolerable evils.

As long as the corruption of American rulers was done by colonials for colonials it was undisturbed. The process by which the burden began to be felt as irksome was largely the story of expansion, and graft played an important, even a necessary, part in that growth.

Piracy faded as a reliable source of income when European navies succeeded in making the eastern seas unsafe for pirates. But land and trade remained. As they were operated in America, they proved that legitimate enterprise is far more fruitful for the discerning grafter than the most highly organized illicit traffic.

The rush for cheap farms, a continuing feature in American life and American graft for more than 200 years after Bellomont resumed the Fletcher grants, was the great fact on which colonial profits rested. In the first half of the eighteenth century the population of British America doubled every ten years. "Moderate quit rents" would, if collected with regularity, have obviated the fiscal measures that aroused the spirit of independence.

Neither revenue nor the needs of settlers, however, were regarded in the distribution of the royal domain. When the entire seaboard from Georgia to New Hampshire had passed into private hands the total quit rents of the thirteen colonies amounted to £16,000. Half came from Virginia and none from South Carolina, whose rent roll had long since disappeared. Yet few men obtained land for nothing, and retired colonial governors swelled the ranks of moneyed men at home.

So did revenue collectors. Yet provincial hatred of tariffs was of such practical effect that customs duties barely sufficed to pay the insignificant salaries of the agents, men so badly recompensed that Governor Hutchinson of Massachusetts observed: "Without bribery and corruption they must starve." For once a patriot corroborated a royalist, and James Otis declared:

"It has been observed that a very small office in the customs in America has raised a man a fortune sooner than a government."

"Incorruption in the best of them," commented the philosophical Governor Bernard of New York, himself no stranger to bribes, "must be considered not as a positive but as a comparative term."

Judges were on the same footing. Experienced litigants never failed to bestow some substantial mark of esteem upon the bench. It had been only a few years since Lord Chancellor Cowper had taken the unprecedented step of refusing presents from the barristers who practiced before him, and his lordship had been roundly denounced by other judges for intimating that the immemorial custom was not hallowed by its very age. How, they demanded, could the

State induce good lawyers to accept preferment unless they could make more than in private practice?

No one was so high in rank as to be above graft or so close to the throne as not to cheat the sovereign. Bellomont's successor, Lord Cornbury, was a cousin of Queen Anne, but he proposed to settle the land question forever by selling (for his own account) all the vacant territory in the province in a lump to two men. New York capitalists were too timid to accept, but they whittled away at the royal domain until in 1743 Governor Charles Clinton appealed to the home government for perquisites to replace his income from such bribes, "there being now no vacant land remaining to grant." This was not quite true, but Clinton felt himself a much abused man as the chances of gain in New York had been grossly misrepresented to him when he took the job. He needed ten years instead of two to make his fortune, although he was the ideal of many of his constituents, one of whom wrote:

"He would have done anything for you within his commission for his bottle and a present."

Clinton's neighbors in Connecticut were in an even worse plight than New York. They really had no public land left, but Governor Roger Wolcott had three sons and was a fond father. His paternal affection enabled the boys to join with some other leaders of society to form the Susquehanna Company. They sent John Lydius, an Indian trader with a reputation unsavory even for his kind, to acquire some sort of title to a tract along the Susquehanna River. Any excuse would be enough for the Connecticut General Court (most of whose members received presents of stock) to vote the company a charter. By just what right Connecticut undertook to grant land in Pennsylvania Governor Wolcott did not say in his written opinion upholding the legality of the deal.

Lydius performed his task so well that the Oneida chiefs denounced him to his face at a conference with the King's

Indian Commissioner, who had the thankless task of attempting to keep the peace between the supposed owners of the soil and settlers who could not be induced to recognize that Indians had property rights any white man need respect. "That man is a devil and has stole our lands," cried the Oneida spokesman, pointing at the unperturbed Lydius. "He takes Indians slyly by the blanket one at a time, and when they are drunk puts money in their bosoms and persuades them to sign deeds for our lands upon the Susquehanna, which we will not ratify nor suffer to be settled by any means."

The Connecticut gentry were impervious to savage oratory. They sold tracts in their new territory as rapidly as possible, leaving purchasers to discover the slender basis of their claims only after they had paid their money and arrived on the ground. Settlers had to fight both the Indians and the Pennsylvania law to confirm their titles. The war whoop shrilled through the night along the Susquehanna; isolated farmhouses blazed right merrily over the corpses of their inmates, whose scalps dangled from the belts of triumphant braves; Indian villages were destroyed in retaliation; a fertile valley was desolate, but some remarkably fine mansions in the best style of colonial architecture were reared in New Haven.

The Seven Years' War breaking out at this time, it was remarked that Pennsylvanians seemed much more inclined to fight Connecticut than France. Quaker pacifism preserved inter-colonial peace, but the animosity engendered by the Susquehanna Company and the graft which accompanied its progress seriously hampered all efforts at provincial co-operation.

Preoccupied with speculation, smuggling and commerce, substantial citizens of New England no longer interested themselves in town meetings. The towns had nothing more to give that was worth a rich man's time. Municipal affairs, relieved of their domination, so apparent in Winthrop's time, drifted into the hands of "the inferior sort." In Massachusetts young John Adams discovered with dismay that local government was controlled by tavern keepers, black smiths and shiftless fellows who seemed to find their account in distributing jobs among their adherents. This first appearance of city machines was deplored by the better classes. Adams very much feared that the meetings at which jobs were discussed were enlivened by the drinking of flip, and in his diary the "smoke-filled room" where nominations are secretly made by shrewd politicians anticipated by more than 150 years the tactics of Harry Daugherty.

"This day," wrote Adams in February, 1763, "learned that the Caucus Club meets at certain times in the garret of Tom Dawes. There they smoke tobacco till you cannot see from one end of the garret to the other. Selectmen, assessors, collectors, wardens, fire-wards and representatives are regularly chosen before they are chosen in the town."

2

The autonomous development of provincial graft came to an end with the Seven Years' War in 1763. The course of the struggle brought America within the ken of British statesmanship. Neither as statesmen nor as men on the make could the King's ministers afford longer to ignore an empire which, in the words of Colonel Fletcher, had fallen to them "so by accident and without fraud, prospect or contrivance." Canada was one of the spoils of war, and the American trade assumed proportions that made it worth the while of even busy men to consider what ought to be done about the colonies. From the moment they bent their intellects to the problem dated the competition which few American bribers were able to meet.

New England's practice of supplying the French West Indies with the provisions that enabled the islands to remain havens for privateers throughout the war also drew the attention of London. The traffic had been carried on under cover of permits for ships to visit enemy ports "to exchange prisoners," a humane trade in which it behooved good men to engage. The permits were hawked about Philadelphia, New York and Boston for as much as 400 guineas until Governor Denny of Pennsylvania "broke the market" by issuing them in wholesale lots at £20 apiece. From motives of prudence, conscientious skippers carried a couple of Frenchmen with them in case they fell in with English frigates. For the duration of the war these perennial passengers enjoyed themselves hugely, living well and making delightful shore excursions as they cruised among the picturesque islands. Prisoners have seldom been better treated.

Remembering this, the rulers of England thought it no more than fair that America help carry the debt burden left by the glorious victory, and then the loss of quit rents began to make history. While their land levy stood at a nominal four shillings in the pound, Englishmen resented the slimness of colonial budgets. Massachusetts, with by far the most expensive system of public works and services in the New World, spent £12,937 10s. a year. New York did very well on an annual revenue of about £4,000. Americans, however, thought taxation a more objectionable form of political extortion than graft. When a man gave a bribe, he received value for it; taxes simply disappeared into the maw of official greed without any noticeable return to the payer.

George Grenville's Stamp Act, then, would have stirred revolt even if it had been introduced by an honest administration, and Mr. Grenville was a typical minister of his day. He had been put into office to inaugurate a regime of economy after the war extravagances of the elder Pitt, but also to elevate the fortunes of what passed for a political party. The public, aware of the extreme vagueness of the leaders' principles, described it more accurately as "the

Bloomsbury Gang," taking the name from the Bloomsbury
section of London which the gang's chief, the Duke of Bed-
ford, was making fashionable. In pursuing the first part of
his task, Grenville roused a revolution. In the course of the
second, he transferred the cream of colonial graft to London. Resentful men at a great distance had difficulty in
distinguishing between the two results.

For once the land grabbers, displaced officials and smugglers found themselves on the side of the angels. For there
were angels. Many men, the "fair traders" of popular speech,
prospered modestly within the law, never having occasion
to seek the favor of officialdom. Many planters and farmers
were content with the rewards of agriculture, untroubled
by visions of vast speculative holdings. Many young professional men dreamed with John Adams, who had confided to
his diary:

"Suppose a nation in some distant region should take the
Bible for their only law book, and every member should
regulate his conduct by the precepts there exhibited! Every
member would be obliged, in consequence, to temperance
and frugality and industry; to justice and kindness and
charity towards his fellow men; and to piety, love and reverence towards Almighty God. In this commonwealth no
man would sacrifice his most precious time to cards or any
trifling and mean amusement; no man would steal or lie
or in any way defraud his neighbor, but would live in
peace and good will with all men; no man would blaspheme
his Maker or profane his worship; but a rational and manly,
a sincere and unaffected piety and devotion would reign in
all hearts. What a Utopia; what a Paradise would this region
be!"

This was written, to be sure, before the author had heard
of the Caucus Club, but greater experience of the world
only deepened his longing for perfection. For "some distant region" he now wrote "America." Such young idealists,

nourished on the classical and modern philosophers, whom they studied as something more than rhetoric, were now unexpectedly joined by the outraged leaders of a threatened economic order.

3

The new era was fittingly summarized in the intimation of one governor that he had determined to "take money in lieu of dirt in future." He was able to do it because graft was increasingly necessary to the well-being of trade. England was insisting that the colonies "buy British," that they refrain from competition with English commerce, that they engage in no manufactures, that they check their normal expansion westward to avoid involving the empire in costly Indian wars and that they demonstrate their gratitude for these restrictions by paying some additional taxes. It was a program that did more than humiliate Americans. It forbade them progress.

Unless they would be content with stagnation and perpetual subordination to the interests of English merchants, they must evade the shackling regulations by bribery or revolt. For ten years they tried bribery. Even as late as October, 1774, Benjamin Franklin was writing from England:

"If America would save for 3 or 4 Years the Money she spends in Fashions & Fineries & Fopperies of this Country, she might buy the whole Parliament, Minister and all."

Franklin spoke from the experience gained in years of dealing at close quarters with a system of government whose outstanding characteristic was an avowed corruption that has never been equaled. The Tweed Ring, the railroad looters, the war contractors and the Ohio Gang of later years were pale, ineffective imitations of the grafters against whom the colonists revolted. The English voter in many a borough sold his franchise for a couple of guineas or enough liquor to keep him drunk for a month. The Cabinet Minister's price was somewhat higher. Both, as well as all the grades in between, yielded to the simplest workings of supply and demand.

Every Prime Minister maintained an enormous slush fund to buy the members of his own party to vote for measures to which they were pledged. At election time seats in the House of Commons were openly advertised for sale by the little groups of electors who then heard themselves described by their purchasers as the bulwark of the British Constitution. As the hustings resounded with the high-minded outpourings of rival partisans during the campaign of 1768, Dr. Franklin wrote from London:

"Four thousand pounds is now the *market price* for a borough. In short this whole venal nation is now at market, will be sold for about two millions, and might be bought out of the hands of the present bidders (if he would offer half a million more) by the very Devil himself."

The pleasant fiction had grown up that only the King was cheated in this process and that a man who amassed a fortune from bribery was essentially a higher order of being than he who grew rich from vulgar trade. The English ruling classes would have been puzzled to devise any means by which bribery might be eliminated. They would have been equally at a loss to understand why anyone should wish the elimination. Some of the landed gentry complained that merchants and the rising barbarian lords of a new industrialism were outbidding their betters in the auction of privilege, but such protests were simply nostalgic longings for a monopoly that had gone.

A few university dons and impractical political philosophers did offer alternatives to corruption. Their literary skill was often admired, their ingenuity highly praised, but the masters of England dismissed as fanciful the idea of a "planned" political economy. Exercises in composition could teach nothing to men who had "muddled through" to greatness. The muddlers were confident results had proved the truth of the theory on which they worked—that government is a scramble for prize money. The elaborate, ceremonial courtesy of social life had no place in the political arena. Here no holds were barred. In private conversation a gentleman could hardly be too prodigal of bows and pompous phrases of respect. But the cultivated son of a noble earl then serving as Prime Minister thought he had advanced a telling argument when he assured a public meeting that the leader of the opposition was a "goggle-eyed son of a bitch."

On this high plane English politics were unexpectedly enlivened in 1768 by a reform bill requiring all newly elected members of the House of Commons to declare on oath that they had not directly or indirectly bribed any elector. Indignant Parliament men remarked that it was introduced by the owner of a borough, whose seat was as much his sacred, inalienable property as his shirt, and who therefore did not need to bribe. His motion was howled down as serving no purpose but to add perjury to the sins of "honorable gentlemen."

Across the Atlantic even successful bribery had begun to lose its charm, resentment of the expense being added to other grievances. In the southern colonies George Washington and Charles Carroll of Maryland were not the sort to submit forever to having their vast projects of settlement at the mercy of freebooters like the Bloomsbury Gang. Dislike of the system was sharpened by lack of practice in corruption. The planters had long ago brought their own governments into complete harmony with agrarian needs. Once they had acquired their plantations they became a ruling caste, governing in the interest of large estates. Bribery in its grosser manifestations had not for some time been necessary to their prosperity.

The continuance of that prosperity was bound up with the development of the West. Land companies were formed to exploit it, but at every turn the eager expansionists were blocked by the philosophic greed (and the desire for peace) of the home government. The whole process was admirably exemplified in the progress of the most ambitious of all the settlement projects, a curious mingling of the visionary and the practical, the Grand Ohio Company.

4

Its history began with murder. In the spring of 1763 William Trent and a group of other fur traders were returning to Fort Pitt from what must have been an unusually profitable expedition, if we may judge by the value later put upon their baggage. They were ambushed by Indians and the few who escaped death or captivity came pelting breathlessly into the fort, glad to save their lives at the sacrifice of their goods.

More than five years later, during negotiations for a "perpetual peace" with the Six Nations, the subject of reparations arose. The claims of the despoiled traders had been bought up by a syndicate headed by the influential mercantile firm of Wharton Brothers, Philadelphia. The elder of the brothers, Samuel, was a sober, hard-headed, industrious Quaker who knew, as did all Americans, that the real estate game could be made to pay. In consideration of his forgiveness and five shillings cash, the Indians allowed the syndicate 2,500,000 acres along the Ohio, although at the same time the treaty makers were establishing a wide neutral zone on the western slopes of the Alleghenies, in and beyond which no white man was to settle. The indemnity land was all within the territory "inalienably" secured to the Six Nations, but Sir William Johnson, Superintendent for Northern Indians and the trusted friend of the Red Man, was a member of the syndicate.

The Grand Ohio Company, formed to exploit these rights, thus had a more substantial basis for a grant than most of its rivals. However, a deed from the King was as essential as the marks of a few Indian chiefs. Wharton sailed for London to negotiate a patent.

He had Pennsylvania solidly behind him, for the seventy-two members of his company included most of the leading citizens of the province. Franklin was among them, and one of his motives for being in England at this time was to prepare the ground for Wharton's coming. The Doctor's title of Agent for Pennsylvania was the least of his qualifications for the task. Of enormous prestige, thanks to his scientific and philosophical achievements, his popularity was strengthened by an easy wit and homely yet graceful manner that were a delightful contrast to the prevailing pomposity in England. He was by long odds the most distinguished American. At this time in his sixties but remarkably vigorous, he took perhaps his greatest pleasure in the infinite variety of the human species. His large, bland countenance was the reflection of the wide tolerance and genuine humanity of his nature. He had already noted:

"There is no kind of dishonesty into which otherwise good people more easily and frequently fall than that of defrauding the government."

A year before the Six Nations agreed to reparation terms, the thoughtful Doctor suggested to the Secretaries of State that a new settlement "in the Illinois country" might be desirable. They expressed mild agreement. The Board of Trade, with which final decision rested, ought, said Franklin, "to be brought over privately before the matter should be referred to them officially." This task he left to Wharton.

The Quaker was well equipped for the work at hand. The credit of Wharton Brothers stood as high in London as that of any American firm. The seventy-two partners had contributed to a fund that was entirely at their spokesman's disposal. And he possessed a talent, shared by a surprising number of American business men in all ages, for calculating the price of a given official.

Mouselike in his plain gray clothes, retiring of manner, soft spoken and persistent, he was conspicuous by his very simplicity in the midst of the powdered, bewigged and beribboned courtiers in their laces, silks and colored coats. Probably they mocked his solemnity, but they found his presents even more magnificent than those given by gentlemen of fashion in mulberry and sky blue. Having paved the way with a general largesse, Wharton moved to the more difficult task of conciliating the powerful.

Thomas Walpole, financier and member of Parliament, was induced to join the company as its "front." He lent it such a dignified façade that the project was often referred to as "Walpole's grant." Shares were given to some other members of the Bloomsbury Gang, and on Jan. 4, 1770, Wharton signed a preliminary agreement with the Lords of the Treasury to buy 2,400,000 acres for £10,460 7s. 3d., about 2 per cent. of its then value. It is to be noted that 100,000 acres of the Indian lands had vanished.

So far the Grand Ohio Company resembled a dozen others organized in various colonies. For all of them negotiations dragged through several years, with money flowing in a steady stream to the languid English placemen who were in no hurry to sign deeds that would end the graft. But a brief conversation between Franklin and Lord Hillsborough of the Board of Trade soon placed the Grand Ohio Company in a class by itself. His lordship, who was then in effect colonial minister, expressed himself as satisfied with the provisional contract but thought the applicants too modest.

"Ask for enough to make a province," he advised Franklin.

The words, repeated to Wharton, fired the vivid imagination hidden behind the Quaker's sober dress and manner. He rose to the occasion with a few pitying thoughts for Virginia rivals—Washingtons, Lees and Fitzhughs—whose Mississippi Company was seeking title to a paltry 2,500,000 acres beyond the Alleghenies. Eagerly the partners figured, conned maps, estimated distances. Boldly they marked out a small empire, stretching for 200 miles along the Ohio River and running south for an even greater distance. Half again the size of Ireland and almost exactly the area of the present State of New York, the territory was reported to be unbelievably rich. No colonial merchants had ever before dared aspire to a tenth as much.

With renewed enthusiasm Wharton set himself to the "vast deal of oiling and greasing" necessary to put the machinery of government in motion. He also evolved a name for the proposed province, a name reminiscent of the imaginary kingdoms of fiction—Vandalia. It was a subtle compliment to Charlotte, George III's German queen, who was supposed to be descended from a King of the Vandals. At times in the course of his negotiations Wharton thought it applied with rather more force to the profligate noblemen, Parliamentarians and secretaries whom he bribed, cajoled and threatened. But the prize was worth the expense. Already settlers were pushing over the mountains in such numbers that the company would be able to recoup its preliminary outlay as soon as its patent was sealed.

Months passed as the Philadelphian propitiated clerks, flunkies, sinecure holders, unofficial but obscurely influential gentlemen. Franklin, whose favorite proverb seemed to be the one about slips between cup and lip, shook his massive head over the delay. At last, on July 3, 1773, a draft was prepared. Payment was to be the same as under the document of 1770, despite the greatly enlarged acreage, a tribute to Wharton's energies and bribes. Suddenly the law officers of the Crown, inspired by the English members of the Mississippi Company, intervened. The Attorney and Solicitor Generals had never in their long careers yet agreed on a point of law, but now both declared the grant illegal.

Wharton replied by quoting Puffendorf and Grotius and the new legal luminary, Blackstone, in a great display of learning. He also drew some more bills on Wharton Broth-

ers, levied an assessment on the seventy-two partners and
renewed his visits to friends in high places. On Oct. 28,
1773, the Committee of Council for Plantation Affairs over-
ruled the legal objections and ordered the patent prepared.
Wharton's five years of toil seemed to be crowned with a
just reward. The scribes would dally a few weeks in hair-
splitting over phraseology, and then would be born the four-
teenth and perhaps greatest of the American colonies—Vandalia.

During the Christmas festivities, therefore, the Quaker
was in a rare state of exaltation. He was so sure of success
that he even regarded with charity the London that was so
distasteful to him. The overdressed fops, shameless ladies of
fashion, festive carousing, hypocritical courtesy and magnificent candle-lit mansions so close to the horrid slums lost
their power to offend when they were so soon to be left
behind. In a few weeks, Wharton rejoiced, he would return
to the delights of honest endeavor, the development of Vandalia and the practical mercantile affairs of Wharton Brothers. Even Franklin was almost optimistic.

As a Quaker, a business man and potential ruler of a
province, Wharton deplored all the loose prattle of possible fighting in the colonies. He thought with Dr. Franklin that a great deal of the belligerent language was supplied by army victualers and gunsmiths. These prospective
war profiteers, said the Doctor, always tried to stir up
trouble, and if they could not involve England in a foreign
dispute were the loudest proponents of a punitive expedition in America.

At this Christmas time, however, pugnacity seemed the
merest talk. It had been the same in '64 during the excitement over the Stamp Act when Americans burned the
houses of tax collectors. Wharton was confident that the
present quarrel over duties on tea would end as harmlessly.
Force was a silly argument for civilized people, interfering with trade and imperiling the success of such meritorious
enterprises as Vandalia. Dr. Franklin accepted this view with

reservations, as usual. The venerable philosopher, his partner thought, did not reconcile himself with sufficient complacency to the realities of British politics.

But it was the Quaker merchant who underestimated reality. At the very moment when he was most sure of the enduring quality of his work in London, the whole project of the Grand Ohio Company had already crashed in ruins. On the night of Dec. 16, 1773, a party of patriots flung some chests of tea into Boston harbor, and doomed Vandalia to become only a name moldering in forgotten archives.

The partners in London were deeply stirred, but in different directions. Franklin, as soon as he learned that the Boston tea party was more than a simple act of vandalism, realized that he was an American—no longer an Englishman. Lightly he cast from him the great settlement scheme on which he had lavished so much time and wisdom. He understood at once that far more important problems than Vandalia were involved in General Gage's military mission in Massachusetts. If the soldier failed, the colonies might be freed from the necessity of bribing every progressive measure through the greedy inertia of London.

Wharton could take no such farsighted view. He lingered on and on in London, fretting at the stubbornness of rebels. Mourning over the fading vision of Vandalia, he never knew that out of the squabbling over taxes, the selfish grabbing for land, the sordid intrigues of smugglers, there had developed an ideal for which his countrymen were prepared to fight. A new and better order of society where honesty and fair play might yet prevail was the goal on which their eyes were fixed as the Revolution got under way with minute men drilling, eloquence flowing, shots sharply popping on the road to Concord and the fine frenzy of independence rising irresistibly toward the spirit of '76.

Passionately these provincials flung their principles as a challenge to the world, and Benjamin Franklin, first citizen of a new nation, was home again in Philadelphia preparing for the Continental Congress a resolution setting forth the

objects that had drawn the Thirteen Colonies together. A
more inspiring Declaration was deemed preferable, but the
first thoughts of the best-informed, most dispassionate American of his day show how largely the new hostility to graft
animated the patriots.

"The British nation," thundered the sage, "through great
corruption of manners and extreme dissipation and profusion, both private and public, found all honest resources insufficient to supply their excessive luxury and prodigality,
and thereby have been driven to the practice of every injustice which avarice could dictate or rapacity execute; And,
not satisfied with the immense plunder of the East, obtained
by sacrificing millions of the human species, they have lately
turned their eyes to the West, and, grudging us the peace-
able enjoyment of the fruits of our hard labor and virtuous
industry, have for years past been endeavouring to extort the
same from us."

In that rather overdrawn indictment, the resentment of
an honest man obliged to carry out a straightforward business project through bribery and influence is plain. To spend
five years and thousands of pounds in order to gain what
Americans considered their rights was beyond the power
or the patience of most men. Yet Vandalia was far from
the only venture thus bound in red tape and expense. Its
history was typical of many others. The backers of settlement schemes, not being the sort to bow meekly before the
majesty of official titles, rose to defend themselves against
corruption.

The English grafters had made the mistake of not giving
value for their bribes, and no graft can survive in defiance
of its reason for being, which is to serve as the handmaid
of progress, or at least of those policies which the dominant
interests of the community believe to be progress. When
the bought official ceases to be the servant of the business
he is paid to protect or expand, he becomes an intolerable
tyrant. That was the meaning of Franklin's diatribe.

IV

THE LAST REFUGE

1

Dr. JOHNSON, DISAPPROVING
on principle of the American Revolution, might have had
the rebels in mind when he offered his famous definition
of patriotism. And in the gloomiest days of the struggle,
when every expedient seemed to fail, the men who refused
to be daunted by adversity could have been forgiven for
reversing the epigram to: "Scoundrelism is the last refuge
of a patriot."

Unprepared, unorganized, often mutually suspicious and
always ill-equipped, the Continentals could only adapt to
their own needs the system they knew best, and that was
founded on graft. Many of them did not like it, had taken
up arms to get rid of it, but fervor and high resolves were
hardly enough to build Utopia overnight. So contractors
robbed the army as a matter of right and custom, continuing the practice by which so many of them had in previous
colonial wars "pinched an estate out of the bellies of the
poor soldiers." Men who uttered the most correct sentiments
when speaking of freedom argued that business was business.

Washington, arriving before Boston in 1775 to assume
command of the army besieging General Gage, found his
soldiers being used to work the farms of their officers instead of preparing to fight. Clothing and powder came in
slowly and with such unexplained deductions that the Com-
mander-in-Chief wrote of the Massachusetts men:

65

"Notwithstanding all the publick virtue which is ascrib'd to these people, there is no nation under the sun (that I ever came across) pay greater adoration to money than they do."

A little later he broke out against the people he had come to defend, crying:

"Such a dearth of public spirit, and want of virtue, such stock jobbing and fertility in all the low arts to obtain advantages of one kind and another, I never saw before, and pray God I may never be witness to again. I tremble at the prospect. Such a dirty, mercenary spirit pervades the whole, that I should not be at all surprised at any disaster that may happen."

Although he was thus armed against surprise at the disasters that were to crowd upon him, it could not be said that the General's prayer was answered. He discovered in the course of the war that Massachusetts men had no monopoly on protestations of morality, love of money or lack of public virtue. To the very end he continued to encounter officers who had to be cashiered "for drawing more provisions and pay than they had men in their company" or "seeking by dirty and base means the promotion of their own dishonest gain" or simply as "defrauders of the public." Occasion for discipline on these grounds was so frequent that the Father of his Country developed a stern parental style in dealing with transgressors.

Non-combatants, hardly more scrupulous than military men, were even more inexperienced in the conduct of enterprises that cost a government money. For 150 years the ways and means to maintain armies and fleets had been the concern of England. Suddenly the colonists confronted the necessity of carrying on a war without a revenue.

Battling through a maze of financial entanglements further complicated by the depreciation of a completely unsecured paper currency, whose collapse was so obviously inevitable when viewed by their descendants but was so inexplicable to them, they came by all roads to the same impasse. The war was being waged against taxes. Every time the Continental Congress mentioned proposals for raising some revenue, the patriots cried indignantly, "What are we fighting for?" In order to carry on, it was necessary to cheat the public on behalf of the government. Printing press money was one way. Requisitioning supplies by force was another. Cheating did not stop at that dictated by public necessity. The opportunity to turn a quick profit is never so clear as in time of war, and revolutionary officials had the imposing English tradition of corruption behind them. But not the least novel feature of the Revolution was the beginning of a new code of political morality, a protest against individual gain at the nation's expense on grounds of principle rather than expediency. The reformers had arrived; the grafters remained.

Sometimes it is difficult to tell which was which. There was, for example, the picturesque figure of the Honorable Samuel Chase, delegate to the Continental Congress from the free state of Maryland. The term "red hot patriot" was not too warm to describe his ardor. Thirty-five years old, tall, solid and strong, with dark, wavy hair falling over broad shoulders on either side of a big-featured, not unattractive face, this Annapolis lawyer had proved himself a furious partisan, a master of invective with a saving grace of persuasiveness lurking behind a violent manner. In later years when he was John Marshall's predecessor as oracle of the Supreme Court, his likeness in countenance and disposition to the learned Samuel Johnson was widely remarked. Irreverent lawyers referred to the distinguished judge, behind his back, as "Old Bacon Face."

Returning in the summer of 1776 from an unsuccessful mission to convince Canada that she was and of right ought to be free and independent, Chase found that Maryland had voted orders to her delegates, including himself, to reject final separation from England. With the belligerence that was one day to earn him impeachment at the bar of the Senate of the United States, he flung himself into a whirlwind campaign to reverse the defeatist decision. The very ferocity of manner, so unbecoming when he had risen to the Supreme Court, cowed those who had triumphed a few weeks before. Almost single-handed Chase bullied and cajoled the electorate. Then, still fresh after exertions that had left his adversaries breathless, he galloped off to carry new instructions to Congress. Over execrable roads, through the heat and dust of midsummer, he covered 150 miles in two days, a feat of horsemanship highly extolled in its time. Although never embalmed in poetry, it was favorably compared to Paul Revere's effort, for it brought the tireless rider into Philadelphia on the very eve of the decisive vote on the Declaration of Independence.

For the next two years Chase served well on innumerable Congressional committees. With eloquence and the resources of a personality that imposed on opponents with the finesse of a bludgeon, he supported Washington against intrigues and cabals. Fiercely he combated talk of any peace that fell short of complete independence. The quality of his patriotism was as indubitable as that of Washington making military history out of the most unlikely material, as that of Adams thundering encouragement to the wavering, as that of Franklin performing his prodigies of diplomacy with a simple zest that made them look as easy as capturing lightning at the tail of a kite.

But patriotism was not enough. In 1778 Samuel Chase still held the same sturdy principles as in '76, regarded himself as the same man who had saved Maryland for freedom, the hero of the famous ride, but lo! here was Alexander Hamilton writing of him in phrases that many of Chase's former admirers were copying.

"It is your lot to have the peculiar privilege of being universally despised," Washington's young aide declared contemptuously. "Were I inclined to make a satire upon the species, I would attempt a faithful description of your heart." Cut by old friends, refused reappointment to Congress, Chase nursed a characteristically hot wrath against purer patriots who thus aspersed him. For after all, what had he done? Nothing more than attempt to corner the flour market. The previous winter the Revolutionary army had frozen and starved at Valley Forge. The troops who survived had developed an extreme bitterness against victualers and clothiers. These gentry devoted themselves too openly to speculating in the variety of paper currencies advanced to them by their government while they sold to civilians—and even to the enemy—supplies that should have gone to the front. Outspoken soldierly comments had affected lay opinion, and the ground was well prepared for criticism when Chase in his capacity as Congressman heard that a French fleet was on its way across the Atlantic to assist the fight against tyranny.

It never occurred to Chase that private use of this information could be regarded as anything but a clever stroke of business, as it would have been five years earlier. He knew that His Most Christian Majesty was sending gold as one of the sinews of war, and would exchange it for bread for his men. Chase had no money of his own, but friends were willing to base a partnership on his knowledge and their credit. They embarked on what was later called a "conspiracy" to execute their corner. They failed, but the price of flour soared alarmingly, with the usual profit to some speculators and the usual suffering on the part of the masses and the army. The newer ideals of government soared, too, in impressive flights of oratory, and Chase was driven temporarily from public life. He returned before the end of the war, enriched by a few years as a dealer in cannon, powder and ships, to be one of the patriots accused by the French Minister of spending most of their time in private speculation based on Congressional information.

The failure of the flour corner was partly due to the fact that Chase was not the only public man with advance tips and a taste for gambling. While the Marylander and his partners were vainly attempting to get complete control of the market, Robert Morris was selling flour to the French at a profit of 50 per cent.

Morris, "the financier of the Revolution," was quite as odd a mixture as Chase. Critics of a later generation were inclined to blame him for harping so much on his "integrity," but a study of his papers reveals that he and they had different definitions for the word. Morris meant only commercial credit, and thought it no sin to boast that his was unquestioned. At the outbreak of the war he was the leading merchant of Philadelphia, and his luck was proverbial. Everything he touched succeeded. Now, a plump man in his middle forties with a baldness that lent him an impressive height of brow, he was a member of Congress, relied upon by his colleagues for financial advice when their own simple trust in the printing press proved unavailing.

Morris had received the first contract for the importation of arms, and had been guaranteed a profit of £12,000. His dealings with the government continued on that plane until in 1779 Thomas Paine was directing his vitriolic pen against the rich man who used a position of public trust for private gain. Morris demanded an investigation and got it. The evidence was uncontested. Paine's charges were substantially correct; the point at issue was whether censure was deserved. The financier for his part made no secret of his belief that should any attempt be made to check "the due influence of wealth" on government, money would exercise its power "unduly" through corruption.

Congress agreed with him and he was exonerated. The reasoning that led members to differentiate between the culpability of Chase and the innocence of Morris was not recorded. No doubt the financier was needed; the politician was not, and the new morality had to give way to practical considerations. At any rate, two years later when Morris was appointed Superintendent of Finances, in sole charge of an empty treasury, Congress specifically authorized him to engage in private trade on the side. He insisted on the condition, explaining that it was necessary to maintain his "integrity."

The system he introduced has been widely admired because against great odds it succeeded. By extremely adroit exchange manipulations, the mingling of his own and the nation's credit, and control over a new bank of issue, Morris made a nice profit for himself and restored monetary circulation to such an extent that even the critical Paine was moved to exclaim:

"We began with paper, and we end with gold and silver!"

In part this result was achieved by taking Hamilton's advice to "unite the interest and credit of rich individuals with those of the state." The Bank of North America was incorporated in Philadelphia with the idea of circulating paper that would be acceptable in trade. Bank notes had been something of a mystery in the colonies, where most banks had been nothing more than an address and a quantity of unsecured promises to pay on demand. Some had even dispensed with the address.

Morris's bank was better than anything hitherto known in America. The charter provided that it was not to begin issuing notes until a capital stock of $400,000 had been paid up. The rich individuals who subscribed never did bother to send in the cash, but Morris was able to use the prestige of their names to print and keep at par millions in notes. It was largely a bluff, but as the one apparently sound structure in a tottering world, the bank earned big dividends for the so-called investors. It also anticipated generations of financial practice in dealing with government.

Not everyone was satisfied with the Morris administration. Individuals who were not rich complained that they were being ruined by an oligarchy of merchants as greedy as the courtiers of King George. "Bill kiting" and "paper mongering" were terms used to describe the financier's methods, and it is true that similar operations in the management of private corporations would have landed Morris in jail, as they eventually did. But in 1783 he reasonably pointed out that men fighting for their lives and property could not be choosy about weapons.

Most of his contemporaries who had a voice in the conduct of affairs agreed. Posterity in a concurring opinion has ruled that Robert Morris shall be remembered as one of the illustrious band of Fathers and that his eight years of financial service to the cause of liberty cover with oblivion the profit he made in that service and three later years in prison.

The United States, in no small part because of his financial juggling, his clever use of graft, had won the right "to assume among the powers of the earth the separate and equal station to which the Laws of Nature and of Nature's God entitle them." It remained only "to form a more perfect union, establish justice, insure domestic tranquility, provide for the common defence, promote the general welfare, and secure the blessings of Liberty to ourselves and our Posterity."

V

"THE CORRUPT SQUADRON"

1

W ASHINGTON'S RAGGED CON-
tinentals, the famous embattled farmers, artisans and clerks,
had won the war. They lost the peace in a backwash of
reaction that is so often one of the penalties of victory. The
right to exploit new lands and old opportunities had been
taken over from the Bloomsbury Gang, but by a race of
something less than saints.

Before the war ended, some of the principles for which
it was fought had been jettisoned. Returning soldiers found
their state governments organized as agencies of materialism
rather than men. Stringent property qualifications deprived
the great majority of the franchise. Of course, they had never
had it before, but the brave words of '76 had seemed to
imply that a new era was being inaugurated.

Most of the revolutionary chieftains, however, did not
understand "equality" to mean universal suffrage any more
than they supposed that "freedom" applied to Negroes. The
new republican state constitutions were drawn up with this
in mind by men like John Jay, an able lawyer and writer
allied to a good many of the wealthiest families of New
York. He was chairman of the committee that drafted the
state's new fundamental law, and he was also author of the
dictum:

"Those who own the country ought to govern it."

In the four years of peace between 1783 and the calling
of the constitutional convention, the states fell into a help-

less confusion more dangerous to trade and even to agriculture than the eight years of war. A desire to escape from the hopelessness of a purely laissez-faire philosophy is plain in the document drawn up by the merchants, planters, and lawyers who assembled in Philadelphia in 1787.

The Declaration of Independence expressed their striving toward perfection. Human rights are its substance; idealism dictated and enthusiasm carried it. The Constitution was conceived in a very different spirit. Here the rights of property are supreme and nowhere except in the preamble is there any mention of personal liberty. (The "rights of man" as distinct from the rights of property were so completely ignored that the first ten amendments were speedily added as a sop to Jeffersonian principles and the persistent idealism of common folk.) Created in a series of masterly compromises over practical difficulties, it was adopted without enthusiasm as a working program.

As it failed to satisfy completely any of the men who made it, so it aroused little affection in the country. Not more than one-third of the limited number of voters qualified by law bothered to declare themselves on "the greatest work ever struck off at a given time by the brain and purpose of man." This general indifference was a tribute to the genius that composed the Constitution. Compromise, no matter how desirable, does not inspire devotion. The preservation of property arouses fanatical support only among the small minority that possesses enough property to worry about.

No one, then, expected the Constitution to inaugurate the millennium. No one could have supposed that it would eliminate graft. But the extent to which corruption would be possible and profitable depended—as did so many other problems—upon the body that was to be built around the framework of the Constitution. The men who offered themselves for the task of construction held three contrasting views, admirably exemplified in the leading exponent of each—Thomas Jefferson, Alexander Hamilton and John Adams.

Jefferson was the most susceptible to words, perhaps because he used them masterfully himself. Spokesman of the agrarians who, if numbers were to be decisive, would dominate the country, he founded his governmental principles on the sands of faith in the essential virtue of common people. As a landed gentleman, he believed that trade corrupted this natural goodness. Apostle of advanced beliefs in the arts and sciences, he was very much a child of the eighteenth century in his certainty that the owners of the soil should rule the nation with Spartan simplicity and fine regard for the welfare of the fellow men. He did not appreciate that Spartan simplicity is the product of Spartan discipline, and Mr. Jefferson did not in the abstract admire discipline. Fortunately he was nearly always able to divorce his practice from his more rigid philosophical theories.

Hamilton was a divinely appointed antagonist for the untidy, versatile representative of Southern aristocracy. The New Yorker's opinion of the abilities and honesty of mankind was low. The illegitimate offspring of a French Huguenot matron in the West Indies by (probably) a Scottish adventurer, he properly looked upon himself as one of nature's noblemen. Such, he maintained, should rule the world. As a very young man he expressed the point of view from which he never wavered:

"The safest reliance of every government is on men's interest. This is a principle of human nature on which all political speculation, to be just, must be founded."

Even earlier he professed to have learned as a fact that the "vast majority of mankind is entirely biased by motives of self-interest." Graft seemed to him an essential ingredient of government.

To this man, just thirty when the constitutional convention assembled, the dominance of agriculture already belonged to a vanished era. Attorney for big merchants, joined by marriage to the wealthy Schuyler family, founder of a bank and an insurance company, the prophet of industrialism, he had not advanced beyond his advice to Morris to "make it the *immediate* interest of the moneyed men to cooperate with the government." Co-operation, by very definition, is mutual. The loose federation admired by Jefferson would not serve growing commercial interests, which demanded a strong regime, highly centralized, attentive to the needs of trade. If the government would look after business, business men would look after the rest of the community. So they argued.

How far Hamilton was duped by such talk is doubtful. Although often acting from respectable, even altruistic motives himself, he never recognized the possible existence of decency in others. Probably he trusted no more in the good intentions of his friends than in the protestations of his enemies. His task, as he saw it, was to entrench capitalism securely in control of the government.

Adams, older than the other two, dispassionate as they could never be, was often as cynical as Hamilton and, paradoxically, even more tenacious of his early dreams than Jefferson. He recognized the evils inherent in the liberalism of the Virginian and the capitalism of the New Yorker. Either system, he thought, would have to be sustained by graft, or what he called "the cohesive power of public plunder."

"In every society where property exists there will ever be a struggle between rich and poor," he wrote. "Mixed in one assembly equal laws can never be expected; they will either be made by numbers to plunder the few who are rich, or by influence to fleece the many who are poor."

Adams, doubting the ability of the masses to use their strength in this class war, supposed that the gentry would "gain more and more continually until they become exorbitantly rich and the others miserably poor." Yet he was also led to this other conclusion:

"The moment the idea is admitted into society that property is not as sacred as the laws of God and that there is not a force of law and public justice to protect it, anarchy and tyranny commence."

It would seem that Adams held out no hope for the poor. But he escaped from the dilemma into which his reason drove his humanity by suggesting that since there must be laws to protect property, there should also be laws to regulate its use. He envisaged a House of Representatives controlled by the poor contending with a Senate of the rich for property rights. Above them in an Olympian calm would be such an impartial executive as John Adams tipping the scales of justice as the general welfare demanded, the arbiter between two irreconcilable forces. With quite as much confidence in his own infallibility as either Jefferson or Hamilton, he never doubted his capacity for this work. With the faith he retained from his boyhood, he knew that God would raise up giants to take his place in future generations.

2

Merely to state the differences between these schools of thought is to indicate the victor. The tighter organization, the intensive concentration of resources, the growing power of money and credit, the greater rewards offered to energy and to graft ensured the triumph of capitalism. In five years and four months as Secretary of the Treasury Hamilton fixed his political system so firmly upon the nation that sixty years of agrarian ascendancy which followed could not dislodge any essential feature.

Without "the cohesive power of public plunder" it would have been impossible, and the strength that forged a world power would have been dissipated in gestures. The moneyed men were only drawn into the orbit of Hamilton's influence in pursuit of their own material advantages. They set up the government of the United States as part of an irresistible urge to establish their class as the managers of national progress. They were grafters, but their graft, from which the crudest extortions of contemporary British practice had been eliminated by the Revolution, shaped the destiny of a new nation.

Jefferson might rally his cohorts with stirring denunciations of "the corrupt squadron," but it was corruption such as the colonies had not experienced. Capitalists no longer needed to buy government favors. They were the government and could bestow those favors freely.

The change was seen at the very first session of Congress. Import duties to provide the mainstay of the new Federal government were worked out in a series of compromises worthy of the constitutional convention. Agreement was followed by an unexplained delay, final passage being gently obstructed by Congressmen who were also importers. They were waiting for their ships to arrive with a summer supply of merchandise tax free. Once they had filled their warehouses, they allowed the tariff to go into effect. They had, of course, already raised prices because of the duties they had not paid.

Senator Maclay, a gruff, rigid, honest equalitarian from western Pennsylvania, was much pained to observe that his colleague, Representative Fitzsimons of Philadelphia, was thus acting in a double capacity as legislator and importer.

"You will always find the merchant uppermost," the Senator mourned.

Evasion of the tariff for a few months was small potatoes. It served only as a rehearsal for the drama in which the greatest Secretary of the Treasury before Mellon put through his program for establishing the nation's credit on a sound basis.

A large national debt might not be regarded at first glance as the most likely magnet to attract the loyalty of moneyed men. But Hamilton knew that once they had become creditors of the government they would insist upon the authority and stability of the Federal regime. In accordance with his principles, he prepared to enlist their support by showing them how to make an enormous profit, but so different was he from British statesmen of the day that he did not want a share for himself.

With characteristic daring he based his system on the almost worthless Continental and state bonds issued during the war. These bits of paper could be bought readily at 5 cents on the dollar or less, and nearly $70,000,000 (face value) were outstanding. Two months before Congress was to meet for its second session, the Secretary of the Treasury advised influential acquaintances that he had a plan for redeeming the depreciated certificates at par. Capitalist enthusiasm for national "integrity" in the Morris sense was reflected in an immediate "marked upward movement" in the recently despised scrip. Rich Senators, Representatives and merchants hastened to get as much of the $70,000,000 as possible before news of Hamilton's program should leak out.

The innocent Senator Maclay noted in his diary the sudden rise which their activities caused. He added that it "could not be accounted for, neither in Philadelphia nor elsewhere." Maclay was one of the minority of Senators to whom Hamilton had not divulged his plans.

Another was Senator Benjamin Hawkins of North Carolina. Jogging into New York over frozen roads for the session of 1790 and cursing the bitter January weather, he encountered two unusually well-mounted groups riding express for the South. Naturally he supposed them bent on escaping from the horrid Northern winter, but they explained that they were bound for Hawkins's own state to buy scrip. They displayed large sums of money for that purpose, and the Senator supposed they had gone mad.

Equally crazy in this foxy way was Representative Jeremiah Wadsworth of Connecticut, who had been Quartermaster General of the Revolutionary Army. He dispatched two fast ships freighted with coin to the Southern states, and soon his agents were swarming over the countryside generously offering to take "worthless" paper off poor men's hands for as much as three or four cents on the dollar.

In New York, Boston and Philadelphia certificates were fluctuating wildly between 25 and 45 cents, but express riders and racing sloops easily distanced the rumors of refunding into the hinterland, while Adams was shocked to hear from his son at home that respected leaders of the Massachusetts bar were speculating with the funds of clients. The hopes of moneyed men soared with the price of scrip and puzzled Southerners thought half New York was engaged solely in the paper trade. Then, on Jan. 14th, Colonel Hamilton's proposals for paying off at par were read in the House, and Senator Maclay was "so struck of an heap" that he could not muster words to record his feelings to his diary that night.

Watching alternately his colleagues and the speculators jammed in the galleries, he could not decide which group was the more jubilant. Many did not wait to hear the end, but poured forth into Wall Street, which that day witnessed the first of a long series of rejoicings over the prospect of everybody getting rich in a hurry. In the uproar of the celebration, the voice of protest could scarcely be heard. But there was protest. The gibe at "the corrupt squadron," which Jefferson would make his own, was being growled angrily in coffee houses and taverns. After a night of brooding over the coup, Maclay recovered his command of the language and predicted that "this villainous business" would "in all probability damn the character of Hamilton as a minister forever."

No one could doubt that members of Congress who were to vote on paying the depreciated scrip at par had anticipated their votes. Their eagerness disgusted many who desired to see the national credit on a high plane. The idea that legislators were not elected to make their fortunes, so novel to men brought up under English rule in the eighteenth century, led several Congressmen to swear solemnly and falsely that they had no share in the speculative mania.

The exact number of gamblers was not known. Jefferson was accused of gross exaggeration when he charged that most of the Senate and a considerable minority of the House were scrip speculators. The Treasury carefully guarded its records from the public, so it was not until a century after the tumult and shouting had died away that the curious were able to discover that Jefferson's figures were so accurate he probably obtained them from a Treasury official. A fire in the department destroyed a good many records just before the Jeffersonians came into power, but enough remain to prove that sixteen of the twenty-six Senators were security holders. In the House twenty-nine out of a total membership of sixty-four were in the same fortunate class. Most of them were active speculators rather than original creditors of the government.

The fire was one of two in government offices that created more talk at the time than mere accidents should. As it became apparent at the close of the century that a Jeffersonian administration was likely, charges of corruption became more specific. Timothy Pickering was accused of having been $500,000 short in his accounts as Secretary of War. Oliver Wolcott, Hamilton's successor at the Treasury, announced that army records would clear his colleague. Pickering had been shifted to the State Department and Samuel Dexter, who had taken his place, was urged to produce the documents. Before he could do so a mysterious fire destroyed them. Adams, in whose presidency the incident occurred, never believed in Pickering's innocence.

A little later Dexter was promoted to the Treasury on Wolcott's resignation, and again his regime was inaugurated with a fire among the records. Ungentlemanly Jeffersonian newsmongers made much of the fact that Wolcott conveniently arrived with a wagon to save his private papers just as the blaze was discovered. The burned documents included many relating to the debt and the refunding. The list of security holders is, therefore, incomplete and there may well have been more interested Congressmen than have been counted. For example, a William Paterson of New Jersey owned scrip, but he is not positively identified as the Jersey Senator of that name. Senator Paterson is not included here among the sixteen who stood to gain by the refunding, although he voted for it.

Meanwhile the battle raged through the session of 1790, the first vote to recognize the debt having far from settled details. The final test of strength came on the proposal to assume state war debts as a Federal obligation. The Senate approved, 14 to 12, five of that body's lesser security holders voting with the minority against their own interests. Greater difficulties were encountered in the House, where there was a smaller proportion of speculators. Hamilton tried to make the issue one of repudiation versus good faith. James Madison, leader of the opposition, retorted with an amendment that almost wrecked the Secretary's careful structure of government by and for moneyed men. Madison proposed that men to whom scrip was originally issued should receive par for what they still held, and all others the highest price quoted before Hamilton reported his funding plan.

The offer, as doing justice to men who had helped win the war, was attractive enough to carry the House by a narrow margin, but Hamilton refused to be beaten. His friends were strong enough to force a reconsideration, and in the short interval allowed him the Secretary worked fast.

He needed two votes and they were hard to get. The mere money incentive had already drawn to his side all who could be influenced by it, but this same session of Congress would select a site for the permanent capital, and that had bargaining possibilities. Hamilton's assistant told Maclay that if he could manage two Representatives from his state, the capital would be located in the Susquehanna valley, where the Senator owned property.

"I constrained my indignation at this proposal with much difficulty within the bounds of decency," the righteous Maclay recorded.

Thus repulsed, Hamilton was driven to apply for his two votes to the most unlikely person in the world—Thomas Jefferson. Washington's chief ministers—Jefferson was presiding over the State Department—were already hopelessly at odds, but Hamilton had learned in the army that weapons can be seized from the enemy.

Walking to Washington's house one day, he drew his rival into conversation. For half an hour they strolled up and down before the President's door. The meticulously groomed, almost dandified Secretary of the Treasury did most of the talking. His carelessly dressed companion stalked gravely at his side, secretly bewildered by the maze of financial complexities into which he was being led. The only thoroughly intelligible part of the discourse was that the nation's credit was in danger and it behooved the whole administration to hang together.

The sage of Monticello ever after maintained that, being recently returned from years of diplomacy in Europe and ignorant of the importance of the issue, he was tricked. Whatever his motives and misfortunes, the deal discussed on that comradely promenade was closed over a dinner at his own table next day. Jefferson agreed to furnish two votes in return for a national capital, signed, sealed and delivered to the Potomac.

On July 16th the site of Washington was approved, Hamilton's obedient Northern gamblers voting with the Southerners. Less than three weeks later Representatives White and Lee of Virginia ("but White with a revulsion of stomach almost convulsive," noted the scientific Mr. Jefferson) changed their votes on assumption, and it was law, 32 to 29. Twenty-one of the majority were speculators.

3

Gaily Hamilton rode the crest of a wave of popularity, the admiring clamor of successful dealers in stock ringing clear over an undertone of grumbling about legislators who voted themselves rich. Of course it was said the Secretary had not neglected his own account in the distribution of paper wealth. Actually his only dealings in scrip were as agent for his wife's family, who profited greatly. He himself was not especially fond of money; he preferred power, and that he seemed to have in abundance. While the funding battle was still undecided, the indefatigable fellow was at work on another project for linking the state to the rich.

The scheme was embodied in a report to Congress on the establishment of a Bank of the United States to be chartered for twenty years. As a medium for issuing a national currency and as a stabilizing influence on the chaotic, local, insecure depositories of the day, the new institution could be useful. But Hamilton did not expect to confine it to such purely financial purposes. The Federal administration was to be strengthened among capitalists by giving them control of the bank and the government's funds.

"To attach full confidence to an institution of this kind," he explained, "it appears to be an essential ingredient in its structure that it shall be under a *private* not a *public* direction—under the guidance of *individual interest,* not of *public policy.*"

A more frankly worded invitation to plunder could hardly have been devised, and the men to whom it was addressed needed no second. As the report was read, Maclay observed that the business men around him in the Senate seemed "magnetically drawn to the contemplation of the moneyed interest." The same influence that passed the funding bill rushed the bank measure through Congress.

Again the speculators paid loud homage to the genius of their leader, and members of Congress hastened to enter the new market for bank stock and scrip. This was established by custom in the shade of an old tree on Wall Street, very handy to the sessions of Congress. Here it was possible to win in a day (and lose in an hour) more than most men could gain in a month of prosaic business. Loss, however, was not mentioned, for the dealers were sure Hamilton had discovered an antidote to poverty, a new credit system that was infallible. Others than gamblers were less confident, and even Hamilton's admirer, assistant and destined successor, Wolcott, confided to his father:

"The sudden accumulation of wealth in the hands of individuals has introduced a mania which has led in some instances to an ostentatious display calculated to excite envy and to recall the unfortunate circumstances under which the evidences of the public debt were alienated to recollection. This, as was to be expected, has induced mad speculations on the part of the fortunate, and ebullitions of discontent from those who have been disappointed."

Slowly these "ebullitions" rolled in from the country as farmers and war veterans and rural shopkeepers learned how they had been cheated of their certificates. The newspapers were full of diatribes, fostered by Madison and Jefferson, against speculators and legislators. "A Farmer" (in unconscious imitation of the M.P. who had been so ridiculed in the House of Commons twenty-odd years before) suggested:

"Would it not be a good regulation to oblige every member of Congress to lay his hand on his heart and to declare that he is no speculator, and that he did not come forward to claim for himself the price of the blood or the life of the poor soldier?"

The men who had mounted the whirlwind of prosperity with Hamilton were impatient of such puerilities.

"The poor soldiers! I am tired of hearing about the poor soldiers!" the House was one day informed by Mr. Wadsworth, he of the fast ships.

His words fanned the fury of former fighting men who

were not apt to regard an ex-quartermaster highly under any circumstances. Only Washington's immense prestige saved the Hamiltonian program, as the Secretary admitted long afterward when he wrote of his chief:

"He was an *Aegis very essential to me.*"

"The President has become, in the hands of Hamilton, the dishclout of every dirty speculation, as his name goes to wipe away blame and silence all murmuring," was the way Maclay put it.

Murmuring was in reality so far from silenced that Washington himself became the object of vilification. He was accused of overdrawing his salary, of conniving for his own profit at "this dirty work," of seeking to be King, of being Hamilton's unwitting or guilty tool. All fantastic, of course, but charges and counter-charges were flung about so freely that no man could escape.

One of the denunciations of Hamilton went beyond innuendo. James Reynolds, of whom nothing much is known except that he was then in jail and had a beautiful wife, accused the Secretary of engaging with him in secret speculations. Reynolds had some letters that plainly showed he and Hamilton shared a sense of guilt. With a chivalry not often copied in politics, three Jeffersonians headed by James Monroe called ceremoniously upon Hamilton to enable him to explain before they laid the incriminating documents on Washington's table. Hamilton had preserved the other half of the correspondence with Reynolds, which proved that his sin had not been betrayal of public trust but adultery with Mrs. Reynolds, a confession that was to rise four years later to help blast his presidential aspirations.

Abuse in the merry winter of 1791, while Hamilton squired the frail Mrs. Reynolds at intimate parties during his wife's absence from town, failed to check what Jefferson called "the rage of getting rich in a day." Stock in the new bank soared to 195; dealings in government securities grew ever larger; the Bank of Massachusetts suspended payment for nearly two months while the son of its president gambled with the funds on deposit. A tree in Wall Street was no longer adequate shelter for the eager dealers.

In March, 1792, a stock exchange was opened a few doors to the west, and a month later the market celebrated the activities of the new institution with a crash. Bank stock plunged to 108 as the first Wall Street bubble burst in a froth of bankruptcies, swindles and recriminations that were to become traditional. The despair of the losers was not alleviated by learning that their representatives in Congress, who had shared in the rise of public securities, escaped the disasters of the fall. Thanks to inside information, they had sold out scrip and stock at the peak.

Some of Hamilton's biographers have deplored the fact that he stooped to unworthy methods to accomplish his invaluable work. Such regrets were misplaced. Hamilton used graft with his eyes open, confident that the good he conferred upon his country was worth the incidental evil. He was realist enough to know that without graft the men Jay called the owners of the country would never have joined with him to restore and maintain Federal credit, that the foundation for genuine national greatness would never have been laid.

4

Even at the height of the boom, some men realized that Wall Street was not the country. Hamilton's brilliant but unsavory manipulations threw off as a by-product a system of westward expansion that carried the descendants of Revolutionary heroes to the Pacific.

The close of the war found the settlements beyond the Alleghenies delighting in a splendid isolation, uncontrolled and cherishing a rude disregard of authority. They and the vast territory in which they lived became the responsibility of the new government, individual states waiving their claims. Speculation in Western lands preceded and was as

rabid as that in scrip. Quite unknown sections of Kentucky
were freely bought and sold at prices higher than they have
ever been able to command since.

It was a regrettable instance of the frailty of good intentions that the framer of an ingenious financial structure of
government could not devise a more satisfactory method of
settling the West than that he inherited from the Bloomsbury Gang. Or perhaps, as an admirer of English institutions and in an unaccustomed mood of humility, Hamilton
did not think he could improve upon it. At any rate, the
old game of land companies and grants was revived in all
its former visionary glory, except that the bribes now went
to members of Congress.

Senator Morris, resolutely pursuing the road to ruin, was
the most ambitious operator in the country. He seldom
troubled with less than a million acres unless he was buying house lots in the future city of Washington. He and
some of his colleagues picked up a good deal of desirable
property there between the date of Jefferson's dinner party
and the vote on the capital.

Morris's holdings were spread over half a dozen states;
his agents in Europe recruited immigrants; he published
pamphlets describing not too accurately the riches to be
won from the soil. This was expensive. His ambition grew
larger than his prudence. He ran out of cash and resorted
to his war methods of financing. The North American Land
Company, incorporated to operate 6,000,000 acres of his
property, issued notes redeemable in specie and secured by
the land. Millions of dollars' worth found their way into
circulation. By the end of 1797 they were coming back, and
Morris had to confess himself in default. Early in the new
year writs were out for his arrest.

"I am a martyr to the times," he told Hamilton.

The Court of Chancery did not share this view. It found
that Morris could never have been serious in his pledges to
redeem his notes. Next month the great financier was in

the Philadelphia jail and no man, himself least of all, could tell the extent of his liabilities. Estimates ran as high as thirty million dollars, half the sum of the outstanding national debt.

For three and a half years Morris lived as the guest of other inmates, too poor to pay for his prison lodgings, a cheerful, negligible old fellow, giving his companions sage advice on thrift and industry, reading letters from those who had lost their money in his enterprises and pacing his measured exercise in the stockaded yard. Carefully he would pick up fifty pebbles at the start, and at each turn of the doleful circle he would drop one. When his hand was empty, the only man alive supposedly able to rival Hamilton's financial ability knew that he had finished his walk and that it was time to go inside.*

Morris had crashed through too great faith in paper. Others arranged land speculations more sensibly, avoiding debt because they did not pay for their land until they resold it. They operated in the manner of John Symmes, who had served with distinction in the war, had been a justice of the New Jersey Supreme Court and a delegate to the Continental Congress. A vision of wealth and power in a new country sent him into Ohio, but he left his base well guarded. He formed a partnership with a pair of Jersey Representatives, Jonathan Dayton and Elias Boudinot, leaders of the Hamiltonian party.

Even before the new Federal Government was set up, the three applied for a million acres between the Miami and Little Miami Rivers. They were equally premature in disposing of it. Symmes had sold a good deal of land there long before Dayton and Boudinot made a contract with the government, although this was signed in October, 1788,

---

* Morris was released under a new Federal bankruptcy law that enabled him to snatch a little property from the wreck of his affairs. Lawsuits over this remnant occupied him until his death in 1806, but the litigation was long suspected of being immortal. It was settled by exhaustion in 1880.

nearly five months before the first Congress met in New York. By some oversight the boundary set forth in the grant fell short of the Little Miami, and Symmes had already sold 20,000 acres in a strip he did not own.

His partners saved him. They secured an extension of the grant to cover those acres and more besides; they had Symmes appointed one of the three judges of the Northwest Territory; they sent him advance information on the funding bill, which enabled the jurist to get a great many certificates at rock-bottom prices in exchange for land. They fought manfully for him when his peculiar sales methods led to complaints and suits. For Symmes would sell a single plot to two or three customers, and so many objected that Washington was inclined to cancel the grant altogether. Dayton and Boudinot persuaded him to allow Symmes to keep the 311,682 acres for which he had actually paid, and Symmes bribed the surveyor in 1794 to run lines enclosing 543,950 acres. Then he went on selling land even outside of that area.

He might have carried on with impunity if he had not made the mistake of quarreling with his partners. They speedily taught him that the protection of Congressional leaders is worth paying for. Settlers who had bought land outside the Symmes grant were encouraged to sue, and won judgments in every case. Appeals to the House of Representatives, although voiced by a new young member named William Henry Harrison, the Judge's son-in-law, were rejected at the demand of the veterans. Bit by bit the choice Ohio lands Symmes had reserved for himself were seized to satisfy judgments. In his will the pioneer was able to leave nothing more than a conviction that a "deepest conspiracy" had robbed him of "the earnings of a long, industrious, frugal and adventurous life." The young son-in-law retired into the wilderness to emerge after many years as "Tippecanoe" Harrison, ninth President of the United

States. By that time the Judge's real estate practices had become standard for operations in the public domain.

Sincere, earnest patriots who remained aloof from the turmoil shuddered at the decay of the glorious Revolutionary principles. Was it for this new breed of parasites, they cried, that they had thrown off the yoke of England? Loudly they bewailed the perfidy of public men, insisting that the new officialdom was as shamelessly corrupt as the British aristocracy.

They were wrong. The graft that called forth these denunciations varied in an important respect from the haphazard corruption of the Bloomsbury Gang. Parliament sold itself to the highest bidder—capitalist, agrarian or feudal. The Hamiltonian majority, disdaining such lack of principle, gave itself freely to the business interests of which Congressional leaders were an integral part. Jefferson proposed only to shift the government to his own class. Jobholders of both parties identified their own profit with the Right.

Proof of the new public ethics was seen in the fate of Symmes's ex-partner, Dayton. His speculations, his repeated votes in support of them, had laid him open only to the political opposition he shared with his colleagues. But when he tried to revive some pre-Revolution tricks, he was no longer within the limits his class would condone. As Speaker of the House, it was Dayton's duty to draw on the Treasury for pay and traveling allowances for members. Between 1798 and 1800 he requisitioned $33,000 for this purpose and retained $18,000.

In the colonies such a thing had been regarded with tolerance. The word "perquisites" would have covered it. Under the new system Dayton found no defenders. Even the amiable Wolcott was aroused and forced the defaulter to make restitution. Dayton was driven ignominiously from public life; unadorned embezzlement had been dropped from the list of entirely respectable political crimes.

VI

THE NEW ARISTOCRACY

1

DISCIPLINED, VICTORIOUS, MA-
neuvering with the precision that cavalry drill sergeants
dream about, "the corrupt squadron" had one fatal flaw—it
was only a squadron. Challenged by even a moderately well-
organized army—of aroused agrarians, say—the troop of
moneyed men would be exposed in the pitiful inadequacy
of its numbers. The host was raised against them by the
inimitable, diverse tactical talents of Jefferson and Burr.

The campaign of 1800, unsurpassed in the quality of the
abuse poured out on both sides, did no more than deprive
the Hamiltonians of the grafting privileges, but their bitter
wails were couched in terms of protest against revolution,
anarchy and spoliation. Thus rapidly do even patriots come
to believe that public plunder is a vested right. Jefferson,
busily organizing propaganda and contributions on a national scale, was dubbed "Mad Tom" in the more polite
writings of his opponents. Their opinion of the dangerous
revolutionary's chief lieutenant was not so simple, and the
filth that was heaped upon his memory has obscured the
man beneath ever since.

The philosophical considerations that so sharply divided
Jefferson, Hamilton and Adams carried little weight with
Aaron Burr. He settled each day's problems as they arose.
Born into the Northern theological aristocracy, he was drawn
to the popular side of every question by his careless affec-
tion for people. He liked everyone and almost everyone

liked him. Passing through a long life of more than common vicissitudes, he retained at eighty the youthful zest for experience that had been his at eighteen. He flung himself with equal abandon and the same gay spirit into political campaigns, dreams of empire, love affairs, lawsuits, family life, speculation and conversation.

In 1800 he was the only man who could boast of repeated successes over Hamilton. As the acknowledged leaders of the New York bar, they had come off with approximately equal honors, but in Hamilton's chosen field of finance Burr had achieved a notable victory. The Bank of New York, Hamilton's own creation, was protected in a monopoly by the refusal of the Federalist legislature to grant any other a charter. The power of a bank in politics was not then disguised to conciliate popular dislike, and Burr thought his party could use one.

He talked, however, about the inadequacy of his city's water supply, recently emphasized by an epidemic. The legislature readily bestowed upon the Manhattan Company, organized by Burr and his political friends, a charter to provide an ample flow of clear water for New York. No one noticed amid the elaborate phraseology of the document a short and simple clause authorizing the use of surplus funds for "operations not inconsistent with the laws and constitution of the state of New York." The Bank of the Manhattan Company was created under that provision and pure water was left to the future. The monopoly of Hamilton's institution was broken.

The rivals met upon a broader field in 1800. New York's electoral votes were expected to decide the issue, and in achieving victory Burr made his great contribution to the American system of government. He also changed the course of a good deal of graft.

The feature of his work that attracted most attention was the conversion of a group of war veterans called the Sons of St. Tammany to an interest in politics. The slender, handsome young lawyer with his charm and the glamor of a higher caste easily dominated the small property owners and artisans of Tammany, who had sought nothing beyond beer and masquerade in Indian feathers. Under Burr's leadership they discovered the grander joys of partisan strategy. Drilled by him as disciplined party workers, they were the nucleus of his attack on the intrenched Federalists. His cohorts of "forgotten men," the fellows who had won independence and were left to wonder what had become of it, elected a State Assembly almost unanimous for the restoration of democracy and agrarian ascendancy.

In those days Presidential electors were chosen by the state legislatures, and for a little time moneyed men despaired. Hamilton himself thought his careful creation of government would be lost, and he urged Jay, as Governor of New York, to call the old legislature into special session to appoint electors pledged to Adams. Any expedient, he said, was justified if it prevented his system from falling into unfriendly hands. But Jay was not the rule or ruin type. He filed Hamilton's letter among his papers with the terse endorsement:

"Proposing a measure for party purposes which it would not become me to adopt."

One hope still remained. In their indifference to the prospect of party government, the makers of the Constitution had written that the man who received the most votes should be President and the next Vice President. Thus Jefferson had served in the second place under Adams. But now the electors were so well disciplined that Jefferson and Burr would each get all the votes of their party's electors, and no more. Final choice would therefore be thrown into the House of Representatives where the Federalists held the balance, and shrewd deals might be arranged to save some part of the administrative machinery for the disconsolate grafters. The Presidency was for sale, and the Revolution's power for reform may be gauged from the fact that there were no bidders. In the contemporary British Parliament, under similar conditions, the frenzied auction that must have taken place would have bankrupted winner and loser alike.

Hamilton, soured by the landslide that had eliminated him as a public figure of any consequence, was scratching away at innumerable letters warning his onetime followers that Burr, the contriver of his political ruin, would use any dishonest expedient to gain power. The great Treasurer was sure Jefferson would make the weaker executive, and he threw all his influence to the Virginian. But Burr had nullified that influence. "The corrupt squadron" that had deployed unquestioningly at Hamilton's commands in the days of funding ignored him now. Moneyed men thought the polished and supposedly conscienceless Burr would be more amenable than the horrid Jacobin, democrat, farmer and anarchist, "Mad Tom" Jefferson.

"The means existed of electing Burr, but this required his cooperation," wrote Senator Bayard of Delaware. "By deceiving one man (a great blockhead) and tempting two (not incorruptible), he might have secured a majority of the States. He will never have another chance of being President of the United States, and the little use he has made of this one gives me but an humble opinion of the talents of an unprincipled man."

Burr's notions of honor rather than any lack of talent kept him from putting in a bid. Jefferson was very busy conciliating opponents and consolidating his position in his own party. Burr maintained a painfully correct, silent demeanor. He knew he could have the highest office in the land, but he was not prepared to stoop for it.

2

The new administration did not take its tone from the Vice President. Rather it seemed a creature of environment,

and that was the city of Washington, muddy, dreary, great
only in promise and ambition, half-built and wholly uncomfortable. Officeholders were still seeking habitable quarters, the embittered Adams was still jolting over miry roads
toward Quincy, cynics were still wondering about Burr's
scruples when the rich individuals whose interests Hamilton had wanted to unite with those of government learned
that Jefferson would not destroy them. He would not have
anything to do with them.

Years afterward when the rivals of 1800 had become reconciled, the ferocity of the struggle buried under two aged
men's memories of the glory of '76, the forthright Adams
wrote in friendly fashion to his successor:

"Your character in history may easily be foreseen. Your
administration will be quoted by philosophers as a model
of profound wisdom; by politicians as weak, superficial and
shortsighted. Mine," he added rather wistfully, "like Pope's
woman will have no character at all."

Men who sought favors from the state were not interested
in Mr. Jefferson's philosophy. The weakness was what they
fastened upon, careless of the fact that it was a philosophical
weakness based on principle. His administration, committed
to the theory that the least government is the best government, left them free. From the lofty plane of his intellectual
superiority, Jefferson was unable to view the mischief that
money grubbers might be working on the lower levels of
practical politics.

Others were not so aloof. The eloquence of Madison as
Secretary of State, the rigid Swiss integrity of Albert Gal-
latin, Hamilton's administrative equal in the Treasury,
matched Jefferson's noble principles. One of those principles, however, was an economy in pay that encouraged
a cheap, petty corruption of lesser jobholders. The revenue
and land offices were not turned over to the plunderers
from a sense of duty, as in Hamilton's time, but the result
was very much the same.

The simplicity of the new regime, reducing expenses of government from $7,500,000 to $4,000,000 a year, cut salaries to a bare subsistence rate. This was a matter of indifference to wealthy planters in high office, but in the inferior ranks of the civil service graft was even more widespread than when the Federalists placed themselves at the disposal of the rich. Old soldiers, clerks and unsuccessful lawyers who carried on the routine of government and whose work threw them into contact with wealthy merchants and land grabbers were entrusted with great responsibility and subject to little control. They were expected under great temptation to observe a more than Cato-like rectitude. That they failed to live up to the standards set forth in Jefferson's more abstract papers for the servants of a free people will surprise only a Jeffersonian.

The corruption reached no higher than Federal attorneys, revenue collectors and customs men. The chief policies of the national administration were bathed in unprecedented purity, with moneyed men carefully extruded. It is easy to imagine the power and wealth they would have garnered if Hamilton rather than Jefferson had conducted the purchase of Louisiana. As it was, the splendid empire passed without graft into the United States to be looted by a later generation. The triumphant President was sure he had acquired across the Mississippi an agrarian paradise into which no capitalist would ever venture, a guarantee that the landholding classes would be forever supreme in the country which he had saved.

3

If Jefferson had been more observant he might have noticed that even in his own time agricultural domination was far from complete. His inquiring and speculative intelligence would also have understood why his administration was so singularly free from graft in the upper register. The

Federal Government no longer had anything to offer that a grafter could sell, for Jeffersonian principles demanded concentration of authority in the states. To the states, then, the grafters turned for office as the wealthy turned for favors —and not in vain.

Watchful in his retirement at Quincy, John Adams saw that power for good or evil had passed from Washington. The course of corruption in the eternal struggle—as he saw it—of the rich to exploit the poor was diverted, not dammed.

"By corruption here," he explained, "I mean a sacrifice of every national interest and honor to private and party objects."

Coldly pessimistic, he watched the men Jefferson ignored sweep the country forward to war and bankruptcy. Coldly disapproving, he observed the philosophy of Hamilton and Jay flourishing in state capitals which professed the Jeffersonian creed. Moneyed men who had served Hamilton and themselves in Congress sought few offices in the states. They found it cheaper to purchase the benevolent support of victorious politicians.

They dealt easily with such machines as the one Burr had created in New York, for after Tammany's mentor removed himself from politics by killing Hamilton in a duel— "Our David has slain the Goliath of Federalism!" exclaimed a vindictive Democrat—his work was taken up by the Clintons. George Clinton had been Governor and succeeded Burr in the Vice Presidency. His nephew, De Witt, was Mayor of New York and a State Senator. At thirty-five he became the leader of his party, and to maintain that position he found it necessary to control the distribution of patronage so that anyone seeking favors should come to him. His method was to crush those who tried to put through legislation for their friends without his approval.

For years every charter that went through the Assembly was paid for. The price of individual votes ran as high as $5,000, that being the amount paid by the Bank of America, successor to Hamilton's Bank of the United States, whose Federal charter expired during Madison's administration. The Democratic Congress refused to renew, and the institution was forced to take shelter under state laws. The same legislature legalized a lottery for colleges in the state—Union and Columbia were two of the beneficiaries. The profits, after expenses were paid, were meticulously devoted to the proper cause. The politicians were content to win all the big prizes.

The pleasure that rich individuals took in dealing with sensible state authorities was not confined to New York. Georgia, too, had politicians and a fertile valley of great extent that attracted almost as much attention from speculators as the Northwest Territory. Four associations known by the euphonious title of the Yazoo Companies were formed to take advantage of the fact that the Georgia legislators of 1795 liked quick and easy profit as much as any Northern Congressman. Men from many states, but mostly from Massachusetts, came into the Yazoo Companies, and they bribed with cash or shares every member of the legislature save one. History fails to record how this lone anonymous incorruptible escaped the net.

A bill selling to the Yazoo Companies for $500,000 a tract admitted to contain 20,000,000 acres and actually comprising 35,000,000—larger than Vandalia or the present state of Georgia—was the result of the judicious partnership of Northern capital and Southern legislative talent. Speculation in the Yazoo rivaled the bank stock bubble, for the land had been bought at a cent and a half an acre and most of it could be sold for 100 times that amount. As one of the biggest land steals ever attempted, it offered a fair target for moralists.

It was also especially vulnerable because most of the legislators had either retired voluntarily to develop their new interests or had been relegated to private life by indignant constituencies. A committee of the legislature of 1796 investigated the work of the previous session, brought most of the unsavory details to light and recommended that the contract be voided. An act to this effect was speedily passed, but the great Yazoo swindle case had only begun.

A nation-wide howl arose from the speculators and their friends. The rights of property however acquired were and must remain sacred, Massachusetts financiers maintained. Georgia would be forever disgraced if she did not keep faith with the men who had debauched her, they said, voicing a plea used neither for the first nor the last time by the beneficiaries of graft.

"For one legislature to declare a former one corrupt is an unprecedented usurpation of the right of trial and judgment," cried Chauncey Goodrich, a staunch Federalist.

The scandal dragged on through the years. A decade after the name of Yazoo had first been pronounced with joy or disgust, the fate of 35,000,000 acres was still in dispute, the Federal courts by that time having intervened to see that the rights of property were protected, and Senator Giles was calling on John Quincy Adams in Washington.

"He said," wrote the former President's son, "if those claims were not totally and forever rejected, Congress would be bribed into the sale of the United States lands, as the Georgia Legislature was to that sale."

Yazoo was finally disposed of by paying the claimants $5,000,000 to give up their loot. The truth of Giles's prophecy was somewhat longer delayed.

4

It took a war to restore the Federal Government to its normal position in the world of graft, nor was that the sorriest feature of the conflict that overtook Madison and the country in 1812. Without corruption, the union might very well have broken to pieces then more irremediably than fifty years later.

Jefferson's eloquent and able successor found that he had to fight, but the resources for doing it successfully were quite beyond his control. America's financial and industrial strength lay in Philadelphia, New York and New England, but the New Englanders were for the moment ardent pacifists. The Napoleonic wars made excellent business for neutrals, and the merchants were reluctant to see their flourishing trade endangered by quarrels over freedom of the seas, border disputes or mere regard for international law. When hostilities broke out in spite of them, they revenged themselves by threats of secession and extortionate charges for everything they furnished the government in the way of naval or military supplies. A rigidly honest bureaucracy would have driven them to revolt, but accomodating grafters kept them soothed with profit.

More irritating to the pride of those who wished to impress America's importance upon a faintly contemptuous England was the state of the army. The United States had been singularly unfortunate in its high command ever since Washington left it. The very first of all Congressional investigations in which with great regularity the nation has probed its political sins was prompted in 1792 by the military disaster that overtook General St. Clair in the Ohio country. The investigators reluctantly reported that a corrupt commissary had sent the expedition out, short of food, ammunition and medical stores, to be massacred by the Indians. Since then the integrity and efficiency of the military establishment had been on the wane.

Typical of the generals who organized the fighting force with which Madison began his war was James Wilkinson, who rose by merit of seniority and a well-oiled tongue to the command in chief. Wilkinson earned a niche in history as the only American soldier of such exalted rank to be a traitor. For years, from his headquarters in New Orleans, he served as a spy of Spain, rewarded with about twice his army pay besides bonuses for such items as inventing evidence on which Burr was tried for treason.

The army he bequeathed to his successors made a sorry showing in the field. In the inglorious annals of the land fighting only two exploits are generally described at any length in the school books. One was Harrison's victory over Tecumseh at Tippecanoe before war was declared. The other, fought after the peace had been signed, made Andrew Jackson the idol of his countrymen. Both were gained by backwoodsmen operating with a minimum of official support, and at that a corrupt commissary nearly cost the Tennessee hero his Battle of New Orleans.

Only four days before his untrained men faced Wellington's Peninsular veterans (fortunately led by Wellington's brother-in-law rather than by the Duke in person), the Kentucky division that was to win the day came into camp. Rejoicing over the timely arrival of the eager warriors was cut short by the discovery that not one in three was armed.

"I don't believe it!" the General shouted in one of those spectacular rages that made him so beloved by men against whom his anger was not directed. "I have never seen a Kentuckian without a gun and a pack of cards and a bottle of whisky in my life."

The unique sight was vouchsafed him that day, and it was only by a rare exhibition of self-control that he was able to write the Secretary of War a comparatively calm account of the missing arms.

"The man entrusted with their transportation has halted on the way for the purpose of private speculations," Jackson reported, and went out to win his victory with what weapons he could scrape together in the city.

No doubt rumors of the peace that had been signed in Europe two weeks earlier had reached the agent in charge of the rifles. If so he can hardly be blamed for stopping to buy cotton while the price was still six cents, because as soon as the public knew of the treaty the brokers were offering sixteen. Some handsome fortunes were won in those few days by State and War Department officials who were the first to get the news.

5

Caught up in the wave of prosperity that rolled majestically across the country in the wake of soaring prices for farm produce, furs and timber, the United States entered upon their first period of general elevation in the standard of living. Comforts of civilization penetrated as far west as Tennessee and Michigan. Immigrants fleeing from the devastation of the Napoleonic wars pushed ever further into the wilderness. Bewildered Indians, driven from one hunting ground to another, were constantly accused of treaty violations for which the only possible atonement was further cessions of rich land on which settlers had fixed their hearts. The best sections remained with the government agents who negotiated the transactions or were held for resale by Eastern magnates for whom the officials obligingly acted.

Jefferson himself believed this process was on the whole desirable, and no doubt he was right. Only a sentimentalist could feel that justice might have been attempted in dealing with the Indians, "a race," as O. Henry's Irishman so happily expressed it, "to which we owe nothing except the land on which the United States is situated."

"To promote this disposition to exchange lands, which they have to spare and we want," Jefferson had written as President, "we shall push our trading uses and be glad to see the good and useful individuals among them run into debt, because we observe that when these debts get beyond what the individuals can pay, they become willing to lop them off by a cession of lands."

Jefferson knew quite well that individual Indians owned no land at all. But the man who had directed the abuse of Hamilton's "corrupt squadron" could philosophize in calmer vein on the advantages of tempting "useful" braves to betray their people by voting tribal lands to pay personal debts.

"You will perceive," he added, "how sacredly it [his advice on acquiring land] must be kept within your breast, and especially how improper to be understood by the Indians. For their interests and their tranquillity it is best that they should see only the present age of their history."

It was, perhaps, as well for the white settler, too. In the booming era after 1815 whole forests were mowed down like grass to make room for salable crops. Sixteen-cent cotton drew the plantation economy steadily westward in ever widening sweeps that still could not catch up with the demand.

Even deeper in the wilderness a former German peddler's agents fought the mighty Hudson's Bay Company on even terms, debauched the Indians and were in curiously secret contact with Federal officials who manned the outposts of civilization. But the European fur market, rousing from years of war stagnation, was clamorous and John Jacob Astor was rolling up the biggest fortune in America. It did not grow quite as fast as his contemporaries supposed because there were such unpublicized expenses as $35,000 in a single year to Lewis Cass, Governor of the Territory of Michigan, for unexplained services to Astor's American Fur Company. The money was well invested for later, as Secretary of War, Cass was to hear, and dismiss, many charges of corruption, extortion, trespass and violence against the company and its representatives.

The rapid expansion westward called for a corresponding increase in credit resources and manufacturing in the East. Industries sprang up to supply the needs of Western settlers, and banks followed thick upon the heels of the factories, offering all the credit facilities anyone could ask. A new race of capitalists arose—men who rediscovered the truism that it is easier to make a fortune from dealing in bonds and shares than from manufacture and distribution.

Old John Adams, conservative, clear-sighted and distrustful, wrote sadly to Jefferson deploring the impossibility under these circumstances of achieving the democracy of which both had dreamed. "An aristocracy of land jobbers and stock jobbers is irremediably entailed upon us, to endless generations," he mourned.

He saw with dismay that any scheming fellow with a few thousand dollars to bribe influential state legislators could become a financier. Once a complacent Assembly granted a charter, it ceased to have control over the operations of a bank. An irresponsible disregard of anything except immediate profit, inconceivable to those who do not remember 1929, seized upon the dealers in credit. They discounted notes for anyone who pleased them, regardless of security. They issued paper money in bales. They fought each other fiercely for the privilege of financing every visionary project whose plausible sponsor spoke in large figures.

The juiciest fruit of this financial hothouse was the second Bank of the United States, a wonderful example of the inability of Jeffersonian philosophy to affect the course of graft or profits. Chartered by a Congress whose members could recall the practical advantages of the first bank, it violated the platforms on which most of them had been elected, but they relied justifiably upon the short memory of voters.

Faithfully the organizers copied the Hamiltonian principle that the bank should have public money to work with but should enjoy strictly private operation. The government directors, a small minority, were persuaded to overlook illegalities from the start. The charter provided that the bank should open for business only after a capital of $7,000,000 had been fully paid up. Actually it opened in January, 1817, with $2,000,000. Dividends were allowed on shares subscribed for but not paid for; directors borrowed the bank's money to speculate in its stock; discounts were made in open violation of the regulations.

It was rather more circumspect than private and state banks. The vast flimsy structure that these institutions erected in a few years towered over the economic system of the country. It could never have been built if corruption had not been its foundation, although the bankers, almost completely ignorant of finance, deluded themselves as much as anyone else. Nothing except their confidence in the paper they printed gave it value, and that confidence was not shared by the despised politicians or grafters, for no hopes of sudden wealth impaired their vision. They were content to dismiss the dangers ahead with a shrug as long as they got their money—specie, not the doubtful bank notes. Unconcerned, they waited for the boom to collapse, ready to appreciate the beauties of a storm from which they thought they were protected.

The crash, surpassing in its disastrous scope anything they had supposed possible, startled them from their attitude of calm indifference. In the spring of 1818 the eminent Baltimore merchants, Smith and Buchanan, went into bankruptcy. Their trade had been excellent, but the profits had been used to speculate in bank stocks. The failure carried a few smaller houses under and shook others more substantial. Packages of paper money held by the Baltimore firm were sent back to the issuing banks for redemption. Their only answer was to put out more. Prices of commodities, which should have been driven up by the inflation, dropped because Europe had ceased to buy American produce, the wars being over and European fields replanted. Desperately the bankers struggled to support their paper with still more paper.

It was no use. In January, 1819, Jefferson wrote that this game of finance had produced "a general demoralization of the nation, a filching from industry its honest earnings wherewith to build up palaces and raise gambling stock for swindlers and shavers, who are to close, too, their career of piracies by fraudulent bankruptcies." The giddy, unreflecting optimism that had buoyed business on a sea of paper turned into an equally unreasoning panic. No one would touch any kind of note. Prices tumbled over each other in a mad race, apparently to see which could reach first a level below the cost of production. In June, John Quincy Adams, Monroe's Secretary of State, noted in his diary:

"Crawford [Secretary of the Treasury] told me much of the information which he is receiving with respect to the operations of the Banks, and the gigantic frauds practising upon the people by means of those institutions."

Crawford apparently thought it no part of his duty to devise some better credit and monetary system. He was too busy lobbying among members of Congress for a presidential nomination, then conferred by Congressional caucus. Meanwhile his Cabinet colleague observed:

"The banks are breaking all over the country; some in a sneaking and some in an impudent manner; some with sophisticating evasions and others with the front of highwaymen."

Five months later the nation's economy was prostrate. In Philadelphia more than half the merchants were bankrupt, three-fourths of the workmen unemployed. Rents had fallen to a third of those charged the year before; beef had dropped from 25 to 8 cents a pound, but thousands of once comfortable artisans were starving and homeless. In Virginia land could not be sold for what had recently been a year's rental.

In the universal ruin the politicians were helpless. The moneyed men upon whom they had relied for loans, stock market tips, retainers and gifts were liquidating, embittered, or in rarely shrewd instances fled to the shelter of inactivity with vast but frozen assets. The next election might subject representatives of the people to the effects of a popular wrath which they believed they had done nothing to deserve. Fortunately the starving masses had not been taught to look for relief to their government, and no one thought it strange that amid the debris of economic disaster the official mind should seek sanctuary in an unsubstantial dream world of its own.

Washington and the state capitals buzzed with talk of political combinations for attack and defense. The grafters who had sold their acquiescence in boom tactics for bribes or support at the polls sought only to keep the price and their jobs. Even in the Cabinet the leading Secretaries intrigued and struggled with each other and Henry Clay in anticipation of the succession to Monroe. The whole administration was shot through with the bitterness of personal feuds, the insane bickerings ot discouraged bidders for the favor of a nation which many thought ruined beyond hope of recovery. It was the period that later chroniclers have chosen to call the "Era of Good Feeling."

VII

"TO THE VICTOR"

1

Sʟᴏᴡʟʏ ᴛʜᴇ ᴄᴏᴜɴᴛʀʏ ᴘᴜʟʟᴇᴅ itself out from the depths of the depression to begin a new era of expansion, but it was a different order of things that emerged. We call it the industrial revolution, and one of its curious features was the elevation of graft from the status of luxury, opportunity or crime—depending on the point of view—to the level of necessity. The oligarchical, dictatorial methods by which the revolution was accomplished in the Old World were largely avoided in the United States by judicious political corruption. The greater freedom of humble individuals, the more abundant life for common folk owed as much to the fact that progress was based on graft as to the more obvious factor of cheap land.

In England manufacturers like Peel combined with the aristocratic successors of the Bloomsbury Gang to impose industrial development and the sacred taboos of trade. They ruled frankly in the interests of class. American capitalists who survived the holocaust of 1819 were less ostentatiously autocratic but just as determined to give their own peculiar law to the business world.

They had picked up bankrupt companies and desirable lands at panic prices and proposed to make their profit from exploitation of the national resources rather than by gambling in them. New processes of manufacture, concentration of capital, improved transportation facilities, made their owners more important to the destiny of the nation than the

merchants and speculators of the previous generation. To
these last, control of the state had meant only increased
gain. Their successors needed control for the very existence
of their enterprises.

The effect was to bend the forces of government more
emphatically than ever to the service of industry and finance,
but the electorate remained overwhelmingly agrarian. Corruption reconciled the two. Thanks to graft, successive administrations ostensibly subservient to demands of farmers
were in practice amenable to the dictates of an increasingly
conscious capitalism that would not be content with mere
talk. Thanks to graft, the gloomy predictions that republican institutions were doomed, voiced by such conservatives
as John Marshall, proved false. For, to serve the contradictory requirements of the country, there arose a race of politicians foreshadowed by Burr, a breed of able, lovable creatures whose faint scruples were no product of social philosophy, to whom public service was a business like any
other.

Among the young men who conned the lessons of the
transformation was Martin Van Buren, star pupil in what
was by far the most practical political school available, the
New York of De Witt Clinton. Son of a Dutch tavern keeper
in Kinderhook, N. Y., Van Buren had observed the down-
fall of Hamilton, the disgrace of Burr, the rise of Clinton.
A youngster making his own way without family influence
or powerful patronage, he had no time for philandering in
the shady groves of political philosophy.

Attracted to politics as a profession rather than by any
urge to do battle for a cause, young Van Buren naturally
allied himself with Clinton. Sent to the Legislature, he became familiar with the system of rewards and punishments
by which a leader maintains his ascendancy.

Had he known that Englishmen were offering the United
States as a horrible example of widening the franchise, he
would have maintained stoutly that democratic processes

were far superior to a regime of rotten boroughs controlled by an effete nobility and the new plutocracy. He was a great believer in democratic processes, but it never entered his head that the beneficent workings of free institutions could be affected one way or the other because an Assemblyman took pay to help a bank. Assemblymen, he would have said, had progressed beyond the stage of development represented in that British House of Commons whose standard bribe was a guinea a vote and dinner every day during the session, "unless the House be upon money or a Minister of State," when of course the price was higher.

Although Little Van was not one to rise superior to his environment, there was in the smiling, handsome young fellow with the innocently cherubic face a force that made him impatient of the autocratic Clinton's domination. Adapting that great man's methods, State Senator Van Buren began to build a machine of his own. His talents were conspicuous, the charm of his personality infectious and his organizing ability unsurpassed. He acquired such an imposing following that, in 1820, he put his own candidate for governor in the field against the mighty Clinton.

Van Buren's acceptance of the standards of his day was admirably exemplified in the statesman he chose to make the race. Daniel Tompkins had held the job during the war, and there was still pending against him a charge of defaulting in connection with war loans. The shortage was nearly $120,000. Van Buren proposed to settle the unpleasantness by voting his nominee $131,250 from the State treasury as fees for war work, and in defense of a very weak claim he rose to hitherto unexampled flights of oratory. His most ardent admirers had never supposed he had it in him. For two days and a half he was on his feet in the State Senate pleading Tompkins's cause. The tremolo stop was pulled all the way out as the honorable gentleman from Kinderhook poured oceans of words over the appalled statesmen. Halfway through the marathon speech Senator

Jeremiah Lott of Brooklyn was seized with fits of such convulsive sobbing that he had to be helped out—it was one
way, of course, to get out—and at the end of the ordeal
his hardier comrades passed Van Buren's bill. A tearless Assembly threw it out.

This dry-eyed economy was not the result of moral scruple,
as was proved when Tompkins got his money by submitting
to Clinton after the election while his sponsor languished
in outer darkness, the penalty for having missed victory by
so narrow a margin as 2,000 votes.

But the ex-Senator was not demoralized by defeat. Pains-
takingly he reassembled the fragments of his shattered machine, and when Clinton died in 1828 no one was strong
enough to dispute the State leadership with Little Van. He
was so popular he nominated himself for governor to give
strength to the Jackson ticket, although politicians knew that
if he carried New York for the hero of New Orleans, his
reward would be first place in the Cabinet.

2

Methodically Van Buren set about organizing the nation
on the model of New York. The enormous enthusiasm for
the picturesque Jackson made his task easier, but also effective was word that the old soldier would reward with
appointive office those who fought for him. Equally useful
was the understanding that moneyed men, who might without assurances have exerted greater efforts on behalf of the
General's foes, would not be unduly molested.

Against an organization so inspired the vast administrative
and diplomatic experience of an Adams—who since the days
of Washington had served his government in high office with
the misanthropic, efficient purity he could only have learned
from his father—was helpless. The operations of the democratic process, as manipulated by Van Buren, deepened
Adams's conviction, formed during the final flurry of in-

trigue that marked the end of the "Era of Good Feeling" and lifted him to the Presidency, that his own ideals were illusory.

"The public history of all countries and all ages is but a sort of mask, richly colored. The interior working of the machinery must be foul," he cried.

A man of Adams's principles was a man unarmed in the struggle of 1828. Jacksonian spellbinders toured the countryside with one eye open for desirable Federal jobs, calling on Heaven to witness that their candidate was the hope of common folk because he was one of them, which was not true. Adams could not disguise his opinion that ability and intellect were better qualifications. The man from Massachusetts kept so aloof that many believed he habitually dressed like a tramp and went barefoot to church, a story that greatly distressed his wife. But Adams was so little worthy of the people's trust that it never occurred to him to use the tale to drum up popularity in the backwoods.

The unimaginative model of official probity was content to be the last man in his office to preserve some privacy. It is a pleasant reminder of the simplicity of his day, soon to be stared out of existence by an aroused national curiosity, that the sixth President of the United States could strip on the banks of the Potomac, pile his clothes on a rock and enjoy a swim without attracting a mob.

The "cohesive power of public plunder" proved just as effective in organizing the masses as Hamilton had found it in rallying moneyed men. The resultant scramble, however, was more conspicuous, for the looters were many more in number and much noisier individually. They were guided by no such general principle as that the owners of the country ought to rule it or that property must be nurtured or that capitalists should have a free hand to develop the national resources. With the simple greed of hogs, so natural as to disarm anger, they hurried squealing to the trough, pushing for place, gobbling up juicy morsels with no other concern than the satisfaction of their own appetites.

When Van Buren drove into Washington a few weeks after Jackson's inauguration, he found the whole hungry horde waiting for him. He arrived after dark, but they swarmed around his coach in noisy demonstration. They had something of the air of loyal followers greeting a chief, but as they trooped after him through the streets and up the stairs of his hotel into his rooms they proved themselves more purposeful. The new Secretary of State lay helpless on a sofa while the office seekers, packed so closely into the place they could hardly move, yapped in chorus about the merit they had acquired in the campaign and the nature of the jobs to which they aspired. For an hour Van Buren tried to get them out so he could rest, and at last it was he who fled, taking refuge in the White House on the pretext of paying his respects to the President.

Next day he set about organizing the distribution of loaves and fishes. Most of them came out of the post office, then introduced to the world as the stronghold of party patronage. Not that any branch of government was overlooked. Officials of all kinds from bureau chiefs to clerks and messengers were turned out in hundreds. More than one poor devil grown old in some clerical position went mad in the grief and rage of summary dismissal, and several committed suicide. Neither pity nor considerations of efficiency in office were allowed to interfere with the inflexible program of Jacksonian democracy. The people now ruled, thundered their beloved leader; let the enemies of the people go.

The friends who took their places were too often men like Samuel Swartwout of New York, to select an exaggerated example, whose help in delivering votes won for him the collectorship of the port of New York. In this post even unenterprising men had raised fortunes in a few years, and Swartwout's ability was such that a mutual friend wrote to Van Buren:

"If our collector is not a defaulter in four years, I'll swallow the Treasury if it was all coined in coppers."

Two-thirds of the national customs revenues passed through Swartwout's hands, and he was an inveterate, unlucky speculator. By 1830 the shortages caused by his private necessities showed plainly in his quarterly reports to the Treasury, but a benevolent Secretary ignored them. For the collector, besides the gratitude due his political prowess, enjoyed the personal esteem of the President. Years ago, as Burr's lieutenant, acquitted in a trial preceding that of his chief, Swartwout had posted General Wilkinson as a coward for refusing to meet him in a duel, and Jackson had always despised the military paragon.

So every three months Swartwout's accounts were accepted, although the deficit grew steadily until his retirement at the end of March, 1838, after one grand operation involving government bonds that brought the total of his embezzlements to the interesting figure of $1,225,705.69. Before the sum was totted up, however, the collector sailed for Europe. A few months later the Whigs were coming into power, "to swartwout" was being used as a synonym for steal and Democratic orators were attempting to disown the fugitive, one Representative shrieking into the record:

"Swartwout was conceived in sin, brought forth in iniquity and reared in fraud."

Postmaster General Barry brought almost as much criticism upon the administration. An experienced dispenser of patronage, he created under Van Buren's direction a model machine that ought to have been the admiration of his successors. But he mixed into jobbery over the letting of contracts to carry the mails so crudely that the President had to let him resign.

Critics who complained of such apparent failures quite missed Van Buren's point. No doubt it was regrettable that the Swartwouts and Barrys could not restrain their cupidity within bounds more or less sanctioned by the criminal code.

On the other hand they were splendid illustrations of the value of party regularity. The whole tenor of Van Buren's seemingly indiscriminate appointments was directed to the one end of lubricating the party machine. He recognized as well as Adams that this is often a dirty business, but he was not fastidious so long as he achieved his object. Every Jacksonian hack in the land knew that his job depended not on fitness for the task, honesty or training, but solely on the zeal with which he supported the national administration. If an incorrigible grafter like Barry, an outright embezzler like Swartwout could go free, no other worker need fear that his shortcomings would hinder his advancement to a position of trust in which he might amass a competence. The defeated party was not slow to copy these tactics, but until they gained power the Whig leaders elaborated ponderous denunciations of the system. Their remarks were scathing, but it remained for a supporter to give the innovation a title. Ardently defending Van Buren in the Senate one day, William Marcy—in whose honor the New York chairmaker, Tweed, had recently named a son—explained the point of view of Democratic chiefs in language the country understood.

"They see nothing wrong in the rule that to the victor belongs the spoils of the enemy," he said.

3

At the outset, there was but one organization that rivaled the Jacksonians in the perfection of its "spoils system." This was the Bank of the United States, and it clashed with the new Federal regime in more than one field. To Jackson, a Western frontiersman with a simpler agrarian formula than Jefferson's, the Bank represented all the Eastern capitalist influences that oppressed the honest farmer. With an unerring eye he fixed upon every evil in the institution. Cheered on by the enthusiastic applause of his constituents

—Jackson would have repudiated any notion that he was supposed to be the President of such people as bankers and manufacturers—he set himself to destroy the Bank. His tactics were those that had won at New Orleans nearly twenty years before. Entrenched in a strong position, he drew the enemy's attack, waited until his own fire would be most devastating and then blasted the foe out of existence. The maneuver was possible because the Bank, like its predecessor, had been chartered for twenty years. The period ended in 1837, but in the interests of financial stability the question of renewal would have to be settled in advance. By withdrawing government deposits and vetoing the bill to re-charter the institution, Jackson scored a complete victory.

Nicholas Biddle, president of the Bank, had been led into the error of overestimating his strength in Congress, where he actually looked for a two-thirds vote to override the veto, for among his papers was a long list of members of Congress and high government executives who had loans, mostly unsecured, from what his foes were beginning to call "the Bribery Bank." The list is admirably non-partisan, containing these examples:

Vice President John C. Calhoun, oracle of Southern planters, once called by Jackson "the noblest work of God"; Henry Clay, elegant spokesman of the backwoods; Daniel Webster, the Voice of New England purity, whether pleading for secession or union, high tariff or free trade; Joel Poinsett, who became Van Buren's Secretary of War; George McDuffie, chairman of the House Ways and Means Committee.

Biddle himself saw more in the struggle than a fight with the aroused agrarians. Against their numbers and clamor he would have matched his control of money and credit, nor doubted the outcome. But other warriors, largely unseen then and usually ignored by chroniclers of the conflict, dealt right manful blows that were decisive in the fray. New York financiers, eager to end the dominance of Philadelphia as a money mart, unostentatiously supported the veto. Repeatedly Biddle wrote that the contest was in reality one "between Chestnut St. and Wall St." As early as 1828 Secretary of the Treasury Richard Rush, as keen a Biddle man as any debtor, warned him:

"You have probably as much or more to fear for the Bank from New York as from Virginia . . . the frog of Wall Street puffs himself into the Ox of Lombard street."

Biddle's financial training did not fit him to cope with such oddly assorted enemies as Jackson and Wall Street. He had begun life in a pleasantly aesthetic, dilettante fashion, won a government directorship in the Bank with an article on finance and had been fascinated by the prospect of power that his new position revealed. As president of the Bank he was inclined to indulge rather too freely in the exercise of authority merely for the joy of doing it.

His principal delegates in the political arena were Clay and Webster. He relied on them to be more than a match for the homespun popularity of Jackson and the smooth tactics of Van Buren. Clay had more influence but Webster was the greater advocate.

The incomparable orator was quite as much the product of his age as Van Buren—both were born in 1783—although he was more innocent than the New Yorker of binding standards of official conduct. Van Buren, while not in the same class as a spellbinder, despite the heroic Tompkins speech, could persuade others but he never fooled himself. Webster was always his own most conspicuous convert, and as his political horizon expanded he was able to carry himself with some degree of sincerity through an amazingly contradictory career.

Adoring audiences applied to him the adjective "godlike," and he did his best to live up to it. But he was a divinity who mercilessly reveals the quality of a people who formed him in their own image. Like Van Buren he was the son of a tavern keeper, but his father had none of the thrifty Dutch virtues to which Little Van had been exposed. From his boyhood, Daniel was accustomed to the idea of debt and he lived with it all his life.

Drifting into the law after a period as a school teacher, borrowing from anyone who would trust him, he speedily discovered a use for a Voice and his singularly handsome, impressive presence. No man of his generation could so dominate an audience, and that was an age when oratory combined the influences now scattered among the screen, radio, stage and syndicated columnists. Webster, who drew up his medium height to look like six feet six, waved the thick black hair back from his great domed head, glared out from under shaggy brows with an aquiline gleam and rolled majestic phrases in tones of such genuine beauty that even his emptiest periods were nobly impressive, talked himself into the position of a great political force.

His legal attainments were trifling; he was always calling on wise old Supreme Court Justice Story for information on the law. His great reputation as a constitutional authority was made in the Dartmouth College case, but the law for that occasion was supplied by more acute minds; Webster furnished the eloquence that moved crusty John Marshall to tears. Since the decision was not handed down for nearly a year after the famous speech, it is reasonable to suppose that the tough old Chief Justice and his colleagues were moved more by considerations of basic law than by the memory of manly emotion. It must be added that with rare modesty Webster himself never claimed the credit of the victory. His $1,000 fee was what had interested him.

Fees, indeed, attracted him to a degree abnormal even in a lawyer. He never got enough, although his practice brought in as much as $25,000 a year, fabulous for a professional man of his day. He was mad to get rich, but his best laid plans drove him ever deeper into debt. At the height of his fame and power he borrowed from everyone and anyone—from a girl who painted his portrait, from a chance acquaintance in England, from his wife's relations, but most of all from Boston bankers. His personal finances were a maze of drafts and acceptances based on no funds, of protested notes and unsecured loans. He paid, when he paid at all, in political services. There is an apocryphal story that once when the national debt was under discussion, Webster, being then in liquor, plunged his hand into his pocket and cried: "How much is it? I'll pay it myself." He was as blithely impractical in settling his own obligations.

The Bank struggle was a welcome event in the annals of the Webster exchequer. The Senator had long been of counsel for the institution, for even more scrupulous men than the godlike one saw nothing wrong in a Congressman who was also an attorney accepting employment from a client on whose existence he voted in the public interest. Henry Clay was also retained by the Bank. Senator Smith, whose failure in Baltimore in 1818 had been recouped, was a staunch supporter of the creditor who held $1,540,000 of his firm's paper. Biddle, a man of no party—"I care nothing about the election. I care only for the interests confided to my care"—noted ruefully:

"The truth is that almost all the misfortunes of the Bank of the United States are traceable, directly or indirectly, to politics. In Kentucky the losses were in great measure incurred by loans to prominent politicians of all sides whose influence procured them undue facilities."

Webster was no more content with legal fees alone than was Clay. The Senator's unsecured loans from the Bank ran up to more than $26,000, and the day after his greatest oratorical effort on behalf of his client and creditor, he accepted $10,000 from Biddle's hand. Throughout the struggle he continued to send the banker confidential information on his colleagues, noting who was friendly and who was treacherous, endorsing many of these communications with his favorite conspiratorial phrase, "Private as murder!"

The Bank went down to defeat, but the triumphant farmers were surprised to find that their troubles did not disappear. A new orgy of corruption enlivened the distribution of government funds removed from "the Bribery Bank." These were deposited in accordance with Van Buren's principles in State-chartered institutions that could be relied upon politically, or as one dispenser of patronage wrote to the Secretary of the Treasury:

"The moneyed institutions exercise indirectly a great influence during elections, for all banks have now been converted into political engines, and we, by the existing arrangement [before Biddle's defeat] furnish our enemies with additional weapons. The Mechanics and Traders Bank [of New Orleans] which I now recommend is, on the contrary, a republican institution, got up to rescue the honest mechanic from the grasp of the opposition, and grant him facilities which he can enjoy without the sacrifice of his elective franchise."

The rescue work was so well done, the facilities granted with such careless generosity, that in the year Little Van reaped the final reward of his labors by succeeding Jackson to the Presidency, 1819 was repeated all over again, preceded by wildly reckless speculation which the banks were delighted to finance. The "honest mechanic" lost both his savings and his job; Democrats and Whigs went into bankruptcy together, and the financial historians are still arguing whether the corruption of the Jackson administration or the corruption of his foes caused the panic of 1837.

4

The fate of the politicians involved in the collapse was only in part commensurate with their deserts. Van Buren, who had driven his political machine into office with remarkable ease over "Tippecanoe" Harrison in 1836, was defeated in 1840 by the same candidate in a burst of righteous indignation and a lurid campaign that was the realization of a politician's dream (not Van Buren's).

At sixty-seven, the bewildered standard bearer of the Whigs was dragged from retirement to epitomize the log-cabin, coonskin-cap, cider-drinking pioneer. The poor old man was the central figure in a riotous orgy of popular fervor beside which Jacksonian idealization of the backwoods primitive was colorless and tame. That Harrison was by birth a Virginian of proud lineage—his father had signed the Declaration of Independence—that his "log cabin" was one of the stateliest, most tasteful mansions on the Ohio, that he was a devoted and by no means contemptible classical scholar, seemed to fit him for the role of champion of the common people against the horrid New York aristocrat, son of the Kinderhook tavern keeper.

The gorgeous farce was played out to a grimly hilarious conclusion when Harrison died a month after taking office, to be succeeded by the Virginia Democrat, Tyler, who had been placed on the ticket solely to snag discontented Southern votes.

The new masters of the country applied Van Buren's spoils system with the same rigor he had employed, and in the most honorable of Cabinet posts, the State Department, appeared the godlike figure of Daniel Webster, still gushing an inspiring felicity of phrase, still plagued by money troubles, still the willing servant of New England bankers and industrialists.

Only one of his old patrons found him ungrateful. Harrison's victory had paved the way for the Bank of the United States to regain its Federal charter. During the Van Buren administration, Biddle had been accommodated with a refuge under Pennsylvania law. He had drawn $400,000 in cash for the purpose—a prosecution for misuse of these funds later failed—and a young man named Thaddeus Stevens engineered the passage of a bill for "the Bribery Bank." Biddle had kept his national organization together and had contributed handsomely to the log cabin and cider campaign.

He was already celebrating his triumph when Harrison died before a charter could be passed. Tyler, true to the tenets of his real party, vetoed the bill and Webster was the only Cabinet member who did not resign in protest. The orator was acute enough to see that Biddle's day was done. He even went so far as to justify the veto, but he did not carry his new principles to the extent of liquidating his debt to the institution that had once commanded his finest phrases. His note remained one of the more dubious assets of "the Bribery Bank" when it failed, dragging Biddle's own fortune down with it.

The Secretary of State had other sources of income. For many years he had been interested in the collection of old claims against Denmark, France and Spain for damages to American shipping fifty years or more before. He had long been in receipt of fees from speculators who had bought up these claims for a few cents on the dollar, but he had an arrangement by which he was to get 5 per cent. of the final proceeds.

His connection with these cases was characteristic of the man and the age. During his first term in Congress as a member of the House Foreign Relations Committee he had discovered forgotten data that strengthened the rights of the claimants. Without making it public, he rounded up holders of the claims, arranged to represent them on a contingent fee and retainer basis and for the rest of his official life was extremely active on behalf of these clients.

Throughout his career, the Voice of New England was saved from the worst consequences of his peculiar business methods by rich Boston constituents whom he so ably represented. On one occasion the leading financiers, merchants and industrial magnates of the section held a meeting to consider Senator Webster's threat to retire because he had to earn money. Statesmanship was preserved for the nation by a purse of $37,000 with no strings attached, so it was said. Such gifts—Webster is known to have received more than one, and sometimes as quite public "memorials" to his services—were reciprocated by more than votes and speeches. He constantly reported to his patrons the progress of measures and government projects in which they were interested. His advance information on the Sub-Treasury program must have been worth a good deal more than $37,000 to the recipients, since it was coupled with a preview of pending tax legislation.

It is easy to sneer with Emerson at the large amount of clay that went into the composition of this national idol or to cry out with John Quincy Adams against "the fallacy of Mr. Daniel Webster, who is perpetually talking about the Constitution while he is indifferent to freedom and those great interests which the Constitution was established to serve." Apparently it is even easier—as biographers of the orator have often found—to ignore his preoccupation with vulgar finance and write him down as a man elevated above common materialism but dogged with money troubles that should never have been permitted to disturb the equanimity of so pure a patriot.

Either method overlooks the conditions of which Webster was the creature. His magnificent command of the spoken word was his own; his pecuniary habits he shared with a multitude, some of whom were luckier than he in speculation. None served so faithfully the class that placed him in a position to exercise his talents. Moneyed men were able to keep control of westward expansion because of the policies Webster so powerfully advocated, although the effects were more valuable after he was dead. He was worth more than they paid him. Good grafters usually are.

VIII

STEALING AN EMPIRE

1

In rapt contemplation of the drama furnished by the furious shadow boxing of rival political leaders, the mass of their contemporaries easily overlooked the working of the spoils system behind the backdrop. While giants such as Webster, Clay and Calhoun grappled and postured in the limelight, unnoticed scene shifters diligently reset the stage that was the nation. When they finished, the vast heritage of the people—the Western wilderness of Washington's day, the imperial Louisiana Jefferson bought, the magnificent estate won from Mexico—had been dissipated.

With insignificant exceptions, the whole of the United States west of the Alleghenies was originally public domain. From the very beginning, it was ostensibly the purpose of every governmental agency to conserve this empire for the general welfare, but the grafters were always at least one step ahead of official policy. The process that had evolved Van Buren and Webster out of the political principles of Jefferson and Hamilton created a race of legislators, departmental clerks, land registration agents and Indian superintendents who had pondered deeply over the wisdom of the sage who preached that hay should be made while the sun shines.

They had not studied the careers of Colonial looters or of Morris, Symmes and the Yazoo speculators but they needed no instruction. Their untutored ingenuity and an ignorant or indifferent constituency were enough.

The sun of popular approval had ceased to shine on the old system of bestowing principalities upon land companies. An era of unrestrained eloquence produced in profusion word pictures of a poor man's agrarian paradise, of free farms, of a government that could abolish taxes by judicious sales of land, but sensible folk recognized the presence of a wide, deep, unbridged gulf between word and deed. In this respect none were more sensible than the official and semi-official gentlemen who exercised the nation's guardianship over the Indians, exposing all those unpleasant qualities easily acquired by men dealing with a despised, inferior race. The belief that the only good Indian is a dead Indian had been firmly fixed by generations of warfare, treachery and injustice, until a Congressional committee, composed of men not notable for their own high ideals, reported that even the Christian churches had been too greatly preoccupied with extorting land and money from the Indians to carry moral weight with the heathen. (This had been true for so long that it passed almost without remark when after the Civil War a pair of missionaries exercised so persuasive an eloquence that one tribe authorized them to collect a $112,000 government draft. The men of God collected in gold; they paid their charges in Confederate bills.)

It must be admitted that the aboriginals were no better served by those of their own race who partook of the newer civilization, for white ways produced such specimens as Allen Wright, a Choctaw who had successfully completed the academic course at Union College in Schenectady, had become a Presbyterian Minister as well as Principal Chief and Treasurer of his nation and was described by one of the great white grafters of the Indian Office as "a full-blooded Indian and a gentleman, whom to know is to esteem." This tribute was paid after Wright, aided by his white admirer, had mulcted the Choctaws of several hundred thousand dollars due from the government, "with," as some more than usually literary investigators reported, "the anxiety of a hungry man for his dinner, but with the dishonor of a thief in the night, and with the eye of a lynx and greed of a wolf."

Under the tutelage of such versatile gentry, the red man was robbed of hunting ground after hunting ground, very largely on the principles enunciated by Jefferson. When a sense of wrong sent him on the warpath, peace treaties provided for the cession of further land as indemnity. When he could neither be tempted into debt nor goaded into war, he was persuaded to sell, and then robbed of the price. All in all, the bewildered Indians signed away tracts totted up by careful calculators to 3,232,936,351 acres—rather excessive generosity, since the total area of the United States falls short of this amount by nearly 1,300,000,000 acres.

To suppose that land thus acquired could be disposed of without graft is to believe in fairies. Sound principles for settlement by pioneers who would actually clear the forest and plant crops were promulgated. The administration of the rules, however, was entrusted to men who had come to regard the spoils system as part of the democratic process.

For many years after sales to big companies had been abandoned as discriminating against settlers and offering too much opportunity for graft, new areas were put up at auction in comparatively small tracts. The open sale was met by equally open corruption. During the administration of Jackson—whose election was acclaimed as inaugurating an era of justice and free land—a vast acreage taken from the Creeks and Choctaws in Alabama and Mississippi was put on the block. The government agents in charge went into partnership with a syndicate of speculators, and other prospective buyers were warned to keep out of the bidding or face real competition. After a few of them—hunters in buckskins, pioneers in homespun, gamblers and planters from the East in tall hats and flowered waistcoats—had seen the tracts they wanted run up as high as $22 an acre, the syndicate was permitted to get almost the entire lot at the minimum price of $1.25. The conspirators then held an auction of their own and pocketed an average profit of $1 an acre.

Most of the settlers were so like their descendants temperamentally that they offered no effective protest. All their lives they had witnessed the working of the truism that to him who hath shall be given. Many of them were westward bound in the hope of escaping from it. That it had caught up with them in the wilderness had to be accepted with such philosophy as they could command. After all, the only sufferer was the sovereign people for whose account the land was being sold, and it is an old story that sovereigns exist to be cheated.

At other times and places the homestead system, whereby comparatively small farms were bestowed freely on men who would work them, was devised to eliminate graft, but civil servants in the land offices were not that easily balked. They were most obliging about writing down the names of men who never came within a thousand miles of their property. In the Milwaukee district, for example, the books at the time of the Mexican War showed 6,441 entries. The exact number of settlers on the ground was forty-four.

So much land lay idle in the hands of speculators that the immediate result of opening new areas to settlement was a food shortage. Those who could not afford graft were driven off the soil or forced to move further west than communications then reached. The first signs of the panic of '37 broke the value of land, but it was too late to help the farmers, and the national economy was so badly off balance that the overwhelmingly agricultural country could not feed itself. In 1830, a year of normal trade, the United States had exported flour and wheat to a value of $6,000,000. In the panic year exports fell to $1,000,000 and yet the yield was so small that $4,500,000 worth of flour and wheat had to be imported. Land under the spoils system had become a speculative commodity, not to be used for growing crops.

Nor was it any considerable item in the Federal budget. Visionaries had looked forward to the day when all the expenses of government would be defrayed by sales of the public land. With millions of acres a year passing into private hands, the tax rate was not lowered. The money for thousands of farms reached the Treasury in a thin trickle. Just before the panic of '37 the reckless speculators paid the government nearly $25,000,000 in twelve months. After the collapse they could do little more than meet the cost of graft. The government's takings swooped to about $5,000,000, slumped still further and throughout the lushest period of westward expansion averaged less than $3,000,000 a year.

2

The millions of idle acres acquired by speculators in their partnership with government officials went far to satisfy the cupidity of minor appointees. More glittering opportunities presented themselves to others in public life. Transportation —the thread that was to bind the nation into unity and become the weave of an alternating pattern of prosperity and depression—suddenly opened vistas of illimitable expansion before a quite unprepared country and its ruling grafters, who saw a new way to exploit the public domain for private advantage.

In the first quarter of the century canals were the delight of modernists. Barges floating on still waters to the accompaniment of stentorian profanity provided mass movement on a rapid scale when compared with the pace attained by oxen tugging small loads through the mud.

In 1829 an even more meteoric velocity appeared on the industrial horizon. At Honesdale, Pa., a piece of machinery closely resembling the tea kettle from which it was derived but grandiloquently christened "The Stourbridge Lion" puffed and clattered over wooden rails. A year later the greatly daring Peter Cooper, sweating with the zeal of a crusader and the exertions of a combination engineer and fireman, actually distanced for a time one of the finest grays owned by the stagecoach line of Stockton & Stokes. The horse won in the stretch when Mr. Cooper's odd contraption broke down, but it was a hollow victory. While Jackson and Biddle were recruiting for their bank battle, the mania for getting places in a hurry, often held to be the distinguishing mark of the American, seized upon the people.

More than restlessness was behind the rapid spread of iron lines. The only possible mechanism for exploiting the national resources, they flung the limits of potential development westward a thousand miles at a bound. Real settlers followed the hunters and trappers, confident that they in turn were only a little ahead of the railroad builders who would make them rich. The frenzy of speculation in farm land was a corollary of the new means of transportation, for soaring values naturally followed the parallel strips of metal into the West.

Among practical men the railroad problem came to overshadow even the fight with the bank, the war with Mexico, the growing bitterness of the slavery struggle. Railroads were what banks would live on; railroads would make the empire taken from Mexico worth having; railroads pushed westward the tide of rival slave and free economies. And the control of this enormous power was vested nominally in the hands of legislatures like that of New York, where charters were purchaseable merchandise, and in a Congress whose most powerful leaders were proud to be the paid servants of financiers.

In retrospect the railroads seem to have become the actual rulers of the West by coups as smoothly worked as a well-planned bank stickup of today, every detail carefully rehearsed and the thieves disappearing with their loot before the spectators can grasp what it is all about. Actually, however, the progress of land grant railroads was neither easy nor swift.

States and local governing bodies were from the first extremely generous, but for more than twenty years Congress repelled with exemplary fortitude every attempt by every railroad company to secure any assistance more substantial than a loan of government engineers to help survey routes. Whig and Democratic Congresses alike turned down all appeals, although some were eloquently phrased and cunningly argued.

The chagrined pioneers of a new industry were justified in declaring the Congressional attitude unprecedented. There was a long list of Federal grants to aid internal improvements, going as far back as 1796 when Ebenezer Zane received three square miles in the Ohio country "in such situations as shall best promote the utility of a road to be opened by him between Wheeling and Limestone." Other highways had been encouraged substantially, and Federal gifts to canal companies exceeded 4,000,000 acres.

The unexpected resistance to the pleas of railroads originated in doubt as to their value. The iron horse might do very well for short hauls, but Congressmen would not trouble themselves with purely local improvements—pork barrel legislation was in its infancy—and the early companies lacked capital and influence to reverse this opinion, although the first of all, the Baltimore & Ohio, used part of the $1,000,000 subscribed to it by Maryland and Baltimore in trying. Nevertheless, a shower of franchises, land grants, charters and bond issues burst from state legislatures with remarkably little priming. Banks had paid as high as $5,000 for a single vote and more for the support of a strong leader. The young railroads were seldom taxed more than $500, and obliging legislators often took that in stock.

Thanks to this generosity, short, unconnected lines began to crawl from city to city in haphazard fashion. The men

who appeared in Washington to urge planned systems over
vast distances were visionaries, enthusiasts, mere technicians
who wanted to develop the country and innocently supposed
that Congress would be pleased to co-operate. They managed
to keep agitation alive until the amazing technological advances made by engineers and inventors in twenty years
convinced the entrepreneurs of Eastern capital that the future of the nation was on wheels.

The Mexican War, the discovery of gold in California, the
suddenly swollen tide of immigration from Europe after
'48, combined to make railroading on a large scale attractive
to moneyed men. The war nearly doubled the area of the
country. Merchants with an eye to the China trade vied
with prospectors in crying for quick transportation to California. Immigrants pouring into New York needed cars to
carry them to the plains and bring back the produce of their
labor. All of a sudden the sovereign people were nearly sub-
merging ordinary politics in the demand for railroads, more
railroads and railroads in a hurry. The method by which
they were attained, who built them and how, who profited
incidentally and where the money came from were matters
of profound indifference to a public firmly convinced that
sufficient transportation would make them all rich.

A few voices piped feebly against the general robust
clamor. John Quincy Adams, who had assigned himself
the thankless role of national conscience, was harping on
the theme that the national resources ought to be preserved
for the benefit of the whole nation, not given to bands of
promoters who promised to build railroads.

Thomas Benton, attractive spokesman of the inarticulate
West, was an even more powerful advocate than an aged ex-
President whose notions of honesty had always been pretty
severe and were now extremely old-fashioned. Benton proposed that government itself build new lines into undeveloped territory for the honor and glory of the nation and
the greater good of Western farmers and ranchers. Congress

and the state legislatures, however, thought themselves unfit for the task. It is impossible to disagree with them. The only trouble was that the gentlemen who came forward to assume the burden were equally incompetent and much more greedy. On Sept. 20, 1850, the Illinois Central became the first railway beneficiary of a Federal land grant under circumstances of which its sponsor, Stephen A. Douglas, the "little giant" of the West, later boasted:

"The Illinois bill was the pioneer bill, and went through without a dollar, pure, uncorrupt."

3

What the Senator meant was this:

In the previous session, his colleague from Illinois, Sidney Breese, introduced into the Senate a measure to confer several million acres upon a company headed by the honorable Mr. Breese's partner, who had a charter but no tracks. Douglas proposed to substitute a grant to the state itself to be used for the encouragement of railways in its discretion, which meant in Douglas's discretion, for he was boss of Illinois.

The Senator was an honest and able exponent of his political principles, but he understood the value of a reputation for being able to do things for big business. In his late 'teens he had lived in upstate New York and had observed Van Buren's methods. He had carried the idea with him to the West, where he built up such an organization that, although he was serving his first term in the Senate, his control of Illinois enabled him to assume a leading role in the legislative drama.

Now his short legs, so grotesquely inappropriate to the massive head and powerful torso, twinkled in and out of lobbies and committee rooms. He thought he had a nice majority for his railway bill. At the last minute, however, the Representatives of Mississippi and Alabama developed doubts as to the right of Congress to give away anything, and their votes defeated Douglas's careful plan.

During the summer recess, the "little giant" set himself to deal with this opposition and fortunately he was in a position to enter the enemy's country without arousing too much comment. His wife had been a Mississippi girl, had inherited a plantation in that state and she and their children were at the moment living there. What more natural than that a weary Senator should seek surcease from his cares in the bosom of his family? Mr. Douglas sought it, but not for long. Soon he was traveling, and his travels took him to the offices of men who controlled a potential railroad known as the Mobile & Ohio.

The backbone of Congressional opposition to land grants was Senator Foote of Mississippi. He had constitutional scruples, but he also had a brother who was a director of the Mobile & Ohio. The brother undertook to manage the Senator if Douglas would guarantee land for the Southern road as well as the Illinois Central. The stage was thus set for the session of 1850. The bill, duly amended, went smoothly through the Senate and Douglas recorded his belief that he could command a majority of fifteen in the House. A good many of his supporters were frankly enlisted "by lending our support to local measures," but who would call logrolling corrupt?

The Senator was in the lobby of the House to witness his triumph when the bill came up. Suddenly and to his horror, he realized that many of his friends were not in their seats. A hasty conning of those present showed an almost certain minority. The clerk was already reading out the title of the bill in the deadly, impersonal tone affected by such officials. Douglas was in an agony of suspense so that he "would have given the world" to be at the side of Representative Harris, his manager for the bill. Fortunately the lieutenant was equal to the emergency.

"Harris, quick as thought, pale and white as a sheet,

jumped to his feet and moved that the House go into Committee of the Whole on the slavery question," Douglas related long afterwards.

In those sultry summer days of 1850, men were always ready to debate slavery. The familiar arguments poured forth that afternoon in accustomed fervor, but in a committee room, undisturbed by such noises, Douglas and Harris were in gloomy conference. Their bill must now go to the foot of the calendar where ninety-seven other measures took precedence. All hope for this session seemed lost.

But perhaps not altogether lost. As long as free soil remained to arouse Congressional passions, the same trick might work again. Douglas himself organized the band of earnest moralists who divided the task of calling for committees of the whole every time the Speaker reached one of the ninety-seven bills. One by one these were pushed back to the tail of the calendar. Legislation languished as the House went repeatedly into those slavery debates by which the session of 1850 contributed so lavishly to the inevitable breach. At last the "little giant's" measure came to the fore again, and this time he was ready. By a majority of three, Illinois received 2,595,053 acres to be used for railroads, and Mississippi and Alabama smaller amounts.

"I did the whole work," declared Douglas, "and was devoted to it for two entire years."

The Illinois Central put a value of $40,000,000 on the gift, and the financiers who took a mortgage on it in return for building the road at a fraction of that amount were naturally eager partisans of Douglas against any such uncouth opponent as the Springfield lawyer, A. Lincoln. But Westerners were not the chief gainers. The capitalist who got the most out of the deal was Morris Ketchum of New York, from whom a young fellow named John Pierpont Morgan was soon to get some early financial lessons.

Politicians who were less scornful of money than Douglas were quick to grasp the real importance of the Illinois

Central bill. For that measure opened the gates to the rail-road builders and stimulated all sorts of other grabs so that within thirty years there remained in all the vast public domain not more than 25,000,000 acres of arable land. In one way and another there had been disposed of, mostly without any return at all, 657,000,000 acres of the best soil in America, more than one-third the present land area of the country. The portion that actually had been sold brought into the Treasury over a period of a century a bit more than $200,000,000, or exactly $113,989,938.82 less than the government had originally paid in purchase money to France, Spain, Mexico and the Indians and for surveying the property.

Douglas had shown the way, and Congress no longer hesitated over the form of encouragement it should extend to railroads. But the terms were not always the same as those of the Senator from Illinois. When he had referred to his project as "pure, uncorrupt," he was comparing it to its successors, not to any ideal principle of conduct such as might be expounded in a Fourth of July oration.

The sponsor of the pioneer bill received neither cash nor shares himself; he traded only votes, not money, in Congress, and he was quite correct according to his lights in saying the measure had not cost a dollar. But his colleagues, watching fortunes accruing from their generosity, were less high-minded. Absorbed in sectional differences, they still found time to steer selected railroad legislation through the mazes of party politics, and they were guided by the same motives of profit that animated the promoters.

They were far too realistic to expect to derive that profit from the actual operation of the railroads they so blithely chartered. That would have been tedious, laborious, uncertain and risky. Only a government could be expected to build roads for the primary purpose of acting as common carriers, but the people did not trust their government's efficiency. The policy of bribing favored syndicates to build railroads—"subsidy" was a preferred word—was felt to be more in harmony with the national genius. Private enterprise was irresistibly attracted, as it was meant to be, by the prospect of so much wealth. Groups of keen financiers gathered hastily to exploit new opportunities for land jobbing and construction financed by state and Federal bonds. The pioneers and experts who alone had the technical equipment or desire to improve transportation facilities were brushed aside, and for thirty years the idea that he might obtain his profit from the carrying trade never once occurred to a railroad magnate. The corruption of public officials was a surer and easier path to success.

4

Throughout the early railroad era, the public was at least as complacent as its representatives. Even reformers—and they were not lacking—found a more congenial target in slavery or, if they wished to crusade nearer home, in the corruption of municipal administrations, which were already in the hands of a race of grafters whose operations affected more directly the lives, health and comfort of the average citizen. Upon these men the nation expended such moral indignation as it could spare from Southerners who dealt in human flesh or Northerners who wanted to deprive slave owners of the sacred rights of property.

In the anxiety to perfect local vote-getting machinery, the principles the machine was ostensibly built to support were forgotten. An unscrupulous man then was at an obvious advantage, and the leader who devoted all his time to a given district carried more weight than a rival who might be called away by private business. So the control of American cities fell into the hands of professional manipulators who had in their gift an empire as valuable as all the land in the West, for they dispensed franchises, undeveloped building sites, contracts, protection in mulcting the citizen. On the graft obtainable from these sources they based their system of civics.

There was nothing much to choose between the large cities of the country, but New York exercised the greatest fascination for the student of graft, partly because of its size, mainly because Tammany Hall lends a continuity to the story that is lacking elsewhere. The Society, lifted by Burr's genius from the pleasantly innocuous activities of a lodge to the grander stage of partisanship, was formally chartered in 1805, and it is cheering to know that its legal objects still remain those expressed at that time—"affording relief to the indigent and distressed members of said association, their widows and orphans and others who may be proper objects of their charity."

Obviously the most practical form of relief was to put "proper objects" on the city payroll or reduce their tax assessments or give them special and valuable privileges. The theory that these philanthropies are carried on most competently by men of business was recognized in Tammany for more than thirty years. Until the panic of '37 at least two-thirds of its leaders were financiers and prosperous merchants.

Although the public services performed by the city were almost non-existent, the number of employees and the cost of government rose steadily all through this period. Repeated disclosures of fraud and even a conviction for some unusually flagrant offense failed to interrupt the progress of the machine. But gradually the bankers and merchants drifted away from prominent positions in the Hall. Some thought they were too respectable to associate with the gang leaders and saloon keepers who provided repeaters and thugs for every election. But for the most part the business men were ousted by professional ward heelers who concentrated on politics, and in the tumults succeeding the panic these gentlemen came into their own.

For a time they did not improve on the methods by which their predecessors had looted the city. Each jobholder took what funds he could lay hands on, sold what privileges were within his reach and bargained for the use of his henchmen to beat up rival voters, smash ballot boxes in unfriendly districts and guard troops of repeaters on their tours from one polling place to another. They kept the city dirty, unhealthy and ridden with crime. They would be even more of a menace to the general welfare whenever they developed a leader capable of imposing some sort of firm organization upon the loose alliance of gangs, contractors, shopkeepers, criminals and idlers.

A rather unlikely environment produced the master mind. Fernando Wood was a Quaker lad from Pennsylvania, his given name a souvenir of his mother's penchant for novels rather than any indication of Latin blood. After a youth devoted to rowdyism, he drifted to unimportant jobs and mercantile adventure in New York, where his business career had not been notably brilliant despite an episode in which he defrauded a partner of $8,000 and successfully dallied with retribution, thanks to the connivance of a friendly prosecutor, until the statute of limitations lapped the peccadillo in the ample mantle of oblivion.

Politics, as practiced in such places as "the bloody ould sixth" ward, offered a more congenial field for his talents. A tall, slender, good-looking fellow with clear blue eyes, a fashionably smooth face and brown hair curling tastefully over his ears, he was always well dressed and smiling. The admiration of "Dead Rabbits" and "Bowery Boys" was won by the very suavity at which they would have mocked in a stranger. But the thugs knew "Fernandy" was one of themselves at heart. They were proud of him, and blindly trusted him to lead them to a promised land of booze and fighting, for they were not fond of milk and honey.

With these men behind him, the graceful young heeler entered Tammany as a power. His talents for organization

and his employment of new methods soon put him in a
dominant position and in 1850, when he was only thirty-
eight, he was his party's candidate for Mayor.

The Hall was indebted to Wood for two innovations that
were to make it victorious in any normal political year.
First was his skillful manipulation of the nominating machinery, which insured for his followers the valuable endorsement of "regular." More important, he recognized the
enormous potential strength of the immigrant vote, and
proceeded to make it his own. For the most part this was
in 1850 an Irish vote. Glancing over the roster of later
leaders, it is difficult to imagine a Tammany that was definitely anti-Irish and anti-Catholic. Yet Wood found it so,
and perhaps his greatest service to the organization was a
lesson in profitable tolerance.

Another feature of Wood's system, although it was not
so exclusively his own, was the sale of nominations, which
his gangster control of conventions made possible. This market provided campaign funds with which he lured the sweets
of office.

Wood failed of election in 1850—Tammany had been
obliged to alternate with the Whigs pretty regularly because the Hall had not hitherto been more closely knit—
but the following year, with no national issues intruding on
the municipal campaign, he was able to put his own Common Council into office. The twenty aldermen and twenty
assistant aldermen—one of them was the chairmaker's son,
William Marcy Tweed, a big young fellow very fine to look
at in his regalia as leader of the "Big Six" fire company—
speedily earned the title of "The Forty Thieves."

Nothing on the scale of their operations had ever been
attempted in a city before. The boodle poured in so fast
that there was no time for concealment, and the disclosures
of corruption bewildered the public. The Grand Jury revealed payment of $50,000 to the aldermen for a Ninth Ave-
nue Railroad franchise. Thirty thousand—young Tweed got

10 per cent.—was extorted from the willing Third Avenue Railroad, and offers to run street cars on favorable terms were laughed out of court when unaccompanied by bribes. All sorts of franchises were openly sold; contracts for paving, printing, building, lighting the streets and selling supplies to the city were awarded to the highest bribers. But low bids must get their innings, and that was when the city sold land. Astors, Goelets, Roosevelts, Dodges, Vanderbilts bought waterfront and other desirable sites for less than New York spent to grade streets in front of the property in order to further enhance its value. Gamblers, thieves, prostitutes and abortionists were on the same friendly footing with municipal officials as were the accumulators of real estate.

By 1854 conditions had grown sufficiently bad to intrude persistently upon the notice of decent but normally indifferent citizens. They protested only against the petty graft and embezzlement, however. The sale of franchises and land still seemed to most of them the proper method of civic development. Wood, who was a born leader for any cause or even for all causes at once, saw they were groping for guidance and boldly offered himself as a candidate for the good people.

"Reform is at home in Tammany Hall," was the new slogan of that organization, and the great moral fervor of the nation's largest city, backed by a little thuggery at the polls, swept the handsome "Fernandy" into office.

A magnificent leading man was lost to the stage when Wood became Mayor. For several months he gave a flawless performance as a great reformer. Saloons closed on Sundays, at least their front doors. Shades were pulled down in the windows of brothels. "Dead Rabbits" and "Bowery Boys" confined their warfare to their own slums. Certain sections of the city were quite safe after dark. New Yorkers ceased to scoff because their Mayor nursed Presidential ambitions.

Tammany was less well pleased with him. The mighty men of the Hall knew their Mayor as well as had old Philip

Hone, who at the time of Wood's first nomination exclaimed:

"There was a time when it was thought of some consequence that the incumbent of this office should at least be an honest man . . . Fernando Wood, instead of occupying the Mayor's seat, ought to be on the rolls of the State Prison."

Tammany resentment was based on other grounds than those of the venerable Mr. Hone, whose own term as Mayor had expired long ago and was no longer of practical concern. What the sachems cried out against was their Mayor's concentration of loot and power in his own hands. Instinctively they knew that Tammany should never permit its leader to use his position for his own advancement in office. That way lay ruin, and not even the wily Wood could induce them to embark upon it. The election of 1856 was the most disorderly yet seen in the city, with axes, clubs and pistols freely used, timid people afraid to leave their homes to vote and a list of casualties that resembled a minor battle.

The Tammany stalwarts failed to beat Wood, but his argument of broken heads and smashed ballot boxes did not convince them. They obtained an amendment to the city charter that forced him to stand for re-election again in December, 1857, and before that day he was read out of the Hall. Even the expedient of naturalizing 4,000 new voters could not win for him, but it took the combined forces of all the other parties in New York to elect Daniel Tiemann. The general opinion of Fernando's honesty may be gathered from the fact that the fusionists of that time accepted the unsavory Daniel, who had been one of "The Forty Thieves," as upholding all that was pure in municipal life.

Joyously Tammany contemplated the ruin of the ambitious one. The Hall began early preparing for the campaign of 1859 by buying one opposition member of the Board of Supervisors, Peter Voorhis, for the modest price of $2,500. Tweed did that work and thus gained for his party complete control of the new registration machinery, then introduced by one side in the hope of curbing election frauds and welcomed by the other as a means of consolidating further the machine's grip on the city.

The sachems proposed to maintain their winning streak by running William F. Havemeyer, a banker who had made a good record as Mayor several years before and was one of the more important recipients of cheap lots. His nomination was a return to the days of business rule, but Havemeyer was popular, able and as honest as the voters had a right to expect.

Strangely enough, Wood did not seem to know that he had been crushed. His enemies had a formidable list of his stealings—he had boosted New York's expenses from $5,000,000 to $8,000,000 a year without noticeable return to the people —but he had the money. Reviled as a traitor to every party with which he had ever been connected, he now ignored the "good people" he so gladly had conciliated five years earlier. While Tammany was packing the registration rolls and boasting of the enviable record of its immaculate candidate, Wood took his Irish, his gangsters, his saloon and bawdy house keepers and his own presentable person over to Mozart Hall and opened a new Democracy. It elected him by 3,000 votes over Havemeyer, despite the vote stealing of his former allies, and as the nation argued itself grimly into civil war, its largest city was again ruled by him of whom John Bigelow, after a lifetime of acquaintance with the great of this earth, could say:

"He was the handsomest man I ever saw, and the most corrupt man that ever sat in the Mayor's chair."

But he was also the man who set the tone for American municipal administration for generations to come, the man who showed that organized graft, able to deliver protection to a theoretically undesirable element and favors to substantial citizens, would command power in communities that preferred private exploitation to the travail of genuine self-government.

IX

THE IRREPRESSIBLE CONFLICT

1

A NEW CUSTOMER WAS IN THE market in the spring of 1861. The United States of America, arming for the defense of union one and indivisible, had a large order to place. The bodies of young men, clothes for them to wear, millions of rations to feed them, horses for them to ride, ships and railways to transport them, guns and ammunition with which they might blast other young men out of a land that could no longer exist half slave and half free—these were commodities for which the insatiable purchaser cried.

The response wrote one of the most inspiring chapters in American history. A moral crusade and an economic revolution were in the making, and both attracted the fanatics. To meet the needs of an abolitionist civilization, the young men poured forth to crush rebellion. Lighthearted, laughing as they roared out the brave, simple notes of "We are coming, Father Abraham, three hundred thousand more" or "As He died to make men holy, let us die to make men free," they marched away, waving to the crowds of cheering, smiling, weeping women in wide skirts and ridiculous bonnets who gathered to bid farewell to the heroes.

The story of their heroism needs no retelling. They were magnificent, touching, splendidly worthy of the homage accorded to their achievements. They have gilded with the glory of their deeds the pages of four years of history.

Some of those pages are not, however, so clean as one

might wish to have them. There are stains, not always of blood. Summoning all its resources for a titanic struggle, the nation learned that it was composed of something less than demi-gods, and this was most apparent in the mobilization of lesser things than lives. The North, however small a part of it realized the fact in '61, was fighting to destroy a form of property and a source of profit. To that end, blood was given more freely than material wealth. Many were willing to risk neither, but some of the very men who most gallantly offered their bodies for cannon fodder clung to the pursuit of gain as long as life listed.

In the first months of the war, when it seemed that the initial Confederate rush would overwhelm Washington and men were hurrying from all sides to save the capital, officers of the new regiments were quite unable to resist the temptation of a bribe, although they knew they might be killed before they had a chance to spend the money. The colonels of the first five regiments of Wisconsin volunteers, urged to make all possible speed, took $5,000 to use a route involving several changes, a good many extra miles at 2 cents per mile per man and a few days' delay. They were not unique.

"I do not think there has been a regiment from Wisconsin where either the military officers of that State or the officers of the regiments have not been paid more or less money for their influence in diverting the travel of their regiments over particular routes," testified President Cass of the Fort Wayne, who had taken part in the auction.

As it was in railroads, so in supplies of all kinds. A select committee of the House, after looking into these matters, spread over many hundreds of pages the sorry tale of peculation. Unhappy generals grappling with problems altogether beyond their experience and training were called upon to win the war with guns that were dangerous only to the men who fired them, clothing that fell apart in the rain, sick and unfit horses bought at enormous prices and shipped halfway across the country to sections noted for the quality of their livestock. They were expected to nourish their men on food paid for but never delivered to the army, and transport that army on ships chartered at exorbitant rates, although condemned as unseaworthy by the navy.

"Such gross and unblushing frauds would have cost all who participated in them their heads under any other government than ours," the committee reported with laudable feeling but an extremely provincial ignorance of other governments.

All countries at war indulged in the same practices. England, long since purged of the Bloomsbury Gang type of grafter, had been helpless through the inglorious Crimean War a few years earlier in the grip of just such vultures as gathered for the feast during the struggle between the States. The notion that a government is a sort of fairy godmother was not to be dislodged from the minds of many Cinderellas in the purchasing departments. They were quite surprised that the rags, pumpkins, sticks and mice that they furnished were not miraculously transformed into sound raiment, gun carriages, rifles and horses for the troops in the field.

Unfortunately the generals, military to the core, ignored vulgar commerce behind the lines. They were such professional fighters as the picturesque Frémont, whose exploits had won California. Commanding in St. Louis, he was a victim of what his own party in Congress designated as "unconscionable and dishonest contracts by which enormous profits are sought to be obtained from the government by a system of brokerage unjust to fair and honest commerce, corrupting to public virtue, discouraging to patriotism and a burning shame and dishonor to the country."

The specific transaction that aroused this indignation marked the first independent entry into the business world of J. P. Morgan, a solid, unattractive chunk of young manhood just turned twenty-four. Much later, when he was as omnipotent as one man can be in the modern industrial world, it was the custom to see in the youngster of 1861 those ruthless, domineering, acquisitive qualities that characterized the mighty financier at the turn of the century. But his was not the master mind. He played only the part of a young fellow with a lot of money and no scruples as to how he made more.

His mentor was a somewhat older man, Simon Stevens, one of the many acquaintances to whom the guileless Frémont gave his confidence. Stevens had come East as the General's agent to buy supplies and fell in with an obscure speculator named Arthur Eastman, who had an option on 5,000 Hall carbines stored in the New York arsenal. The weapons had been condemned as worthless four years before, so Eastman could get them for $3.50 apiece. The terms were cash, which neither Eastman nor Stevens possessed, but Frémont's agent undertook to raise the needed sum in return for Eastman's agreement to resell at $12.50 per gun.

On Aug. 5, 1861, Frémont in the midst of many troubles was cheered by one hopeful communication. Stevens reported that he had 5,000 rifled carbines, "new," fully up to government standard, available at $22 apiece. The General, undeterred by the fact that he had no authority for such purchases and perhaps ignorant of the limitations on his power as a commanding officer, telegraphed an order to buy and ship by express at once. Meanwhile Stevens had taken young Morgan into partnership on the deal, and Frémont's telegram convinced the banker that profit was certain. The next day Eastman took the carbines from the arsenal, 4,996 of them, presenting a Morgan draft in payment.

Only then did he discover one of the reasons why the government was selling so cheaply. The carbines were not 'rifled, but this was a defect that a little time, work and about $1 per barrel could remedy. Eastman had it done, and two weeks after Frémont had begun to wonder about his fine new guns, the first shipment left New York. The second was delayed until the conspirators—Stevens was now an aide de camp to Frémont with the rank of Major—learned that the earlier lot had been paid for at $22.

Even such amateurs as Stevens and Eastman had spotted the lack of rifling. What they did not know was that this particular Hall model had a firing mechanism so devised that it was about an even chance whether the soldier who used it sent a ball in the general direction of the enemy or blew off his own thumb. The weapon had been condemned originally for this peculiarity after repeated accidents. While Stevens and Morgan were reckoning their profits, Frémont's men were learning at the cost of several thumbs that Major Stevens had not told the exact truth agout the standards attained by his purchase. Payment of $58,175 on the second lot of carbines was refused.

Such words as "treason" and "bad faith" were later used in pointing out that the government had sold for $17,486 on Aug. 7th what it had agreed the day before to buy for $109,-912. But even at twenty-four Morgan was a hard man to balk of profits. His influence arose mainly from the fact that at this time his father's London banking house was important in war financing. So, very insistent upon his rights, he was heard at the War Department, but his subordinate part in the transaction was seen in his withdrawal from the case—something he would never have done in a deal of his own making—and Stevens was left to win the appeal after five years despite an intervening confession to bribery in another connection. Morgan's role remained passive to the end. He simply offered stolid refusals to disclose the nature of his contract with Stevens. That, he said, was his own very private business.

2

At the head of the system of which Stevens took such shrewd advantage stood the figure of Lincoln's first Secretary of War, Simon Cameron. As the President and his Cabinet elaborated plans to preserve the Union, no face around the table mirrored the majestic sadness of that time so well as the sensitive features of Cameron. Most of his colleagues were bearded in various degrees of luxuriance expressive of the owner's taste and temperament, but the Secretary of War needed no hirsute adornment to emphasize the distinction of his countenance.

The oldest man in the Cabinet, sixty-two, he was almost as tall as the President and could have sat for the portrait of one of those wise, kindly, pitying Scots dominies of whom Barrie wrote. His thin, longish white hair capped a magnificently domed forehead, beneath which deep-set gray eyes seemed to reflect the sorrows of the world, while the small, thin-lipped mouth curved in an expression of mild benevolence.

No one who knew "General" Cameron—he had been adjutant general of Pennsylvania in his thirties and the title clung to him all the rest of his ninety years—was deceived by this gentle yet imposing appearance. For he had created a political machine that was even closer than Tammany to the realities of life. Without altogether realizing the magnitude of his achievement, he was establishing the "Pennsylvania system," the open domination of politics by the industrial and financial interests of the state.

This development was bound up with Cameron's own career. He had combined banking, railroading and iron making with the practice of politics; they had made his life both full and happy. His political education dated from the Era of Good Feeling when he had been a printer employed for a short time in Washington. Then he had become a newspaper publisher in Harrisburg and won the state printing contract. As the owner of a press, he was better equipped than most of his contemporaries for banking, and soon he was running off his notes with the best of them. The young "General" also financed several profitable canals and railroads, and in 1861 his fortune was estimated at $5,000,000, one of the largest in the country.

Unobtrusive public service accompanied the accumulation of wealth. Although an attractive person, liked by men who most abhorred his principles, Cameron never boasted any devoted mass following. His strength lay in the manipulation of more popular leaders and the adroit mobilizing of industrial support behind his own bandwagon.

He began life as a Democrat but, as Lincoln once observed, "not Democrat enough to hurt him." In 1845 he had somewhat disrupted his party to secure a Senate seat, beating the official Democratic candidate by winning in obscure ways the support of the opposition. His treachery was punished by two successive refusals of the legislature to send him back to Washington, and in 1857 he became a Republican.

The new party was rather discouraged that year over the Senatorial outlook, for the Democrats held a majority of three in the legislature. It was felt that the Republican nomination would be an empty honor. The newcomer to their ranks, however, informed the caucus that by a curious chance he could command exactly three Democratic legislators. They were non-transferable, but if he should be the Republican choice, he could be elected. The caucus, incredulous, appointed a confidential committee to check the claim, and it was even as Simon had said. Three Democrats and the solid Republican bloc returned him to the Senate.

The incident made him strong enough to be a decisive factor at the national convention of 1860 and won him a place in the Cabinet. He had bargained for that with Lincoln's campaign manager at Chicago, although the candidate did not hear of it until after the election. Then Lincoln was perturbed. The Cameronian reputation was so well established that the President-elect hesitated long before carrying out the promise. Only the advice of other party leaders and the plain fact that the "General" could and probably would wreck the administration if passed over, led to his inclusion as Secretary of War.

Now, with the country hastily engaged in creating an

army in the face of Southern rebellion and a strong Northern minority feeling that war was unjustified, Cameron applied his own political methods which, unfortunate as they may have been for troops in the field, established the Secretary's Republican machine as the organ of Pennsylvania industry. His whole system was summarized by a later Congressional finding:

"The evidence pointing to a criminal collusion between government inspectors and contractors are many and of the strongest kind."

Cameron's chief assistant in the War Department was Tom Scott, on leave of absence from the Pennsylvania Railroad. Scott's generosity to selected lines was characterized by the investigators as "outrageous and indefensible." But the profits of Cameron's road and the Pennsylvania doubled. Others did not do so well.

"There seems to have been a studied effort to destroy certain railroad competition," remarked the House Committee.

John Tucker, also a Pennsylvania railroad president, was the Secretary's chief purchaser of army transports. Tucker chartered or bought a great many unseaworthy vessels at enormous prices on which government officials took such extravagant commissions that the thrifty Cornelius Vanderbilt was shocked. The old freebooter appeared before the committee very angry because "these thieves," as he called them, had demanded money before they would let the Commodore overcharge the government for his ships.

Perhaps "old Corneel" was disappointed that he had not done quite so well as that other shipping man, Marshall Roberts, who enjoyed some fame as the owner of the *Star of the West,* which failed to relieve Fort Sumter. Roberts sold the army two new ships at $100,000 each after the navy rejected them. One of the vessels foundered on her first trip; the other barely made port and had to be abandoned, but Roberts cleared a net profit of $89,000 less commission to

Tucker, who knew of the navy's adverse report when he
agreed to take the ships.

Wherever investigators turned they found the same conditions, but the strangest story they heard was that of "Gen
eral" Cameron's old journalistic supporter, Alexander Cummings. He had published *The Evening Bulletin* in Philadelphia for many years but in 1860 he went to New York to
found *The World* with Manton Marble.

Early in the war he received a letter from his friend, the
Secretary, asking him to make some purchases for the army.
Patriotically he agreed, whereupon a fund of $2,000,000 was
placed at his disposal. The publisher did not think it odd
that no one ever told him what the army might need; it
never occurred to him to consult the quartermaster, although
he was sometimes in that officer's quarters, and he admitted
he never questioned the complete accuracy of any man's
selling talk.

For the most part he relied upon inspiration. One day he
watched troops entraining for the South and reflected that
the garments suitable to New York in spring would be
uncomfortably warm when the gallant fellows reached Rich-
mond, as he did not doubt they would in a few weeks. Mr.
Cummings was admirably prompt. Before the sun went
down upon his zeal he had acquired 19,680 pairs of linen
pantaloons for $17,220 and 1,670 dozen of straw hats at the
bargain price of $4,145.68. Some days after the shipment had
proceeded south to astound a long-suffering commissariat,
Cummings mentioned the matter to the quartermaster. He
was genuinely pained to learn that soldiers did not wear
straw hats and that linen pantaloons were regarded as inappropriate for active campaigning.

"But then," he testified philosophically, "I had ceased to
purchase."

An equal nonchalance was evident in the publisher's accounts. The committee, poring over bills for boxes of her-
ring, imported beverages, butter, cheese and other groceries

confidingly bought by Cummings from an "expert" who turned out to be a hardware salesman, could find no records for about $140,000 of the late $2,000,000. Their witness comfortably assured them the sum must be covered by vouchers.

"What vouchers, and who has got them?" asked the committee despairingly.

Under the circumstances one may admire the restraint of their proposed resolution that the War Department's purchasing system "is injurious to the public service and meets the unqualified disapprobation of this House."

It was equally objectionable to the President, who perhaps had not forgotten some of the gossip once heard from Thad Stevens. Stevens and Cameron had come into the Republican party from opposite sides, and were never reconciled to their diverse origins, although they were in the same service. In conversation the Representative had relieved himself of some unkind expressions.

"You don't mean he'd steal!" exclaimed Lincoln, who had formed an accurate estimate of his aide's probity and knew that common theft was not one of his failings.

"He wouldn't steal a red-hot stove," retorted old Thad bitterly.

It was the sort of joke that helped make Lincoln's task bearable. He thought the Secretary of War should have a little fun, too, but the gentle Simon was not amused. He raged, and in his rage sent off an impulsive demand for a retraction. Unfortunately he found Stevens only too ready to oblige.

"I said you would not steal a red-hot stove," the apology ran. "I now take that back."

Lincoln could put up with lack of humor in his official family, but he could not condone the Secretary's application of Pennsylvania business methods to the conduct of the war. In January, 1862, he wrote a brusque note informing Cameron that his name was being sent to the Senate as Minister to Russia and that Edwin M. Stanton would be Secretary of

War. It was a disgrace and meant to be. But in the interests of party harmony and perhaps because he was moved by some tears that the "General" summoned into his fine eyes for the occasion, Lincoln relented so far as to accept a resignation.

Cameron's departure—he actually went to Russia for a time —failed to improve official standards of honesty. Nor was the unwilling diplomat as crushed as his enemies had hoped. In 1863 he returned to his railroad, his bank, his iron works and his place among the leaders of industry.

His war services were appreciated at home, for his colleagues knew he had done his best for them, that he was himself no cheap bribe-taker, that his brief administration of the War Department had fostered home industry. They rallied to Cameron and the "Pennsylvania system," and the carefully curtained back room of the ex-Secretary's bank was the scene of some practical political meetings, such as the one at which, a state legislator testified, Cameron promised him $20,000 for his vote. These gatherings, very much like those Tammany heelers held in the back rooms of saloons, were so successful that it was not long before a select committee of the Pennsylvania House reported:

"Unlawful means were employed to secure the election of Simon Cameron to the Senate of the United States."

That was a mere detail. The important thing was that in 1863 the genial, gentle, stubborn old man was back in the Senate, never again to have his rule questioned in Pennsylvania.

3

Victory in a war on the scale of that between the States calls for at least four great leaders—a man to inspire the people with confidence in the sanctity of their cause, a man to win battles, a man to organize the cold materialists who are not susceptible to faith and a man to raise the money.

The North produced Lincoln for the first task, Grant for the second, Cameron and his successors for the third, and in Jay Cooke found the essential financial wizard. Until this Philadelphia banker took over the job of marketing war loans, the unsystematic efforts of the government and assorted agents brought meager results, while *The Bankers' Magazine* deplored the "unfortunate rush for profit." Failure was in the air; defeatists were crying out to let the South go and good riddance, but some patriots actually proposed that capital be conscripted in the same way as men. The blasphemous idea was dismissed so decisively that Representative Kellogg of Illinois protested:

"I am pained when I sit in my place in the House and hear members talk about the sacredness of capital; that the interests of money must not be touched. Yes, sir, they will vote 600,000 of the flower of the American youth for the army to be sacrificed without a blush; but the great interests of capital, of currency, must not be touched. We have summoned the youth; they have come. I would summon the capital, and if it does not come voluntarily, before this republic shall go down or one star he lost, I would take every cent from the treasury of the states, from the treasury of capitalists, from the treasury of individuals and press it into the use of the government."

This was wild talk. The employment of Cooke was much more to the taste of the majority. He was not then one of the country's greatest bankers, but he came from Ohio and his brother, Henry, a newspaper editor, was an ardent supporter of Salmon P. Chase, former Governor of their state and now Secretary of the Treasury. Cooke established a branch in Washington, put Henry at the head of it and solicited Federal business.

The Treasury was lucky to get him. A vigorous, intelligent man in his prime, about whom there was nothing eccentric except his whiskers, Jay could look further ahead than immediate profit on a bond issue. He wanted to make himself the dominant financier of the country, and in the government's necessities he saw his opportunity. He was content to make little or nothing if he could convince the business world of his fitness for large undertakings. Worth more to an astute banker than any commission was the information Henry obtained at the Treasury, where he was so much at home that the uninformed supposed him to be Chase's confidential secretary.

The public fought for Cooke's issues. His methods, new then but copied by generations of bond salesmen after him, took every advantage of the speculative wave that was the accompaniment of war profits and war graft. The advertising possibilities of press and public meeting were exploited fully for the first time. Paid space in the papers, select dinners and hampers of choice wines for editors, market tips to financial writers, insured the success of the war loans. Money poured in almost as fast as purchasing officers could spend it, and another brother, Pitt Cooke, wrote admiringly to Jay:

"The country owes you a debt of gratitude as great as it did to old Robert Morris."

It was true. Cooke's methods, even, were similar to those of the Financier of the Revolution, allowing for improvements in advertising media, and both men met the same fate through a belief that they could adapt to private ventures their success in public finance. That end, however, was mercifully hidden from the banker, who soon regarded himself as set above all normal laws. He blithely promised that bonds would be paid in gold, although bought with paper which was at a 40 per cent. discount. This was not stipulated in the acts authorizing the loans, and added just 40 per cent. to the cost of the war. Congress later balked at the expense, but Cooke declared with every evidence of sincerity:

"I shall ever insist that the pledge in my advertisements and the advertisements of my agents was equivalent in equity and honor to any of the loan laws, and Senators and Representatives who deny this are dishonest to my mind."

His operations, bringing in hundreds of millions, were the backbone of victory, but many people believed he made too good a thing of it. One conversion loan was sold at such a premium that an individual described by brother Henry as "an eccentric and witless member of Congress" endangered the whole system by proposing the government save the premium by issuing its own bonds. The reference is the first, but not the last, in the fraternal banking correspondence to James G. Blaine of Maine. His plan was not adopted, but criticism did not die. Men saw that the House of Cooke emerged from the war far wealthier than any of its former superiors and more powerful than any had ever been before. But Jay explained:

"I think people will begin to understand by and by that Jay Cooke and his firm didn't make money out of the government, but made money as they had a right to make it out of the prestige which their own successful efforts gave them."

Which meant that the confidence inspired by his government operations enabled him to sell other securities on which the profit was greater. This, in sum, was Cooke's subtle graft. He linked the authority, the solidity and the future of the Union to his own establishment, and used the excessive premiums for promotion work that advertised his bank as much as the bonds. In all the manifold business fields into which the government was driven by its war needs, it was best served in the marketing of its bonds, largely because Jay Cooke had a vision of future greatness.

4

He was not the only one so inspired, although he ranked among the most honest. Others were sufficiently detached from the war to anticipate the needs of a nation at peace. To many of them that meant transcontinental railroads, which would not only tap the Far West but would make more accessible the rich trade of the Far East. Such plans were years old, but only when the public was absorbed in greater excitements could Congress establish a policy that offered an empire to the most unscrupulous financial buccaneers available.

Douglas's Illinois Central bill was to be the model, but improvements had been made in legislative technique during the intervening ten years. Legislators expected more than traded votes for local measures; promoters expected more than land.

The people, breathlessly awaiting news of victory and defeat, naturally ignored the routine progress of railroad laws. Before Lee surrendered, therefore, few concerned themselves with the details by which four lines to the coast had been chartered and generously subsidized—the Union Pacific, Central Pacific, Texas Pacific and Northern Pacific. Of these the first achieved most notoriety, but the Central deserved most.

It was one of the more luxuriant products of the California climate, a lush, exotic growth from an exceedingly unpromising seed. Reorganized as the Southern Pacific, it was to rule the state for half a century, but it was the creation of four adventurers who knew no more of railroading than how to bribe their way to a charter.

Of strangely diverse and complementary talents, the four met on the common ground of desire for great wealth. All of them were in the prime of life but they, no more than young Morgan, thought of going to war. When they came together in 1861 they did not discuss the stale news arriving by courier and clipper ship from the battlefields. Their only interest in the great crusade was that it made the need for a railroad more obvious and distracted attention from the means by which the project could be launched.

Their financial resources were on the surface laughably inadequate. Collis P. Huntington and Mark Hopkins could contribute to the venture only the credit of a moderately successful hardware store in Sacramento. Leland Stanford's shop in San Francisco was worth as little, and his legal education was for the moment no asset. Charles Crocker, although the loudest of the four, a monstrous squat creature of more than 250 pounds with a voice like thunder, probably had the least worldly goods, for he was one of those men to whom the prefix "ex" seems always to apply. He was at this time an ex-iron worker, an ex-peddler, an ex-prospector.

Between them they managed to raise not quite $200,000, enough to have built perhaps ten miles of the hundreds they projected. However, they were not so simple as to expect to use their own money for building, even if they had had it. The $200,000 was quite enough for the purpose at hand, Huntington believed. The partners confided their savings and borrowings to him when he departed for Washington in 1862. They then incorporated the Central Pacific Railroad Company with a nominal capital of $8,500,000, not a penny paid in.

All of Huntington's $200,000, the entire working capital of the Central Pacific, was laid out in bribes to Congressmen or others with influence, and one day a gallery observer noted that a bill for a transcontinental railroad had passed while the lobbyists were "looking down on the scene like beasts of prey." The public was not interested, but Huntington sent word to his partners:

"We have drawn the Elephant."

It was an understatement. The Central Pacific had thrown its $200,000 upon Congressional waters and lo! it had returned in the form of a land grant for 9,000,000 acres and a loan of Federal bonds for $24,000,000. This was coupled with a grant of 12,000,000 acres and $27,000,000 to the Union Pacific, the plan being that the two lines of track should meet somewhere in Utah. There was a provision that the government's $24,000,000, payable in installments upon completion of short sections of the road, would be secured by a first mortgage on the whole line. This did not worry Huntington as he set out for home.

The four partners were practically penniless, but they had their charter, and the popularity it won for them swept

Stanford of the fine Eastern manners into the Governorship of California. They knew none of them need ever want for money again, and in a few days it began rolling in. The route of the Central Pacific was put up at auction. Any town, no matter how remote, could insure the road's passage through its streets at a price. No town that did not pay, however advantageously situated, need expect to see a railroad. At $150,000 from the smaller places to San Francisco's $3,-000,000, the cities and counties pressed their money into the empty pockets of the four, and soon Stanford's brother, Philip, was scattering gold pieces to cheering voters on election day.

Building could now begin, but there was that troublesome matter of a first mortgage. Within two years it had occurred to the California quartet and to the promoters of the Union Pacific that this obligation would be hard to evade and might discourage potential purchasers of stock. So once again Huntington set out for the East. This time he took more than $200,000, and in Washington he met the Union Pacific agents engaged on a similar mission. The session of 1864, enlivened by so much of acrimony and joy in the prospect of victory that could not now be long delayed, unostentatiously passed another railroad bill. Generously Congress agreed, after a good deal of priming that almost broke the four partners again, to accept a second mortgage and leave the first free as bait for investors.

Both sets of promoters then adopted the same tactics. They formed construction companies and, as railroad boards of directors, voted to themselves, as builders, contracts to lay the rails at about double the cost. The contracts were secured by a first mortgage. Meanwhile they sold to an eager public as much stock as possible—stock in the railroads, not the construction companies. The result was that the actual operation of the roads could never earn interest on the excessive first mortgage, let alone dividends or the government's claim. The lucky owners of the construction companies would be able to foreclose, take the two lines of subsidized track for their own and retain the profits.

It worked so well that Huntington, Stanford, Hopkins and Crocker took in $79,000,000 from stock, government bonds and cash contributions from localities. Although their complete ignorance of engineering caused them to waste and be cheated of nearly three-fourths of their expenditures on actual construction, they emerged with a profit of $36,000,000, plus millions of acres of farm land, water front terminals, town sites, mines and forests. The government held a $24,-000,000 bag; share holders found they had nothing more valuable than wall paper; four adventurers had achieved autocratic dominion over the destinies of a "free" people, but members of Congress jingled a great many California gold dollars in the pockets of their tight-fitting trousers.

X

THE GOLDEN AGE

1

Lincoln's warning that the nation could not exist half slave and half free had been a splendid slogan for the emancipators. That it was also a profound economic truth was less generally appreciated by a people preparing for a great forward material movement after the interruption of war. Industrial greatness was achieved eventually, but only through long and bitter strife revealing that the nation could not exist half a modern mechanized state and half an eighteenth century agrarian commonwealth. The South had learned that an outmoded economy withers in the face of more efficient methods. It was now the turn of the West to con the same unpalatable lesson.

Such studies are not easily mastered. Public opinion clung with the tenacity of innate conservatism to the old ways. Many of the very men who were creating an interlocking system of vast industrial organization sincerely believed that their ideal was a return to the prosperous, graceful, leisurely life uprooted by the war. Of course it had never been quite the paradise they remembered, but they yearned for it in their hearts while they strove with brains and hands to found a new order, far more promising in its potentialities for service to mankind, if only it could be guided to that end.

The guide unreflectingly chosen was graft, but the choice was implicit in the confusion caused by mixing the professed ideal with the practical application. Everything, including the deficiencies we lump under the heading of human nature, encouraged corruption. Nothing less could have induced public officials to turn over the national resources to private exploitation. Without graft the nation must have done without the new means of transportation, for instance, or embarked upon a policy of state socialism unknown to most of its citizens and repellent to the rest.

Four years of war had developed in the victorious North sufficient rancor to abet the vicious system of reconstruction loosed upon the prostrate foe by an alliance of crusaders bent on racial equality and carpetbaggers bent on plunder. The bloody shirt became a banner that rallied its millions, but the business of meting out injustice to the vanquished was no more absorbing than the struggle of returned soldiers to recapture their places in the economic system, or the efforts of non-fighters to perpetuate war profits by control of peaceful enterprise. All were willing to use graft to achieve their ends.

Yet the crazy, uncurbed post-war speculation, the rush to develop new industries and new frontiers, were mingled with a nostalgia for a Rousseauean simplicity that had never existed except in the imagination. The combination led voters to demand of their leaders only that the South be made to repent, that the rest of the country be enriched and that the administration return to the Jeffersonian ideal of the less government the better. These demands were not incompatible with graft; rather they led so directly to it that a year after the war the rigidly upright Indiana Republican idealist, Representative George Washington Julian, had become "more and more disquieted by the signs of bribery I see."

They were signs of the times. No man could win election to public office, except perhaps in Pennsylvania and some other Eastern industrial strongholds, unless committed to the cause of "the common people." But once in place, he was subjected to the unremitting pressure of a growing capitalism's powerful economic interests. To minimize the resulting friction, dangerous to the life of political machinery, there was only one lubricant. It was applied so lavishly that George Hoar of Massachusetts, himself a Republican of soundest principles, after serving a little more than one full term in the House, delivered this indictment of the government of which he was a part:

"In that brief period I have seen five judges of a high court of the United States driven from office by threats of impeachment for corruption or maladministration. . . .

"I have seen in the State in the Union foremost in power and wealth four judges of her courts impeached for corruption and the political administration of her chief city become a disgrace and a by-word throughout the world.

"I have seen the chairman of the Committee on Military Affairs in the House rise in his place and demand the expulsion of four of his associates for making sale of their official privilege of selecting the youths to be educated at our great military school.

"When the greatest railroad of the world, binding together the continent and uniting the two great seas which wash our shores, was finished, I have seen our national triumph and exultation turned to bitterness and shame by the unanimous reports of three committees of Congress that every step of that mighty enterprise had been taken in fraud.

"I have heard in highest places that the true way by which power should be gained in the Republic and the true end for which it should be used when gained is the promotion of selfish ambition and the gratification of personal revenge.

"I have heard that suspicion haunts the footsteps of the trusted companions of the President. . . ."

This was a prosecutor's summation, but it can hardly be considered severe for a decade that saw the "Reconstruction" of the South, the spectacle of Cabinet members fleeing to private life before exposure of frauds, the Crédit Mobilier scandals, the Whisky Ring, the gold panic conspiracy, the apotheosis of Tweed and at last the election of a proven perjurer as President, a fitting finale to the golden age of graft.

2

Republican leaders who wrapped themselves smugly in the mantle of Lincoln's political canonization while they resolutely ignored his policy, after the manner of those who had expounded the gospels of other prophets, were not likely to overlook corrupt opportunities for fastening their grip on power. The criminal cynicism with which they connived at the plundering of the Confederacy indicated their limitless capacity for maladministration. The best of them were recklessly ready to use any means to maintain the ascendancy of their party.

Their cry of patriotism, their vociferous concern for the welfare of freedmen as voters, their frenzied waving of the bloody shirt, were the elements in a smoke screen behind which industrial and financial giants captured effective control of the country. Occasionally the strong wind of a more than usually vigorous public protest blows the veil aside and we catch a glimpse of the real operations in the open. One such moment was afforded to Julian on a swing through the country, and although he was among the most radical of the "rule or ruin" radical Republicans, he saw whither his party was tending and wrote:

"The saddest part is that public officials, both State and Federal, are in league with the capitalists in making the rich richer and the poor poorer."

The process was being carried out in nothing so completely as railroads, for they were then by far the most important factor in industrial development. Among the rich who were getting very much richer and doing it very swiftly were the incorporators of the Union Pacific, who had acquired control of a company called Crédit Mobilier of America, which owned nothing except a charter drawn in the widest possible terms. Through this agency the promoters paid themselves from the Union Pacific treasury $93,546,-287.28 for construction of the road. As directors of Crédit Mobilier they spent $50,720,958.24, including bribes to protect their $43,000,000 profit. One of the first threats to this program was the chief engineer, Peter A. Dey, who in 1864 sent in his estimate for the first 100 miles of road across the Nebraska prairies from Omaha. He figured $30,000 a mile, but that allowed for only reasonable gains. He was told to revise his calculations upward.

Dey was one of those single-minded technical men who do not appreciate the technicalities of business, and when he found that his estimates were to be the basis for the Crédit Mobilier extortion, he regretfully resigned "the best position in my profession this country has ever offered to any man." He was succeeded by General Grenville M. Dodge, who could figure anything and whose ethics were not so rigid, especially after 100 shares of Crédit Mobilier stock were placed in the name of Anna Dodge, his wife.

Dividends totaling 1,055 per cent. were paid between April, 1866, and December, 1868, so the co-operation of such stockholders as the new chief engineer was understandable. But danger still persisted. Under the terms of the charter, there were five government appointees on the board of directors, and members of Congress had been chosen. Furthermore, each twenty miles had to be approved by government commissioners before the Federal subsidy was handed over. Damaging legislation might hamper the work just when the profits were mounting dizzily into the millions.

Later the manipulators of the construction contracts tried to justify their gains by the plea that they had ventured their personal credit at great risk to accomplish an undertaking of paramount importance to the nation. In fact their own investment was negligible and was returned to them twofold within sixty days. Thereafter the Federal subsidy paid all expenses.

Naturally graft alone made the huge profits possible. One government commissioner received an outright bribe of $25,-000 and government directors of Union Pacific were invited to a small share in the takings of Crédit Mobilier. The only possible hitch remaining was the danger of Congressional action. To guard against this, one of the Crédit Mobilier ring, Oakes Ames, was sent to Congress from an obliging Massachusetts district.

He found in Washington a distressing propensity to meddle. As the Union Pacific pushed its tracks ever further west and it was obvious even to the most seasoned doubters that the line would really be completed, some statesmen spoke of fixing rates. Others feared possession of millions of acres of land would take the minds of the directors off actual operation of the railroad. There was talk of resuming the grant.

The company prepared to answer these arguments. In January, 1868, the Crédit Mobilier turned over to Ames 200 shares of its stock without recording the use to which he should put it. Other shares were delivered to President Thomas C. Durant on the same terms. A few days later Ames wrote from Washington to the company's headquarters in New York that he would place his shares "where they will do the most good for us. I am here on the spot, and can better judge where they should go."

Within a month he had noted in a small pocket book the names of twelve of the most influential members of the House to whom he had given stock, and be it noted that this was the Crédit Mobilier stock of the "insiders" which carried the profits, not the Union Pacific stock which anyone could — buy and would be sorry for later. The lucky Representatives included Speaker Schuyler Colfax, Blaine, Garfield of Ohio, Boutwell of Massachusetts and "Pig Iron" Kelley of Pennsylvania. Some of Durant's shares were credited to Representative Brooks of New York, Democratic leader of the House.

Still Ames was not satisfied. A proposal for an investigation had been barely averted by the masterly parliamentary tactics of Colfax, leading Ames to point out to his associates that the money spent on the Speaker had been well invested. They could feel fairly safe, but Ames liked to make sure.

"We want more friends in this Congress," he wrote on Washington's Birthday, "and if a man will look into the law (and it is difficult to get them to do it unless they have an interest to do so) he cannot help being convinced that we should not be interfered with."

Once he had the stock well spread around, he lost his fears of interference, "for I have found that there is no difficulty in inducing men to look after their own property." That Representatives should own stock in companies for which they legislated seemed entirely proper to Ames. He once retorted to a colleague who questioned his motives:

"You stated that we in New England were not as pure as you were in Pennsylvania; that you did not own a share of bank stock, and that you thought no member of Congress ought to. Well, I am not so pure as that. I think a member of Congress has a right to own property in anything he chooses to invest in."

Mr. Ames did Pennsylvania too much honor. Most of the Representatives from that State held views about property no whit different than his own. But when he used the word "invest" in connection with ownership of Crédit Mobilier stock he was stretching a point. "Invest" implies that the investor puts up some money, but Brooks and the twelve Republicans were not inconvenienced to that extent. The stock they took at par—worth 350 in the open market—had accrued dividends of something more than par value and paid 625 per cent. within the next year. Thus, when Garfield "bought" his ten shares of Crédit Mobilier, the transaction consisted in Ames's paying him $329. The same was true of the other "investors," although some of them got more than Garfield.

Representative Kelley, who acquired his nickname through a fanatical devotion to raising the tariff on pig iron, put through his deal with Ames while both were waiting for an F Street car one day. He was later disarmingly frank about it, but the arrangement had been so friendly, not to say casual, that it quite slipped Kelley's mind, or so he testified. One fact was unforgettable; there was no legislation put through that session of 1868 to which the Crédit Mobilier could object, although the public, which had bought millions of Union Pacific stock, was royally bilked, for the company could never hope to earn a return on the amount paid to the Crédit Mobilier.

Only vague rumors of these proceedings were afloat when on May 10, 1869, the entire nation joined in elaborate celebration of the road's completion. A golden spike was driven home by a silver sledge at Promontory Point in Utah, marking the end of the greatest rail-laying feat in history up to that time—1,775 miles in five years, mostly through unsettled country where the chief advantage of any railway at all, according to the eminently sensible General Sherman, was a solution to the military problem of Sioux tribes.

"So large a number of workmen distributed along the line will introduce enough whiskey to kill off all the Indians within 300 miles of the road," he wrote his brother, the Senator.

That comprehensive result was not quite achieved, but then some of the other expected Utopian consequences also failed to materialize.

3

The election of 1868 had meanwhile removed Ames's qualms. Colfax rode into the Vice Presidency on Grant's coattails, and several of his fellow members of the Crédit Mobilier ring were elevated to the Senate. They did not find themselves out of place there, for the general opinion of Senatorial integrity was such that one obscure but talented lobbyist made a comfortable living selling votes in the Upper House, where he knew no one.

This canny fellow offered the support of any Senator to any measure. He asked only $500, payable after delivery of the vote. Opponents of the bill received a similar offer. The lobbyist collected no matter how the Senator voted, and even if he abstained, the ingenious faker billed each side $250 on the plea that the best he could do for his client was to persuade the Senator to absent himself.

Into this political atmosphere, General Grant moved in a blaze of military glory that quite obscured for most of his contemporaries his unmitigated ignorance of civil affairs. "Paid for but not bought" is an epigram that has been applied to those diverse masters of politics, King Charles II and Mirabeau. Grant, who was no politician at all, might be described as bought but not paid for.

Of a wonderful simplicity and candor, he was ever conscious of his own lamentable failures in the business world. They had instilled into his impassive stolidity, weakening the very real firmness of his character, an enormous respect for the accumulators of wealth. He could no more understand how they made their money than they could grasp how he won battles.

His first independent act of administration was to appoint as Secretary of the Treasury the greatest merchant in the country, Alexander T. Stewart, who had this much in common with Hamilton, that he was an immigrant of Scottish ancestry. Despite the pleasing analogy, the law clearly forbade the employment at the head of the Treasury of a man with so many interests to conflict with those of the government. Stewart offered to satisfy legal requirements by executing a deed of trust in which he relinquished all business affiliations. This Grant submitted to Chief Justice Carter of the District of Columbia Supreme Court.

"The Chief Justice gave a brief, adverse, oral opinion, and in language not quotable upon a printed page," recorded Boutwell, who was later to fill the office that the Senate refused to Stewart.

Admiring the wealthy, Grant was naïvely gratified when he visited New York in the June after his inauguration on the way to a peace jubilee in Boston to accept the hospitality of two very rich men, Jay Gould and Jim Fisk. They had a national reputation, one that led Senator Sherman to refuse to meet them socially. But Grant was not troubled by petty conventions.

He could not know that Gould and Fisk were preparing to use him in a magnificently daring enterprise, more impudent than anything they had ever attempted before. That was saying a good deal. The partnership in the last few years had provided New York with an entertainment that was almost worth the millions they charged for it. Now they were great figures in the world, each wielding his power in characteristic fashion.

Gould—"a heap of clothes and a pair of eyes," Fisk once called him—desired nothing better than to be left alone to work out elaborate schemes for unloading worthless securities or acquiring control of new corporations. Fisk preferred to display the evidence of his success in gaudy uniforms, bevies of showy women driven behind equally showy horses, fantastic offices over his ornate Grand Opera House, gems, dinners, mistresses—the complete playboy.

They were best known as the rulers of the Erie Railroad, which they had plundered and manipulated with every resource that Gould's fertile imagination could invent. They were the only men who had ever beaten old Vanderbilt to a standstill on his own ground. In their memorable battle with the Commodore for control of Erie, they had dumped shares on the market by the thousand, Fisk printing them himself on a hand machine as fast as Vanderbilt's brokers could buy them.

"If this printing press don't break down, I'll be damned if I don't give the old hog all he wants of Erie!" Fisk exclaimed, sweating at his work.

With a suitcase full of currency the pair had beaten the

sheriff to the Jersey ferry by one jump, after the Commodore learned that he had bought more Erie stock than was supposed to exist and still did not have control. Then the inconspicuous Gould slipped up to Albany with a million in cash. He returned with pockets empty save for an act legalizing everything he and Fisk had done. The eminent jurist, George G. Barnard, later Gould's paid servant, called the measure a bill to legalize counterfeit money, and whatever Barnard's other judicial faults, he was a good judge of that sort of legality. Even so, Gould had been lucky or his million would not have been enough, since some State Senators demanded and got $100,000 apiece. But at the last minute Vanderbilt withdrew from the legislative auction; "I'm sick of the whole damn business," he cried.

Since then, only a little more than a year before Grant's visit, the partners had been looting Erie to the tune of millions, putting its stock up and down to squeeze shareholders, nearly doubling the outstanding amount of stock in four months and allowing operation of the road to sink to such low levels that men began to speak of the frequent accidents as "Erie massacres." But Fisk, assuming with delight the title of "Prince of Erie," and the unobtrusive Gould had taken precautions against interference by public bodies. On their board of directors sat Boss Tweed of Tammany Hall and Peter Sweeny, his chief lieutenant.

The Erie was running so smoothly in every way except as a common carrier that Gould had leisure to consider the gold market, which had exercised a fascination over speculative minds ever since paper money began. Almost all the great financiers of the period gambled in it more or less, to the despair of importers, who needed the metal in their business. They had to make payments to Europe in gold—the United States had never yet known a "favorable" balance of trade—and Gould's little plan was nothing less than to squeeze them in a corner.

Careful study revealed that there was only about $15,000,-

ooo of gold in the New York market. Erie's resources, backed by a bank the partners owned, were more than ample to take care of that. But to execute a corner, the passive co-operation of the government was needed. The Treasury could throw $100,000,000 on the market, and it would be sound economy to do so if the price of gold soared to anything like the figure Gould had in mind. In the spring of 1869, therefore, the Erie pair laid the basis for government co-operation by taking into the deal a Wall Street speculator, Abel Rathbone Corbin. He was small fry compared with the lords of Erie, but he was Grant's brother-in-law.

The details of the scheme were well worked out when the unsuspecting President came to New York as house guest of the Corbins. Gould called on him, and Fisk offered one of his Fall River steamers to convey the presidential party to Boston. Grant accepted, and on the night of sailing the flamboyant Fisk was host on board the vessel at one of the ornate dinners that delighted his soul.

Leading bankers and merchants were invited to see on what good terms the partners were with the administration. At table, Gould turned the conversation to finance. He held forth with unaccustomed eloquence on the duty of the Treasury to allow gold to rise freely. As one inspired by patriotism, he explained that this would enable farmers to get higher prices for their crops, would help the railroads that moved the crops and assist business in general. Others disagreed, and the discussion proceeded merrily until someone thought to ask whether the President had any views on the subject. Grant, who was quite capable of applying common sense to any problem and was not as entirely lacking in a grasp of business as he and his friends believed, replied that a good deal of the nation's prosperity seemed fictitious.

"The bubble might as well be tapped one way as another," he added as he puffed his cigar.

"His remark," said Gould, "struck across us like a wet blanket."

But he refused to give up. When Grant returned to New York, discussions were resumed, and again Gould pleaded for the farmer. At last, on Sept. 1st, the President wrote Secretary of the Treasury Boutwell, the former Crédit Mobilier Congressman, that the government should not sell gold while crops were moving. Boutwell, on vacation, duly telegraphed these instructions to Washington, and they were transmitted to General Butterfield, head of the New York sub-treasury. The very next day Gould began his corner, and his first purchases included substantial blocks for Corbin, Butterfield and General Horace Porter, Grant's secretary.

Gold was, however, curiously hard to lift. Fifty-five million dollars in buying orders only raised the price from 135½ to 140½. Corbin was worried, but Gould salved his fears by paying him $25,000 on account of his paper profits. Fisk proved more difficult to manage. His very sure instinct for a rascal told him that Grant was not one. He could only be convinced when Gould assured him that Mrs. Grant was to share in Corbin's holdings, and then he wanted more than his partner's word for it. He was, therefore, admitted to hear Mrs. Corbin hint in ladylike fashion at the same thing and one of his henchmen, W. O. Chapin, was entrusted with a letter from Corbin to Grant on the gold situation. The messenger was to carry this missive to the President's retreat in the Pennsylvania mountains and report whether the advice was pleasing.

Chapin was speedily introduced to Grant's presence by Porter, handed over the letter and waited for Grant's reply. The imperturbable smoker merely puffed and nodded and walked away, whereupon Chapin hurried to the telegraph office and dispatched this message:

"Delivered all right."

But when Fisk received it, it read:

"Delivered. All right."

The punctuation made all the difference, and the Prince of Erie plunged into the market. His heartiness did more than Gould's quiet buying to convince the Street that the partners knew something. Fisk's unshakable conviction that the President himself was in on the deal was contagious, and as they watched the burly figure roaring out his confidences, men remembered a recent night at the opera when the Grants, Corbins, Gould and Fisk had occupied the same box to hear Offenbach's "La Perichole."

Corbin's letter, however, had disturbed the President more than Chapin guessed. Even Porter, whose holdings on Gould's books stood to net him a fortune, apparently did not know how his chief felt. But on Wednesday, Sept. 22d, the day gold closed at 140½, Mrs. Corbin received from her sister a note hastily scribbled in pencil:

"Tell Mr. Corbin that the President is much distressed by your speculations and you must close them out as quickly as possible."

That evening when Gould called, Corbin was sitting at a table under a lamp, bending over this paper, and he later testified that Gould could have known of its contents only by peeping over his shoulder.

"But I think him too much of a gentleman to do that," the old speculator added.

Supposing that Corbin was right in his estimate of Gould's delicacy, the leader knew the game was up when his host refused $100,000 to remain in the market. Quietly Gould took his leave, and he spent Thursday making his own preparations, which did not include informing Fisk of Corbin's withdrawal or Mrs. Grant's letter. So on Thursday gold continued to rise, while Grant from Pennsylvania was instructing Boutwell to sell and the only business in New York was being transacted in mounting hysteria on the exchange.

The 24th, known in the colorful history of Wall Street as Black Friday, was the day Fisk had chosen for the big coup. Early in the morning he paraded a couple of his harlots through the narrow thoroughfare where such forms of display are frowned upon, and offered to bet all and sundry that gold would go to 200, a figure at which he proposed to make the shorts settle. He seemed well on his way to that goal, for his brokers were carrying everything before them in the gold room. This was a magnificent apartment adorned with a marble fountain gushing streams of the clear water that made up so large a part of the value of the stocks in which the brokers dealt.

No one paid any attention to the beauty of the scene that morning as Fisk's agents shrieked their bids and importers, screaming replies, saw themselves crashed into bankruptcy in an hour. The price was rising so rapidly, 144 to 150 to 155, that the telegraph indicators, geared for changes of an eighth, were literally burned out by the pace. An inferno of shouting men, rushing up to bathe their sweating faces in the fountain before tearing round and round with yells of fury, was in the full swing of madness when one of Fisk's bull-throated spokesmen overtopped the clamor.

"One hundred and sixty for any part of five millions," he bellowed.

The sheer magnitude of the bid silenced the noise, and as the same thunderous voice made the same mad offer, but at 161, the water could be heard plashing quite sanely in its basin. Again the bid—162 for any part of five millions—and suddenly in the fearful hush the ruinous farce was ended.

"Sold a million at 162," calmly said James Brown, a Scots banker with excellent connections and a clientele of leading merchants, and if anyone had been interested in the time of day he would have noticed that the hands of the clock stood at 11:53.

Three minutes later gold had dropped twenty points, and most of those who had not been crushed in the rise were trapped in that stupendous fall. At 12:10 General Butterfield signed for a telegram, mysteriously delayed for an invaluable half hour, ordering him to sell the gold in the subtreasury. On the Street, men who were not completely stunned were shouting for the blood of Gould and Fisk, while young Albert Prince Speyer, one of the Erie brokers, had quite gone off his head, button-holing bankrupts on the curb and offering to sell them millions at 160. Barricaded in offices guarded against the mob of traders by Erie thugs, Fisk was raging against the background of his partner's impenetrable silence. Gould had begun the day with instructions to his private brokers to sell gold down to 135. Thereafter he never spoke once, determined, he explained, not to open his mouth so that no one would be able to quote him.

Meanwhile men began to wonder who knew that the government was preparing to sell. Boutwell's telegram was sent at 11:42, and the time of Brown's offer took on significance. General Butterfield had "anticipated" the order by a few minutes, entering the market on his own hook to sell $700,000, a transaction that netted him $35,000 in half an hour. But in the rage against the Erie partners few could spare epithets for lesser gamblers. Lynch spirit was abroad in the Street that day, yet among the betrayed none was so outraged in his feelings as Jim Fisk. He was sure the President's family, official and otherwise, had accepted their graft and then run out on the deal.

"The moment I got up street that afternoon," he related, "I started right round to old Corbin's to rake him out. . . . I was too mad to say anything civil, and when he came into the room said I:

" 'You damned old scoundrel, do you know what has happened?'

"This was of course after everything had blown up. Said I:

" 'Do you know what you have done here, you and your people?'

"He began to wring his hands, and, 'Oh,' he says, 'this is a horrible position; are you ruined?' I said I didn't know whether I was or not. . . . I knew that somebody had run a saw right into us, and said I:

" 'This whole damned thing has turned out just as I told you it would; I considered the whole party a pack of cowards.'

"And I expected that when we came to clear our hands, they would sock it right into us. . . . He was on the other side of the table, weeping and wailing, and I was gnashing my teeth.

" 'Now,' he says, 'you must quiet yourself.'

"I told him I didn't want to be quiet; I had no desire to ever be quiet again. He says:

" 'But, my dear sir, you will lose your reason.'

"Says I, 'Speyer has already lost his reason; reason has gone out of everybody but me.' "

The Congressional committee to which Fisk told this tale was, in response to popular outcry, inquiring into the circumstances of Black Friday. The chairman was Garfield of Ohio, whose ten shares of Crédit Mobilier stock were not yet public knowledge. The opportunity for a rising statesman to make his mark was too good to resist, and Garfield met the occasion with a Ciceronian eloquence which inspired in his report such reflections as:

"The malign influence which Catiline wielded over the reckless and abandoned youth of Rome finds a fitting parallel in the power which Fisk carried into Wall Street, when, followed by the thugs of Erie and the debauchees of the Opera House, he swept into the gold-room and defied both the street and the treasury. Indeed, the whole gold movement is not an unworthy copy of that great conspiracy to lay Rome in ashes and deluge its streets in blood for the purpose of enriching those who were to apply the torch and wield the dagger."

The committee resolutely explored the mazes of finance, and the majority discovered that all the government officers had remained pure. General Porter and Butterfield said they had never authorized the conspirators to buy gold. Fisk's charges were declared to be the groundless calumnies of a villain.

But the minority, the two Democratic members of the committee, pointed out that their colleagues had balked every effort to find out just what share, if any, these officials and the President's family had borne. Grant politely declined an invitation to appear and the Republicans rejected with horror a proposal that Mrs. Grant and Mrs. Corbin be asked to explain. The Democrats admitted "it was a delicate matter to call upon the gentler sex," but thought it might be done in the interests of truth and justice if they were interviewed in their own homes "with a due deference to their sex and position." The majority, however, ruled, and today it is impossible to disagree with the minority's finding that on the evidence permitted before the committee, one can neither convict nor acquit.

Of course the chief conspirators came out unscathed except in reputation, and of that they had little to lose. Gould actually made money, thanks to timely selling orders. The Prince of Erie discovered that he had not been a principal at all but was acting throughout as the agent of a not very well-known broker, William Belden, who obligingly passed through bankruptcy to settle the account. But Fisk's certainty that he had bought the President of the United States, and very cheaply too, convinced the financial community that politics had developed no defense against a determined bribe. The assaults on the Grant administration were redoubled until graft became the normal method of approach.

4

In his quest for favors, Gould would have done better to deal with Congress, as he learned later in his career. He understood the legislative mind, and capitalists were assured of less publicity in the lobbies of the Capitol than in the White House. Therefore, the greedy, crowding into Washington in such numbers as to submerge the more formal society of pre-war years, turned for sympathy to the legislators.

"You can't use tact with a Congressman," one of the few unbribable Cabinet members of that time told young Henry Adams. "A Congressman is a hog! You must take a stick and hit him on the snout!"

And the country was soon chuckling at Mark Twain's quip: "There is a Congressman—I mean a son of a bitch . . . but why do I repeat myself?"

These allegories from the animal kingdom ignored the fact that the graft was great because the work it fostered was great. The country, for all its professed yearning toward simplicity, was in a hurry to grow up to its broad frontiers. Government support in the shape of land grants, concessions, franchises and subsidies was essential to the exploitation of national resources by private enterprise. Nothing in the history of the country or the philosophy of its people indicated that this support could be anything except purchasable merchandise.

Senators and Representatives were no more unusual in their greed or ancestry than the Goulds and Vanderbilts who bribed them. Business wanted to buy favors from the state; politicians wanted to sell. That, in the absence of any deterrent to trade, makes a market.

In the Washington of Grant's day, Collis Huntington spent $200,000 to $500,000 a session, and barely outbid Tom Scott, now of Texas Pacific. Other railway men were in town. Manufacturers sought tariffs. Concession hunters hungered for mining rights, timber rights, mail subsidies. Contractors spurred the demand for public improvements. All these people needed legal advice, and most of the members of Congress were lawyers. Fees, gifts, market tips and campaign funds were to be had from an almost infinite variety of sources.

And then, to make the legislative feast complete, Jay

Cooke acquired control of Northern Pacific. Of course it was not yet a railroad, merely a charter and a grant of land confirmed only after a campaign so expensive that Jay complained to brother Henry:

"I hate this lobbying."

Henry did not. Confirmation of the land grant was in the form of a joint resolution and Henry had enlisted the backing of some of the best men in Congress. Speaker Blaine, no longer considered "an eccentric and witless member," was accommodated with loans which, Jay lamented, were most inadequately secured, and his campaign fund was swelled greatly by the House of Cooke. Senator Ramsey of Minnesota led the forces in the Upper House. General Porter, fresh from his purification by the gold panic investigators, accepted a present or fee of $4,666.66 "with alacrity," said Henry, who added that the nation's law makers were "hungering for arguments more substantial than the good of the country." These were supplied, and on April 20, 1870, Henry exulted:

"We have been at work like beavers, and have whipped the enemy on every vote so far—in most cases three or four to one. We let the other side do most of the talking and we do the voting."

Next day the resolution passed the Senate 40 to 11. In the House five weeks of delay followed, largely because of the philosophic opposition of Ben Butler, plunderer of New Orleans during the war. This military hero had nothing against the Northern Pacific, but he should have been bought; he expected to be bought; it was customary to buy him. Jay, however, refused to descend to some levels, and the rapacious Butler was well below the limit. He remained in opposition, and the resolution passed by only 107 to 85.

The President made no difficulties. He was one of Jay's great friends and relied on Porter a good deal. He was touched by the banker's thoughtfulness in arranging little parties and sending gifts to the Grant offspring. He sincerely believed no one could run a railroad so well as the financier of the Civil War.

He signed and Cooke began adapting his war propaganda to the arts of peace. Once again gifts and messages and advertising contracts poured into newspaper offices, and Sam Wilkeson, a publicist with a literary style way up in G, produced some prose lyrics so convincing that the author himself stirred with a desire to go to Minnesota "right off." He restrained his ardor, content to sell Northern Pacific bonds on commission, and the more extravagant literature of the Florida boom was anticipated so thoroughly that skeptics spoke of the district as "Jay Cooke's banana belt." It was some time before anyone knew that a few of the earliest settlers, equipped for a land said to possess the wonders without the discomforts of the tropics, froze to death that winter. But Cooke was indignant when the few who had been there—and returned alive—intimated that Minnesota and North Dakota might be rather cold in January.

Despite the puffery, the "banana belt" attracted little real money. The public failed to rise to inducements that had moved them to place faith in the Union's credit during the war. Northern Pacific was reaping the reward of the corruption that had made its own and other subsidies possible. The grafters who had signed over to the plunderers the rights of government and shareholders had ruined the market for railway securities. Europeans were being warned by their own officials that American railway bonds were dangerous, for foreigners had lost hundreds of millions, providing an "invisible" import that went far toward adjusting the country's unfavorable trade balance. Local investors were all too well informed about Erie and were hearing disquieting whispers about Crédit Mobilier.

Only millions could be raised for Northern Pacific where tens of millions were needed, and the House of Cooke spread itself thin to cover the work in the Northwest. So thin that in 1872 Jay wished to retrench on campaign contributions and complained that every politician seemed to look to him for financial backing. Henry warned him it would be impossible to economize on the national legislature, and added: "Blaine is so persistent in this matter that I feel it is important that he should be conciliated. We are not yet through all our fights in Congress. However unreasonable in his demands he may appear to you to be, my conviction is irresistible that he should in some manner be appeased."

The appeasing of Blaine and many others forced Cooke to dip into the funds of his depositors, and still Northern Pacific bonds sold slowly. At last nothing short of a cash subsidy from the government could save him. The press, deprived of tips, presents and dinners, broke out into a rash of complaints about "corrupt land grants" and railroad building in the wilderness.

It was bad luck that at this juncture the papers were also able to drag into the light of day details of the Crédit Mobilier, and they ruined Cooke. While members of Congress spent the short days of January, 1873, rushing for shelter, there could be no question of further advances to railways, although Jay could not for the life of him see why the fugitives should not come to his assistance. He had made no crooked contract with himself, but men were too angry to discriminate between him and the Union Pacific. Honest editors and envious capitalists, not to mention Western settlers and buyers of stock, were clamoring for the truth and on Jan. 6th Henry watched Representatives "squirming, dodging and filibustering" on a proposal to make the investigating committee's hearings public. Soon Congressional leaders were on the stand, lying and evading and excusing, while the bond market fell all to pieces and stocks tumbled in panic.

Only the industrialist Ames seemed to think his transactions had been nothing out of the usual legislative line. He told the whole story quite honestly and frankly, to the committee's obvious embarrassment. He listened, registering scorn, while one after another the men he had bribed called on heaven to witness their purity.

"I never owned, received or agreed to receive any stock of the Crédit Mobilier or of the Union Pacific Railroad, nor any dividend or profits arising from either of them," Garfield swore.

Pig Iron Kelley informed the committee pompously that "I have challenged my memory in vain" for any recollection of the details so freely given by Ames. Other gentlemen's memories were similarly impervious to self-catechism, although Vice President Colfax, after several prolonged sessions with his conscience, suddenly recalled a very odd bank deposit which coincided damnably with Ames's testimony. It came to him in a blinding flash of revelation that a $1,000 bill had been sent to him unsolicited and unexpected through the mail, the gift of an eccentric printer (since dead) to be used for Colfax's expenses in the coming campaign. Colfax had forgotten all about it until that very moment, but once his memory started working it provided an elaborate series of details.

After listening to this sort of thing for several days, the committee decided that "Mr. Kelley then understood that the money he received was a balance due him after paying for the stock," and that "the facts in regard to Mr. Garfield are identical with the case of Mr. Kelley." Similar findings were reached about the other gentlemen, but by a marvelous exercise of logical faculties the investigators concluded that none of the Republican stockholders had any corrupt motive "or was aware that Mr. Ames had any. Had it appeared that these gentlemen were aware of the enormous dividends upon this stock, and how they were to be earned, we could not thus acquit them."

Although it was thus ruled that the Republicans had not been bribed, the committee decided that Ames had bribed them and ought to be expelled from the House. The case of Brooks was also different. He was found guilty, apparently of being a Democrat, for the evidence in his case was like that of the others, and his expulsion was recommended. The House concurred in the committee's report, and everyone agreed that Ames summarized two thick volumes of testimony and argument when, after hearing the vote that deprived him of his seat, he said:

"It's like the man in Massachusetts who committed adultery, and the jury brought in a verdict that he was guilty as the devil, but that the woman was innocent as an angel. These fellows are like that woman."

In the face of such exposures Jay Cooke found it quite impossible to sell Northern Pacific securities in sufficient quantities to replace the immense advances his bank had made to his railroad. He cried out that all who doubted the value of his stock were "copperheads," just as he had denounced anti-war men a few years before. He thought the government owed it to the general welfare to come to his rescue, but the grafters were too frightened to repay with that sort of service the money they had received at Cooke's Washington branch. Not even Blaine dared propose a cash subsidy for Northern Pacific.

Confidence in Cooke and bonds and railroads and government vanished together, and on Sept. 17, 1873, Grant was entertained for the last time at Jay's country estate, Ogontz, whose splendors had been hymned by scores of newspaper writers. The President spent the night, and at breakfast next morning his host received news that the bottom had fallen out of the market. He maintained an unconcerned demeanor until he had put Grant on a train for the West; he preserved his calm until he reached his own office. But at 11 o'clock the great banker, the wonderful optimist of the "banana belt," the super-salesman of hundreds of millions in paper, was collapsed in tears at his desk while long-faced clerks were locking the doors of Jay Cooke & Co. upon a startled world.

The jolt toppled the whole uncertain financial structure,

for the bubble of which Grant had spoken so casually four years before had not been tapped; it had exploded. Within a few days the crash was spoken of as a panic. Manufacturers and merchants went bankrupt by thousands, and suddenly it occurred to them that the graft by which they had once profited was bad.

Their social vision might have been further sharpened if they had not become conscious of the newly unemployed, hundreds of thousands of starving, homeless, bewildered citizens who were shivering in doorways that winter, prowling through alleys in search of garbage, dying in the frozen gutters. They were oddly pacific, but their mass—110,000 in a New York still short of 1,000,000 population—terrified the element of the community that remained "substantial." Radicalism was a specter that haunted those who still had houses and food. Ragged men were obviously dangerous, and wherever they gathered were mercilessly clubbed by the police. A mild suggestion that a rent moratorium would ease the crisis was met by *The World* with the flat assertion that this was a communist plot to rob the landlords.

5

Such terrors speedily quashed the incipient revolt against the grafters, and the panic of '73 was scarcely an interruption in the career of corruption. The politicians only had to graft a little harder to make both ends meet. The fate of the Crédit Mobilier Congressmen did nothing to deter them and the failure of Cooke did not end their opportunities.

Post office officials kept in pocket money by letting contracts for new buildings on a cost plus 15 per cent. basis, a species of plum that was to delight a purer generation. The Treasury was entering into an agreement with John D. Sanborn, one of its former secret service men, to collect delinquent taxes for a fee of half the takings. Mr. Sanborn, finding bad debts hard to collect in those times, merely levied $427,036.49 in current taxes on selected corporations. But the government should not have complained; when he made the division he generously handed over the odd cent.

Some other agents of the department were doing even better out of an arrangement with a group of distillers for the evasion of the tax on spirits. General John A. McDonald, supervisor of internal revenue, and General Orville E. Babcock, Porter's colleague in Grant's secretariat, were joined in this "Whisky Ring." The government lost millions in taxes, and in the end Babcock almost lost his freedom. He was saved by Grant, who refused to allow the prosecutor to promise the small fry immunity in return for state's evidence, so that it was impossible to prove conspiracy.

Babcock won the same sort of vindication as Porter and Garfield, but other members of the President's official family were less fortunate. The first whose luck failed was the Attorney General, George H. Williams. He had once been nominated by his friend, the President, to be Chief Justice of the United States, but before the Senate could vote on confirmation, it was learned that the contingent funds of the Department of Justice had been used to buy a carriage for Mrs. Williams and supply the wages and liveries of her servants. Her husband's name was withdrawn, but he continued as Attorney General until early in 1875 it began to be whispered that his wife was being paid to get Federal prosecutions dropped.

"Landaulet" Williams, as he had been called since the carriage incident, resigned rather than face the rumors, and he was followed within a few months by Secretary of the Interior Columbus Delano, whose trouble was land frauds. Delano was succeeded by Zach Chandler, "Xantippe in pants" to his irreverent contemporaries, a man so rich as to be above money bribes but, as chairman of the Republican National Committee, the chief spoilsman of the administration. The department, therefore, continued to operate on a system of favoritism.

Meanwhile the Navy had been slowly disintegrating from its high war efficiency, and as Grant began his last year in office a House committee tried to find out why. One of the reasons was the quality of supplies furnished to the fleet by a Philadelphia company which had taken Secretary of the Navy George M. Robeson into partnership soon after he entered office. The company's books defied analysis by accountants, but there was no doubt about the Secretary's own finances. A lawyer of slender means, Robeson in four years at the head of the Navy banked $320,000.

The investigators recommended impeachment, but 1876 was a presidential year; the party was faced with real opposition, and anyway the doubtful honor of being the first Cabinet officer ever to be impeached had already fallen to Secretary of War William W. Belknap. Two state trials at once was a little too much for Congress to face.

The specific charge against the General—he was a Civil War product, too—was selling the monopoly of trade at Fort Sill. It had been exposed in *The New York Tribune* four years before with no practical result save to reduce the Secretary's cut from $6,000 a year to $3,000, so poor Belknap might be regarded as a victim of the depression. He also had sentimental claims to sympathy, for on his side was the romantic interest of a lovely lady, indeed of two lovely ladies. The public, however, was oddly callous to this appeal, and even his lawyers felt called upon to excuse him with the plea that a man in office is like a dead body at the bottom of a pond, "he becomes buoyant by putrefaction and rises as he rots."

Belknap had risen far. He had been in Grant's Cabinet from the beginning, and the extremely mixed society of post-war Washington owed a great deal to him. He had appeared at the outset of the administration with a very handsome, sprightly bride, and officialdom is always grateful for the rare favor of good looks in a Cabinet member's wife. Mrs. Belknap was popular, her home tasteful, her parties elaborate, her clothes the envy of a small army of lesser women—and even of some who would have asserted their equality. There is a hint of domestic discord in the cry of the well-to-do but careful Senator Bayard:

"I own my house in Delaware; I own my house here; I have no rent to pay, but I cannot afford to dress my wife as these Cabinet Ministers' wives are dressed."

Mrs. Belknap died, but the home of the Secretary of War was only briefly desolate. Her sister, equally beautiful, equally fond of clothes and entertainment and equally extravagant, moved in to care for the widower in his bereavement and remained, to the joy of all who loved gaiety, as his wife.

It was through these ladies that Belknap had met the merchant to whom he sold the Fort Sill post tradership. In 1872 *The Tribune's* stories failed to inspire official action but by 1876 the soldiers, mulcted unmercifully at the garrison stores, forced their woes upon the attention of Congress. Suddenly the Republicans acted, hoping to cleanse their party of at least one spot in time for the coming election. Harsh things were said on the floor, and on the morning the House debated his impeachment, the Secretary was hurrying to Grant with his resignation. He got it safely accepted only an hour and a half before the articles accusing him were voted.

He hoped thus to avert further inquiry, but the Senate ruled against his plea that he could not be impeached after he had resigned. Through the spring it debated details, and then thoughtfully set the trial itself for the hottest days of summer. In July Washington fairly sizzled as the Hayes-Tilden campaign got under way to the accompaniment of torrid blasts of oratory from the Belknap hearings. The ex-Secretary, the panic so evident on the day of his resignation replaced by a pomposity that even the heat could not wilt, was painted as an exceedingly gallant figure. He had, counsel intimated, taken upon his manly shoulders the guilt of his wives who, in their innocent eagerness for new gowns, had entered into dealings the nature of which their sex barred them from understanding. Counsel practically dared gentlemen to insinuate that delicate females could know the difference between right and wrong.

The plea, partly successful in the gold panic investigation, might have had tremendous effect in that age of deference to and contempt for what orators loved to call the gentler sex. But this time the testimony clearly showed that Belknap had signed in person for his quarterly bribes and had been very active in working up the romantic line of defense.

In the end, the vote of 37 to 25 fell five short of the two-thirds needed to convict, most of the minority carefully explaining they meant to express no opinion of Belknap's guilt but believed his resignation removed the case from their jurisdiction. They had been powerfully swayed, too, by the closing defense argument, which neatly summed up the political morality of the period:

"That the present Chief Magistrate has taken large gifts from his friends is a fact as well known as any other in the history of the country. He did it openly, without an attempt at concealment or denial. He not only received money and lands and houses and goods amounting in the aggregate to an enormous sum, but he conformed the policy of his administration to the interests and wishes of the donors. Nay, he did more than that; he appointed the men who brought him these gifts to the highest offices which he could bestow in return. Does anybody assert that General Grant was guilty of an impeachable crime in taking these presents, even though the receipt of them was followed by official favors extended to the givers? General Grant's wealthy friends in New York gave him money not with any evil design upon his integrity, but because it was a pleasure to themselves; and the President appointed them to office afterward not because they had bought his favor, but because he thought the public good required it."

Perhaps it was partly due to this august example that mere exposure, even though it might ruin individuals with ease, failed to achieve permanent reform. But the main reasons for the system's survival was that it remained profitable to the dominant economic interests. Not until a more efficient substitute could be developed would there be an end to the golden age of graft.

XI

A BUSINESS ADMINISTRATION

1

THE GENERATION THAT PRO-
duced the Washington of the '70s, so distasteful to sensitive
moralists, had not exhausted in the capital either its ingenuity or its economic reason for being. There was plenty
left over to supply local government, and the transit of William Marcy Tweed across the political heavens was a lurid
glare beside which the stellar grafters of the Grant administration glimmered but faintly.

It was one of Tweed's unique achievements that he relegated the handsome Fernando Wood to the background
when great corruptionists are considered. Yet the chairmaker's son lacked some of the talents for thievery that distinguished the Mayor. Tweed surpassed the equally willing Fernandy only in the application to existing political
machinery of the business principles that elevated Astor,
Vanderbilt and Gould to fame and fortune. No one could
steal an election so neatly as Wood. But his younger rival
brought to the task of government a high measure of organization, system, the generally admired commercial virtues of thoroughness, attention to detail, enterprise and a
not quite infallible intuition of how much the traffic would
bear.

Born and reared in New York's Cherry Hill section, he
never cherished any illusions about how the city was run,
but he was neither shocked nor saddened by his knowledge.
Growing up in the heyday of Van Buren's spoils system, he

was fourteen when Jackson's Collector of the Port introduced into the language the verb "to swartwout." As a voter Tweed witnessed the beatings, free-for-all fights, ballot box smashing and other symptoms of contemporary democracy. Although a Democrat in a Whig district, he himself was never molested at the polls, thanks to a massive frame— more than six feet, nearly 250 pounds—and a reputation for being a likely lad with his hands.

Apprentice in his father's shop at eleven, partner in a brush factory at nineteen, married at twenty-one, he remained aloof from civic affairs for five years more, until in 1849 the organization of a new volunteer fire company threw him into the way of becoming the great master of dirty politics.

His size, skill and good nature made him Assistant Foreman of Americus Engine Company No. 6, the "Big Six" of small boys' admiration. Soon he was foreman and commanded the devoted allegiance of seventy-five red-shirted volunteers who regarded their fire-fighting bond as more sacred than party ties.

Tammany needed such men, particularly to lead forlorn hopes in the Whig Seventh Ward, and in 1850 the Hall persuaded Tweed to make the race for assistant alderman. He lost by forty-seven votes, a better showing than was expected. But he had no taste for moral victories. Nominated for alderman at the next election, he split the opposition by inducing the principal of a girls' school to enter himself as an independent Whig. The scholar took enough votes from the regular candidate to reverse the 1850 decision. Young Tweed was elected with a plurality of forty-eight.

Unfortunately for New York, the body in which he took his seat was that Common Council known as "the Forty Thieves." There Tweed speedily learned of profits far larger than those of the most successful brush manufacturer. Zestfully he flung himself into the mastery of this new business, and so impressed his colleagues with his commercial ability that in his first term he was one of the leading negotiators for graft on their behalf.

A term in Congress failed to alter the rising politician's conception of government as an organized system of plunder. It did teach him that there is little in the game for any but the leaders. The operations of Tammany were more congenial and more easily manipulated to his advantage, for he saw that the duties and opportunities of an elected official in the city bore no relation to the principles and program for which he had been chosen. Slavery and states' rights were just as hotly contested in a municipal campaign as if the Mayor were going to have something to do about them. Genuine local issues—transportation, street improvements, public health, schools, crime prevention and so on—were discussed only by irresponsible theorists.

A Mayor and Council elected on a platform of maintaining Southern rights and discouraging immigration were conveniently unpledged in regard to any of the matters with which they would actually deal. But if the good people of New York were more interested in the extension of slavery than in the paving of their roads, the operation of their public utilities or the administration of justice in their own town, Tweed was not. He studied civic problems to such purpose that at the outbreak of the war he was a leader in Tammany, unofficial chief of the Board of Supervisors and admittedly a professional politician, having given up his factory. He was one of the sachems who failed to keep Wood from the Mayoralty, but an augmenting swarm of ward heelers, back slappers, gang leaders and people who wanted to do business with the city were calling him "Boss."

The title was a tribute to the man's potentialities as yet rather than to his actual power. Wood still ruled, but in the unobtrusive political realms of bar parlors, "clubs" and the sacred precincts of Tammany Hall, the insiders could see how Tweed was undermining the handsome Fernandy. The Irish were lured back. The gangs were brought into line. The war chest was filled. The vast bulk of the "Boss" exuded confidence as he organized the fight for November, 1861—a fight as bitter as those on the Southern battlefields. Tammany was as anti-war as Wood, and Tweed himself was on the ticket for sheriff, spending all he had in the world, something more than $100,000, to win that lucrative post. He woke up the day after election a penniless man and still only a supervisor. A fighting Irishman named O'Brien, who had run away from Bull Run on the eve of the battle, was more to the liking of a "copperhead" constituency than one who had never gone to war at all. The "Boss" lost two to one to the deserter, but Wood too had fallen. While he and Tammany fought each other to a standstill, a Republican, George Opdyke, slipped into City Hall with 600 votes to spare, very much a minority choice of the people, or at least of the tally clerks.

Oddly enough, defeat riveted Tweed's hold on the Hall. He was able to show his bruised and discouraged followers how to retain the spoil despite their rout. He himself still held the Board of Supervisors. With Wood out of the way, Tammany could also control the aldermen, and a simple majority was sufficient to pass any measure over Opdyke's veto. The city treasury continued to run through the pockets of the same people in a way that seemed very wonderful to them, and they gave Tweed full credit.

He wanted cash as well. He got it by applying the non-partisan principle to the Board of Supervisors. This body had been made up from the two parties in equal parts so they could watch each other, but the "Boss" organized them on business rather than political lines. The distinction between Republican and Democrat, never so odious as in war, was abolished. The Board, controlling the purchase of supplies by New York County, permitted merchants to deal with any supervisor they liked so long as they paid sufficient graft.

"And through that one member," Tweed explained later, "they were talked to, and the result was that their bills were sent in and passed, and the percentages were paid, sometimes to one man, sometimes to another."

Mayors might come and go, but as long as supervisors and aldermen could dominate the city, Tweed was content to let the glory of executive office gild whom it might. Capitalists in search of franchises and real estate, merchants with wares to sell to the city, promoters who wanted streets extended to their undeveloped properties, lawbreakers in need of protection knew that business would be facilitated by going direct to the "Boss." He was in such demand that he had to open an office, and on the door he painted the legend "Attorney-at-Law." The right to use this honorable title had been conferred upon him by his tame jurist, Barnard, under the polite custom then prevailing that permitted such eminent citizens as Supervisor Tweed to dispense with the trivia of bar examinations.

Lawyer Tweed had an extremely respectable clientele, and his fees were more respectable still. By the end of the war he could remember his squandered $100,000 without regret. He had put the city's affairs on a strictly business basis so that no opportunity for graft could be overlooked by mischance. He established the methodical custom of a fixed rate of fraud for every bill, and in time the proportion was $2 in graft for $1 in goods or services. The division of the loot was worked out with arithmetical precision.

To business men like Vanderbilt and Astor, this efficiency was gratifying. When Astor wanted a bit of waterfront or an easing of his tax assessment, he found Tweed bought and sold in a way the millionaire could appreciate. When Vanderbilt needed a court order in a hurry or a special bill or a joker in a franchise, he could rely on the "Boss" to have it in stock.

Before Grant moved into the White House, Tammany had widened its field to include the whole state. Its man, John T. Hoffman, was Governor; it controlled the Assembly and could buy the Senate; all New York City was in its hands, and Supervisor Tweed had become State Senator Tweed. While railroad builders, tariff mongers and carpetbaggers crowded into Washington, the great New York financiers or their agents were more likely to be found in the rooms of Senator Tweed's ornate, hospitable suite in Albany.

Although only minority leader, he had enlisted his fellow Senators in a compact order of grafters so well drilled in legislative maneuvering that their grateful constituents conferred upon them the title of "Black Horse Cavalry." This "corrupt squadron" was the one with which Gould dealt when he came to Albany to straighten out his little difference with Vanderbilt.

The master of Erie was not one to pinch pennies. He drew the "Boss" away from the Commodore's New York Central by the present of a block of Erie stock, a directorship and a retainer of many thousands as counsel. Not the least of Tweed's "legal" services was to place Justice Barnard at the disposal of the Erie partners. Barnard had been harrying them on Vanderbilt's behalf, but now he turned at a word from Tweed. In emergencies, the Supreme Court of the State of New York was held in the rooms of Josie Mansfield, first mistress to the Prince of Erie, where His Honor was frequently entertained. It was a pity to interrupt those festive dinners with the dull judicial process of granting an injunction against a rival road or group of stockholders, but at least Barnard wasted no time on hearings.

Financiers were not the only source of income for the "Black Horse Cavalry." Tweed decided to give New York City a "home rule" charter, and his colleagues, who had never heard that there was honor among thieves, held him up in a way that did credit to his teachings. They cost him $1,000,000, but the "Boss" did not begrudge the money. The new charter gave the city much more latitude in taxing and spending.

New Yorkers hailed Tweed as a benefactor when he

brought them this document. Home rule stirred the people
to great enthusiasm. It sounded fine and independent, and
also simple. With the indifference Tweed had foreseen, the
better citizens left details to their elected officials. They rejoiced without thought of who was going to spend the new
revenues, and even *The Times* joined in the chorus of praise,
saying:

"Senator Tweed is in a fair way to distinguish himself as
a reformer."

Better informed or more alert men than *The Times's* edi-
torial writer knew that the charter delivered the city into
the hands of its grafters. Greeley was one who saw the truth
and wrote it, but in his preoccupation with national affairs
neglected the dirt in his own front yard except for an occasional backhanded blow at what was already being called
the Tweed Ring.

This band, completed dominated by the "Boss," num-
bered three other chief figures. A. Oakey Hall, Tweed's
Mayor, a man of fashion and wit—at least he liked to think
of himself in those terms—was the chief in office and the
least in all other respects. "Slippery Dick" Connolly, the
Comptroller, and Peter Sweeny, who became Park Commissioner under the new charter, were old associates of Tweed,
who now took the office of Commissioner of Public Works,
an appointive post. In these four jobholders centered all
municipal authority.

On paper the system appeared to provide a beautiful balance, with the Mayor watched by the Comptroller and both
subject to the scrutiny of a Board of Audit, composed of
themselves and the Commissioner of Public Works. In practice, the million Tweed cast upon legislative waters to obtain the charter returned to him within a few days. In a
few weeks, the Ring split $15,000,000, mostly from contracts
for the County Court House, which cost about four times
the $3,000,000 it was worth. The bill for plaster alone was
$1,826,278.45 and served as part of the inspiration for an

illustrated nursery rhyme, very popular in its day, which ended:

> This is BOSS TWEED,
> Nast's man with the brains,
> The Tammany Atlas who all sustains,
> (A Tammany Samson perhaps for his pains)
> Who rules the city where Oakey reigns,
> And formerly lord of "Slippery Dick,"
> Who *con*troll'd the plastering laid on so thick
> By the Comptroller's plasterer, Garvey by name,
> The Garvey whose fame is the little game
> Of laying on plaster and knowing the trick
> Of charging as if he himself were a brick
> Of the well-plaster'd House
> That TWEED built.

Plunder was so plentiful there was no time to keep an accurate account of it in the jealously guarded books of the city. Therefore estimates of what the Ring stole vary from $30,000,000 plainly traceable to $50,000,000 based on a guess at what their unrecorded dealings should have netted. Their activities, however, cost New York more than $200,000,000—more than all the loot of the Crédit Mobilier, Southern Pacific and Erie manipulators put together—without considering the intangibles of bad government, wasted resources or unfulfilled city plans.

The Ring's success was clearly due to the business genius of its leader. The chief merchants of New York had long ago endorsed him in fulsome phrases. The financiers were his friends and associates. The so-called opposition was as much his to command as the Tammany cohorts. For being regularly beaten, the Republican leaders received rewards they could hardly have earned if they had won.

But there were meddling folk who did not appreciate the blessings of a business administration, who would not tolerate in government the system of which they highly approved in private endeavor. Among them were such politicians as Samuel J. Tilden and journalists like George Jones, owner of *The Times*. Both were bent on smashing the Ring, but for a long time their foe sneered at or ignored them.

In the autumn of 1870 *The Times* began asking embarrassing questions about the source of Tweed's millions. For nearly a year Jones thundered accusations which he could not support by solid evidence. For the most part he could be answered by equally empty words. But his charge that the "Boss" was afraid to make public his Comptroller's accounts was so true as to be uncomfortable. With a great flourish, therefore, the Ring appointed an investigating committee. Six of the city's wealthiest and most respected residents were invited to inspect the books and report on the state of municipal finances. The six were so rich as to be above ordinary temptation, but they were also large owners of real estate, subject to the vagaries of the tax assessor and presumably grateful for that officer's forbearance. The current John Jacob Astor was their chairman.

Much later it became painfully obvious that the records showed plainly the fictitious names credited with large sums for imaginary services, the padded expense vouchers, the gift of city property to low bidders. But Mr. Astor and his associates published for the delectation of their fellow citizens and the benefit of the Ring a long paper extolling the probity of the existing regime.

"We have come to the conclusion and certify that the financial affairs of the city under the charge of the Comptroller are administered in a correct and faithful manner," their statement ended.

This interpretation of the figures supposedly examined by the Astor committee was not easily reached by less gifted mortals. In the summer of 1871 some transcripts from Connolly's books, made by employees either for blackmail or sale, fell into Jones's hands. He published them, and Tweed's elaborate, efficient structure of organized corruption, proof against all the normal vicissitudes of politics, fell to pieces and died of mere exposure. Sweeny fled. Connolly and Hall hastened to save themselves by confession. Tweed, defiant and overconfident of his hold on courts and juries, allowed himself to say for publication:

"Well, what are you going to do about it?"

"Hang them!" was an answer shouted by a crowd at Cooper Union.

That mass meeting, led by fierce reformers, shrewd politicians, indignant professional men and mercantile magnates suddenly alarmed at the rising cost of government, gave decent folk a rallying cry and an organization to make their voices heard. By the end of October Tweed knew that he had lost the courts. Even Barnard deserted him, and on a very black Friday the "Boss" was in his office waiting to be arrested on a complaint signed by Tilden. Gould waited, too, and when the sheriff arrived, the silent ruler of Erie was ready with a real estate bond of $1,000,000. A few days later most of the Ring's henchmen were defeated in a wave of popular fury that even gangsters at the polling places could not check, although Tweed kept his Senate seat.

For more than a year adjournments and delays put off the hour of reckoning, while accomplices and partners of the Ring bargained for immunity. Not all were successful. Barnard was impeached and convicted. Justice Albert Cardozo, father of an even more distinguished jurist, resigned before the Senate could remove him. In January, 1873, coincident with the Crédit Mobilier revelations, the "Boss" himself was on trial, still confident as he sat with his array of notable counsel—Elihu Root was one. Twelve of Tweed's peers listened for three weeks to the extremely complicated evidence which conclusively proved his guilt, but they were unable to agree.

"No jury will convict me," the accused boasted.

The prosecution outsmarted him. At his next trial, held in November amid the panic of '73, detectives thwarted efforts to tamper with the jury panel. After very little deliberation, the foreman announced a verdict of guilty, and the one-time master of New York, looking many more than his fifty years and even larger than his 280 pounds in the flabby degeneration of his once athletic figure, was on his way to a cell on Blackwell's Island.

It was a well-furnished cell, with especially widened windows, and Tweed spent thirteen months there. He was not to know freedom again except as a hunted fugitive. His term served, he was rearrested in a civil suit for $6,000,000 brought by the State. Bail was set at $3,000,000, and now there were no Goulds or Astors to come to the fallen leader's rescue. He moved from Blackwell's Island to Ludlow Street, and from January to December, 1875, enjoyed the comforts accorded to debtors of means, driving out for exercise and dining at his own home in the company of keepers.

Then, three weeks before Christmas, he wearied of this regimen. Giving his guards the slip at his house, he reawakened New York's flagging interest in his fate by disappearing mysteriously. For six months he lay hidden, made his way to Cuba and boarded a Spanish brig for Vigo. Someone squealed, and the new Atlantic cable was used to carry word of his impending arrival on European shores. Disguised as a sailor, he was engaged in scrubbing the deck when Spanish soldiers found him on the ship but they recognized him from one of Nast's cartoons. This, depicting a Tweed in prison stripes collaring a couple of juvenile offenders, gave the Spaniards the impression their man was wanted as a kidnaper, and he was promptly jailed.

Brought back on a United States warship, he again occupied his comfortable room in Ludlow Street. A confession of most of his stealings in return for what he understood to be a promise of release aroused some hopes, but the expected order never came. A few days after his fifty-fifth birthday, Big Bill Tweed was dead, victim of the delusion that the people really like to be governed badly in the interest of their governors.

During the years of his imprisoment, he had leisure to observe the contrast between his own place in public esteem and that held by the Ring's partners outside politics. It puzzled him. They had all been business men together, but no one could think of terms harsh enough to fit Tweed, while Gould, Astor, Vanderbilt—men who had made even greater profits from the system than he—were acclaimed as wizards of finance worthy of the respect and envy of the community.

As for his own view of his career, the "Boss" went boldly on record during the embarrassing formalities that marked his entrance into the county jail. He had murmured his name, age, color and nationality, but when a flustered clerk inquired his occupation, Tweed forgot the brush factory, the law office and his corporate directorships. Quite clearly, realizing that in one word he was summing up his status and achievements, he replied:

"Statesman."

XII

HONEST GRAFT

1

AMID THE CRASH OF FALLEN reputations, men said hopefully that the exposure of the Tweeds and Belknaps would put an end to shameless bribery. An aroused citizenry, burning with indignation (when not laughing at the governmental follies) demanded a house cleaning. The voice of the sovereign people was plainly heard calling for honesty in public life, and the will of the voters must not be thwarted in a democracy.

Corruption would have been banished promptly, no doubt, if only economic necessity had yielded to popular wrath. But hard facts are notoriously clamor proof, and one of the hardest existing facts was that the industrial community had found no substitute for bribery. Graft paid dividends and in addition the people got their railways, factories, roads, public buildings, pensions for old soldiers. They also got a depression, but after a couple of years its effects were passing and Tweed's brand of statesmanship was still supreme. The combination of panic and scandals had only so much influence that the party of Reconstruction, railway jobbery and the Grant Cabinet had to steal the election of 1876 for the honest if dull Hayes. It was done by shameless frauds in Southern states and an extra-constitutional electoral commission to confirm them.

Four years later popular wrath had faded; normal views on corruption prevailed, and the Republicans were able to put a Crédit Mobilier Congressman in the White House.

Exactly the same circumstances restored a shattered, apparently ruined and disgraced Tammany to power in New York. The golden age of graft survived its most notorious exposures because private enterprise knew no other way to deal with public servants.

Nowhere does this appear more clearly than in the correspondence of Collis Huntington. Despite the scandals which were breaking all around—perhaps because of them— the master mind of Southern Pacific averaged $600,000 a year in bribes merely to protect privileges that had cost originally only half as much, and he was getting tired of it.

"I think this coming session of Congress will be composed of the hungriest set of men that ever got together, and the devil only knows what they will do," he wrote of the men elected in '74.

Before they went out of office he was satisfied that those who opposed him "can be switched back with proper arguments." But he did not value Congressional talent at its then market price, and complained:

"It costs money to fix things. I believe with $200,000 I can pass our bill, but I take it that it is not worth that much to us."

If Huntington was dissatisfied with Grant's last Congress, words almost failed to express what he thought of Hayes's first, "the worst set of men that have ever been collected together since man was created." Admirably non-partisan in this crisis, the great lobbyist wrote of a California Representative:

"I notice what you say of Luttrell; he is a wild hog; don't let him come back to Washington, but as the House is to be largely Democratic, and if he was to be defeated likely it would be charged to us, hence I think it would be well to beat him with a Democrat; but I would defeat him anyway, and if he got the nomination put up another Democrat and run against him, and in that way elect a Republican."

Fortunately for the political future of Mr. Luttrell, he became amenable to Southern Pacific influence, and long before the election, Huntington's wrath had been turned from him to Representative Piper, "a damned hog any way you can fix him."

A large part of Huntington's increasing expenditure was due to the efforts of the unbuilt Texas Pacific to get the same governmental support that had been lavished on its rivals. Tom Scott of the Pennsylvania was the organizer of the prospective line, and the intolerant Wendell Phillips commented on his methods:

"The members of twenty legislatures rustled like dry leaves in a winter's wind as he trailed his garments across the country."

Congress rustled with the rest, and Huntington recognized the unpalatable truth that the national legislature might at any time subsidize a competitor to the existing transcontinental monopoly.

"Scott is prepared to pay, or promises to pay, a large amount of money to pass his bill," he mourned.

Huntington's letters carried a continuing burden of the writer's fear of Scott's industry and the expense and worry of keeping legislators in line. At last, in March, 1877, three days after the inauguration of Hayes and "the worst set of men that have ever been collected," came the triumphant note:

"I staid in Washington two days to fix up the Railroad Committee in the Senate. Scott was there, working for the same thing; but I beat him for once, certain, as the committee is just what we want it."

The troubles of those who deal with Congress are never over, as Huntington would have been the first to admit. Hardly had the Scott menace been eliminated than a greater rustling was heard among the leaves, and from the legislative bushes emerged the silent, enigmatic, highly dangerous figure of Jay Gould. Branching out into the transcontinental field, the New Yorker turned up in December, 1877, in control of Texas Pacific.

Congress saw him coming, and the price of votes leaped so high that Huntington groaned. Why, he demanded, if Gould had to get into this game couldn't he have worked through an agent? It would have been so much cheaper for all concerned, for the size of Gould's bribes was proverbial. The spendthrift, said Huntington, had offered $16,000 for one mere Representative! The Californains were saved a lot of needless expense only because Gould thought it would be easier to loot the already bankrupt Union Pacific than to fool with a new line. He went off to browse in that pasture, where only he could feed, all others believing the possibilities of profit exhausted. He left on the eve of a new era in plunder.

2

By playing off Southern Pacific against Texac Pacific and Gould against the field, Congress had satisfied some of the "hunger" which seemed to Huntington its most distinguishing characteristic. But the more secure the former hardware merchant became in the power he owed to bought government favors, the more he resented the necessity for continuing to pay. His fellow industrialists shared the feeling, and by the 'eighties they were strong enough to do something to relieve it.

During their rise to greatness they had had no other weapons than raw bribes and tricks. Once they acquired firm control of the nation's industrial expansion, however, they could exercise political influence through more efficient means. The railroads were vulnerable only while they were being built. They dominated the territories they served after they were in operation. Coal, steel, oil, textiles and similar sovereignties, puffed to giant size by the accelerating technological progress of the machine age, held similar sway in their communities. The cold logic of finance capital ex-

posed the wastefulness of the golden age's indiscriminate
bribery and, more effective than reform idealism, evolved
a substitute which the philosopher of Tammany Hall,
George Washington Plunkitt, shrewdly denominated "honest
graft."

This was the reward offered for favorable interpretation
of the law rather than payment for violations. In form,
honest graft had the aspect of legitimate transactions; in
practice, it was the elevation to office of politicians who
would carry out "sound" business policies from conviction.
Their election might not be cheaper, but it was more reliable and therefore more attractive than the doubtful
method of arguing with unbelievers after the polls had
closed. The honest grafters were lawyers who habitually
drew fees from private interests seeking government aid,
contractors who consistently won bids for public works,
executives of big corporations sent into public office to represent their companies rather than their constituencies, machine bosses who recognized the short-sightedness of double
crossing their industrial allies.

The chief complaint against the Congresses of Grant and
Hayes was that they would not stay bought, and that was
dishonest graft. The bribers themselves added to the clamor
against the low estate to which public morals had fallen,
and as new rulers rose to power they proposed to end the
treachery. The open buccaneering of Vanderbilt was being
replaced by combinations among the younger masters of
capital, who thought haphazard bribery, so likely to end in
betrayal after all, was as old-fashioned as ruthless throat cut-
ting. They preferred to attach their policies to the platforms
of the dominant parties and scratched their ballots as dis-
criminatingly as Gould, who once testified:

"I am a Democrat in a Democratic district and a Republican in a Republican district."

Even Chauncey Depew, spokesman for the Vanderbilts,
could see that a new period in the relations of business and

government was at hand, one that would abolish any fundamental differences in party principles. As an orator he was opposing the incipient demand for State and Federal commissions to regulate railroads. But the more he argued, the less he was convinced. He could not escape the impression that regulation might be a good thing if the right sort of capitalist regulated the regulators. Seizing upon the arguments of his foes, he even converted the old Commodore's son, William, author of the phrase "The public be damned."

Depew and other executives were acute enough to see that the economic force of which they had gained control by bribery had a more subtle political influence of its own. Railroads had already tasted of this power. Rockefeller's Standard Oil was an independent empire. Blast furnaces and the drab black mounds of a thousand coal mines cast their gloom over the Pennsylvania landscape as young Andrew Mellon, Frick, Carnegie and a dozen others rode the crest of a wave of hysterical production.

Immigrants could not be recruited in Europe fast enough to man the Eastern mills, lay tracks to the new centers of industry, run up the grim tenements of a thousand slums. Fortunes skyrocketed to dizzying heights, and the masters of great corporations, far more genuinely than the press, could have claimed to constitute a fourth estate in the land —if they had not been so certain that they were really all the other three as well.

Although their public utterances frequently gave the impression that these gentlemen were not aware of any progress since the war, they understood better than they liked to have it known that a new capitalist era was opening. This was to be seen in the gathering of the small savings of thousands to be put at the disposal of one. Investment trusts and insurance companies with vast resources were pools from which increased production could be drawn. The stocks of hundreds of industrial undertakings were widely scattered so that the men in control were no longer the owners of any considerable share, except in a few unique corporations like Standard Oil. Corporate organization had traveled the business cycle back to the model of the Virginia Company of London.

The sense of responsibility among the great of the 'eighties was, furthermore, exactly that of Smith, Sandys and Argall. This has been made abundantly clear in dozens of studies of the multi-millionaires, who have been characterized as modern robber barons, buccaneers of business, plutocratic pirates and plain thieves. But their view of the nature of private enterprise was shared by all except an extremely small minority of their contemporaries, a fact which enabled honest graft to thrive.

The most nobly principled railroad president of that generation of whom we have any extensive record was Charles Francis Adams, Jr. Of the fourth generation of a family unique for its record of unblemished public service of a high order, his own achievements in this field were by no means inconsiderable. Nourished in the tradition of two Presidents and the example of his own father, Lincoln's brilliant Minister to England, Adams held just as lofty notions as had his great-grandfather about "the cohesive power of public plunder." But the reader of his autobiography will seek in vain for any indication that he differed from the successful financiers he despised in his concept of business aims. President of the Union Pacific from 1884 to 1890, he seems never to have thought that his commercial activities had any social significance.

"I took the position advisedly, and from purely selfish considerations," he says.

He left it, he adds, "with a consciousness of failure, but a deep breath of relief." He was distinguished from his colleagues only because a sense of responsibility to fellow directors, not to the public, arose within him at times. He regretted even this, referring to himself rather apologetically as "absolutely the victim of the duty delusion, laboring under the foolish idea that I owed some sort of obligation to my company."

The folly was not shared by other executives. Furthermore, they applied their business principles to politics, which Adams never dreamed of doing. They found that as they and the government were drawn closer together in more or less avowed recognition of the fact that they had common interests, they were able to bring public policy into line with industrial needs (as interpreted by the lords of industry). They were also spared a good deal of the cruder forms of bribery because the encouragement of manufactures and transportation had become a feasible political program that office seekers dared avow from the standpoint of private profit as well as public policy.

This indispensable factor to a system of honest graft was due to a weakening of the popular distrust of the new economic forces, a revolutionary change made possible by the same dispersion of ownership that reared the vast corporate structures which the Morgans and Mellons were beginning to impress with the stamp of their peculiar genius.

As the heavily watered stocks were launched upon financial seas, the presence of widows and orphans among the shareholders was discovered by astute campaigners. From a thousand platforms the role of industry as the protector of the otherwise defenseless was rehearsed by voices that faltered artistically as they touched upon the reliance of a man's little ones upon steel and coal stocks. Politicians were defied to tamper with the savings of mothers or the dividends of babes.

The new era was marked by the rise to power of two leading figures of the golden age, both tarred with the Crédit Mobilier brush but both willing to forget it and both proven supporters of the owners of the country. They reaped their reward in the election of 1880, and soon Blaine's charming wife was writing to her daughter:

"Your father and I have picked out Garfield's Cabinet

for him [the writer's husband headed the list] and have devoted to him for two mornings our waking, but not risen, hours. Oh how good it is to win and be on the strong side!" This was such a common sentiment that it completed the harmony between government and business. Cuddled together in its comfortable warmth, the politicians and industrialists discovered a community of interest that was above crude cash considerations.

3

The proponents of honest graft already had two models—the Southern Pacific in California and Cameron's Pennsylvania machine. The Western example was the more desirable, for government in the Far West was a department of the railway, whose employees filled all offices, from sheriff to governor.

Elsewhere in the country, however, no one industry was big enough to dominate all the rest, and the politicians had a chance to express themselves. Cameron's system, therefore, was recognized as the best obtainable in an imperfect world. The gentle Simon acknowledged no single master. He served a class, and although he retired shortly after the close of the Grant administration in a gesture of paternal fondness, he provided an adequate successor in the person of his son.

James Donald Cameron, trained in business and politics by a careful father, had at the Senator's suggestion succeeded the unlucky Belknap. The young Secretary's promptness in ordering Federal troops to the aid of Florida and Louisiana Republicans had enabled the party to turn those two states from the Tilden column to that of his rival in 1876, but the ungrateful, upright Hayes refused to keep him in the War Department. Old Simon, angered by the snub and unwilling to interrupt his boy's promising career, resigned his own seat and ordered the Pennsylvania legislature to elect Don.

The new Senator took his father's place in the councils of the party and at the head of the State machine, where he was seconded by Simon's best lieutenant, Matthew Quay. Their clever combination of the coarser methods of Tammany and the arrogant autocracy of the Southern Pacific made Pennsylvania a Republican bulwark for decades. The Camerons did not soil their hands with dirty money for the protection of saloons, bawdy houses and criminals. They shared no fraudulent bills paid by city or state. They did not bribe petty politicians of local influence. They simply permitted all these things in exchange for a regularly delivered, overwhelming Republican majority. With their power at the polls safeguarded by an army of contented ward heelers, thugs and minor jobholders, the Camerons could devote themselves to what they understood to be the real business of politics. This, they supposed, meant the fostering of Pennsylvania industry, which they served with a loyalty bribery could not have purchased.

The Pennsylvania delegation to Congress was on the firing line of every tariff fight. Franchises and important contracts for State construction were awarded with more restraint than Tweed had used, and with more regard for the political future. When a prominent mill or mine had a dispute with its workers, State police were supplied to ram home with club and bullet the doctrine of company slums, twelve-hour shifts and starvation pay.

Don Cameron never panhandled Carnegie, Frick or Mellon for his rewards. But business was thrown to his railway and his bank. When a particularly prosperous corporation was in the making, Don and Matt Quay bought (and paid for) a few shares at promoter's prices. It was infinitely more respectable than the older custom of giving Daniel Webster $10,000 handouts. It was also better business.

Cameron fought for his party and his party's backers with a force of which Webster had been incapable. Not that Don was an orator. He never spoke if he could help it, scorn-

ing the cheap popularity of the platform. He preferred
the accolade of the powerful to any amount of huzzaing in
the streets. His effectiveness was displayed in caucus and
committee where the power of a disciplined state machine
lent emphasis to his few remarks. His methods were demonstrated in the great tariff fight of 1882-83.

Sheer oratory here went for nothing. Of all the flood of
words loosed by impassioned speakers, the only phrase of
the long debate still remembered is that in which Senator
Beck compared Hoar of Massachusetts to the soil of his native state, "poor by nature and exhausted by cultivation."

Cameron took no part in such pleasantries. He was arguing and threatening in quiet corners, demanding a "reasonable" tariff on iron. He was so enraged when the rate was
fixed at only a little less than the most rabid ironmaster
could ask that he tried to wreck the whole bill, and succeeded in reducing the majority for it to one. Time showed
that the tariff was quite high enough. The new steel works
rising in a lush growth were kept running at profitable capacity. Their masters forgave Cameron for not bringing them
the moon, and their campaign contributions continued to be
the sinews that bound the machine together.

The close relation between the new school of political
leaders and their colleagues in bank and factory prevented
some of the abuses that had made the post-war era a reproach to moralists. But the moneyed men were obtaining
what government favors they desired without scandal and
often with the approval of such public opinion as was
allowed to express itself. There might have been another
opinion if the workers had been as free as they were told.
They had votes, but the Pennsylvania manufacturers mar-
shaled their hirelings on election day with military precision, forcing the men to elect the very candidates most
opposed to proletarian interests. Chauncey Depew admitted
he was one of the very few large employers of his genera-

tion who did not coerce his labor at the polls, and considered himself a very advanced liberal on that account.

4

The neat distinction between honest and dishonest graft
was drawn a great deal in the 'eighties and 'nineties. Blackmail, protection money from prostitutes, thieves, gamblers
and saloon keepers, outright pay for a vote—these were
dishonest. They might add up to a large sum, but the individual pickings were comparatively small. Honest graft
was where the big money lay. The operation was succinctly
described by the philosophical Plunkitt, who offered as explanation for his comfortable fortune:

"I seen my opportunities and I took 'em."

The opportunities were strictly business. Contracts for
government work, wise use of advance information on legislation and, above all, co-operation with industrial and financial magnates—these were the paths to wealth. No man
trod them more knowingly than Plunkitt's patron, Richard
Croker, who spread his influence over the entire business
and political life of New York and died a British country
gentleman, a millionaire, owner of a Derby winner, something of an Irish patriot and as firmly convinced of the
correctness of his principles as years before when he had
declared before an investigating committee:

"If you can show me where I have taken a dollar from
this city, you can cut that right arm off—or encouraged it
either."

Dick Croker, the most autocratic boss who ever ruled,
died only a few miles from his birthplace. But the magnificent buildings, blooded stock and fertile fields of Glen-
cairn were really in another world than the blacksmith's hut
in County Cork. At the age of three, the boy became a
resident of New York's East Side. He achieved a little elementary schooling before he grew big enough to work in

a machine shop, and but for his strength and pugnacious spirit might have spent the rest of his life trying to attain the dizzy rank of foreman.

Of no more than middle height but abnormally broad and powerful, he found his relaxation in using his fists on other lads. He packed such a terrific wallop and was himself so indestructible that in his 'teens he was the leader of the Fourth Avenue Tunnel Gang and a figure in his district. His prowess attracted the notice of sporting politicians, and when Dick succeeded one night in knocking all the teeth out of an opponent's head, he was a made man. In the cheering audience was no less a personage than Sheriff Jimmy O'Brien, the Bull Run deserter who had conquered Tweed.

The fighter made his political debut under O'Brien's tutelage in the campaign of 1864. He led his Tunnel Gang in various forays at the polls and even voted—the straight Democratic ticket—although he had not yet reached his majority. Within a year he had made such strides in what he saw would be his life work that at the election of 1865 he voted seventeen times.

A further political apprenticeship was served as an attendant in Justice Barnard's court, and at twenty-five the squat young gangster with the black, bristly hair framing a rather ill-favored countenance was an alderman. He also drew a salary as an underling of "Slippery Dick" Connolly until the Tweed regime went down, but he lost only his job. His rank in the Ring did not warrant the honor of notice in the scandal.

No longer attached to the city payroll, he applied himself to the task of getting back. To this end he placed himself and his heelers at the disposal of the one man who saw that from the ruins there might arise a new and stronger Tammany Hall.

This practical visionary was John Kelly, another East Side Irish youth who had climbed to political eminence by the judicious use of a good right cross. Three terms as sheriff enabled him to retire when he found himself at odds with the Ring. While his former colleagues were squirming on the witness stand, absconding or "squealing," Kelly was in the Holy Land, meditating on religious truths, piously buying pictures for the new St. Patrick's Cathedral and reflecting that the sobriquet of "Honest John," which he had bestowed upon himself in an expansive moment, ought to be an asset under the new conditions at home.

Kelly knew that if he stressed his integrity often enough, it would be taken at face value by many. Of course it would not impose on fellows like the reform Mayor, William Havemeyer, who had come in after Tweed's fall. Havemeyer inspected a good many of the back records of the sheriff's office and wrote indignantly to Kelly:

"Fraud permeates every part of your bills to such an extent that one honest spot would be a sort of relief."

Honest John might have pointed out that the Havemeyer fortune, garnered in real estate, sugar and railways, owed a good deal to the system that made sheriffs rich. The rejoinder would have been a waste of words. Kelly preferred to devote himself to rallying the demoralized Tammany statesmen, at which he was so successful that two years after Tweed's arrest he elected young Croker coroner, a job worth $15,000 a year.

From this vantage point, Dick watched his leader introduce the principles of honest graft. Organized assessments for nominations were augmented by campaign contributions from prominent business men, reputable and otherwise. This levy was within the law and united all in a common effort to elect a whole ticket. Those who worked hard were rewarded with contracts and real estate tips, but the outright thievery of the Tweed Ring was reduced to unobtrusive proportions.

A brief spell in prison interrupted Croker's study of this engrossing subject. The battling coroner was accused of killing an opposing thug during one of the campaign fights of 1874. There is little doubt that he was innocent of the actual shooting but preferred to take his chances in court rather than implicate a friend who was guilty and might have been proved so.

"I never carried a pistol in my life, and never will as long as I can use my hands," was Croker's defense, and it was good enough to win a hung jury.

He did not seek vindication by standing for public office, although he was not brought to trial again, which was a boon to the Croker exchequer. Court appearances were expensive, even allowing for the $4,000 contributed by Abram Hewitt, millionaire son-in-law·of Peter Cooper and a man with statesmanlike ambitions.

Absence from official employment served Croker well. He devoted himself to building up Tammany's strength in his own district and in his spare time helped Honest John run the city. They made an odd pair as they sat in what had come to be known as the Boss's office at the Hall. In feature, figure and manner they resembled each other closely. Both were broad, simianly heavy, powerful ex-pugs who had abandoned the use of their hands for anything more arduous than counting money. They even wore their whiskers in the same style, and Croker became as sparing of words as Kelly, and as unyielding once he had determined on a course of action. Tweed had talked too much; his successors never made that mistake.

Under Kelly's supervision, Croker learned not only the science of governing the country's largest city, but also how to profit by the honest graft that was the perquisite of his unofficial position.

"I have got nothing to hide at all, and if anyone tells me of a nice stock to buy, and I can make a little turn on it, I am going to do it, and I have done so," he told Frank Moss, counsel for a legislative committee investigating municipal affairs.

Croker's half of a real estate business which bought land where new streets were to be opened netted him between $25,000 and $30,000 a year. Of his Wall Street speculations, his share in a firm of auctioneers employed by the city, his contracting company and his office for bonding municipal employees he would not speak. They were private. Croker thought it reasonable that Tammany men should stand by one another, that officials he elected should throw business his way. Moss, interpreting briefly the Boss's scheme of politics, suggested:

"Then you are working for your own pocket, are you not?"

"All the time; the same as you," was the reply.

"If it is an honorable business, you are always willing to do it?"

"I am not prepared to go into any other business at present," Croker answered. "I have all I can do now."

Everyone knew Croker's real business was governing New York. Everyone knew, too, that he was an able executive who saw to it that his subordinates devoted themselves all the year round to their work. They might not pay much attention to the duties for which the city hired them, but they were everlastingly doing favors, carrying on practical charity, getting jobs for workmen, standing between poor offenders and strict retribution. In return they asked only votes, and it was small wonder that the masses preferred the rule of the Hall to the cold, unsocial dominance of reformers whose sole aim seemed to the people to be the closing of saloons and whorehouses.

"Good government" programs included nothing that really improved the lot of the underprivileged. The economic favors that Tammany sold were given away to the same men by the reformers. So New York was prepared to put up most of the time with a good deal of open vice, crime and miscellaneous disorder in return for tangible benefits conferred by the machine.

Early in the 'eighties, Croker began to take over the ailing Kelly's work, and by 1886 he reigned alone, still cultivating the silence he found so golden and bringing to the top of the political heap a prize assortment of strangely profane gentry who were more afraid of Dick Croker's frown than they had been of his fists in the good old days.

His first independent action was to pick his own candidate for Mayor. The choice surprised district leaders. For Croker nominated and elected Abram Hewitt, steel magnate, rapid transit entrepreneur, philanthropist and contributor of $4,000 to a Coroner's defense fund. The general, uncharitable view of this action was that Croker wished to reassure the electorate by offering a respectable figurehead. But the ex-pugilist was not the man to underestimate his strength. He must have known that he could elect any fairly eligible candidate that year, and he chose Hewitt from more generous motives than his enemies were willing to admit.

Croker, pupil of Honest John and critic of Tweed, was satisfied to give New York as good a government as he conveniently could. His principles were exactly those of the self-made business leaders of whom the country was proud. His business was managing that extremely large corporation, the City of New York. Like Carnegie or Frick or Rockefeller, his primary aim was power and wealth. After that he was even more willing than they to consider the public interest.

Unfortunately he found, as did the kings of oil and steel, that independents got in his way. The independents had to be removed, and in doing it neither Rockefeller nor Croker was any more concerned with the general welfare than a Vanderbilt. The politician, however, could not be quite as ruthless as Standard Oil. The sovereign people would not tolerate the crude exercise of power in their service that they condoned in private enterprise.

The foes Croker felt called upon to crush did not include the ostensible Republican opposition. That, in the person of Tom Platt, "the Easy Boss," was a business-like ally, to be knifed on occasion but essentially a partner in political commerce. Platt, tall and thin and shrouding his keen practical sense under an air of gloomy piety, made his deals with Tammany by which both profited. There was at least as much truth as poetry in the satirical verse in which Croker was made to protest about investigators:

> They'd pry into our bonding scheme,
> And find out how we skim the cream
> Of all the business—that's no dream—
> Myself—and Platt.

Such a man was no more Croker's real rival than the railways that furnished rebates were the enemies of Rockefeller. But the Hewitts of politics were 'dangerous. The new Mayor wanted to head the city government, not just accept the honors. So at the end of a term, Croker dropped him for a real Tammany stalwart, Hugh J. Grant, who was elected handily, although Hewitt split the Democratic vote by running as an independent.

Grant was docile, for Dick had raised him from an alderman and had made him a sheriff, an act of kindness which so stimulated the new official that he remembered he was little Flossie Croker's godfather. Flossie was celebrating her second birthday when Sheriff Grant became obsessed with what he called this "great responsibility." He hurried to the Croker home. After some urging, Flossie was persuaded to toddle across the floor to see what the nice gentleman had brought, and Dick Croker's heavy scowl was lightened by a beam of paternal fondness. Little Flossie took her present very prettily, although it was only a plain white envelope, and the $5,000 in bills inside made small appeal to a two-year-old. Next year the charming ceremony was repeated but when, as Mayor, Grant had to testify to it, he was obviously ill at ease as counsel pried into his ten-

derest feelings. He insisted he had done no more than he
ought, and cried awkwardly:

"I think if you will look over the obligation that one
accepts when they become a godfather—of course, I must
say that I feel very delicate about discussing such a subject here, because it is a matter that I always considered
sacred until this committee saw fit to go into it."

As Croker consolidated his control, there were fewer
transactions of this sentimental nature. Directorships and
blocks of stock, without any godfather nonsense about them,
replaced envelopes containing cash which alone could never
have piled up the $5,000,000 fortune he left when he died
in 1922.

It was typical of the popular indifference to the real
sources of power that although Croker's regime was repeatedly investigated by hostile committees, the machine
was never smashed. The press, the preachers and the people
occasionally worked themselves into frenzies of indignation
over exposures of vice and crime. But these spectacular
evidences of corruption were mere by-products of honest
graft. Croker's privileges in his "private" affairs were the
causes of other evils. In order to maintain his position, the
Boss was obliged to allow subordinates to make their profits
in ways he himself scorned.

Each investigation spread on the record the same story
of protection sold to the underworld. Each burst of popular indignation seemed to mark the end of the system.
A few years later the process would be repeated. The larger
business interests, unmolested, continued under any administration.

Perhaps the most picturesque of the reforming gentry was
the Reverend Dr. Charles Parkhurst. A fashionable clergyman preaching to a congregation that included Boss Platt
at the Madison Square Church, he was horrified to discover
that drink, women and fighting were the chief preoccupa-

tions of many of his fellow citizens. He decided Tammany was to blame.

In search of proof of his charges, the Doctor hired a detective and explored the underworld. His lurid descriptions of the spicy scenes he witnessed were in the finest manner of Presbyterian theology and they forced one more investigation upon the city. They also lost the Madison Square Church a parishioner, for one Sunday the preacher expressed the opinion that Platt was a great deal worse than Croker. The "Easy Boss" could not accept this comparison with the ex-fighter, gambler and follower of horse races. He promptly changed his place of worship.

Dr. Parkhurst's revelations stirred the wrath of the people. The reformers announced that the city would be purified forever. But none of them suggested how the girls who were to be driven from the closed bawdy houses should live. Certainly not on the wages offered by the pious followers of Dr. Parkhurst, for most shop girls who had no other help had to eke out their starvation wages by prostitution. Nor was the comfort of religion an adequate substitute for the saloon, sad as the fact might be. Working men wanted a little more variety in their lives than the day's labor and a sermon. In the absence of accessible parks, movies, sports facilities, libraries or recreation grounds, nothing was left except the bar, the brothel or a bit of a set-to along the docks.

This state of affairs did not spring from the ignorant greed of policemen and ward heelers. But the reformers were so outraged that men actually took money to wink at human frailty that they could advance no further in their quest for dragons to slay. New York, roused to a righteous indignation that stopped far short of the real culprits, followed Dr. Parkhurst's crusade as blindly and hopefully as the little children of the Middle Ages marched forth to conquer with the innocence of faith the armed might of the infidel.

The virtuous streamed to the polls, carrying some of the godless with them in the hysteria of the moment, and as the year 1895 opened in what was confidently expected to be the millennium, William Strong was in the Mayor's office and a vigorous young Harvard graduate named Theodore Roosevelt was hurrying from Washington, where he had been a Civil Service Commissioner, to head the police department.

Certainly here was an alliance that would work the miracle if anything could. Strong was a merchant so eminently respectable that it was supposed the thieves, madams and gamblers would rush for the nearest ferry on the day of his inauguration. Roosevelt, burning with an ambition unknown to his stolid forebears, proposed to make the world a better place for mankind and the name of Roosevelt famous all over the remodeled universe. But Tom Platt, who had taken no share in the victory of his party, regarded the new Mayor as only "another of the fellows who wore a little bunch of whiskers under his chin." The Police Commissioner was just an impetuous youngster with a mustache and teeth.

The "Easy Boss" was justified in his opinion that the reform business would come to nothing. The ostentatious honesty of the merchant and the fiery zeal of the Harvard idealist managed to harry a few street girls, close some saloons and break up a great many pinochle games in back rooms. The gutters were cleaner and some of them safer after dark, but slums were no more livable than before; sweat shops blandly repudiated the idea that health regulations could apply to them as they did to bars; wages for thousands remained at or below subsistence levels.

Dick Croker "sat out" during the Strong administration, a happy exile improving his British estate and taking his gift for silence to Newmarket and Epsom Downs. He had a very pleasant time indeed during two years remembered with anguish by Tom Platt as the period when the boss of the party in power couldn't get a friend appointed to a street-cleaning job. Cables of advice and encouragement were Croker's only contribution to New York politics as the reformers wondered why all their good intentions somehow failed to change the nature of man.

Clean government, confined entirely to the morals of the lower classes, had become so distasteful that in 1897 Croker was able to elect a subservient nonentity, Judge Robert Van Wyck, as first Mayor of Greater New York to the tune of a new popular song, "A Hot Time in the Old Town Tonight," and an even newer chant, "Well, Well, Well, Reform's Gone to Hell!" The business of the City of New York was back in the hands of the old firm, the firm which *The World* with a good deal of truth represented Croker as calling "Myself & Me." Under that title the paper printed verses recording the Boss's admissions before an investigating committee and concluding:

> They've had us on the witness rack;
> Now we'll seek pleasure at the track,
> And if we lose, why we'll come back—
> Myself—and Me.

But Croker came back only to lose the election of 1901 to Seth Low, his second defeat as against fifteen victories, and to retire definitely from politics thereafter. No regrets marred the twenty remaining years of his life, for to a British editor he once explained that Tammany's power was honest graft, the reward for being the one municipal organization willing to devote all of its time and energy to the service of the people.

"I do not remember ever having done anything that I ought not to have done," he said. "For I have done only good all my life. . . . If we go down into the gutter, it is because there are men in the gutter."

XIII

LAND'S END

1

W HILE POLITICIANS AND IN-
dustrialists were discovering in the East that the greater
good and higher morality alike dictated a careful coddling
of capitalist enterprise, the victims of the system dreamed
of the last frontier. The ultimate mass flight from inexorable
economic laws that were increasing the gulf between rich
and poor was on. The fatal alternation of boom and depression had driven successive waves of pioneers into the
wilderness to develop new resources for the next periodic
upturn. During the early days of honest graft, the human
debris of Eastern industrialism pushed to the Pacific and
the Rio Grande. In the deserts and valleys of the Far West,
the cycle that had begun with the landing of a handful of
Englishmen at Jamestown was completed.

The unquenchable optimism of adventurers led them to
suppose that the last of the public domain that was worth
a poor man's labor would be distributed in a more equitable
manner than had been employed in previous generations.
"Out where the handclasp's a little tighter, out where the
sun shines a little brighter," the confident ranchers, farmers
and hunters moved to unoccupied areas and began a new
life. They thought their work on the land would establish
title to it, for were not the politicians constantly proclaim-
ing that the West was held as a sacred trust for the landless
poor?

Of course the landless poor did not go west alone. With

them, they later complained, were lawyers and speculators from such "eastern centers of population as Peoria and St. Louis." The California gold rush had sent ahead of them a choice collection of plunderers of whom the Southern Pacific quartet was a shining example. Even earlier there had been the semi-feudal civilization of Spain, inherited by Mexico. As the pilgrims in search of the wide open spaces drifted into the strange land of exaggeratedly tilted mountains and vast dry plains, they found the normal pioneer hardships complicated by problems of previous claimants.

The treaty of peace with Mexico in 1846 contained the usual clause that property was to be respected by the new sovereign. Just what titles existed in the western empire no one knew, and the Mexican records were to prove a most unsatisfactory source of information. Meanwhile outgoing Mexican officialdom reaped a final harvest before jobs and perquisites should be taken over by the conquering gringo.

Governor Pio Pico of California distinguished himself by offering Mexican deeds at closing sale prices. He did almost everything but put up a "Must vacate" sign. Pico belonged to a governing class that had never encountered the theory that government might be in the interest of the governed. He did not know there was a widely held belief that public lands were for the benefit of the public. So he passed out land grants in return for any consideration that could be obtained.

Even after he was obliged to move to Sonora in the face of advancing American troops, even after conclusion of a peace his income continued. His associates in office were accustomed to mock at him as an ignorant ranchero who could scarcely sign his name. They jested about his really remarkable girth, his fatuous amiability, the cast of countenance that betrayed a more than usual admixture of Negro blood. But Pico, however deficient in the loftier exercises of Castilian courtesy, possessed a grasp of political essentials. Also he still had a supply of official paper.

He drew up on that paper formal grants of land newly incorporated into the United States. These were pre-dated a few months to be valid under the treaty and sold to a varied lot of gamblers and ranchers. Since the business was transacted without benefit of maps and several hundred miles from the scene, the boundaries were of necessity set down in the vaguest terms. Purchasers, however, were assured that this was an advantage. They would be able to claim almost anything under the descriptions signed by Pico.

Other Mexican officials were as generous. A small army of "antedaters" locked sealed Mexican documents in their strongboxes to await the day when increasing population would make the lands worth having. They succeeded in creating such confusion that in New Mexico alone claims involving more than 8,000,000 acres were not finally settled until 1904, and in 1930 Congressional committees were still investigating Mexican land grant frauds in California.

The possibilities of litigation were enhanced by the existence of some grants that were not fraudulent. Many gentlemen of Spanish descent and a few early settlers of other nationalities held titles that were sound, but they had often extended their original boundaries by means that were decidedly open to question. The resulting court work was so lush that Hubert Howe Bancroft, a Californian of wide experience and keen observation, wrote:

"The usual fee for securing to the occupant a title was half the land, while with a bill of extras he [the attorney] might easily sweep up the other half. He was not much of a lawyer in those days who had not a Mexican grant in his pocket, the title to which his clients had paid for."

The stakes were high and the wheel of fortune turned with its usual fascinating speed. Potential millionaires won and lost in bewildering succession, and one of those who played the land game most spectacularly was the colorful and confiding Frémont. He operated on such an extensive scale that even before the Civil War he boasted somewhat ruefully:

"When I came to California I was worth nothing, but now I owe two million dollars."

Frémont had paid $3,000 for his Mariposa Estate, a more straightforward beginning than most claims could show. His turned out also to be the only large new grant in the gold fields. As the Forty-Niners came storming round the Horn and over the mountains, disregarding any man's rights in their craze, the upkeep of his invaded grant ruined the gallant general. The Mariposa Estate tainted his career in the Senate where he and his father-in-law, Benton, were not believed to be wholly disinterested in their attitude toward land legislation. His holdings seemed to offer Frémont the prospect of enormous wealth, and he pursued the mirage with a recklessness that had made him an incomparable explorer. He ignored details, such as the fact that Spanish grants like his never included the mining rights. The General lost Mariposa and with it most of his popularity in California.

At the same time there was a noticeable slump in Mexican paper. A speculation that failed relieved the actual improvers of the soil temporarily of their fear of losing the fruits of their work. Since many of them were lulled into a false security, the reverse suffered by the grabbers encouraged immigration and greatly increased the value of later grabs.

The case that settlers hoped would become a precedent involved a myth known as the Mission Dolores grant. The document that was the basis of the claim recited that in consideration of paying the debt of the mission, one Padre Santillan, a parish priest, should receive a tract of land. The amount of the debt he had so long ago assumed was not stated, but the compensation was 15,000 acres, most of it within the city limits of San Francisco and worth almost anything the claimants cared to mention. There was a good deal of excitement among the owners of city property, but this was allayed when in 1859 the United States Supreme Court held that the rights supposed to have been purchased from Santillan's heirs had never existed and the whole claim was fraudulent.

2

The Mission Dolores decision checked the speculators in the Southwest only momentarily. The clever Easterners from Peoria and St. Louis saw that the grab had failed for want of graft that could have prevented the case from reaching the untouchables on the Supreme bench. But they knew their day would come again. Throughout the later gold rush and the Civil War they traded busily in Mexican deeds, and a surveyor-general of Arizona later reported:

"The great majority of these grants were abandoned in good faith for a period of from ten to twelve years . . . no value was attached to them either by the [original] principals or their heirs in Mexico."

As yet there was not sufficient population in the territories to tempt the determined land grabbers to make an issue of their demands. But they were preparing the ground to assert their claims, and a year after the Mission Dolores decision they got what they wanted. Congress, in an act generally unnoticed in the rising tide of the slavery agitation, established a precedent by confirming one of the better claims, one on which all the land lobbyists had concentrated.

"Congress laid the egg in 1860 which was hatched by the Commissioner of the Land Office and the Secretary of the Interior in 1879," declared the one-time radical Republican, Julian, transformed at the date of this remark into a Democrat and Federal surveyor-general of New Mexico.

As the transcontinental railroads had established the basis

for their later plunderings in the heat of war, so the South-western speculators dug the foundations for their fortunes while most of their countrymen were absorbed in the epic struggle for the Union. During the days when most men's thoughts were with Lee marching across the rolling Pennsylvania countryside toward Gettysburg, a young lawyer named Stephen B. Elkins arrived in New Mexico.

He had been hailed by the friends of his family as a promising youth. In 1860, at the age of nineteen, he was graduated at the head of his class from the University of Missouri. He served for a time in the militia in the early stages of the war, rising to captain and studying law on the side. But opportunities for rapid advancement toward anything except martial glory were lacking in Missouri just then. Elkins had more prosaic ambitions, and the year 1863 found him surveying with youthful eagerness the prospects of one who was in on the ground floor of New Mexico.

There was gold in those hills which reared themselves in the splendor of improbable colors across the landscape, not yet the wonder of Eastern tourists. The budding lawyer, however, was no more attracted by the arduous chore of gold-hunting under the burning sun than he had been by military life. He speedily realized that there was an easier way to tap the resources of those magnificent distances.

"Elkins' dealings," wrote Julian after an exhaustive study of the land office records, "were mainly in Spanish grants, which he bought for a small price. Elkins became a member of the land ring of the territory, and largely through his influence the survey of these grants was made to contain hundreds of thousands of acres that did not belong to them. He thus became a great land holder, for through the manipulation of committees in Congress, grants thus illegally surveyed were confirmed with their fictitious titles."

Elkins's youthful charm, legal talents and business acumen alone could not account for the influence of which Julian wrote. The young stranger, realizing that politics would be a major element in the disposal of desirable tracts, became imbued with a rather vociferous public spirit. He hastened to learn Spanish and so ingratiated himself with the local citizenry that within a year he was a member of the territorial legislature. Successively District Attorney, Attorney General, United States Attorney and Delegate to Congress, he combined politics with land grabbing so happily that in 1875, while serving in Washington as the representative of New Mexico and his own real estate interests, he could aspire to the hand of Hallie Davis, a West Virginia heiress whose father, Henry Gassaway Davis, was not only his State's richest man but also one of her United States Senators.

Among Elkins's earliest acquaintances in New Mexico was an ornate and hospitable frontiersman, Lucien Benjamin Maxwell. Elaborately formal and delighting in magnificent display, Maxwell was one of the finest flowers of the old Southwest, preserving the most picturesque of Castilian colonial traditions. From his old Spanish manor house on the Red River he ruled a principality comprising most of what is now Colfax County, a good deal larger than the State of Delaware. Over the vast unfenced range, his flocks wandered in the care of guitar-playing Mexican herders. Hundreds of peons respectfully uncovered when Don Lucien rode among them.

Their homage and the grave ceremonial of his relations with the Mexican landowners was very gratifying to Maxwell, who cherished the old-fashioned rites of a dying civilization with all the greater fervor because he himself had been born and reared in the simplicity of Kaskaskia, Illinois. As a young man he had anticipated Greeley's advice. He gained some reputation on the frontier as a hunter for one of Frémont's expeditions. He was proud, too, of the friendship of that Western hero, Kit Carson.

When Elkins first heard of the lord of the Red River, Maxwell was really exercising only a sort of regency. He had married one of the local Spanish belles, Luz Beaubien, whose father, Carlos, had in partnership with Guadelupe Miranda acquired a grant to what they said was nearly 2,000,000 acres. Maxwell devoted himself to developing this property as a sheep ranch without bothering about his father-in-law's title, although it was common knowledge to all who were interested in Southwestern lands that Mexican law limited grants for a single individual to eleven leagues, roughly 48,000 acres. However, there was no one to raise a protest when Beaubien and Miranda multiplied this by about twenty and pooled their resources. After the fashion of the frontier, the two regarded possession as all the law they needed.

The year that Elkins entered the New Mexico legislature, Beaubien died. Maxwell, buying out the other heirs to the property, became the owner as well as the manager of the entire estate—owner, that is, if he could make good his title. It might have gone unquestioned in his lifetime had gold not been discovered among the hills where his flocks had fed in lonely security.

At first the discovery hardly presented itself to Maxwell in the light of a major disaster. He entertained rosy dreams of becoming wealthier than he already was. He ought to have known his countrymen better. Their notions of law were even more sketchy than his, and in the rush for gold they were accustomed to look upon sounder titles than the Beaubien-Miranda grant as non-existent. News of the strike along the Red River spread across the Southwest, and before the sheep baron knew what was happening, the prospectors swarmed in upon him, prepared to shoot it out with any purveyor of mutton on the hoof who might choose to interfere. They qualified their opinion of such pacific citizens with a rich profanity, and Maxwell's vaqueros were no match for the hard-bitten, reckless survivors of many a pitched battle, saloon brawl and claim dispute.

Maxwell might have had old-fashioned ideas but he was not stubborn to the point of folly. His flocks were melting away as the miners over-ran the land, driving the sheep from water, winning gun fights with the herders and casually shooting animals whenever they had a taste for fresh meat. The boy from Kaskaskia knew the Southwest well enough to recognize defeat, and he looked around for a way out. His friend Elkins, rising young politician and fellow land-owner, was in a position to help. Maxwell agreed to turn over his estate to men better able to defend it. The Maxwell Land Grant and Railroad Company was duly incorporated with Stephen B. Elkins as president.

That was when Elkins went to Washington, where he encountered the representatives of many another land-grabbing syndicate. But the Delegate to Congress with a record of half a dozen years as a territorial law enforcement officer was in a better position than most, and was welcomed by Washington society. Good-looking and bronzed by the romantic sun of New Mexico, he was an amiable raconteur of tales about the frontier. The capital liked the contrast between the primitive roughness which Easterners associated with the territory he represented and the rather polished manners of the Delegate.

He penetrated even to the exalted circles where Hallie Davis had her being, and his social success did him no harm when it came to pushing the claims of the Maxwell Land Grant and Railroad Company. However, the pretensions of minor land grabbers were necessarily delayed by the larger affairs with which Grant's Congresses were dealing. There was also the annoyingly persistent detail that Beaubien and Miranda could not under any possible interpretation of Mexican law have become possessed of more than about 5 per cent. of the area Elkins claimed. The discrepancy could be adjusted by a simple act of Congress, but the measure had to be brought forward while the public was exciting itself over Crédit Mobilier revelations and Jay Cooke's "banana belt" was carrying the banker to ruin.

When it came to the point, charm and good looks and

the bribes that the company could afford were not quite enough. In the general debacle of '73, the Maxwell company drifted into difficulties. The property was unproductive, with the prospectors still roaming over it at will and the "railroad" part of its title quite without meaning, apparently added only to make the ensemble impressive. There was one last recourse, however, for a hard-pressed American. European stock markets were full of eager capitalists seeking speculative outlets despite governmental warnings against railways in the United States because the country was too powerful to be subjected to the usual methods of "intervention" to safeguard investments.

In the Netherlands the fact that the president of the Maxwell Land Grant and Railroad Company was "the Hon." Stephen B. Elkins seemed to inspire confidence. With funds received from this source, the backers were able to recoup, but it was too late to save the company as well. In 1875 the corporation, its title still unconfirmed, drifted into bankruptcy, and the ruined ranch on the Red River was sold for taxes. The purchasers included Stephen B. Elkins.

The government, with unusual foresight, had sold only the amount to which Beaubien and Miranda would have been entitled under Mexican law. Confirmation of the remainder was still to win, but the reformed syndicate had a more influential chief than a territorial delegate. It had Senator Davis's son-in-law, for in the year his company went bankrupt Elkins married. The beginnings of frank harmony between business and politics also advanced the opportunity for a favorable settlement of the Red River question. All the land grabbers wanted to see Elkins win a precedent and they got it "under circumstances," said Julian, "indicating the remarkable readiness of the Commissioner of the General Land Office, as well as the surveyor-general, to serve the claimants."

Elkins and his friends received in 1879 title to 1,714,764

acres, surveyed and patented. The fierce miners had moved on to other unfortunate areas. Squatters who followed had spent several years improving homesteads on the Red River, but they were not fighting folk. The "real" owners could step in and claim it all.

"It was," said Julian, "a wanton and shameful surrender to the rapacity of monopolists."

It was also the beginning of Elkins's life as an absentee landlord. He would always retain his interest in New Mexico and his affection for the West. But in the East wider opportunities presented themselves, and the ex-frontiersman was a citizen of West Virginia, treading carefully in the trail blazed by his father-in-law. It was a safe and honorable path, leading to the accumulation of millions in his own right, a seat in Harrison's Cabinet and sixteen years in the Senate as a champion of the industrial interests of the country.

3

Elkins's success had, as Julian said, hatched an egg that kept the politicians of the Southwest in funds for years and made the purchase of land from anyone except an established grantee a gambler's undertaking. Officials, remarking the dizzy heights of wealth and influence to which Elkins had soared from humble territorial beginnings, worked harmoniously with the speculators, who now began to produce the old Mexican grants in bundles.

Out of forty-nine that were passed upon by Congress in this period, forty-seven were approved, although almost all of them were stretched to many times their original limits. One, Julian discovered, "was invented by the surveyor-general and made legal by the hasty act of Congress confirming it." The people who had settled and improved the land were ignored by their representatives. When Julian took over the land office, he traced between 8,000,000 and 9,000,000 acres illegally granted in New Mexico alone.

The upright old gentleman set himself to expose the causes of what he called "this monstrous piracy of the public domain," and he soon learned that it was "carried on under the forms of law and through the machinery of a public office," the one over which he now presided. But the corruption was more widespread than that. For years, he reported, the speculators in spurious and illegally amended grants controlled the Federal Land Commissioner.

"It would be an extravagance to assume that they have not exercised a shaping influence over the action of Congress touching these claims," Julian added.

Nor, he warned, were their activities to be considered entirely in the past tense. The grant owners "have not yet retired from their fruitful field of operations in Congress. They have their allies in both Houses." Elkins and other speculators were supreme in the territorial legislature and worked in harmony, he declared.

Julian's reports read like the fanatic denunciations of a partisan scandal monger, but they were backed by figures. They were also supported by the similar findings and experience of his neighbor surveyor-general, John Hize of Arizona. Hize was alarmed by the persistence of a go-getter who called himself Addison Peralta-Reavis and asserted he was the owner of 1,300,000 acres on the Arizona-New Mexico border. He declared that the land office records themselves would show the validity of the claim. Since it had already been investigated and set aside as baseless, Hize was astonished. But sure enough, conspicuous among the papers was a document purporting to be a survey and patent of the property. No one could remember having seen it before, for the very good reason that it had never been there. On analysis it proved to be a not very clever forgery.

It might be supposed that this would have ended the case. But the claimant with the hybrid name was not easily discouraged. He decided to revise his figures, and the next year he explained that no doubt the survey had been forged in order to cheat him, as he was really entitled to 5,000,000 acres.

The history of this grant varied in some details from the usual run, being at once older and less well founded. It was based on a rumor that in 1758 the King of Spain had conferred a vast estate upon Don Miguel de Peralta, a loyal servant. For the next century and more nothing further was heard of this gift. Then in 1871 one George W. Willing, Jr., wandered into the real estate office of James Addison Reavis in St. Louis. Willing spun an interesting yarn of having bought from Peralta's heirs the rights to an estate on which there were a good many settlers. Whatever Willing had given for these rights—the whole transaction rested upon his unsupported word—he did not have enough left to prosecute his case. Reavis, eager for adventure, accepted an invitation to a visit in Arizona. He came back with a deed signed in blank by Willing. That gentleman, protesting that the paper had been stolen from him by his guest, was unable to prove it and relapsed into obscurity.

Reavis's troubles were just beginning. He need not have been a very experienced dealer in real estate to understand that a deed from Willing was not worth much in itself. Some evidence of the King's generosity would be helpful. So would hints as to where the boundaries of the alleged grant began and ended. Reavis wound up his affairs in St. Louis and ventured forth into the wilderness.

His movements during the next twelve years were never minutely traced. He said he had spent some time in Mexico establishing from the records of that country the existence of the grant. He had certainly obtained somewhere rather venerable-looking documents written in Spanish. Nor was there any doubt that he diligently prospected for a site in what the Land Commissioner later called "the garden district of Arizona." He not only found the land he wanted, but he met a woman who actually bore the honored name of Peralta. She was a Mexican Indian with no visible signs of Spanish blood, but Reavis decided she must be the last descendant of Don Miguel, which no one appeared to dispute. He promptly married her and hitched the valuable patronymic by a hyphen to his own.

Only then, in 1883, was he ready to strike. He produced before the land office the evidence of his rights. There was his wife's name, the Willing deed and the documents written in Spanish. He left these things with the officials and hurried out to the garden district to cash in. Even before his case was taken up, he succeeded in extorting several hundred thousand dollars from settlers as well as $50,000 from the Southern Pacific for a right of way. This last puzzled observers, for the Southern Pacific was not in the habit of allowing itself to be bullied. However, it developed that Collis Huntington was backing Reavis as a private investment, and the railroad's $50,000 was the price of his share.

Unfortunately for his dreams of a fortune, Reavis underestimated the value of time and political fences. His twelve years of preliminary work were evidence of his leisurely methods. Two years spent in shaking down the settlers instead of getting politicians to confirm the Peralta grant proved fatal to his hopes. For in 1884 the Democrats elected Cleveland, and the spirit of civil reform, already given a good push forward by that veteran spoilsman, Chester A. Arthur, was in the air. When Reavis finally urged a decision on his claim, he was horrified to discover that the new land office people were not susceptible to the usual influences.

Failing at bribery, he slipped his forgeries among the Arizona records, and when that failed him he maintained the struggle with all the arguments he could think of, reinforced by Huntington's lobby. But the territorial land offices had passed out of the hands of the speculators. The Peralta claim marked something besides the end of an era of territorial advancement. It was a symptom of the beginning of a new standard in public office. Slowly there was growing into existence a body of public servants who, safe from the wholesale dismissals of the spoils system, really believed that they should be loyal to their employers, the people.

Reavis did not understand this. He did not appreciate the fact that the success of Elkins, for example, was due to the astute mingling of public and private business. Unable to buy the land office, Reavis boldly insisted that his case be decided on its merits. That request was granted, and in 1889 the surveyor-general pronounced the claim a forgery. Reavis sued in the United States Court of Claims for $10,-000,000 as a protest against this judgment. The court was quite as incorruptible as the land office. It not only agreed that the Peralta papers were forged but recommended that the plaintiff be prosecuted in the criminal tribunals. The great $10,000,000 case ended in 1895 when the claimant started a two-year prison term.

But hundreds of other claims were still pending, and at intervals the successors of the speculators discovered new evidence on which they tried to "muscle in" on prosperous towns, improved ranches and fertile orchards. Sometimes they succeeded, until at last in 1930 a Senate committee, called to deal with a plea that the more outrageous Pico grants in California be upset, decided that innocent purchasers of land might be protected. The committee did not deny the frauds, but pointed out that they had been committed so long ago that any penalty inflicted would fall on men who had bought land in good faith.

The decision, just and reasonable after so many years, had been urged nearly half a century earlier by the speculators themselves. When Julian proposed to oust grantees who had obtained their property by deceit, the land grabbers cried out that such procedure would unsettle all titles. The argument, which they conveniently forgot when they themselves were dealing with squatters, was said by Julian to be "quite as ridiculous as if a den of counterfeiters, suddenly taken into the clutches of the law, should insist that their consignment to the penitentiary and the confiscation of their tools would 'unsettle' the currency."

For the most part, however, the strange plea prevailed, the Peralta and Mission Dolores failures being exceptions. Elkins, the forty-seven out of forty-nine successful claimants before Congress and the territorial grafters had gotten away with everything except desert, mountain, swamp and a few tracts suitable for national parks. Land's end had been reached, and frontier days were over. Only dry farming, irrigation and the discovery of oil were to give value to what the land grabbers had left of the public domain.

XIV

"REMEMBER THE *MAINE*"

1

T̲HE FRONTIER WAS GONE EX-
cept as a carefully preserved museum piece for tourists, but
expansion was not so readily balked. Business had never
been better than at the end of the 'eighties, and the imagination of men who were becoming cramped even in the
West soared easily over the sea. While European chancel-
leries watched in mild concern, imperial ambitions, rather
thinly disguised under the plea of "manifest destiny," stirred
in American bosoms.

Spain, from whose once omnipotent empire newer powers
had carved their colonies, recalled that before the Civil
War the "Yanquis" had talked freely of annexing Cuba.
As this talk revived thirty years later, the government of
the infant Alfonso XIII accounted it one of God's mercies
that the panic of 1893 and the ensuing domestic excitement temporarily diverted the American public from
thoughts of conquest and gave full scope to Grover Cleveland's will to peace. The depression—it followed just such
an orgy of speculation encouraged by a complacent government as had distinguished the panics of 1792, 1819, 1837,
1857, 1873—startled the country as a phenomenon unique in
history, but one man saw the cloud's silver lining.

Marcus Alonso Hanna, calm amid a storm of crashing
fortunes, observed business and political prospects with satisfaction. The success of a long-cherished plan for the proper
government of the country was more than likely, he thought.

Mr. Hanna, who would have doubted the sanity of anyone who called him a visionary, dreamed of an administration operating openly, frankly, loyally, in the interest of private enterprise. If that was graft, he was prepared to have his foes make the most of it. In 1893 he could see events falling into a pattern so favorable to his aims that he might almost have designed it himself. Enthusiastic admirers and implacable enemies said he did.

Mark Hanna was a product of the new entente between industry and politics. The son of an Ohio physician turned business man, Hanna at twenty-five headed a leading Cleveland wholesale and commission house, a rival to that of John D. Rockefeller. Both young men devoted themselves to business during the Civil War, but Mark had a liking for company and fun. Rockefeller, undistracted by trifles, saw opportunity first, and in 1862 started an oil refinery, a move Hanna did not copy for two years. Standard Oil soon bought him out, and he entered a coal and iron business headed by his father-in-law.

For nearly twenty years thereafter, Hanna took only so much interest in politics as to vote, serve on honorary committees and help his party—Republican of course—at the polls on election day. A clear-faced, vigorous man with dark, waving hair and a cascade of whisker falling from just under his lower lip, he was indistinguishable from thousands of other moderately successful fellows.

He had early experienced at his mines the advantages of a government that was the dutiful handmaiden of industry. It was the days of the Molly Maguires, those reckless workingmen who were spreading terror among the respectable by revolutionary insistence on the right to live. A succession of wage cuts brought the Ohio miners out on strike in the spring of '76 and hysterical employers, who had other plans for centenary celebrations, protested that this was anarchy, un-American, a menace to property. The National

Guard came down to protect the experiment of strike break-
ers at a mine Hanna controlled, and union leaders were arrested in high-handed military fashion. Then one day a
volley crackled sharply in the faces of a band of starving
strikers who somewhat embarrassed the troops by being entirely unarmed. The aim of the soldiers was unexpectedly
good; a miner fell with a bullet through his head—"trying
to escape" ran the already familiar phrase—and in Cleve·
land a small Hanna heard the first oath ever uttered by his
father in the presence of youth.

"God damn militia, anyhow!" he cried fervently.

Mark Hanna was a kindly man. Also, he proposed to
operate his mines after the Guard departed, and he spoke
sharply to the politicians. Without any more killings, unless one wished to count deaths from disease and starvation,
the strike was broken. Hanna was in Canton for the sequel
when twenty-three of his former employees went on trial
for their crimes. The mine owner was impressed by a local
lawyer, Major William McKinley, who had undertaken their
defense despite a hostile court and the overwhelming preju-
dice of his friends. McKinley won acquittals for all but one.

A few years later Hanna became the operator of Cleveland's street cars. Control of the City Council was as essential to the success of the enterprise as wheels on his cars,
and soon his enemies were calling him boss of Cleveland.
It was not strictly true in the sense they meant it. Hanna
was not personally interested in the local machine, city
jobs or municipal contracts. He wanted only franchises,
and in return offered his services as a sort of chief of staff
to petty captains no one of whom was strong enough to
control Cleveland alone. By 1888 he had mastered politics
so thoroughly that he was selected to manage the campaign
of John Sherman, Ohio's elder statesman, for the Republican presidential nomination. Benjamin Harrison, grandson
of "Tippecanoe," won the prize, but Hanna learned the

most important political lesson of his life—that an issue which touches business in the pocket is worth enormous campaign contributions.

The tariff was the big talking point of 1888, far outweighing Cleveland's honest administration and civil service reform. Protected industries, rising to the defense of their subsidy, were ready to pour fortunes into the fray. Hanna, serving on a national committee to solicit funds, noted for future reference that manufacturers seemed to have no sales resistance at all. The Republican army, supplied with more money than ever before, advanced irresistibly to November and victory despite a Democratic argument that rings rather oddly in modern ears. The tariff must be lowered, said the Cleveland supporters, because the government was amassing a surplus larger than it could spend. The tariff added to the hoard, taking money out of circulation and working—so they said—all manner of hardships upon business.

Business, however, did not know it was being hurt, and the Canton lawyer who had defended Hanna's miners wrote a tariff bill whose preposterously high rates were dictated by the manufacturers who benefited from them. Major McKinley won the governorship of Ohio and Hanna's friendship, but Cleveland carried off national honors in 1892 in a reaction against the blatant schedules of the McKinley Bill.

Another partial result of that tariff was less demoralizing to the Republicans. The panic of 1893 greeted Cleveland at the outset of his second term, and his opponents found comfort in the thought that the bulky New Yorker with a conscience reminiscent of the elder Adamses would have to deal with a depression. No matter what he did, his critics were pleased to reflect, it would be unpopular with many and probably not very gratifying to the rest. After that, Hanna believed, it would be possible to lift his principles of honest graft to new heights.

2

Actually Cleveland's policies had no bearing on the election of 1896. Hanna carefully engineered the nomination of McKinley and set the stage for a smooth campaign on prosperity, protection and the expansion implicit in "manifest destiny." But a few days later an eloquent and beautiful crusader touched off the country's smoldering discontent with a couple of fervent sentences, and startled Republicans, no longer confident of coasting to victory on the lingering effects of the depression, found themselves fighting what many believed to be a forlorn hope under the drooping folds of the gold standard.

William Jennings Bryan, alight with fanaticism, had stolen the issue from his foes. In the name of the free coinage of silver and the great Jehovah, he was rousing a torpid citizenry to a flaming belief that something should be done for their benefit besides quadrennial flattery. To horrified financiers and manufacturers east of the Mississippi, this was rank revolution. They dreamed of guillotines at night and declaimed about "monetary heresies" by day, incidentally reviling as traitors those silver mine owners who had spent $289,000 to elect delegates to the Democratic National Convention which had caused all the trouble.

Surrounded by business men who grew white at the mention of the terrible Bryan, Hanna kept his head. Through the heat of midsummer, while the "boy orator" was sweeping the people off their feet, Hanna organized a drive to educate the masses to McKinley and gold. That took some doing, for "the Majah," as John Hay called him, had an embarrassing record of mild bimetallism. The tariff was the only issue on which he had ever declared himself uncompromisingly, and that was a dead duck as Bryan raged over the West, shaking his locks at frenzied audiences and declaiming with religious zeal about crosses of gold.

In July Hanna knew he didn't have the votes. But he

thought he could get them, and not necessarily by outright purchase either, if he had enough money to spend. Propaganda could do it, if laid on thick enough, and Hanna sallied forth to get the wherewithal from men of wealth who were so frightened they reminded him of scared hens. To them the man from Cleveland spoke soothingly. A shower of checks and bills answered his confident assertion that he would elect McKinley if he had adequate funds for "education."

He got millions, the first time such sums had been used in a campaign. His speakers, pamphlets, press releases poured over the land in an unprecedented flood that almost drowned even Bryan's tireless oratory. More than $10,000,-000, perhaps as much as $15,000,000, went into that stupendous, almost forgotten argument, leading some party stalwarts to worry about a possible popular resentment of lavish spending.

"I wish Hanna would not talk so freely about money," one fearful lieutenant complained.

But the captain ignored the plea. He made the grand tour of Wall Street, talking about money all the time. Then, as the cool autumn days seemed to take a little of the fire out of the Bryan ferocity, Republicans began to hope again. They said reason reasserted itself. The Democrats preferred to believe the sinister and corrupting influences of the enemy's money power betrayed the people. Certainly the gods of politics were on the side of the better paid battalions.

The jubilant victors, counting the margin of their November majority, were in an ungenerous mood. In New York, Whitelaw Reid's *Tribune* discovered that the incendiary, blasphemous Bryan had been making war on the Ten Commandments and the paper, which had been badly frightened, now exulted:

"The people won. Truth won. Righteousness won. God won. The moral law was vindicated in affairs of State."

Of course it would have been more accurate to say that the checkbooks won, graft won and the right of the corruptionists to plunder the country was vindicated in affairs of State.

The glorious triumph had left the conquerors without a policy. They only knew—Henry Adams told them so—that a new era in the world had dawned. The gold standard had been saved; the tariff was secure; the friends of religion and private exploitation of public resources were in office; there would be a complete break with the past, that past of which Adams wrote:

"One might search the whole list of Congress, Judiciary and Executive during the twenty-five years 1870 to 1895 and find little but damaged reputations."

3

A good many of those reputations were in the throng that clustered in some confusion around the stocky figure of Hanna and the deceptively aquiline sternness of the President-elect. What were they going to do? McKinley himself was willing to do nothing. His Secretary of State, the venerable Sherman, bereft of the advice of the General and carrying into the new era odd memories and manners of a Washington that had been dominated by a slave-owning aristocracy more than forty years ago, was equally content with inaction. But his colleagues had promised the country prosperity and thought they ought to make motions.

Signers of campaign checks, however, warned against any interference in the domestic field. So, as the year faded out in pleasant anticipation of the following March 4th, thoughts returned to the possibility of a crusade that had been exercising many minds when 1896 was new. The tempest of Bryanism had passed—only for the moment, young Mr. Roosevelt feared—and as the air cleared, the conscience of America could discern Cuba still struggling to be free. The political year, ending peacefully in the pursuit of a policy, had begun with a good deal of strenuous debate over our duty to neighbors, and Senator Henry Cabot Lodge had injected into a highly rhetorical address on common humanity the more practical note:

"Our immediate pecuniary interests in the island are very great. They are being destroyed. Free Cuba would mean a great market for the United States; it would mean an opportunity for American capital invited there by signal exemptions."

That was a pleasant thought, even if the "signal exemptions" should have to be imposed by force upon an unwilling people. It became even more attractive after the inauguration of Major McKinley and the era of prosperity. "Manifest destiny" again crept into the oratorical periods. At last Republican leaders understood this new world they were to build for their business men. Imperialism, not yet a word anathema to liberals and radicals, was to be its substance.

The determined expansionist policy coincided with a discovery by the men who had filled Hanna's war chest that their increasingly complex industrial machine was a dynamic, not a static, force. Markets must expand, with comfortably augmenting profits, or they must contract, involving the magnates in losses and their country in a depression. So business in general listened approvingly to Senator Lodge and remembered that Spain still had some other possessions in far places. Those islands in the East, what were they called? Oh, yes, the Philippines. An admirable market.

The politicians liked imperialism for its fine, resonant tone, soothing to national pride. Of course it would probably mean fighting, but nothing serious, and many agreed with Roosevelt that "this country needs a war." Mr. Roosevelt, just released from his police duties in New York by Croker's triumph, was belligerently carefree, adding that for his part:

"I don't care whether our seacoast cities are bombarded or not."

But there were those who did care, and one of their few representatives in Congress, after listening to his colleagues predict that it would be an easy matter to lick Spain, interpolated the bitter question:

"How many lives do you want to sacrifice to do it?"

Apparently he was no patriot.

Of course prospects of new markets, even the magic sound of imperialism, were not likely to appeal to the people who would have to fight the battles, pay the bills and sacrifice the lives. Besides, only the most rarely frank of mortal statesmen ever admit publicly that they are bent on conquest solely for the sake of booty. Certainly the grave, kindly, God-fearing gentlemen who advised Major McKinley shrouded the harshness of facts in a veil of exalted ideals, and before long it was apparent that the great heart of America was moved by the struggles of a brave people against foul oppression. A glorious sentimentality, fed on manufactured atrocities and endless talk of duty to humanity, completely hid from the nation the brutal truth that it was embarking upon as unjustifiable an act of aggression as history can show, largely at the command of the interests that had paid for the political victory of '96.

The shipyard owner who had contributed $400,000 to the campaign clamored for action; Congress threatened to declare war no matter what the yielding statesmen in Madrid might reply to the pacific McKinley's representations, and public opinion as expressed at mass meetings endorsed the stand. Roosevelt, relegated to the Assistant Secretaryship of the Navy in one of those fruitless efforts to condemn him to obscurity, was elaborating plans for a cavalry regiment and warning Commodore Dewey in China to be ready to seize Manila, although the value of that port in freeing Cuba was not immediately discernible.

Joseph Pulitzer of the *World,* master of sensation, was

very anxious for a war, just a little one, he hastened to add, that "would give him a chance to gauge the reflex in his circulation figures." Mr. Pulitzer's supremacy in his own field was being threatened by a millionaire youth (or "blackguard boy," as Mr. Godkin's *Nation* called him) who had been invited to leave Harvard not so long ago. William Randolph Hearst was outdoing the older expert in hiring reporters to invent stories of Spanish sadism.

With so much combustible sentiment in the air, it does not at this distance of time seem surprising that at 9:40 on the evening of Feb. 15th a mysterious explosion sank the battleship *Maine,* ostensibly on a courtesy visit to Cuba, in Havana harbor. To an exceedingly ill-informed public in the United States, that unexplained disaster (we know no more about it now than they did then) was very sinister. A howl for blood arose and McKinley's convictions, never proof against what he took to be the voice of the people, were forgotten. Two months after the *Maine* went down, and despite the fact that Spain had desperately accepted every demand made upon her, the United States were in a very muddled state of war.

4

In the first fine careless rapture of an as yet bloodless conflict, the confusion was apparent only to a few responsible officeholders, and they had no idea of its extent. The rest of the nation was happily confident that the navy and a noisy vociferation of "Remember the *Maine;* to Hell with Spain" would blast Spanish power from the face of the Western world.

Those private interests which had forced the country into active hostilities were delighted. Pulitzer discovered that his circulation responded to the stimulus with a reflex positively convulsive; the day after the declaration of war he sold 1,300,000 copies. Roosevelt's pet project for a regiment of cowboys and college men was on paper, and in the papers, too, progressing from "Teddy's Terrors" through a period of "Rocky Mountain Rustlers" to the final, immortal "Rough Riders." * Contractors, armament makers, horse dealers, clothing merchants, food salesmen, politicians and assorted busy-bodies descended upon appalled officials in Washington in a flood that almost swamped the ship of state.

Even Russell Alger, the Secretary of War, who had been a field officer in the Civil War and a mogul of Michigan politics ever since, was amazed by the number of exceedingly influential persons who wanted very special favors. All day long he had to receive a steady procession of petitioners seeking war orders, military preferment, camp sites, protection from mythical Spanish raiders, jobs, assurances on pious or temperance or medical grounds. Alger mournfully recorded the fact that most of these people were so troublesome but so inescapable because of their high rank that he could get at the real work of his department only in the evenings and on Sundays after church. His experience was not unique, and his colleague, Secretary of the Navy Long, wrote:

"It is interesting to note how every section of the country, although all are patriotic, has an eye on the main chance."

Perhaps more interesting is the method by which the purveyors to army and navy converted the holy crusade—for so most Americans sincerely regarded it—to their own profit. The boodlers and grafters did not, as in the Civil War, permeate the entire military machine; colonels and quartermasters for the most part exacted no spoil; the practice of splitting commissions with government officials was far from general; bribery was at a minimum.

Truly this was a gratifying state of affairs and should have commanded public applause. It might have done so had not the waste, inefficiency and avoidable losses of men and

* In their ever memorable campaign around Santiago, the only member of that regiment who rode was Theodore Roosevelt. The rest walked.

money been even more glaring than in '61. The troops were as badly clothed, worse fed and as neglected hygienically despite impressive advances in medicine and, theoretically, in administration. But the profits were, if possible, greater. Government purchasing departments were learning just what the political victory of '96, that fairest flower of honest graft, had meant. Business in that hysterical year had bought the government, and the delighted representatives of industry, in Washington to keep "an eye on the main chance," found themselves among friends. The most favorable contracts were signed without argument or commission, even when officials knew that the government was being victimized. After all, the administration had been elected to do what it could for business. That seemed to mean business should dictate war contracts.

As the crusade to free Cuba began at a distance of 10,000 miles with the Battle of Manila Bay, the price of everything the government needed soared to the skies. An obliging commissary made little protest, and the sovereign people were too busy contemplating the glory of their arms to bother about the harshly material aspect of how that glory was nourished in the field.

The subservience of politicians to actual and potential campaign contributors was more complete than could have been bought by outright bribery. The political argument convinced officials who were otherwise incorruptible, while more cynical grafters did not care what the world called it, just so they got money. Therefore ship owners were permitted to break agreements with the navy and boost the price of colliers needed by the fleet. The packers were allowed to supply horrible, nauseating messes called canned beef from which even hungry men turned in disgust. Contracts were let at high rates for tropical clothing that was delivered only when the troops returned from Cuba to face a Northern autumn.

In its effect on the army, this subordination of military

aims to business and political influences was far more deplorable than any simple, wholesome graft. Grafters do not clamor for credit; they are content with cash. The upright representatives of the market place hungered for a share in the glory. They forced upon the fighting forces the burden of conducting a war in accordance with the political exigencies of the moment. Fortunately Spain fought on the same principle, and Madrid had developed a capacity for blundering that an inexperienced nation like the United States could hardly hope to match.

A study of the tactics and strategy of the conflict leaves an odd impression of two countries desperately striving to shunt victory into the lap of the other. In such a competition Spain's almost complete lack of resources and a virtually non-combatant fleet were decisive factors against a wealthy nation equipped with battleships whose guns fired real shells.

The war, declared on April 25th, ended in an armistice on Aug. 12th, and in that time the country was treated to a wonderful demonstration of a great national effort conducted in the interest of imperialist industry and a jingo press. In Southern training camps the volunteers sickened by thousands and died by hundreds because politics dictated the selection of unwholesome sites. Supplies ceased to command the interest of government agents after they were paid for, and the Santiago expedition of 17,000 men was sadly equipped for a tropical campaign.

The troops, however, were so eager they actually fought for place on the transports, and these high spirits continued until the moment sixteen days after the embarkation when the first brush with the enemy on Cuban soil took place, to the considerable surprise of the high command, at Las Guasimas. It was a happy little skirmish, giving Colonel Roosevelt his first taste of fire and his first praise for gallantry in action. It also witnessed the marvelous resurrection of "Fighting Joe" Wheeler, a Confederate cavalry hero, now at sixty-two Major General Joseph Wheeler, U.S.A., who in the flush of victory was waving his hat and shrieking with unreconstructed fervor:

"Come on, boys, we've got the damn Yankees on the run!"

After that, the campaign progressed in slightly more conventional fashion. Its triumphant close, however, was dictated more by Spanish defeatism and a desire to go home than by any display of strength on the part of the Americans. To be sure, there was a glorious charge up San Juan Hill, which gave the United States a President even if it did not effect the fall of Santiago.

For that achievement, the country was indebted to the political situation in Spain and a consummate bluff put up by Commanding General Shafter. Madrid decided the state of public opinion called for a naval battle, so Admiral Cervera led his little fleet to suicide against the overwhelming superiority of the American ships outside Santiago. Shafter, 300 pounds of unhappy general suffering through the tropical July in a woolen uniform, thereupon talked the not unwilling Spanish commander into surrender. The enemy, ignorant of the disease sweeping through the American lines around the city, made only one condition; his troops were to be sent back to Spain at the expense of the United States.

General Shafter leaped at the chance to overcome a hostile army of superior numbers by the bloodless expedient of paying its passage money home. The farce was completed when the Spanish Line, in which the Spanish government was interested, ignored the state of war to bid $513,000 for the job against $1,312,915 by the other transatlantic companies, which thought there could be no competition. The War Department was unmercifully assailed for saving $800,000 and "giving the Spanish Government money instead of bullets."

Shafter never reaped the reward of his skill. The poor fellow, military in every inch of his great bulk, had failed to cultivate the politicians, nor was his figure appropriate to parades of martial glory. Worst of all, he had actually cursed that high priest of journalism, Richard Harding Davis. War correspondents of such eminence expected military operations to be conducted with a view to suitable publicity. The unromantic Shafter had dared to damn Davis for trying to lead a landing party. After that the General was studiously written down by the reporter and his outraged colleagues.

So General Shafter was ignored. But the war was over; Colonel Roosevelt was famous; the United States had an empire, and Mr. Pulitzer was ruefully counting the cost of his (and Mr. Hearst's) little flutter in martial enterprise. It had not paid. The expense of press boats and cables offset most uncomfortably the fleeting honor of increased circulation, and Pulitzer admitted he did not care if he never saw war again.

He had a far more congenial topic at his hand. Spain was beaten, but mismanagement went on, and as the ragged, hungry, tottering heroes came north to be mustered out, the results of the political crusade for liberty and wider markets impressed themselves unfavorably upon a country that had developed a taste for excitement. Charges and counter-charges took up the space formerly devoted to "Spanish atrocities." Rejoicings over heroism and Santiago and Manila Bay faded before the outcry against corruption and murder.

The effect upon the November elections was likely to be disastrous. McKinley, his war and prosperity both won, moved hastily to save the reward of his success. Full inquiry was promised and a fact-finding commission of impressive names appointed. This body succeeded in allaying the tempest until after the electorate had been duly recorded in favor of the Republican party, short and successful wars, a place in the sun and big profits. Then the investigation proceeded.

At its head was that veteran railroad builder, Grenville

Dodge. Time was no object, and witness after witness droned on the sorry tale of inefficiency, recrimination and excuse, General Nelson Miles, conqueror of Puerto Rico in a campaign whose only casualties had been caused by his food supply, gained immortal fame by coining the expression "embalmed beef" to describe the stuff the commissary and packers had furnished him. The intricate process by which the entire equipment of a 200-bed hospital got mislaid for weeks was spread over many pages. Letters and complaints poured in, and a dealer in canned goods begged the commission to refrain from so much detail since the trend of the hearings was "unfortunate for the reputation of American tinned meats abroad."

Of other reputations the commission was more tender. It had been denied the right to subpoena witnesses, to force anyone to testify or to promise immunity. There could be no serious effort to thrash out the charges of corruption under such circumstances. General Dodge would ask his witness in effect:

"Did you ever take a bribe?"

The witness would answer solemnly in the negative, and that phase of the investigation was over. The commission was able to report quite honestly:

"There has been no evidence before us that anyone in or connected with the War Department has dishonestly received a dollar."

Virtuously the commission turned its back on suggestions that there might have been profiteering and influences of which the public would disapprove. There was no consideration of whether the free hand so chastely extended to the business community was not as corrupting in its effects as the outmoded bribery of the Civil War.

Yet it was tacitly acknowledged that because the pursuit of gain was so intent, fatalities from disease in the army had been ten times those from battle. Our fighting superiority to Spain had been proved at a cost of 280 killed in action.

Deaths from typhoid, yellow fever, malaria and dysentery, the scourges of the camps, reached 2,910 in five months. There were no figures on the thousands turned back into civilian life wrecked in health, many of them to die in the midst of their appalled families who had envisaged quite a different return of the heroes. But by then there were other things to think about. The Twentieth Century was at hand, and mankind was exhorted to look forward.

XV

"THE CHRISTIAN GENTLEMEN"

1

ONLY FOUR YEARS HAD PASSED since the last new era had been ushered in by the triumph of sound money, but another was at hand, for the Twentieth Century was to be faster in many ways than its predecessors. The eras could succeed each other with greater rapidity. McKinley set the tone for the latest when he explained why the Philippines became the spoil of a purely altruistic war and how an American army happened to be suppressing Filipinos who wanted to be as free as Cubans or more so. The incongruity was the will of God, he told a delegation of Methodist missionaries, who were no doubt edified to learn that the United States acquired a colonial empire in direct response to prayer.

"I walked the floor of the White House night after night until midnight," the President informed his clerical audience, "and I am not ashamed to tell you, gentlemen, that I went down on my knees and prayed Almighty God for light and guidance more than one night.

"And one night late it came to me this way—I don't know how it was, but it came."

"It" was the divine revelation that the islands could not be given back to Spain nor allowed to fall to any European country nor left to their own untutored selves. So, the Almighty seemed to hint:

"There was nothing left for us to do but to take them all, and to educate the Filipinos, and uplift and civilize them, and by God's grace do the very best we could by them as our fellow men for whom Christ also died. And then I went to bed and went to sleep and slept soundly."

God was a comparatively late recruit to the cause of imperialism, contributing His recommendations only long after "the Majah" had reached the same conclusion without heavenly assistance. Months before he had taken to walking the floor at night and nearly two years before his explanation to the Methodists, McKinley jotted down a private memorandum that bore no mark of supernatural collaboration.

"While we are conducting the war," he wrote, "and until its conclusion we must keep all we get; when the war is over we must keep what we want."

Few Presidents have mirrored their generation so successfully as McKinley. The serene appropriation of divine approval for aims that were of the earth earthy was by no means invented at this time, but never in this country had it been quite so smugly applied to commercial transactions. Small children in that period imagined their God as a venerable party who ran the universe from an office six days a week and donned silk hat and frock coat on Sundays.

This was in the image of those who visibly conducted the affairs of this world, building up a vast power that revised the methods if not the objects of graft. The political agents of the larger industrialists, placed in office to serve business, were asked only for tariffs and blindness. Men who could carry out this program were in line for advancement. So there was no government interference with J. P. Morgan's steel trust, the spreading Standard Oil, the sugar and beef barons, the budding aluminum monopoly of a scantily publicized Pittsburgher whom the financiers of the Smoky City were beginning to call "Uncle Andy" Mellon.

They and a thousand like them were pyramiding companies and stocks in amazing fashion to create such intricate structures that they could never be untangled. John Sherman died as the Twentieth Century opened, but his anti-trust law appeared to have predeceased him for all practical purposes—except when labor unions were accused of striking in restraint of trade. The financiers no longer raided each other with joyous abandon, for they were growing class conscious, recognizing a community of interest. In that bond of cold, unfriendly fellowship they included the politicians, particularly Senator Mark Hanna of Ohio. After the election of 1900 a great peace settled over the partisan camps. Even Colonel Roosevelt was quiet, sidetracked into the Vice Presidency where, the men who put him there fondly believed, he would fade gently from public memory. The short session of Congress was chiefly notable for Hanna's gallant effort to pass a ship subsidy bill in the interest of a prospective merchant marine. The legislators adjourned without doing anything about it, the proposed beneficiary being too feeble an infant to make its way through the Capitol, and through the long summer of 1901 the talk was mostly of Morgan's billion dollar giant, half steel and half water.

Then in September a pistol in the hands of a madman popped sharply during the gaiety of the Buffalo exposition, and they took McKinley to a private house to die while Hanna's usually smiling face was streaked with tears as he waited outside the door.

The way opened before Colonel Roosevelt, and for a moment it seemed still another new era was about to begin. Certainly there would be action; the Colonel was noted as a man of action, and once again the country thought it discerned the inscrutable workings of a Providence that could be credited with a tender regard for Roosevelt's career.

The new President, however, despite an engaging flair for the spectacular and an impulsive manner, was a practical person. The reformers, who counted him as one of themselves, descended upon Washington to help him achieve the gentle Utopianism that was the intellectual craze of the day. A mild clamor for trust busting swelled to audible proportions, but Senator Hanna was still a welcome guest at the White House, and Roosevelt was experiencing the sobering effects of an office that carries unbounded responsibility but is fortunately not equipped with unlimited power. The capitalists, after a breath-taking moment of uncertainty, heard the Colonel speak of "good trusts" and thought he was likely to prove a sensible fellow after all.

2

Reassured that he was not going to upset the bargain by which the government kept out of the market place, the Eastern railroad and coal leaders, dominated by J. P. Morgan & Co., considered the time ripe to crush once and for all that dangerously un-American thing called unionism. Anthracite miners had dared suggest that some small part of the increasing profits of the pits ought to go into wages. The operators, who had come to regard their workmen as an inferior race of cattle imported in bulk from Europe, supposed that a desire to bargain collectively was a germ imported with them. But through painful years the "cattle" had built up an organization. When the mine owners refused even to discuss terms or grievances, the fierce, blackened army of delvers in the earth swarmed to the surface, swore in a variety of tongues to stand firm for their rights and the great coal strike of 1902 had begun.

Neither for the first nor the last time, the unlovely coal country saw the horrors of economic warfare. The ragged miners and their families starved grimly in tents and shacks. The operators, far from the scene, sent reinforcements to their normal armies of hired thugs, who were far rougher than anything a Tammany boss could muster at an election riot.

In New York, Morgan spoke briefly in the privacy of his

office, and "Bet-a-Million" Gates emerged to offer 100 to 1 that the strike would be broken. But Gates was a crude and vulgar fellow, as coarse as Morgan himself. Another of the great financier's creatures spoke in more becoming phrases. George Baer, president of Morgan's Pennsylvania & Reading Railroad, one of the largest anthracite operators in the field, turned from a sharp rejection of arbitration to say:

"The rights and interests of the laboring man will be protected and cared for—not by the labor agitators, but by the Christian men to whom God in his infinite wisdom has given control of the property interests of the country. Pray earnestly that right may triumph, always remembering that the Lord God Omnipotent still reigns."

It must have surprised Mr. Baer very much to learn that the Deity he worshiped was not a sort of glorified member of the Coal and Iron Police. Still more bewildering was the suddenly intransigent attitude of the national administration. Roosevelt, no longer proving sensible from the standpoint of his party's financial backers, was suspected of a desire to show his sympathy for the miners in concrete form. Perhaps that was to be expected of him, for he was one who valued the cheap plaudits of the multitude. But when Mark Hanna was found to be infected with the same heresy, the Baers might well become alarmed.

The process by which Hanna discovered that there is another philosophy, not necessarily depraved, than that which guided him as mine owner and traction magnate was the inevitable result of political experience. He had entered public life as the conscious servant of business and still regarded himself as such, but he had been brought into contact with new ideas. And, remembering the Ohio strike of 1876 when he had the militia out to fight the union, he was no longer willing to quote William Vanderbilt and let it go at that.

Had he remained in Cleveland, devoting himself to private affairs, Hanna would have kept the opinions of a Rocke-

feller or a Morgan and merited the nickname of "Dollar
Mark." His first years in politics had been entirely dominated
by an attitude that would have been intelligible to any of
Grant's Cabinet. In 1890 he had urged Ohio's Attorney General to drop an anti-trust prosecution against Standard Oil
because some of his friends were involved. He pointed out
that "in these modern days most commercial interests are
properly and necessarily taking on the form of organization
for the safety of investors and the improvement of all conditions upon which business is done." He added:

"There is no greater mistake for a man in or out of public place to make than to assume that he owes any duty to
the public or can in any manner advance his own position
or interests by attacking the organization under which experience has taught business can best be done."

Since then "Dollar Mark" had learned as a politician dedicated to honest graft that an occasional deference to public
opinion and at least a pretense of considering the general
welfare was necessary to preserve the existing system. Indeed, he had acquired a genuine interest in the general welfare as a corollary of prosperity. Not the least of the services that men such as he rendered to big corporations was
the modifying of arrogant methods, a measure of protection
against their own abuses.

Hanna knew, for example, that Republican platforms
should contain anti-trust planks, drafted by such reliable
statesmen as Senator Foraker, who took $44,000 in "legal
fees" from Standard Oil during the period when he was
the plank's author. Hanna knew that execution of these
laws should be in the hands of Attorneys General like
Philander C. Knox, one of Mellon's lawyers. Hanna knew,
too, that a stubborn defiance was not the best way to meet
labor's aspirations, and he therefore became in the eyes of
his one-time peers as rabidly red a radical as Theodore
Roosevelt, who wrote to him during the coal strike:

"I feel most strongly that the attitude of the operators

is one which accentuates the need of government having some power to supervision and regulation over such corporations."

This sentiment would have been nothing less than socialism to the "Dollar Mark" who had wanted an anti-trust suit against Standard Oil dropped. But the Senator Hanna of 1902 saw nothing startling in it. To the great indignation of substantial citizens in New York he actually argued there on behalf of the union and advised stockholders to demand that their officers arbitrate. This form of pressure, often irresistible when exerted upon Congressmen, was singularly ineffective in relaxing the uncompromising attitude of Morgan and Baer. Hanna was told that his efforts were being construed as "mischievous" interference.

"You tell them that if I hear any more of that kind of talk I will go to New York, hire Carnegie Hall and give them something to talk about," snapped the Boss of the Party, stung by the suggestion that he who had done so much for both business and politics was no better than a meddler.

Hanna's attempt to make the operators see reason gave him the air of a liberal, but he was just as staunch a defender of finance and industry as ever, perhaps more so, although he dimly recognized a certain responsibility that capital owed to society for the right to go on multiplying itself. He argued that trusts were desirable, but he thought labor should be organized on a similar scale. He did not convince the operators, who still felt that their campaign checks had bought the government to do their bidding without question.

Then, as stocks of coal in the cities dwindled, the sovereign people spoke. They cried that they would be frozen for no other reason than because J. P. Morgan believed "men owning property should do what they like with it." Eight years before in an exactly similar situation the people

had cried in vain to their servants. At that time George
Pullman had wagged a white chin whisker and muttered
stubbornly that he had nothing to arbitrate. The railroad
strike had spread, and public opinion damned Mr. Pullman
with fierce invective. But business was still sacred, and President Cleveland had moved the army. The strike died out
in blood and tears while Eugene Debs with remarkable good
humor and impeccable manners began a six months' jail term
for having been right.

Surely, the bankers who controlled the coal operators believed, their own Mark Hanna and Republican President
could be no less unmoved by popular clamor than a mere
Democrat. But between 1894 and 1902 some of the politicians had begun to doubt that the most ruthless methods of
exploitation on a national scale would always be submitted
to in spineless apathy. Others, applying the "honest" rather
than the "graft" part of their system, had reached the conclusion that government really ought to govern. They were
ready to check the overly arrogant campaign contributors
for their own good.

Roosevelt, therefore, proposed to use the army as freely
as Cleveland, but in a new way. The horrified Baer learned
that in spite of his appeals to God, in spite of Scripture and
in the face of religious sanctions, Federal troops would move
into the fields and work the mines for the public unless he
and his fellows agreed to arbitration.

The idea of sitting in the same room with the officer of
a trade union so angered this Christian gentleman that he
was content to let the Lord and Roosevelt fight it out. But
his own master, Morgan, was a man of little faith. He saw
that one step toward nationalizing a basic industry might
very well be followed by another. He avoided the first step
by a surly consent to a mediation conference and Baer's
fear of contamination was allayed by referring to Labor's
representative at the meeting as a sociologist.

3

The heavens did not fall because the miners won a slight increase in wages, and as the Roosevelt administration pursued its entertaining course, Mr. Dooley explained to Mr. Hennessy how the President felt about corporations. " 'Th' trusts,' says he, 'are heejoous monsthers built up be th' enlightened intherprise iv th' men that have done so much to advance progress in our beloved country,' he says. 'On wan hand I wud stamp thim undher fut; on th' other hand not so fast.' "

In this spirit Roosevelt decided to prevent the Northern Securities Company from carrying out its plans for a Northwestern railway monopoly. The merger would have benefited public and operators under the sort of regulation that was to be effected a few years later, but the President, who cheerfully admitted a complete ignorance of economics, wanted to bust a trust, and Northern Securities could be busted without seriously inconveniencing anyone, although Morgan, director of the movement, came down to the White House to voice a famous expression of his idea as to the relationship between business and government.

"If we have done anything wrong, send your man to my man and they can fix it up," he told Roosevelt.

Attorney General Knox, present and designated by that faintly contemptuous "your man," retorted that illegality could not be "fixed up." Northern Securities lost the ensuing action and the case set a precedent for a great many dissolutions of trusts, most of them not effected by Roosevelt. This stormy campaigner actually inaugurated just twenty-five anti-trust suits in seven and a half years. His conservative successor, Taft, to whom the support of big business was flung in its darkest hour, began forty-five in four years.

The achievements of these two administrations were based on the newly elevated standards of graft, that a little gentle pressure should be exerted when the governmental partners of the capitalists feel that their friends have gone too far. But the use of public office for private ends had hardly been abolished. Throughout his career, Roosevelt sought the aid of Tom Platt, had recognized that gloomy gentleman's claims to patronage. He was fulsome in praise of Matt Quay of Pennsylvania. He had conferred a lucrative job upon James Clarkson of Iowa, once unrestrainedly denounced by Civil Service Commissioner Roosevelt for reckless use of the spoils system in the post office. President Roosevelt excused Clarkson's "occasional removals" for political considerations as "in no way to be criticized." The "occasional removals" consisted of displacing 32,000 Democratic postmasters who should have been protected by civil service regulations.

It was clear that the Platts and Quays could keep Roosevelt in line fairly well even if he sometimes rebelled against Baer's Christian men. His war chest for the campaign of 1904 was, therefore, well filled. Hanna died early in that year, but a worthy successor was found in George Cortelyou, Secretary of the new Department of Commerce and Labor, in which there had been established a Bureau of Corporations that might awake from its slumbers any day. He was a persuasive solicitor with a memory from which all recollection of sums contributed soon vanished. Since it was the practice to burn the national committee's books after election, this forgetfulness was convenient.

"The man who was to run this campaign had to be a man of my type," Roosevelt explained.

Thinking this was the case, Morgan and his partners gave Cortelyou $150,000, Standard Oil $100,000, E. H. Harriman $50,000 for himself and $200,000 he had collected from others, Jay Gould's son $500,000. Some of them felt they had been cheated, for soon after Roosevelt was launched on his second term the packers, several railroads and Standard Oil were sued in the Federal courts. They all escaped, even Judge Landis's fine of $29,000,000 against Standard Oil being reversed. But many of the wealthiest Republicans were sure Roosevelt was an ingrate who accepted campaign graft and then betrayed the cause that supported him. Henry Frick, recalling a secret conference at the White House, sneered:

"Why, Roosevelt fairly went down on his knees to us in his fear of defeat, and said that he would be good and leave the railroads and the corporations alone if we would only give him this financial help. We did, but he didn't stay put in his second term. We got nothing for our money."

Frick accounted it as nothing that they got an excuse. As the panic of 1907 began in a stock market crash, unemployment, suicides and the other phenomena of depression, the bankers assured the country that Roosevelt's "policy of hostility against corporations" was to blame. The President had in a happy moment coined the phrase "malefactors of great wealth," and the men who had given of their thousands thought him most impolite.

They took their revenge. Cortelyou, elevated to the Secretaryship of the Treasury, conferred upon Morgan almost dictatorial powers and $25,000,000 of government funds to throw into the call money market. Lack of any central banking system forced Roosevelt thus to rely upon the men he had been publicly denouncing and his humiliation was complete. He could have blamed it on the financial influence which had for years prevented the government from adopting some form of control over the nation's credit system.

Oddly enough the panic did not end until Morgan had acquired the enormous resources of the Tennessee Coal and Iron Company for United States Steel. He extorted a promise that in this emergency the anti-trust laws would be ignored in order to save a large brokerage house that was overloaded with Tennessee Coal and Iron stock. So the steel corporation got about a billion dollars' worth of property for $45,000,000 and the panic was permitted to subside.

The spectacle of manipulation and irresponsible financing, plain during the depression, was emphasized by investigations that sought to learn its causes. Roosevelt voiced a popular sentiment when, nearing the end of his term, he proposed a program of genuinely advanced reforms "social security," rate regulation for utilities, restriction of stock speculation. He was also attacking the power of the courts to set aside what he called the will of the people, and he anticipated the argument that he would hurt business with:

"The 'business' which is hurt by the movement for honesty is the kind of business which, in the long run, it pays the country to have hurt. It is the kind of business which has tended to make the very name 'high finance' a term of scandal."

The scandal, in the view of men like Henry Havemeyer of the American Sugar Refining Company, was caused by political interference. Early in the century Havemeyer testified that the government ought to have nothing to do with any corporation.

"You think the public has no right to know what its earning power is or subject them to any inspection whatever?" a not very grammatical investigator asked him.

"Yes," was the reply, "that is my theory. Let the buyer beware; that covers the whole business. You cannot wetnurse people from the time they are born until the time they die. They have got to wade in and get stuck, and that is the way men are educated and cultivated."

It was an ideal of education and cultivation that failed to appeal to the country. Roosevelt and other politicians of the semi-advanced school saw that it would be safe to put themselves at the head of a movement to end the irresponsible dominance of the great capitalists. Safe, but—since the power of an industrial-financial system is not something to be stopped in its remorseless progress by mere words—perhaps not very effective. Regulation of corporations, thanks to the grafters, was to be done by friends.

The Christian men who controlled the property interests

of the country fought every inch of the way in blind, short-sighted defense of their profits and power. They would have been smashed had not their conscientious employees in public office repudiated the Havemeyers and Baers in the spirit of true loyalty to their masters. The high price of honest graft was justified when its practitioners proved, as Depew had said years before, that the right kind of regulation could achieve added security and gains for business.

XVI

DRIVING THE RASCALS OUT

1

WHILE ROOSEVELT WAS TILTing with the windmills of Wall Street, a band of even stranger knights roamed the country seeking to rescue fair cities from ogres who held them in durance vile. Spurred with rage against every evil, they rode a hobby of perfection in government. A bewildered succession of municipal bosses—practical politicians all—were jolted out of the placidity of accepted corruption by a handful of penmen whom the suddenly harassed statesmen (when most polite) called lunatics. These madmen appealed from the conservatism of an established order to the conscience of the nation. They sought no office themselves, and in proportion to their disinterestedness, which had been woefully lacking in earlier reformers, they were believed.

The public, never at a loss for a picturesque name to fling at its heroes or its villains, fastened upon these modern crusaders the title of "muckrakers." They accepted the unsavory word as a badge of honor. They were laughed at or reviled, according to the accuracy with which their shafts hit the mark, but they aroused an interest in local government that gave a new twist to graft and politics. They provided the basis for the reforms that Roosevelt called the "New Nationalism" and Woodrow Wilson was to designate as the "New Freedom."

The volunteers in this holy war started with a premise which at first they thought unassailable. They held to the simple theory that the democratic system of government ordained by the fathers was the best that human wit could devise. Yet any man who walked the streets with his eyes open could see that in practice it was less than perfect. The logical conclusion was that it had been perverted by scheming, selfish, greedy criminals. Nor were the students of government reduced to finding "John Doe" indictments. They could and did name the culprits—Croker and his successor, Charlie Murphy, in New York, Boss Butler in St. Louis, "Doc" Ames in Minneapolis, "Hinky Dink" Kenna and "Bathhouse John" Coughlin in Chicago, and so on through the railway guide.

These men were cast as the villains of the piece, and the drama was written in that uncompromising, unreal theatrical style which recognizes no gradations of virtue. The characters are entirely pure and noble, or they are scoundrels of deepest dye, which makes it easy for the author. The difficulty with the municipal plot, however, was that the players obstinately refused to fit themselves to the mold prepared for them.

Lincoln Steffens, the Lancelot of muckrakers, pursuing the Grail of honest government over the land, was among the first to encounter this strange recalcitrance. The machine leaders simply would not conform to diabolical specifications. Steffens, whose early training left him quite unprepared for the corruption he encountered in his journalistic progress through New York, assumed that Croker must be rather more devil than man. But as he studied actual conditions he reversed himself. Behind the machine he saw the tacit support of a vast respectability, of one of whose symbols, the reform Mayor Strong, he wrote:

"His ideas of integrity, ethical perhaps in a merchant, were downright dishonest in government."

The muckraker found that Croker was doing a businesslike job of ruling the city and was not entirely delighted with the sale of protection to vice and crime. Taxed with responsibility for such scandals, the Boss had echoed Tweed's "What are you going to do about it?" The papers branded the sentiment as arrogant defiance, but Steffens thought it the expression of a politician's honest puzzlement. Certainly neither Steffens nor Croker nor the outraged editors could answer. No one offered an acceptable substitute for government by and for those business men who had the time for it.

"If we get big graft, and the cops and the small fry politicians know it, we can't decently kick at their petty stuff," Croker told Steffens.

Everywhere it was plain that the "petty stuff," which enraged the populace far more than larger but less picturesque steals, depended for its continued existence upon the graft given and taken in the interest of "clean" business. The experience of widely scattered reformers proved, to the surprise of every one of them, that legislation of real benefit to the people was resisted not by the crooks and grafters but by respected mercantile and professional leaders.

Ben Lindsey, fighting for underprivileged youth in Colorado, had the bankers, merchants, clergy, lawyers and teachers arrayed against him in an almost solid block of aroused righteousness. The decent people of Denver were mortally afraid that Lindsey's child welfare program was going to cost them money. An increased tax rate, they wailed, was confiscation. They quoted Scripture about the sacredness of property. They were indignant when it was pointed out to them that there was something about little children in the word of God, too. Lindsey won, but not merely because his cause was just. He had an army with him, an army of corrupt politicians, grafting police, bribe-giving saloon keepers and inarticulate laborers. The crooks had nothing to gain one way or the other, so they judged the question on its merits and plumped in a body for Lindsey and the kids.

In St. Louis, Joseph Folk, a prosecutor with some of the fire that animated more literary muckrakers, moved to the governorship of Missouri by exposing and attacking the corrupt machine that ran his city, but he knew that in the wider field of his ambition he had failed. The city, the state, the whole nation, applauded as he laid bare the connection between municipal officials and the underworld. A sudden hush fell when he applied the same tactics to brewers and transit companies.

"For a time," Folk commented bitterly, "I had the whole-hearted support of the press, the Chamber of Commerce and the business men of the city. As long as I was after Boss Butler and the grafters in the city council, I was a hero. But when I started to prosecute bankers who were involved in a city franchise, the press turned against me. The prosecutions were bad for business, people began to say; they gave St. Louis a bad name; they should be dropped."

That was the invariable result of every one of those campaigns organized under the slogan "Drive the Rascals Out." While the drive concentrated on professional boodlers, the better element approved. As soon as the attack carried on into regions of city life where the evil had its root, there arose the cry "bad for business." It was one that neither reformers nor politicians could successfully resist. Hostility to legitimate profit was as fatal to a public man's career as adultery. Both had to be practiced in secret if at all. Only those who did not expect to stand for re-election or hope for appointive office, like Roosevelt after 1904 and before 1912, dared suggest that there might be a kind of business it would pay to have hurt.

Gradually the muckrakers learned that their original demand for a business government was not the triumphant solution that it at first appeared. For business men were already in politics, and Steffens for one was coming to the conclusion that this was what ailed politics. His disillusionment was chronicled in such powerful fashion that one is apt to consider his case unique. But it was paralleled by that of many others, among them a young Cleveland enthusiast, Frederic C. Howe.

2

Howe, sitting under Woodrow Wilson and James Bryce at college, had taken his ideal of politics from those master theorists. With eloquence and a wealth of scholarship, they had drawn for him a picture of the perfect commonwealth. Here, they said, the destinies of society would be entrusted to the gentlemen, a godlike, impartial, disinterested race ruling benignly for the good of all. Young Howe, entering upon the practice of law and failing to be attracted by the profession, kept this charming vision in the back of his mind.

But, alas, Wilson and Bryce had not told him where the ruling gentry were to be found and how they were to be elected. Their pupil thought he caught a glimmering of the answer to this practical difficulty when one day a group of Cleveland's "better citizens" suggested that he be a candidate for the City Council. He accepted eagerly, and plunged at once into the most exciting municipal campaign 1901 could offer.

It was the year Tom Johnson was becoming Mayor of Cleveland for the first time and, in the process, taking from the redoubtable Hanna control of his own city. Without much regard for party labels, Johnson called himself a Democrat, largely because the machine in office was Republican. Howe, partner in the corporation practice of the martyr Garfield's sons, was naturally a member of their party. But he was drawn irresistibly to the attractive personality of his nominal opponent.

Johnson was something new in American politics, a converted robber baron of business who had turned to public service rather than private charity to relieve his conscience. In the buccaneering 'eighties he had drawn a fortune from one of the most piratical of fields, local rapid transit. As a dealer in franchises and an operator of financially topheavy street railways whose profits were as large as their service was bad, he had no superior. He might have left many millions of dollars and a hastily fumigated reputation for philanthropy if he had not at the height of his career met Henry George, the single-taxer. Johnson, the plunderer, listened to George's keen thrusts at an economic system that was too much taken for granted. He read, studied, thought and from the meditative cocoon burst Tom Johnson, reformer.

He was a far more dangerous opponent than his teacher or the muckrakers or cloistered theorists who dallied with the same principles. He knew exactly what he was talking about when he attacked the evils of municipal government, for he could speak of them in the first person singular. He had bribed common councils; he had engaged in the intricate process of over-capitalization; he knew all the tricks because he had used them. Now he offered to give Cleveland the benefit of that experience, to operate public utilities owned by the city in the interest of the people.

Howe, who was running on a platform of what he still called a "business administration," was soon in the Johnson camp. He was amused because some of the heelers in his ward, whom he had been denouncing vigorously, were quietly working on his behalf. Apparently they did not realize what he stood for, he told himself, and with their professional help he was elected.

One of his first acts as a public man was to introduce, at Mayor Johnson's request, a bill to enfranchise a natural gas company that offered to supply the city at 30 cents per 1,000 cubic feet. Cleveland was then paying 80 cents to a company that manufactured gas from coal. Obviously the new offer was a fine thing, and Howe in his innocence did not anticipate any objections at all.

It was a time of surprises. The first came when a delegation of coal merchants visited him to ask withdrawal of his bill because it would ruin the trade of those who sold fuel to the artificial gas company. Howe explained patiently that his measure would benefit all the 300,000 people of Cleveland. He was genuinely shocked when his visitors brushed aside this argument, insisting that the important point was their private gain.

They were not, Howe observed, unique. The artificial gas company advanced as a serious objection to ruin the fact that it had an investment of $12,000,000. Howe did not think it stood a chance against the plain advantage of the city, but to his amazement many of the "reform" councilmen, the upright citizens committed to economy, efficiency and honesty, were against him. They defeated his measure by a single vote.

Then, in a turmoil of angry members, one arose to reveal the fact that a well-known physician had offered him $2,000 to vote against the natural gas franchise. It was too much for Howe. He had supposed that the giving of bribes was confined to saloon keepers, licensed thieves and paving contractors. But here was evidence that nicer folk stooped to it too. In a white heat of indignation that still permitted him to note he was the only person present thus aroused, he delivered himself of the opinion that the man who paid for a vote was as low a specimen of humanity as he who received the money. There must have been some who agreed with him, for on a second roll call his bill passed.

The reformer's elation was short-lived. As he walked out of the council hall, two known grafters, members of what Cleveland called "the notorious thirteen," blood brothers to New York's "Forty Thieves," accused him of being a double-crosser. They were corrupt and dishonest but a traitor was to them loathesome. Howe also valued loyalty and resented the gibe. Whereupon the grafters pointed out just what he was betraying, and they found it hard to believe he did not know it. By the irony of politics Councilman Howe had been nominated, financed and elected by the artificial gas company. Its officers had labored under the misapprehension that a partner of the young Garfields must be one of the "best people."

Howe's disillusionment was still incomplete. Next day a committee of bankers and merchants called upon him, more in sorrow than anger, to point out the error of his ways and reclaim him to the principle of a "business administration" for municipal affairs. One of them was an individual for whom Howe had always entertained profound respect, a member of the Charity Organization Society and "identified with almost every good movement in the city." This gentleman explained that he and his friends had been pained by Howe's intemperate remarks about men who paid bribes.

Public utilities, the charitable one asserted, were constantly being victimized by unscrupulous politicians. Without bribery it was impossible for the companies to get "the things they ought to have." Howe thought it over and saw that they were right. It was difficult to distinguish blackmail from bribery and no doubt, as his friends said, corruption was inseparable from the private operation of utilities. With that argument his visitors succeeded in creating one more advocate of municipal ownership.

At this stage of his career, Howe put grafters and respectables on a joint level of honesty. Other campaigns led him to modify his views still further. Leaving the municipal ownership fight to Johnson, he undertook a more congenial crusade. Alleviation of slum congestion, more parks and playgrounds, new schools, public baths and dance halls, these were the reforms on which he set his heart. Almost to a man, the best people of Cleveland sprang to arms against him.

The erection of public baths was arrant Socialism, squealed the Chamber of Commerce. Howe's campaign to remove "Keep off the grass" signs in the parks and let the people get some real fun out of them, was termed vandalism. The conception of lawns as purely ornamental was cherished by good citizens who could remember that red

revolution in the shape of Coxey's army of the unemployed
had been squelched by the happy device of arresting the
leaders for walking on the grass.

In the course of years, Howe won most of his points,
without converting the well-to-do. "Reform" councilmen
voted tirelessly against their former colleague but Howe,
like Lindsey, found support among the despised grafters.
The harsh things he had said about "the notorious thirteen"
never prompted them to retaliate against his pet measures.
The ward heelers and the bribe takers were with him.

"They knew better than I did where the children lived
and where they had to play," he wrote. "On measures where
there was no money moving they voted right; while repre-
sensatives of the east-end [respectable] wards often voted
wrong."

It came down to this: The machine leaders had to be paid
to defeat municipal ownership, labor legislation, adequate
health regulations, better schools, new parks, decent hous-
ing, aid to the needy, "the more abundant life." Business
men in politics were eager without bribes to oppose anything that raised taxes or threatened private enterprise.
They wanted to stop paying graft, but keep all the favors
graft bought. They demonstrated that the perennial demand for business methods in government was as logical as
a cry that penitentiaries ought to be run by criminals.

3

Whenever the people could be brought to understand the
absurdity, genuine reforms were promptly instituted. This
happened after one of the muckrakers decided to put his
studies of the stockyards into a novel. A reading public
accustomed to nothing saltier than the fiction of Mrs.
E. D. E. N. Southworth reacted to Upton Sinclair's "The
Jungle" with a cry of horror such as "Uncle Tom's Cabin"
had drawn from a previous generation.

It could not be ignored. In May, 1906, the Senate passed a bill to establish Federal inspection of packing houses. The men who ruled the stockyards disclaimed any improper influence in Congress, but they kept the measure from coming to a vote in the House until Roosevelt, who was not a candidate for re-election, permitted himself the luxury of wielding his "big stick." He was a practical politician as well as an occasional crusader, and he knew better than to waste his time arguing with the people's Representatives. He went over their heads to inform the stubborn packers that further lurid details, sufficient to ruin their already crippled export trade, would be made public unless the agents of the beef trust in Congress dropped their obstructive tactics. Orders went out from Chicago, and opposition to the inspection bill collapsed.

Forced thus to yield some of the profits of the graft that enabled them to dictate to Representatives, the masters of cash and credit assailed the politicians as subversive foes of honest private enterprise. But they were not so angry as to seek a divorce from government. For, while minor inroads on the sacredness of private property were being made in inspection bills, the same politicians who were guilty of them were allowing quite unregulated companies to seize control of two new forces that were to remake the world.

Water power and fuel oil were advancing to rival older industries, and as the lusty young giants sprang into ungainly growth, observant men saw that the looters of previous generations had overlooked something. Oil was generally found under land that had always been considered so worthless that some of it had been left to the Indians, and the best power sites are hardly the most desirable farms. Consequently at this late stage, the government unexpectedly had some assets, and neither Republican nor Democratic politicians had been as thoroughly imbued with socialistic principles as the more rugged individualists among the business leaders affected to believe. Power sites were handed over without thought or question to men who promised to bring electricity into homes and shops.

ιDespite immense popular agitation against monopolies that already existed, there was little effective effort to establish control over the new monopolies that were being created. This was not altogether the fault of the monopolists, for as early as 1898, Samuel Insull was urging "conditions of public control, requiring all charges for services fixed by public bodies to be based on cost plus a reasonable profit." Coupled with the monopoly Insull was also demanding in a field still fretted by competition, such carefully restricted regulation would have hampered him not at all and would, he hoped, pacify consumers.

He failed at that time to arouse any enthusiasm for a dull, theoretical problem. Just as the Civil War generation had clamored for railroads, regardless of how they were financed or managed, so their children were fascinated by the fairy tale quality of the new power, which seemed to offer every poor Aladdin in the country a plentiful supply of magic slaves.

Some of the pitfalls that had trapped an earlier public were avoided, however, thanks to the fact that a few of the guides were both alert and honest, qualities that had been completely divorced in those eager slavery disputants who had approved the transportation grabs. In 1903, for example, Congress passed a bill presenting to private interests all rights to the exploitation of Muscle Shoals, Alabama. This was in the tradition of the "golden age," but Roosevelt vetoed the measure, thereby preserving an issue for a later generation to fight about. He explained that he would prefer to see Congress adopt a policy "under which these invaluable rights will not be practically given away."

The oil men were in a more favorable position than their fellow entrepreneurs of power, for they could follow the trail blazed by Rockefeller. The manner in which he had enforced his monopoly by fraud, corruption, violence and intimidation had been spread before the public by muckrakers and courts. Students of Standard Oil methods could see plainly that control of distribution was the secret of success; production might then be left to such free competition as was possible for rivals who had no means of their own of getting the product to market.

The sudden expansion that came with the gasoline motor was too rapid even for Standard to cope with, and new interests had to be admitted to the field. Among them were the Pittsburgh Mellons. "Uncle Andy" and a few other "independents" soon reached an amicable agreement with the older colossus. Prices were to be fixed by Standard and competition was kept down by judicious control of the pipe lines through which "black gold" went to the sea and which were too expensive for any genuine independent to build.

The share that corruption of public officials played in making the rules of the game was admirably exemplified when the Mellons marked the new era of 1900 by entering the oil business in a large way. The greatest gusher up to that time, the Spindletop dome, brought in to the accompaniment of fire and fury on the Texas plains, fell into the hands of one Colonel Guffey, a veteran oil speculator and picturesque old ruffian who dressed and talked and acted like a Western gambler of the cinema that was to be. He went to the Mellons to finance the almost uncontrollable burst of oil, and in its early days he was allowed to head the company that became Gulf Oil. The Colonel complained years afterwards that "they throwed me out," but until then he was a big man in Texas and he had learned politics fighting Matt Quay in Pennsylvania.

"Governor Hogg [of Texas] was a power down there and I wanted him on my side," Guffey related.

The recruit was enlisted by giving to a syndicate of which he was a member the lease that developed into the Texas Oil Company. It was a princely favor, and the Texas legislature refrained from threatened interference with leases, operations, pipe line control and other trifles. Gulf Oil, thanks to that forbearance, was launched on a course that was to lead to such an intricate maze of profitable subsidiaries that in a quarter of a century W. L. Mellon would be unable to say just what positions he held in the various offshoots. He knew he was president of Gulf Oil, the parent holding concern, but as for Gulf Production Company, "My position . . . I think, is chairman. I am not sure. . . ."

The "hands off policy" which permitted a few corporations to dominate the oil fields also opened the gate to wild cat speculation and swindles surpassing anything known in the most lush period of railroad financing. That policy, however, did not come naturally to men in public office. Governor Hogg, for example, was a conservationist, a foe of monopoly and a liberal until he joined an oil syndicate. His legislature's first reaction was to establish strict supervision over new companies. But they were all reasonable men. Soon it was again impossible to tell whether the statesmen were blackmailing the industrialists or being bribed by them. The distinction, with regard to the ultimate disposal of petroleum and power, is academic.

4

The sorry drama of a plundered public domain was not revived in its older, cruder version because the roles that had been played of old by the grafters of land office and homestead bureau could no longer be filled. Vast stretches of patronage had been removed from the grasp of rival partisans, and security of tenure enabled an army of jobholders to create a precedent for efficient service. They were not the public servants whose work made the greatest stir in the world, but they were tangible evidence to support optimists who think mankind capable of self-improvement. Comparison between the average appointee of Andrew Jackson's day and his successor, who kept his post even when Wilson came to power at the head of a hungry party that had fed for sixteen years in the wilderness, underscores the change.

To maintain the system of honest graft by which alone the newly important national resources could be turned over to private exploitation, the exploiters were obliged to look higher than permanent jobholders. If they looked to the Senate, they could feel at home. Although plunderers like Samuel Swartwout had given way to a Samuel Stratton, who created the Bureau of Standards and raised it to a level of efficiency that few industrial organizations can match, Webster and Clay had been succeeded by Henry Cabot Lodge and Boies Penrose. As one studies the careers of those four men, time stands still.

Lodge, the "scholar in politics," the upright and righteous, was credited with being unbelievably learned in the history of his country, but he was well satisfied with the morals of the political system he adorned. In 1915, eulogizing Charles Francis Adams, Jr., who had just died, he referred approvingly to that gentleman's share in the exposure of Erie corruption half a century before. Said the Senator:

"It is difficult now even to imagine such a situation."

Adams himself, brushing aside mere forms and moral sentiments, had in 1912 offered a more reasoned analysis.

"As to the so-called transportation abuses," he wrote, "if any real progress to more satisfactory conditions has been made, a knowledge of the fact has not reached me."

Lodge, however, could ignore facts as easily as Webster. The scholar was the true successor of the orator as representative of Massachusetts mill and bank. He had parted with Roosevelt, the friend of his youth, on the issue of loyalty to the men who own the country, and those "Dear Theodore"-"Dear Cabot" letters no longer flitted back and forth to illumine their era for posterity. Untroubled by the financial worries that had dogged Webster, the cultivated Lodge was personally incorruptible, but his true likeness to the Voice as the servant of industry may be measured by the fact that he would have been proud to have his name linked with that of the godlike Daniel. He was as active, too, in lending government support to private enterprise.

Boies Penrose was altogether a different sort of animal, a living refutation of the theory that what this country needs is a leisure class devoted to politics. A Philadelphia aristocrat of rather more than life size, he entered on a public career as a reformer by way of Harvard. That about completed his resemblance to Theodore Roosevelt. A taste for honest debauchery, a sense of humor and a natural cynicism drove Penrose from the ranks of the just into the arms of Matt Quay. He was soon that astute corruptionist's chief lieutenant and destined heir to the machine built by old Cameron.

Sufficiently wealthy to satisfy the desires of his Gargantuan appetites, he was not greedy for money. He did relish the appearance of power, and he towered over the Pennsylvania ward heelers as much mentally as he did physically. He liked to refer in pseudo-Nietzschean fashion to the "natural law" that superior intellect ought to rule the world, and he gave himself as an example of the superiority. A jackal among rats, he thought of himself as a giant among men. He must have found that attitude hard to maintain on his visits to Smithfield Street, Pittsburgh, where he was as deferential as his nature permitted in the presence of real power embodied in the mild, wispy Andrew Mellon.

Throughout the storms and passions of the long struggle for the regulation of big business, Lodge and Penrose scorned to pay lipservice to the aspirations of the multitude. They remained unmoved as, after some oddly progressive gestures from the conservative Taft administration, Roosevelt's "New Nationalism" gave way to Wilson's "New Freedom." They looked with contempt on the host of reforms—income tax, Federal Reserve system, labor legislation, rate fixing—and they saw to it that in the execution of these measures the donors of campaign funds were protected.

After all, their political machines still functioned. Regulation might be imposed, but the apparatus of regulation remained in safe hands. The influence of bosses of the Penrose stripe assured nomination of corporation executives or corporation lawyers to most of the new commissions, so that the effect of reforms was to strengthen industry for new opportunities, which was of course one of reform's avowed aims. It was much more carefully fostered than the other avowed aims, such as promotion of the general well-being.

Harmony between the discordant objectives of plunderers and conservationists was achieved so naturally, so painlessly, that there ought to be a prettier word than graft to describe the process.

XVII

OVER HERE

1

Leaders of american capitalism still muttered that regulation outraged basic principles of liberty, yet they developed increased efficiency through the stricter organization imposed upon them. Wall Street sneered at "political banking" but the Federal Reserve system achieved partial stabilization of credit. Financiers lamented the old freedom, while judicial interpretation of the anti-trust laws tended toward the theory that mere size is unassailable, a ruling established firmly when United States Steel won a dissolution suit.

As Europe's imperialist and commercial rivalries sent her hurtling down the road to war, benevolent supervision by the Roosevelt-Wilson commissions eliminated some of the worst abuses of unfettered American competition and strengthened the industrial fabric of the United States for the burden of world power. The supervision it owed to the muckrakers, the benevolence to the grafters.

The fact that the regulatory machinery was for the most part not operated on the old lubricant of bribery is evidence that it was in harmony with the economic needs of the time and could use the lighter oil of honest graft. Had the new government bodies been the hindrance that bankers and factory managers called them, the commissions could not have survived so easily, for it was still no part of the nation's philosophy that profits should be harmed. Another factor in the higher level of honesty was that Federal spending was comparatively small; only occasionally, as in the appropriations for river and harbor improvements or new post offices, were bribes worth the giving. Cities and states were the organizations that spent enough on public works and services to make graft remunerative, and in this field the New Freedom wrought little better than the New Nationalism. The muckrakers had convinced themselves but not the people that local administrations were corrupt because it paid certain businesses to keep them that way. So little impression had the sensational books and articles of two decades made upon the public that many well-intentioned folk still thought it a pity the heirs of tainted fortunes—young Goulds, Vanderbilts and Astors with their social point of view conditioned, by their economic interests—did not volunteer in the service of municipalities in sufficient numbers to oust the bosses.

Gentlemen, it was said, did not care to risk their good names amid the abuse and suspicion of dirty politics. A cynical attitude toward dirty politics was proper for men who wished to be thought sophisticated. Yet without that leaven of dirt, the clash between government and business over Wilson's reforms would have been so greatly intensified that American industrialists could not have won so swiftly or so surely the dominating world position that was soon to be theirs.

In the summer of 1914 that future was by no means as obvious as it seems in retrospect. The futile diplomacy that preceded the outbreak of hostilities led to gloomy forebodings. When the armies began to move, the shock of war was reflected in instant slackening of business activity in the United States.

But slowly, while national attention was fairly well divided between the German troops seeking to break through to Paris and a Boston baseball team rising from last place to a championship, the country began to hear of war profits. Industrial shares crawled upwards in the stock tables. Fac-

tories worked overtime to keep up with the demands of
Death, who was working twenty-four hours a day. The over-
weening confidence of a boom period infected the usually
timid masters of capital. Rush orders had to be filled for
nations too busy fighting to bother about the cost, and impatiently the beneficiaries brushed aside the Secretary of
State's pronouncement a few days after war began that any
loans to a belligerent would be "inconsistent with the spirit
of true neutrality."

That Secretary was William Jennings Bryan, who held
fewer terrors for Wall Street than in 1896. Successful men
could not take over-seriously the dicta of one who had been
beaten as often as Bryan. Beauty and power had departed
from the orator with his hair, and Easterners who had once
clutched their check books at the mere mention of his name
now mocked his old-fashioned views of morality and life.
When he told financiers they ought not to make money out
of the war, they shrugged and turned to other officials, for
even in a Democratic administration there were some who
recognized the call of business. Able Wilsonian lawyers
found a wealth of precedent and legal lore to support the
argument that loans were in complete accord with neutrality.

A ruling to that effect, in spite of Bryan, was followed by
a lush scramble. In three years J. P. Morgan & Co., agents
for the British government, placed war orders of $3,000,000,-
000 and in arranging the credit to carry them took a profit
of $30,000,000. Billions of dollars of the American securi-
ties held in Europe were resold here. As the Allies became
increasingly dependent upon supplies from this country, the
center of world finance and industry moved across the Atlantic to New York.

The spokesmen of government watched the change with
approval. They were pleased that the stock market reported
steady advances. Factories hummed, and as the supply of
raw labor from Europe ended abruptly, wages rose too.
Almost as much as the mass slaughter in France, it became

the wonder of the world that American workmen (some of them) were achieving decency and comfort and a few luxuries.

It seemed a triumphant refutation of Bryan's notions of neutrality, yet the new prosperity was leading the country unconsciously on to war. In effect the investors had gambled on an Allied victory. As the deadlock on the Western Front tightened, business grew apprehensive. Bryan had been right; it was not possible to divorce public policy from economic facts. Our enterprising, adventurous capitalism had persuaded the government to permit evasion of the overwhelming sentiment in favor of real neutrality. The business executives had won commercial supremacy for the nation. It was up to the people to protect the gains.

Bankers did not ask for war in so many words, of course. They only wished to tread the alluring road that led to it. The second J. P. Morgan, lacking his father's fierceness, although resembling him in many other respects, headed the financial community in pyramiding Allied commitments, but he was not the bloodthirsty ogre that his enemies pictured. There can be no doubting his sincerity when, accused of driving the nation into the shambles for the protection of his bank and his clients, the gruff, silent, aloof man cried:

"Do you suppose I wanted to get my own son into the war? He went though."

It appeared the lesser evil. Peace, if accompanied by Allied defeat, would involve the ruin of America's place in the sun of prosperity. There was no turning back, and a wave of preparedness propaganda was the first acknowledgment of a determination to defend war profits. The motives, as usual, were mixed. The dominating one, also as usual, was seldom voiced but powerfully affected the thought of great numbers of citizens who were quite sure they were guided by abstract principle only.

As in the war with Spain, an idealistic slogan was found.

In 1898 Americans burned with a desire to free Cuba. In 1917 their sons would be satisfied with nothing short of freeing the whole world. In 1898 stories of Spanish atrocities and the explosion on the *Maine* had been used to stir public opinion, although a declaration of war did not follow for months. In 1917 fictitious German atrocities and the torpedoing of the *Lusitania* fulfilled the same function. These wrongs and a determination to avenge them could be trumpeted abroad, and played decisive roles. Other reasons for participation in the war were not allowed such wide circulation lest they cool the hot lust for battle.

There was, for example, the long cable that on March 5, 1917, the day after he had been inaugurated for his second term, Wilson received from Ambassador Walter Hines Page in England. Mr. Page was a great Allied sympathizer, rather more useful to the country in which he was serving than to the country he represented. He had received flattering attentions in London and was an ardent interventionist. His scholarly mind, however, was not altogether fixed upon the cause of saving British civilization. His cable was a cold, reasoned argument that had nothing to do with democracy, self-determination of oppressed peoples, the Teutonic menace to Shakespeare and Chaucer or our moral debt to France. Page was concerned with other debts.

He began by pointing out that Great Britain had reached the end of the capital which for nearly three years had financed the Allies. Further purchases in the United States could only be paid for by shipping gold, which domestic needs and the German submarine campaign prevented. Page had been informed that in this crisis "trans-Atlantic trade will practically come to an end. The result of such a stoppage will be a panic in the United States." The only solution Page could see was Federal government credit to finance boundless purchases.

"Of course we cannot extend such a credit unless we go to war with Germany," he added with calm simplicity.

With the enthusiasm of a partisan he outlined a rosy prospect for American business, if not for American lives, should this procedure be adopted.

"We could keep on with our trade and increase it, till the war ends," he predicted, "and after the war Europe would purchase food and enormous supply of materials with which to re-equip her industries. We should thus reap the profit of an uninterrupted and perhaps an enlarging trade over a number of years and we should hold their securities in payment."

Even an administration that professed a belief in open covenants openly arrived at could not publish such a communication, although Wilson recognized the truth of his Ambassador's analysis. The eager dealers in credit had blown the war prosperity bubble all by themselves, or perhaps some too pliable members of his government had supplied a little air too. But the whole country would suffer with these men if the bubble were to be pricked. Three days after reading Page's message, which of course was only one among many similar influences, the President called Congress to a special session to declare war.

2

As the motives that had led the nation into the mess were said to be nobler than those that had prompted any previous national effort, so the conduct of the war was to be without blemishes that had dimmed the glory of earlier crusades. Under the leadership of the man who had taught Reformer Howe that a nation's politics should be run by its gentlemen, the people of the United States would unite in one common, altruistic, heroic, altogether splendid adventure. The youth would give his life, the capitalist his time and money, the scientist his learning, the business man his organizing ability.

The vast machinery of a modern industrial state clearing

decks for a fight lumbered heavily into action and patriotism was to keep all energies directed to the one ideal for which, Mr. Wilson informed the world in his stately prose, America did battle. Patriotism had never been adequate to this purpose before, but in 1917 mankind lived in the New Freedom.

There was even the legend of a new chivalry arisen from the bloody filth of Flanders where burrowing armies watched children recently snatched from schools engaging in single combat among the clouds. The world thrilled to the spectacular duels of these knights of the machine age flashing in the sun or perhaps plunging darkly to earth in a streak of blackish smoke. The United States, proud of its unsurpassed mechanical progress, doubted not that American airmen in American planes would soon be making the heavens unsafe for Germans.

This ideal doubtless animated a group of leading citizens of Dayton, Ohio, who on April 9, 1917, three days after the declaration of war, incorporated the Dayton-Wright Company. Its aims were to build a plant, hire technicians, produce fighting planes for the army. The best known of its five incorporators was Orville Wright, pioneer of flying. The only other of whom the country knew anything was Edward A. Deeds, around whom the aerial phase of war preparation was to center.

Deeds had achieved his reputation as an official of the National Cash Register Company. This enterprising firm had captured its market by such ruthless competition that in 1912 Deeds and some of his associates were convicted of violating the Sherman Anti-Trust Act. Criminal prosecutions under this statute were sufficiently rare to create wide interest in the case. None of the defendants served sentences, since the verdict was upset in the Circuit Court of Appeals, but Deeds's name was remembered.

In 1917 he was a fine example of the efficient executive with the square jaw and regular features magazine readers had learned to associate with the type. Forty-three years old, he had played a considerable part in the industrial growth of Dayton. His thin-lipped mouth spoke authoritatively; his eyes were steady behind rimless glasses as he made important decisions; his thinning hair revealed how well shaped was his head. He knew nothing about airplanes, but he was credited with other qualities fitting him to head the Dayton-Wright Company.

He did not become an officer of the firm. Patriotism called, and a few days after incorporation papers were drafted he was on his way to Washington, one of the army of busy fellows who offered their services at a dollar a year—and up—and were hailed by the press as sacrificing private interests for the good of the country. Doubtless this was not Deeds's understanding. He was not likely to suppose that his interests and those of the nation could clash. He proposed to build up a young but essential industry, and his own prosperity would be no more than an indication of the benefits he had conferred upon his fellow citizens.

Nevertheless, there were signs of a faint misgiving as to the interpretation that might be put upon his actions. Some of his earliest dealings were accompanied by strict injunctions to avoid publicity, although they were hardly military secrets. No less an authority than Charles Evans Hughes was later to term at least part of his operations as "neither candid nor truthful."

Deeds, in the midst of the turmoil of a Washington preparing for its stupendous war task, found time to keep in touch with folks at home. In April he was the first civilian member of the Munitions Standards Board, was soon transferred to the Aircraft Production Board and then placed at the head of its production division, the most important cog in the machine. More than a billion and a half dollars were appropriated for the aviation program, and in the sheer intoxication of dealing with nearly astronomical figures, the business patriots gave free rein to their fancies. Of Mr. Deeds his chief, Secretary of War Newton D. Baker, said:

"His imagination peopled the sky with airplanes."

The need, however, was for something more substantial, and various optimistic statements without any basis in fact emerged from the Deeds offices. After August, 1917, they were issued over a signature that might be expected to reassure a warlike people, for in that month the man of imagination was commissioned a colonel, and then "Mr. Deeds went to town." The spending of a billion and a half made no appreciable addition to the sky population in the war zone, it is true, but on March 27, 1918, an American-built plane was actually in France. It was the only one there, and Senator Thomas inquired bitterly:

"How did that one get away?"

Nearly five months later, on Aug. 12, 1918, the first American-made planes to fly over the German lines—eighteen of them—took off for their initial flight. A group of Senate investigators traced these "disappointing results" to the fact "that the airplane program was largely in the control of the great automobile and other manufacturers who were ignorant of the practical problems."

Colonel Deeds had not really been as impractical as the Senators seemed to think. Almost as soon as he reached Washington he had been active in plans for a flying field at Dayton. Langley Field was already there and more than $2,000,000 had been spent on it. There was, however, another tract of land, McCook Field, and of this Edward A. Deeds was the owner. He was also part owner of New Field and some of the land had been acquired by his former business associates on telegraphic advice from their colleague in the capital.

The Colonel's conduct, deplored by Hughes, was considered quite correct by Baker, for Deeds had meticulously disposed of all interests that would enter into his dealings on behalf of the government. His land, his shares in the Dayton-Wright, Delco and Dayton Metal Products companies had been transferred—to his partners and his wife. The stock transfer to Mrs. Deeds, made on Oct. 13, 1917, was dated back to Aug. 28th, the day her husband entered the army. His associates bought his Dayton Metal Products stock with notes for $500,000 which, Hughes reported more than a year later, "are overdue and unpaid save to a small extent." It was in response to Deeds's insistence that these transfers were bona fide sales that Hughes used the expression "neither candid nor truthful."

McCook and New Fields were bought, including about twice as much land as the government needed, and in Dayton factories buzzed with war orders. The airplane company with which the Colonel was no longer officially connected got its share. The Aircraft Board recommended in June that Dayton-Wright get a contract, and it was so drawn that the firm stood to win profits of $6,350,000 on a $500,000 investment. Hughes estimated that under no circumstances could it gain less than $3,500,000, not counting "generous salaries" —$30,000 and $35,000 from the one subsidiary alone—paid to each of Deeds's former partners.

Officers of the company apparently had been too busy with these negotiations to prepare their plant for production. The $500,000 capital was not paid up until December. Meanwhile Deeds was sending to the private address of one of his old partners confidential information on departmental regulations about contracts. As soon as the stockholders had paid their $500,000, the government furnished $1,000,000 and promised $1,500,000 more to speed the work of equipping the plant. At this time the Witteman-Loomis Company of New Jersey, which had been making planes for years, was unable to get any army orders at all. Nor were all the ambitious, unbuilt factories as lucky as that in Dayton.

"Companies assured of capital and factory space have

been denied contracts because they were not going concerns," the Senate investigators reported, "while other companies in similar conditions have received contracts."

The reason for this was geographical. Nearly all the civilian personnel of the Aircraft Board hailed from Detroit or Dayton. Most of the orders went to home town boys. Detroit's automobile factories and trained labor supply explained in part the favor shown to that city, but the argument did not apply so well to Dayton. There the only noticeable advantage was Orville Wright, and it might have been easier to move him than to move a factory and corps of workmen.

Those who thought the scarcity of American planes over the fighting lines revealed the waste of a billion and a half failed to give credit to the Aircraft Board's real achievement. The Liberty motor, developed under its supervision at government expense but remaining the property of private manufacturers, represented a notable advance in aviation. It was unsuited to the most pressing military needs, being too heavy for combat planes, but no one doubted it would be an extremely valuable asset in commercial flying. It had first call over the ships the army had to fly.

When Hughes completed his study of the Aircraft Board's activities, he was in no doubt as to where he should place the blame. He bluntly recommended the court martial of Colonel Deeds for "false and misleading information" regarding production of planes and for advising his former associates on deals with the Colonel's department.

"This highly improper conduct demands the attention of the military authorities," the future Chief Justice affirmed.

The war had been won by then without much aerial assistance from the United States, and Baker gave the Hughes report the attention he thought it merited. He held an inquiry of his own and decided to do nothing. After all, Colonel Deeds was soon to retire into civil life, where he would be welcomed back to National Cash Register as president

at $100,000 a year. The imagination that had peopled the
sky with airplanes could devote itself to less adventurous
pursuits.

3

Visions were no monopoly of the Aircraft Board. There
had been dreams of tanks, the weapon even newer than
planes, and a country so eminently machine-minded as the
United States was expected to show the world something
stupendous in the way of mechanized warfare. Actually the
A.E.F. suffered from a shortage of the mobile monsters,
having only what the British and French could spare, since
the first American product did not reach France until nine
days after the armistice was signed.

Domestic manufacturers also did well by not making
shells and artillery. The Ordnance Department's war bill of
$5,879,508,656.02 included $827,450,214 on a group of contracts which netted exactly 20,000 shells for the army, and
$478,828,345 for forty-eight 4.7 inch guns, twenty-four 8 inch
howitzers and thirty-nine anti-aircraft trucks.

Of course these scant results of tremendous effort and expense were due in large part to the unprecedented demands
of an unprepared nation arming for battle without any
qualms about the cost, but it was odd how seldom private
business shared the losses. The confusion and waste were
generally laid to the politicians; the business men, at least,
credited successful achievements to the fine enthusiasm with
which they threw themselves into the government's work.
Of that enthusiasm Deeds was only one example among
many.

Whether he and his colleagues realized it or not, the fact
was that a war was almost as effective as a panic in bringing
on consolidation, co-ordination and centralization of industry. In the emergency, measures of unprecedented government control were adopted, far surpassing anything the
muckrakers had dared hope for, but the dictatorship was

in the safe hands of business leaders, who as government men decided what would be a fair price for themselves as industrialists to charge for their wares. There was no complaint from them as their cherished principles of liberty went by the boards.

The Wilsonian reforms went too, laid aside "for the duration." If the country as a whole found little to admire in the combination, it may have been because, as a House Committee pointed out at the end of the war, the dollar-a-year men had organized whole industries in violation of the anti-trust laws.

"Competition was at an end," said the Committee.

That seemed to the legislators a great evil, but the plea of national necessity was accepted. The logical conclusion that if the trust form of organization proved efficient in war it ought to work equally well in peace did not commend itself to a public that had lived through the effects, described by the Representatives as "heartless profiteering." Such men as Bernard M. Baruch, who as chairman of the War Industries Board had unrivaled opportunities for observation as well as for assisting in the work, dissented.

"We are on the threshold of a new era," he reported to the President when his work was done. "During the whole course of administration a single flagrant instance of abuse by an American business man of the confidence of his Government is yet to be discovered."

This statement emanated from a capitalist who was as disinterested as a man of his wealth could be, who owed allegiance to no combination or industry since he had achieved riches by independent market operations. Yet he had himself found steel plates selling at 16 cents a pound at the time the United States entered the war and had forced the price down to 3½ cents, which still yielded a handsome profit. Mellon's aluminum monopoly was getting about 60 cents a pound in April, 1917, but agreed to the demand of Baruch's board that it accept 32 cents f.o.b. The stuff cost 17½ cents to make.

Baruch was justified in thinking there was such a thing as progress. In 1861 the entire military and civil administration had been shot through with bribery to provide war profits. In 1898 the politicians, loyal servants of industry, gave those favors away. In 1917 business simply moved in and took over the departments conducting the war on the "home front."

The full effects of this comparatively subtle graft were not apparent until after the armistice. Then the scramble for profit, unchecked by patriotic scruples or regard for appearances and sharpened by realization that the end of war contracts was at hand, grew so hectic that Baruch might have been tempted to revise his opinion. But Baruch's board had been hastily disbanded and one of the most effective emergency controls "let go" just when the expert services of its personnel might have mitigated the greed of those who were taking a last advantage of a rich uncle.

It was estimated the United States entered into 100,000 contracts during the nineteen months of hostilities, and thousands were unfilled on Nov. 11, 1918. Obviously they could not be canceled out of hand; the resultant panic would have been worse than war. Washington had to settle on a basis that would interrupt the transition to peace-time production as little as possible.

How the dollar-a-year men interpreted this is best followed in a study of the "cost-plus" contracts. In thousands of cases the administration had been unable to set a price and therefore agreed to pay all costs plus a percentage for the contractor's profit. The costs of ships, munitions, supplies of all kinds, were of course raised to the highest possible level and hundreds of millions were deliberately wasted so that tens of millions might be collected in profits.

A group of Representatives who studied a vast mess of corruption in the huge ordnance budget plodded through heaps of testimony to the conclusion that the powder plant built at Nitro, W. Va., represented "the greatest waste of material and labor that this subcommittee has had the opportunity to observe."

This job had been let on a cost-plus contract to the Thompson-Starrett Company of New York, one of the foremost firms in its field. It built an enormous plant and a small city at Nitro—unfortunately not in time to produce powder for war purposes—and the members of Congress who studied the feat found that the cost to the government had been about $60,000,000, including the price of expensive lumber used to burn other unwanted materials and a scale of wages so high that it provoked sarcastic comment. These wages had been paid to hundreds of syphilitic, epileptic and insane workers who were brought to Nitro apparently for the sole purpose of treating them in the excellent company hospital. It was a noble philanthropy, but the contractors collected their percentage of profit on the cost of hospitalization, medical fees and drugs as well as on the wages.

After the armistice the company recruited several carloads of workmen in Montana, paid all their expenses to West Virginia, kept them less than a week and shipped them back again. And of course the "plus" part of the contract was applied. In 1919 the whole $60,000,000 Nitro plant, together with nearly $10,000,000 worth of equipment, was sold for $8,551,000.

The story of Nitro was repeated in part at Old Hickory, Tenn., where the Du Ponts built another powder plant at a cost, to the government, of $90,000,000. E. C. Morse, a shrewd business man who was Director of Sales in the War Department, sold Old Hickory for $3,500,000, resigned his office and admitted to the House committee that he was considering a tender of the general managership of the company that bought the plant from him. After his experience on the witness stand, however, he decided to capitalize his war connections in other fields.

Mr. Morse, Mr. Deeds, the rest of the temporary army officers and dollar-a-year men, were well pleased with the results of their crusade for democracy. They had won the war and expanded the industrial-financial system of the country to fabulous dimensions. That their methods were akin to Plunkitt's honest graft was, perhaps, hidden from them. Only if a government not composed of industrial leaders should attempt to copy their war-time setup would they see in it a corrupt and vicious machine.

4

In the exultation of victory and disappointment over the peace, the most valuable administrative lesson of the war was largely missed. This was the plain fact that security of tenure under civil service combined with responsibility exercised in the revealing glare of a national spotlight worked powerfully for honesty. Eighteen thousand new millionaires were produced by the war, the income tax figures showed, but none of them were among the permanent Federal servants.

The way these people handled enormous public funds without any taint of graft was unique in American history. So unique that for a long time it was hard to believe. Yet the Senate committee that investigated Baker's department as the war closed produced no story of systematic corruption. Even the Republican administration that moved in on the ruins of the New Freedom was unable to reverse the verdict. A Bureau of War Transactions was established in the Department of Justice, but the civil service emerged from its ordeal there in surprising contrast to the money-grubbing patriots hastily recruited at a dollar a year or a colonel's pay. Some petty theft, some suspicious approval of sub-standard articles by a few inspectors, were uncovered, but the Attorney General announced:

"I found no reason to bring indictments against a single one whom I was urged to prosecute."

That Attorney General, to be sure, was Harry M. Daugherty, but an exhaustive examination of his conduct in office brought out no evidence to indicate that in these cases his opinion was based on anything but the facts.

The contrast between the permanent jobholders and their temporary colleagues was plain and understandable. Civil service had developed a genuine standard of conduct in the departments, a standard that was noticeably lacking in private business. The United States had achieved a bureaucracy, with all the qualities of such an organization. Private enterprise remained an amoral field in which every man's ethics were his own. The civil servant who accepted part of a salesman's commission, received gifts and market tips in exchange for information, borrowed from men who did business with his department, knew that his acts were dishonest. The same practices were so common in the world of commerce that individuals who refrained from them were in many instances rather pitied than admired.

General acceptance of this variation was indicated in popular verdicts, those of juries as well as the more nebulous pronouncements of public opinion, on grafters and those who debauched them. Repeatedly the bribe taker was condemned and the bribe giver exonerated, evidence that in politics alone of the fields of human endeavor the pimp enjoys a higher moral standing than the prostitute.

At the time Daugherty was unable to find grounds for indictments against public men, his department unearthed sufficient information to recover $8,500,000 from private beneficiaries of war contracts in civil suits. This was admittedly a small part of the overcharge, but when a Daugherty finds the civil service blameless and can uphold criticism of private business, the divergence in ethical standards is obvious, for he would have jailed any employee of a Democratic administration who had been as culpable as the many commercial companies he proceeded against.

It was the custom then and for years afterward to sneer at bureaucracy for its obvious faults and to ignore its equally obvious virtues. Yet only in a bureaucracy can men trained in government be sufficiently secure in their jobs to devote their time to doing them well and honestly. The habit of speech that has made bureaucracy synonymous with death and decay was fostered by those who were afraid of the reforms a powerful civil service might achieve, for it remained as true as it had been in the day of Croker or Tweed that many men preferred to deal with a corrupt than with an honest official. Yet it was increasingly clear that the problem of efficient public operations was to keep a bureaucratic machine functioning in accord with the will of a responsible administration in the interests of the people, and that graft would be one of the evils thereby eliminated. Left to itself, the bureaucracy would petrify into an automaton devoted to ironclad rules. But the war proved that it need not be simply that.

The vast expansion of the machine during hostilities was made without deterioration of standards, but the responsible administration needed to guide the machine was lacking. The American system of politics was not designed to place in power men with specific orders to carry out definite programs. This was left to other influences than the mandate of the electorate, and so far as these influences were devoted to private ends, graft of one kind or another was essential. The corruption of the bureaucracy had vanished, but the corruption of those who directed the bureaucracy was still possible.

That this should have been true need surprise only those who accept unthinkingly the oft-repeated assurance that business methods would improve the government. The theory that if you say a thing often enough it becomes true made a little Frenchman named Coué famous. It also accounted for the widespread belief that business men are more honest than politicians. Yet the world of private enterprise remained, ethically, in the period of Fletcher and the Bloomsbury Gang. The practices that were almost universally condoned in commercial transactions—as corruption had been in eighteenth century England—were recognized just as universally as hideous betrayals of trust in public officials. Politics had achieved notable ethical progress. Business lagged far behind.

XVIII

NORMALCY

1

THE LEADERSHIP PREDICTED
for American industry by Ambassador Page did not carry
with it the crescendo of profits that should have been the
reward of greatness. In fact a definite if brief post-war depression gave warning that prosperity is never inevitable.
There was some comfort in the thought that Europe was
in sorrier plight, for America's desire to save the world had
faded with the band music and four-minute speakers. In its
place were more prosaic ambitions, some of which could only
be realized through graft.

The whole nation was bending its energies toward getting public support for private aims. Farmers wanted to
maintain high food prices. Manufacturers wondered how
they could keep government as a cash customer. Financiers
worried about the disposal of their new oceans of credit.
Labor planned to extend the benefits of war wages to peace.
There was no place for the New Freedom; every interest
was trying to capture government for itself, and in 1920
every interest thought it had succeeded.

The country had done with theorists and dreamers. President Harding, with the jovial figure of Harry Daugherty
at his elbow, was obviously a return to the plain American
in high office. Men who had achieved fame and fortune by
a shrewd understanding of plain Americans swarmed around
him.

Despite the hopes of farmers and workers, it was evident

that he was going to preside over a business administration, and three problems assumed paramount importance. First, the task of preserving the American market for domestic manufactures without sacrificing the foreign field. Second, liquidation of the war, disposing of accumulated stocks of materials, caring for the disabled, satisfying newly organized veterans and restoring to private hands the enormous confiscated assets administered by the Alien Property Custodian. Third, distribution of the burden of maintaining greatly increased responsibilities of government and retiring a national debt of thirty-two billions.

None of these had been political issues in the campaign of 1920. They were merely left in the lap of the incoming administration, and long before Harding drove to his inauguration beside the shattered Wilson, it was clear that his methods would not only be pre-war but pre-Spanish war. Normalcy, which Candidate Harding had offered as a Nirvana for a weary world, making it the keynote of his campaign, was obviously a state where give and take between government and business could be carried on apart from the excessive scruples of the civil service.

A dying generation returned to power in the Harding landslide. The imposing figure of the President-elect was just that—a figure. Real authority was vested in a group of statesmen whose politics and morals were distinctly nineteenth century. Any liberal or even modern tendencies that some of them may have displayed in their fiery youth had long since given way to complacent rigidity.

Daugherty, who had created his friend Harding in the image of William McKinley, had learned politics from Mark Hanna, and nothing else. The Gargantuan Penrose, who had never progressed beyond the Cameron-Quay tradition to Pennsylvania industry, died shortly before the inauguration but with the assistance of another servant of the mighty, former Attorney General, now Senator Philander C. Knox, the Mellon lawyer, had already impressed the old machine upon the national administration with a grip no scandals could shake.

In their group, too, was Senator Lodge, still finding it "difficult even to imagine" the corruption of a previous generation. Before he died in 1924 it should have been easy for him, because the solution he and his fellows gave to their three fundamental problems insured a wide understanding of all forms of graft. The voice of those who had financed the Harding campaign with a lavishness unknown since Hanna had toured Wall Street was heard in every point. To protect the nation's leadership in world industry, the Republicans adopted the policy of the averted glance. Charles Evans Hughes at the head of the State Department inspired confidence in the rectitude of our foreign relations on a plane far above the practical negotiations of such men as Harry Sinclair, who noted that "in Latin-American countries they always want a little grease." The only wonder is that Sinclair should have used the qualifying "Latin."

In the domestic field, industrialists wrote their own tariff, which was passed by representatives of farmers whose inflated land values were collapsing as a Europe more or less at peace began to raise its own food. But the farmers had contributed only votes, not campaign funds. A protective tariff for manufactures, a few kind words for agriculture, a benevolent interpretation of regulatory laws, an amiable disregard of private financial operations abroad (except for an occasional use of the marines)—these marked the return to normalcy.

Liquidating the war was even simpler. Harding knew a couple of pleasant fellows who would attend to it.

Taxes and the debt burden were as delightfully settled. By great good fortune it would be possible to enlist Andrew W. Mellon, a name Harding had never heard. But when its magic significance was explained, he found it easy to believe a man possessed of as many hundreds of millions as the shy Pittsburgher must know all about money.

The result of this practical government by practical politicians was naturally the familiar one which Senator Lodge supposed to be embalmed in history. It bore a strong historical likeness to the corruption of Reconstruction days that had so aroused the Senator's ire.

Once again reaction to a sustained period of war idealism stripped moral pretenses from the scramble for government favor, protection and contracts. Again the flowers of Federal spending attracted the bees. Again the war-inflated masters of industry were preparing to take over new fields, but pride in their prosperity was insufficient to convince public opinion that business ought to have whatever it asked for. Business, therefore, was reduced again to bidding for the good will of statesmen who had been elected on quite other grounds. These factors so outweighed the exodus of the dollar-a-year men and the presence of a fairly incorruptible permanent officialdom that it was Harding's misfortune to be compared to Grant at least as often as to McKinley.

He was fully as unfortunate in his chief appointments. The new unit committed to the enforcement of prohibition, not yet under civil service rules, set a modern record for wholesale graft when 8 per cent. of its personnel had to be dropped for malfeasance or were actually convicted of corruption during these years. But on a percentage basis the much-reviled dry agents were a purer lot than the President's Cabinet. Of the original ten in that august body, one was jailed, one owed his escape to a hung jury, two resigned under fire and another suffered for years from income tax trouble.

2

Warren Gamaliel Harding of Marion, Ohio, brought to the White House the governmental ideals of the isolated small town of the era before cinema and radio. Years in public office, including eight in the Senate, had not altered his conception of politics as a sort of glorified poker game. In 1920 he raked in the winnings of the great national jackpot with serene satisfaction and began arranging the chips in a new, complicated design.

"You know," he told a friend after he discovered the pile was hard to handle, "before I was elected President I thought the chief pleasure of it would be to give honors and offices to old friends—I thought that was the one big personal satisfaction a President would get. But you know," and Harding appeared to be sincerely grieved, "you can't do that when you're President of the United States; you have to get the best man."

The combination of Harding's friendliness and sense of duty brought to Washington an odd assortment. The Ohio Gang, so miscalled from the President's fondness for friends of earlier days, promptly established a system reminiscent of the golden days of General Grant.

The best men—"best minds" was the term popularized by the President—included some very able, upright citizens whose services were eclipsed in the shadow cast by a few of their colleagues. For graft was to provide the chief publicity of the Harding administration. Secretary Fall, Secretary Denby, Secretary Mellon, Postmaster General Hays, Attorney General Daugherty, Alien Property Custodian Miller, Director Forbes of the Veterans Bureau—these were the names in the headlines.

An atmosphere of romantic fiction, strangely unromantic and sordid in real life, was imparted to the conversations of mystery men who turned out to be extremely commonplace, to code messages, to suicides of men in confidential posts, to behind-the-scenes activities of ladies of surpassing loveliness (until we saw their photographs), to clowns tragically grappling with fate and being twisted into figures of fun at whom a cynical, farce-loving nation roared.

Testimony, the unfolding of history by the leisurely method of Congressional investigation and court trial, numbed by sheer weight the national moral sense. Volume upon volume the record rolled from the presses, making a total verbiage unequaled in the annals of graft, but it was made of more than paper and ink. Living witnesses provided it in a seemingly endless procession. Defiant, timid, blundering, sharp, virtuous or guilty, loquacious or dumb, they all contributed to the unlovely picture, with here and there in the confusing shower of recrimination and excuse one desperate phrase dropped with startling simplicity:

"I refuse to answer on the ground that it may tend to incriminate me."

On almost every page is the dark, all-pervading smear of oil, since the best endeavors of ten generations of land grabbers had failed to alienate entirely the national resources. Considerable tracts that had been left contemptuously to the public as fit only for Indian reservations or possible dry farms of a remote future were actually the caps of oil fields. Both Taft and Wilson had set aside some as reserves for the navy's fuel.

As the demand for gasoline and fuel oil increased, a continuous propaganda sought to force these proven areas into the hands of private producers. The fight had been so close that Josephus Daniels and his Assistant Secretary of the Navy, a smiling young fellow named Franklin Delano Roosevelt, sat up by turns in the galleries all through the closing days of one session of Congress to prevent laws affecting the reserves from being slipped through in the haste of a dying House.

While the convention delegates of 1920 were sweltering in Chicago until their chiefs could select a candidate, there had been rumors that a new oil policy might be expected. Leaders of the industry bulked large in the political market place for a time and were seen in the smoke-filled rooms where the insiders met and where Daugherty had predicted that Harding would win. Then they dropped into the background. There they remained, even when the new Secretary of the Interior was named.

This was Senator Albert B. Fall, a stalwart of the old land-granting breed from New Mexico where men as old as he remembered Elkins. But the oil reserves were the property of the navy and Fall's views on the subject did not seem of much importance. Nor had his integrity then been questioned. After half a lifetime of public service in high judicial office at home and the Senate in Washington, his only asset, aside from political prestige and a Cabinet officer's salary, was a large but rundown ranch. A careful picture of the formal Southwest, spare and tanned, with long mustaches and a grave manner, he was the poorest but not the least imposing of the new Cabinet.

His interest in oil was more than academic. In his adventurous youth he had gone prospecting with Edward L. Doheny, who had since become president of the Pan-American Petroleum Company and possessed of vast interests in the West and Mexico. A quiet-spoken, mild gentleman with the bluest eyes George Creel ever saw, Doheny had ideas about the oil reserves and attached little importance to the accident of his having been always a Democrat.

When the triumphant Republicans moved into Washington, the price of oil was rising. The big companies were competing eagerly for the output of new wells, and the barren acres of the naval reserves beckoned alluringly. In charge of them as Secretary of the Navy was Edwin Denby. With the jaw of a fighter and the brow of a thinker, he was in fact delightfully pliable, trusting and receptive of Fall's advice.

Before he had been in office a month, he alarmed his Bureau of Engineering chief, Admiral Griffin, by saying the reserves ought to be transferred to the Interior Department because all public lands should be administered as a unit. Griffin protested that the oil reserves were no more public lands than the navy yards. He and other officers knew what usually happened to the public lands, but they bowed with proper discipline to their superior. At the end of May, 1921, Harding signed an executive order transferring the reserves to the Interior Department, and within ten days Fall was writing to his blue-eyed friend, Doheny:

"I have notified Secretary Denby that I shall conduct the matter of naval leases, under the direction of the President, without calling any of his force in consultation unless I conferred with himself personally on a matter of policy."

With the game in his hands, Fall was not content to turn the reserves over to his and his party's friends out of sheer devotion to principle, although his terms were modest enough. He appears to have decided from the first to do business with Doheny and Harry Sinclair, an ex-hackdriver who had crawled up from the muck of the oil fields to a commanding position in the industry and on the racetrack. A much younger man than Doheny or Fall, he was of the type the success story magazines liked to call a rough diamond. If he had any scruples, they were not divulged to a curious public, but he was equally free of delusions of grandeur. Not even a term in jail embittered him.

He was to get the Teapot Dome reserve in Wyoming. Doheny was in line for Elk Hills in California. Both contracts went through the Interior Department in much the same way—hastily, secretly and without competitive bidding. Each lessee figured his profit would amount to $100,000,000. The government was losing property with an estimated value of $500,000,000.

The principal difference in the two deals was in the method of compensating Fall. Doheny, as an old friend, trusted the Secretary. On Nov. 28, 1921, he sent in his first offer. On Nov. 29th Fall telephoned that he was "ready to make that loan." On Nov. 30th Doheny's son put $100,000 in a little black bag and carried the money to Fall in Washington. The final lease giving Doheny just what he wanted was not signed until a year later.

Sinclair, more businesslike and less friendly, paid only after delivery, but he paid more. He also got prompter service. He delivered his proposals formally in February, 1922, and the lease was signed on April 7th. It was the day after Senator La Follette, who had been hearing rumors, called for copies of executive orders concerning the reserves and the same day Fall published a denial that he had executed any leases at all. Then, although La Follette introduced a resolution to investigate, Sinclair turned over to Fall's son-in-law $233,000 in Liberty Bonds in two installments during the month of May.

Two unfortunate circumstances disrupted the profitable nature of the transaction. In the first place, the head of the Senate subcommittee for La Follette's investigation was Thomas Walsh of Montana, a patient and acute prosecutor. Secondly, Sinclair's Liberty Bonds had been derived from a private oil deal so very unsavory that it shocked the fumigated conscience of a Rockefeller. Sinclair, Colonel Robert W. Stewart of Standard Oil, James O'Neil of Prairie Oil & Gas and H. M. Blackmer of Midwest Refining had made a little agreement with their own companies reminiscent of the Crédit Mobilier and destined to become as famous. They contracted to buy $50,000,000 worth of oil and in a simultaneous contract sold it to their own companies at a personal profit of $8,333,333.33.

This profit came to them in Liberty Bonds in an intricate process by way of Canada. Sinclair, forgetting that bonds bear traceable numbers, used some of them to pay Fall. He also turned over, with what willingness no one was able to tell, $185,000 of the same lot of bonds to Will Hays, who had retired as Postmaster General to be Czar of the Movies, to help pay the Harding campaign deficit. The voluntary nature of the gift was questioned not only because it was by far the largest made, but because it came a few days after Senator Walsh began his hearings on Teapot Dome.

"The synchrony suggests at once that the extraordinary sum yielded up at that critical time by Sinclair was not altogether voluntarily donated, and that either hope or fear, if not gratitude, stimulated his generosity and accentuated his devotion to the principles of the Republican Party," Walsh commented.

However that may have been, the relation between campaign contributors and campaign managers was too complicated for the committee to unravel and the investigators turned, no doubt with relief, to those candid witnesses, Doheny and Sinclair.

"I have always considered that Liberty Bonds were practically cash," said Sinclair.

"I am just an ordinary, old-time, impulsive, improvident sort of prospector," said Doheny.

The impulsive fellow added that $100,000 meant no more to him than $25 or $50 to ordinary mortals, but Walsh pointed out that $100,000 might be little to Doheny and a tidy sum to Fall. The Supreme Court affirming that the leases had been made through "fraud and corruption," on which ground they were canceled, agreed with Walsh and the navy recovered its oil.

Before this final result was achieved, the country was regaled with one sordid revelation after another, leading up to a memorable day in February, 1924, when the former Secretary of the Interior—he had offered his resignation a month after completing the oil leases and before the exposures began—was forced to take the stand after a prolonged series of blusterings, falsehoods, cringings and attempts to plead ill health.

The committee room was crowded as the onetime elder statesman entered. All over the country men were waiting for the result of the meeting between the Westerners, Fall and Walsh. A brilliant cross examination by the Senator, the connoisseurs thought, would be matched by an equally pyrotechnical explanation from the former Cabinet Minister. Talk fell to a murmur as Fall came slowly forward to take the stand.

Illness and more than illness had changed the old Senate leader. The healthy tan was gone, the firm brown cheeks sunken in yellowish folds, the erect carriage stooped. Senator and Secretary Fall had permitted his pride of place to be reflected in his clothes. Always in the days of his arrogance he had been a little too carefully dressed. Those who had not seen him since stared in surprise and pity at the shabby figure moving painfully toward his inquisition. His suit looked as if he had slept in it. An old and obviously broken man, he settled himself in a chair, shrinking from the silence of the crowded room. Motionless, almost breathless, the audience waited for the duel to begin.

It began and ended on Walsh's first preliminary question. Fall answered with a prepared statement in which he refused to testify "on the ground that it may tend to incriminate me."

That was all. The committee could have no use for Albert B. Fall unless he waived immunity, and he rose to go. No one moved except his lawyer, hurrying forward to lend a supporting arm to the sorry figure of his client. Slowly the two retreated through the hushed crowd, Fall tottering slightly despite the aid of counsel and a thick stick, his gaze fixed on the floor.

There was no sign of triumphing over the fallen. Those who cast cautious glances at their neighbors noticed that all seemed to partake of the shame of the central figure shambling out of their sight. But few saw anything save that painful progress toward the door, a doleful march to which the only accompaniment was the mournful tap of the cane and a hissing shuffle as Fall failed to lift his feet clear of the ground. At last he was gone, and behind him the implications of his brief statement were settling into the minds

of his hearers. For the first time in history, a member of
the President's Cabinet was on his way to prison, and the
audience could still hear, growing fainter as it receded down
the corridor, that sullen tap, scuffle . . . tap, scuffle . . .
the muffled drum beats of a nation's humiliation.

3

Even before this climax of degradation, there was a popular but sadly unscientific belief that Harding had been killed
by the anguish of knowing too late the sort of graft his
friends had brought to his administration. The kindly, handsome, friendly man had long since drained the pleasure of
his place. He had showered offices upon his friends, and in
the summer of 1923 he was asking men he thought he could
trust "what a President should do whose friends had betrayed him." He repeated the question on a trip to Alaska;
when he reached San Francisco on the way back he was
ill, and on Aug. 2d, while his wife was reading to him,
he died.

Years later Herbert Hoover pronounced what was perhaps the kindest funeral oration that could have been devised. Harding's Secretary of Commerce, elevated to the
Presidency, was speaking at long-delayed dedication cere-
monies of a Harding memorial in Marion, Ohio, surrounded
by the dead President's fellow townsmen and with Harry
Daugherty on the platform behind him.

"Warren Harding," said Hoover, who was to discover that
there are depths of unpopularity to which no mere grafter
ever sinks, "had a dim realization that he had been betrayed by a few men whom he had trusted, by a few men
whom he had believed were his devoted friends. . . . That
was the tragedy of Warren Harding."

"Dim realization" was mild. In some cases it must have
amounted to horrid certainty, for while Fall was being
cautious, not to say secretive in his financial relations with

Doheny and Sinclair, members of the administration even closer to its head were less discreet.

The first to create a scandal of national proportions was one of the good fellows so dear to Harding's heart, Colonel Charles R. Forbes, a hard-drinking, crap-shooting braggart and a smoking car raconteur of parts. His reckless, brilliant war record was a recommendation in those days, and the only reason for suspecting him of any fitness for public office. However, he had held fairly high posts in Hawaii and while there had impressed Senator Harding with his hospitality, his geniality and his stories. He had also performed some vague but noisy services during the campaign.

On the basis of these claims and talents, Colonel Forbes was appointed Director of the Veterans Bureau, in charge of building hospitals for disabled soldiers, disposing of surplus stocks and generally fulfilling a grateful nation's promise that invalid and crippled heroes should want for nothing.

Forbes made scarcely any effort to conceal the predatory nature of his regime. He rioted across the country, gaily levying tribute of liquor, cash, hotel accommodations, women and presents from anyone who wished to sell sites for hospitals or obtain contracts. He returned to Washington and plunged into negotiations to loot the enormous store of hospital supplies collected during the lavish war years at Perryville, Md. To the Budget Bureau he submitted a list of damaged goods to be sold. When this had been approved he inserted a much longer list of new supplies in perfect condition and the same day sold the whole lot without any attempt at competitive bidding at 10 to 20 cents on the dollar.

While thus robbing the government—he was buying sheets for his hospitals at $1.03½ each and selling exact duplicates in unbroken packages for 20 cents—Forbes neglected to play fair with his subordinates. He and the chief counsel of the Bureau, Charles Cramer, had been partners in a $25,000 fee paid by the grateful seller of a California hospital site,

and Cramer expected to share in the supply loot, too. But
while he was in the West, his wife telegraphed to him:
"Think it necessary you return at once. Think Colonel
is a traitor. Has ordered Perryville cleaned out this week.
I am seeing General S. in your behalf tomorrow."
Mrs. Cramer saw "S." and thereby spoiled the graft. A
few days later General Sawyer, the Marion sanitarium
keeper who had come to Washington as the President's personal physician and adviser in Federal hospitalization, protested to Harding about the unseemly haste in emptying
Perryville. Forbes managed to square himself then, but two
months later, in January, 1923, Sawyer again protested, and
this time the President was convinced. Goods that the government would have to spend $5,000,000 to replace had
been sold for a little more than a tenth that sum.

This could not be met by boasting or a funny story. Complaints against Forbes had passed beyond the official family
and there was a buzz on Capitol Hill, where Walsh was patiently preparing his case against Fall. But Harding had
never acquired harshness. He permitted Forbes to retire to
Europe and send his resignation from there, two weeks before the Senate voted to investigate the Veterans Bureau.
Twelve days later the scandal broke wide open. Cramer shot
himself through the head, leaving no other explanation than
a sort of ode to death clipped from a newspaper. Forbes
brazened it out to the end, that being eighteen months in
Leavenworth as the cellmate of Dr. Cook, who improved
the time by proving to the Colonel's satisfaction that Peary
had not been first at the North Pole.

4

Forbes was, in a sense, Harding's personal tragedy, but
one even closer to the White House was on the defensive
at the same time. The House Judiciary Committee was
holding hearings on a motion to impeach Attorney General

Daugherty. The charges failed, but the talk unleashed was disturbing to the "vindicated" man's best friend, inured though he was to the savagery of political attack.

The outcry against Daugherty had been loud before the inauguration. Neither his legal attainments nor his political reputation offered any grounds for assuming he could carry out the duties of the government's chief law officer. Criticism subsided in the optimistic, trustful days that greet every new administration, but before long Harding could read in the newspapers revived denunciations of the man who had made him President. Rumors were flying about Washington with the lushness natural in a place where nearly half the population comes into contact with confidential information.

It was said that Daugherty served as the chief go-between in deals with big business. This in a Cabinet that included the pious Hays, the fabulous Mellon, Banker Weeks of Boston and Fall was fantastic, although based on the nubbin of truth that Daugherty was doing his best. Immunity from anti-trust prosecutions, pardons, liquor withdrawal permits for bootleggers and assorted favors were supposed to be on sale at the Department of Justice. If that was a mistake, some of the shrewdest denizens of the underworld and equally astute leaders of business had thrown their money away.

The extent to which Daugherty profited could never be established. He banked with his brother, Mal, in Ohio, and the records of his account had been destroyed. One investigator, before he was denied access to the bank's papers and before destruction was complete, saw deposit slips for $74,000 in the Attorney General's name.

"The tax returns of Mr. Daugherty show that he had no property; he was in debt more than he was worth when he became Attorney General," pointed out Senator Brookhart, chairman of the committee that investigated the imitator of Hanna. "The evidence again shows that we found in his brother's bank live certificates of deposit to him of nearly $75,000, which would be accumulated within these two or three years on a $12,000 salary."

If Harding knew of his friend's sudden prosperity, he did not question its source. But the evidence came uncomfortably close to home when early on the morning of May 30, 1923, in the Attorney General's suite at a Washington hotel, they found the body of a man named Smith, the head grotesquely resting in a wastebasket. Daugherty had spent the night at the White House while the obscure sharer of his apartment was firing the shot that was to make him nationally famous.

Jess Smith in life had done all his shining by reflected glory. To the public he was an unidentified face in group pictures of the mighty, his most striking characteristics being devotion to the Attorney General and a fondness for being photographed with Harding. He had sold a small department store in Washington Courthouse, Ohio, Daugherty's home town, to accompany his friend to the capital. They shared living quarters, card games and the privilege of calling the President "Warren." Jess seemed no more than a handyman who took messages, did the shopping, shunted undesirable visitors aside and helped the Attorney General into his overcoat. But those who had business with the Department of Justice knew he could facilitate intricate negotiations.

He prospered amazingly. One of his single deposits in Mal Daugherty's bank was $63,000 in Liberty Bonds. He sold liquor permits and protection to bootleggers in larger quantities than he could deliver. Considerable sums paid to get estates out of the hands of the Alien Property Custodian were delivered to him. Whether or not it was possible for Daugherty to live so intimately with his henchman and remain ignorant of these payments and promises was a question on which juries twice disagreed.

There was, therefore, ample grounds for Harding's sorry

bewilderment when he went to Alaska. But the worst revelations were reserved until after his death. He was spared the chagrin of witnessing the indictment of Daugherty—forced out of the Cabinet by exposure of his methods—and of Alien Property Custodian Miller. The two were charged with conspiracy to defraud the government in turning over $7,000,-000 in American Metals Company stock to European claimants whose agents gave $391,000 in Liberty Bonds to John T. King, a Connecticut Republican leader who died a week before the indictments were returned.

The prosecution contended this sum was divided among Daugherty, Jess Smith, Miller and King. Fifty thousand dollars' worth were traced to Miller and the same amount to Jess. Daugherty's lawyers were quite willing to admit the guilt of the two dead men, and their client declined to testify. He offered the familiar formula that testimony "might tend to incriminate me," and the additional excuse that his honor would not permit him to discuss his relations with President Harding. The same scruple applied to his dealings with Mal Daugherty, who was later sentenced to ten years for embezzlement, misapplication of funds and a string of other offenses against the banking laws. Two juries convicted Miller and failed to agree about the former Attorney General.

Juries were kept pretty busy with Harding's Cabinet officers and their friends, performing their tasks with the unpredictable light-heartedness usual to twelve good men and true. One set convicted Fall of accepting a bribe from Doheny. Another decided on the same evidence that Doheny had not bribed Fall. Since the $100,000 transaction was not denied, the verdicts seemed to establish that Fall thought he had been bribed, but that Doheny never had any intention of bribing him.

The impulsive, improvident old prospector fared better than his fellow oil lease beneficiary. Sinclair fought harder for what he considered his rights, with the result that in

March, 1927, he heard himself sentenced to three months in jail for contempt of the Senate after refusing to furnish information. In the autumn of that year he was on trial for conspiracy, a charge that Doheny had already shown was difficult to substantiate. But Sinclair, trying to make assurance doubly sure, hired Burns detectives to shadow his jury and, presumably, influence the verdict. This time it was contempt of court, and the sentence was six months, which Sinclair served in the District of Columbia with great good nature. But he could not be convicted of bribing Fall.

The unsavory episode of the oil leases, with its accompanying divergence in the fate of the principals, brought into sharp relief that moral progress of which Senator Lodge had been so proud. Two generations had passed since the Crédit Mobilier scandals. Then, too, the malefactors had been thoroughly investigated. Then, too, they had been haled before more substantial tribunals than the bar of public opinion. But in the 'seventies the man who gave the bribe was guilty, the man who took it innocent. In the 'twenties we had advanced beyond all that. Now the man who gave was exonerated; he who took, the culprit. Oakes Ames had won a posthumous moral victory.

5

An administration that could survive the scandals breaking over the grave of the martyred Harding had to have qualities that appealed to the nation. Coolidge, even with a Cabinet purged of Daugherty, Denby and Fall, could hardly have won the vote of confidence he achieved in 1924 without offering the sort of government people thought they wanted, or could be fooled into thinking they wanted. And the fine essence of that government, superdistilled in one brain, was Andrew W. Mellon.

Behind the screen of the more picturesque and imprudent activities of his colleagues, the unobtrusive millionaire was accomplishing with characteristic quiet efficiency the fundamental revisions in policy toward which the others blundered so tragically. All of them were trying to encourage the new era of expanding profits, and if graft went with it, why, that was as it had always been. The section of the community which shared in the profits would be sufficiently grateful to overlook the graft if the collectors would be a bit more decorous than Fall, Forbes and Daugherty. The Secretary of the Treasury was nothing if not decorous.

On a scale that dwarfed even the half billion dollar oil scandal, Mellon directed government to the service of private interests. No one brought him money in little black bags, however; no one paid his hotel bills; no one sent him cases of liquor or bevies of women; no one gave him Liberty Bonds. He did not need these stimuli.

Most of the Republican leaders of his time went back to the McKinley era for political inspiration. Mellon antedated them by a full century. He was destined to be compared ad nauseam to Alexander Hamilton, and although his enemies would never admit it, the analogy was sound. In matters of basic principle, the quiet, unsociable, thrifty financier, so oddly compounded of diffidence in manner and ruthlessness in action, was a reincarnation of Washington's brilliant, improvident, adventurous aide. Mellon embraced in its entirety the Hamiltonian theory that government ought to draw the moneyed interest to its support, and by the same means that the first Secretary of the Treasury had applied with success. Of course Mellon personally profited to a far greater extent than Hamilton had done or wanted to do.

For nearly half a century Uncle Andy had devoted himself with single-minded intensity to carrying on the work begun by his father, Judge Thomas Mellon. This loquacious, hard-headed jurist was the typical barefoot boy of the success story. He had bought and sold, foreclosed mortgages, taken shrewd advantage of the weaknesses of his fellow men and

preached to his family the virtues of saving, hard work and
sobriety.

Of his eight children, the sixth, Andrew, was his best
pupil. At eighteen the boy went to work for his father at
$75 a month—his last salaried post until he entered govern-
ment service—and although it was the panic year of 1873
he acquitted himself so well that he was made a partner.
Before he was thirty he had taken over most of the Judge's
interests in coal, land, steel and banking and was well on
the way toward the two billions at which the family fortune
was one day to be estimated.

By 1920 the shy Andrew was an aging and lonely man.
His two children were at school. His wife had long since
left him—she said that after nine years of life devoted to
money grubbing she couldn't stand it any longer. But then
she was Irish, granddaughter of Peter Guinness, the brewer,
and a lover of company, gaiety and the pleasant feudal philanthropies of her class. Ten years after their divorce, her
former husband was ready to quit Pittsburgh too. Perhaps
he remembered that his venerated sire had once written:

"The only way a person can do is to get as much out of
the government as he can, and that seems to be the best
policy now among the Cabinet et al."

Of course Andrew Mellon had long ruled a political as
well as a financial and industrial domain. He had learned
about it in as realistic a school as the Tammany of Croker
and Murphy, in the days when William Randolph Hearst
was a reformer and had with his usual felicity of phrase
exposed some of the operations of a system he did not then
like. In a telegram to Editor Brisbane, Hearst remarked of
the Tammany setup:

"It is true . . . that the judges go hat in hand to Mr.
Murphy, but it is also true that Mr. Murphy goes hat in
hand to Mr. Ryan [of rapid transit and oil] and Mr. Ryan,
who instructs Mr. Murphy and appoints the judges and
governs the people, has his hat on all the time."

Mellon, too, had his hat on all the time, and his whisper was louder than the bellow of Penrose. Yet something more than the acquisitive instinct led the Judge's son into public service. His manifold affairs ran themselves; his great industrial enterprises were monotonously successful in accordance with the infallible Mellon formula by which wealth, like the amoeba, reproduced itself over and over again. The process was scarcely more interesting than cellular division under the microscope, but the manipulation of national finances to the applause of the enlightened moneyed interest might be more satisfying than the pyramiding of millions in the obscurity of Smithfield Street.

Nevertheless he did not appear eager; he never did; eagerness was no part of the Mellon technique, nor of the Mellon temperament. But he "went down to Washington," as he phrased it, and only after he got there discovered, he said, that his place in the industrial world made him ineligible for the Treasury. Besides the general prohibition against engaging in commerce, which Grant had found insurmountable in A. T. Stewart's case, the members of the Federal Reserve Board, of whom the Secretary of the Treasury was chairman, were debarred from having pecuniary interest in any bank they were supposed to supervise.

"That relieved my mind," Mellon said much later. "There was a door that I could go through gracefully, and not become Secretary of the Treasury."

He confided his scruple to Knox, but the Senator brushed it aside.

"Oh, there is nothing in that," he assured his client. "The Supreme Court has decided that. There are two decisions that clear up that question. One of those cases was at the time I was Attorney General."

Knox promised to arrange the details, and his plan bore a strange resemblance to the Stewart memorandum which Justice Carter had pronounced unworkable in strong language fifty-two years before. With one grand gesture, Andrew Mellon divested himself of a catalogue of fifty-one directorships and a medley of corporation offices, put his bank stocks in his brother's name and announced himself qualified for the Treasury. On March 4, 1921, twenty days before his sixty-sixth birthday, he was sworn in, the first of the Cabinet to enter. Eleven years later the reluctant Secretary was the only survivor in the Cabinet of that band of ten and it was found extremely difficult to pry him loose.

Whether or not Uncle Andy's divorce from trade was as complete as the law contemplated was a question that could not be set at rest, even by his statement that his active connection with Mellon companies "was severed in 1921 as completely as if I had died at that time." The records of his department would indicate that he was an exceedingly lively corpse.

The fine impartiality of a chairman of the Federal Reserve Board was supposedly assured when he "sold" his bank stocks to his brother, Richard B., for $10,520,495. He took a note bearing 5½ per cent. interest, just the amount of the dividends being paid on the stock, but Hughes was not asked to decide whether it would be "candid or truthful" to describe such a transfer as a bona fide sale.

Richard Mellon was the ideal debtor. When the dividends rose to 7 and then to 8 per cent., the interest on the loan rose with them. In 1930 Andy's son, Paul, assumed the obligation and the stock without any advance in price, although the shares of Union Trust, foundation of Mellon financing, had increased in value from $2,750 to $20,000. At this time Richard discovered that in the fluctuation of dividends and accruing of stock rights he had inadvertently netted about $300,000. This he insisted—so it was testified after he was dead—on returning to the Secretary of the Treasury.

"I do not care to profit by this," he told his brother's confidential man of business, "and I want to pay Andy the entire amount of earnings that I have received, over and above the interest that I have paid."

This, declared an admiring lawyer, retained by Mellon at great expense, displayed a motive "so commendable that it must even yet be recorded in high heaven in R. B. Mellon's favor." A less enthusiastic Bureau of Internal Revenue, probably not so well acquainted with heavenly bookkeeping as were Mellon lawyers, considered it merely collusion.

In successful defense of this transaction as a sale within the meaning of the law, the same legal luminary who had won Doheny's acquittal exhausted a deal of fly-blown eloquence and some real ingenuity. But the people, who had in their own little business affairs another meaning for such simple words as "buy" and "sell," were never permitted to know the exact nature of the brotherly trade until after Mellon had ceased to hold office.

However, the technicalities of his qualifications were as nothing beside the Pittsburgher's odd conception of a public trust. His spoken and written words on the subject were conventional enough, but his real philosophy could be judged more accurately from his official acts and policies. Here the industrialist never seemed to realize that it would be possible for the national interest to differ from that of Aluminum Company of America, Gulf Oil, the Koppers companies, Pittsburgh Coal or Union Trust.

"He is the only man that the big interests, the Rockefellers and Morgans, will not bluff," Daugherty said he told Harding in urging Mellon's appointment.

The Rockefellers and Morgans would not need to bluff Uncle Andy. They could trust him. He gave them an administration dedicated to the service of the wealthy as no one since Hamilton had dared or been able to do. Accumulation was so greatly accelerated, surpassing anything ever known before, that the Mellon family fortune grew from an estimated six or seven hundred millions in 1920 to two billions in the depression year of 1931, Uncle Andy's last in the Treasury. It was an administration that fulfilled the

classic definition of graft—the perversion of public office to
private interest—with a grandeur that was never surpassed.

6

Of course the growth of the Mellon estate was not entirely the result of the Secretary's official practices. But
they played their part, and a sufficiently large one, in this
as well as in piling up the fantastic wave of speculation
that reached its crest and broke in a thunderous roar of
panic on the financial beach in 1929. The Mellon principle of taxation freed individuals and corporations of great
wealth from a burden that might have checked the un-
bridled expansion that was for some years the party's pride.

Mellon's attitude toward tax laws was frankly expressed
when it was later charged by the Department he left behind
him that he had "planned, schemed, contrived and devised
a comprehensive scheme and plan of tax evasions and tax
avoidance while he held the office of Secretary of the Treasury of the United States." Specifically it was alleged that
Uncle Andy in paying $647,559 for 1931 had defrauded the
government of which he was a part to the extent of about
$2,000,000. Explaining the process by which his tax was
computed, Mellon declared:

"The result was what I think was a fair amount for me
to have paid the government in that year."

Taxpayers with incomes less susceptible to legal jugglery
were not allowed the luxury of offering what they thought
was fair. The law fixed what they were to pay, and Secretary Mellon was the chief administrative officer of that law.
In his own case he interpreted his obligation at a little less
than 3 per cent. of his total income or 8 per cent. of what
was estimated as his gross taxable income. A three man board
of tax appeals finally ruled that most of the deductions were
legal.

These excursions into individual economy were part of

the program that became known as the "Mellon Plan," described with enthusiasm and accuracy as the best of its kind since Hamilton. For eleven years Secretary Mellon labored to reduce the tax burdens of the wealthy and to mold the national administration into an agency for the service of industrial and financial enterprise. When he took office, the surtax on a few of the largest fortunes in the country was 65 per cent. Corporations were subject to an excess profits tax on net earnings above 8 per cent. The war had been the excuse for these encroachments on a man's right to do as he pleased with his money, and the war was over. It was not paid for, but Mellon thought thirty billions could be found eventually in the lower brackets.

His first report—almost as startling as Hamilton's famous one on public credit—proposed repeal of the excess profits tax, reduction of surtaxes to 40 per cent. at once, 33 per cent. later and 25 per cent. eventually. A series of nuisance taxes was to replace in part the lost revenue. His relief to income tax payers, however, stopped short at $66,000; he favored retaining the high rates on all incomes below that figure, apparently on the ground that such trifling sums could be put to no genuinely useful purpose.

"I recommend this reduction," he told critics, "not to relieve the rich but because the higher surtax rates have already passed the point where they can be collected."

Even in that Republican honeymoon year there were men who believed it was the Secretary's duty to enforce the law rather than confess himself powerless to collect more than those in his own income tax bracket, in their generosity, cared to contribute. These visionaries forced some concessions, since Uncle Andy's colleagues lacked his quiet stubbornness and courage. He would have defied a whole nation of people with less than $66,000 a year. But when Harding finally signed the new bill, surtax rates had gone down only to 50 per cent., although excess profits taxes were abolished. Mellon's personal saving, aside from that achieved by his corporations and family, amounted to more than $500,000 a year. For the admittedly bad business period of 1921, under the old rates, he had paid $1,492,883. For 1922 he paid $950,958, and for 1923 his tax was $895,000. It was small wonder that cynics could say pityingly of Fall: "Did he only get $100,000?"

Still Uncle Andy was not satisfied. In 1923 he launched another tax reduction campaign, but threw a sop to the rabble with less than $66,000 a year, while proposing to cut the surtax to 25 per cent. Almost the entire financial community rallied to him; only such rare exceptions as Senator Couzens, who derived his million a year from tax exempt securities, insisted business was not suffering from oppressive burdens. This, indeed, was obvious, for the country was marching toward an unparalleled boom with a few voices crying in the wilderness that the need was for greater purchasing power and distribution of goods rather than the multiplication of means of production. But Mellon could not be swayed by mere facts from his insistence that high surtaxes discouraged enterprise and could not be collected anyway —a contradiction to which he remained stubbornly oblivious.

"Ways will always be found to avoid taxes so destructive in their nature," he said.

He knew whereof he spoke better than he ever cared to reveal publicly. In the files of the Bureau of Internal Revenue was a letter addressed to the Secretary at about this time by Commissioner David H. Blair. It began:

"Pursuant to your request for a memorandum setting forth some of the various ways by which an individual may legally avoid tax, I am pleased to submit the following, which has been prepared by a member of the Income Tax Unit of this Bureau."

Then are detailed twelve loopholes in the income tax laws—distribution of property among the taxpayer's children in order to get into lower brackets, sale of stocks for deductible paper losses, division of corporate profits in the form of non-taxable loans rather than taxable dividends when the stock is closely held in the family, formation of family trusts, partnerships and so on—all the tricks that were enabling former employees of the Bureau of Internal Revenue to make handsome fees as private consultants on the regulations they had helped draw up and interpret.

"I think," observed Senator La Follette the younger, "if Senators will take the trouble to read the annual statements of the so-called 'Mellon companies,' they will find that all of them have been adopting this procedure ever since."

Certainly Uncle Andy had employed most of these tax reduction methods in his personal returns, which explained his payment of 3 per cent. on a gross income of more than $20,000,000. One of many examples cited in his return for the single year 1931 gives the clue to the entire process.

At the end of December, Uncle Andy gave some thought to the tax it would be fair for him to pay and decided to take a few losses. He settled on a block of Pittsburgh Coal stock that had cost him about $6,000,000 and at the then market quotation was worth $500,000. A loss of $5,500,000 was just what he needed for his tax return, but Pittsburgh Coal was the biggest concern of its kind in the world, a foundation stone of Pittsburgh industry and of Mellon power. Uncle Andy had refused two years before to accept $10,000,000 for the stock, representing a figure some twenty points above the highest boom quotation. For his block exactly matched that owned by his brother, and the two together were 51 per cent. of Pittsburgh Coal common. When, therefore, Uncle Andy blithely sold such a fundamental interest at the depressed market, one might wonder if he really meant it.

The sale was arranged, according to Mellon, in a casual conversation on the last day of the year with the president of his Union Trust Company, a man Uncle Andy had made almost with his own hands. Exactly 118 days later one of his children's holding companies, advised by the same confidential secretary who had attended to the actual transfer of the shares to Union Trust, bought back the entire block. Although the market had declined meantime, the price was $500,000 plus 6 per cent. interest for 118 days, plus the cost of the transfer stamps. In a Union Trust memorandum the difference appears as "interest" rather than profit on a sale.

This and several other transactions in which after much maneuvering the only result was a loss for Uncle Andy's tax return while essential ownership remained unchanged were traced through a maze of family companies so involved that even the great financier frequently confused them one with another when trying to explain just how they worked. Most of these deals met with the approval of the tax appeals board, for Commissioner Blair had been right about the legality of the loopholes.

On the witness stand in 1935 an aged Uncle Andy, displaying as much embarrassment as was possible for a man so conscious of his rectitude, denied he had ever made any considerable study of tax avoidance methods or had any knowledge of the Blair memorandum. If that was true, he had certainly misled the country when in fighting for the Mellon plan in 1923 he spoke of tax avoidance with the assurance of an expert. At least one profound article on the subject appeared under his signature. The Blair document bolstered the arguments the Secretary was using at that time, although he did not publicly employ the data, and it is odd that neither he nor his counsel remembered such an innocent motive for the paper, if that was the motive. Perhaps the Mellon memory easily shed anything connected with his rare defeats, and in 1923 the famous plan went down before the assaults of its foes. Surtaxes were kept at 40 per cent.

Two years later, with Coolidge elected largely on the issues of lower taxes and prosperity and with the Harding scandals mercifully ignored by all except irreconcilable

Democrats, Mellon achieved his objective. Paeans of adulation rising with almost no dissenting voice from the press and spokesmen of business enfolded the gray, dour little man in a fulsome atmosphere which led even him to expand to something approaching geniality. Surtaxes dropped to 20 per cent., inheritance taxes to the same figure. Gift taxes were abolished, the capital stock tax repealed, the clause giving publicity to returns deleted. The Secretary and his family were saving several millions a year, and before another gift tax could be imposed, he would have time to place enormous wealth in the names of his children and their corporations, safe from his own collectors.

7

To just what extent the reckless boom of the late 'twenties was due to the work of its Pittsburgh apostle is hardly capable of exact analysis. It is, however, plain that the full tide of speculation, greed and folly would not have been possible without the complete sympathy of the man who molded the nation's tax policy, controlled the flow of credit as chairman of the Federal Reserve Board and offered in his own devotion to the creed of accumulation an example for the rest to follow.

Equally difficult to assess are the benefits that accrued to the Secretary solely by virtue of his official position, for he was not the only industrialist upon whom the government smiled. Furthermore he had always obtained his share of consideration before he took office. So perhaps it is only an unsavory coincidence that the favors showered upon his companies during his term reached impressive totals. To list a few of the simpler instances is as good a way as any to illustrate the interplay of public service and private interests (graft, for short) under a regime that delights to honor its millionaires.

Uncle Andy's personal saving in income tax was a small

part of his gains. Under his guidance the Bureau of Internal Revenue became what Representative Garner of Texas with pardonable partisan (Democratic) exaggeration called "the greatest Santa Claus in history." This was a novel role for the wisp of a man from Smithfield Street, but he dispensed his bounty with a verve that did credit to the softer side of his nature.

The gifts took the form of tax refunds in accordance with esoteric regulations evolved by officials of the Bureau. A surprising number of the men who drafted the rules retired quickly to become highly fee-ed advisers on tax matters, and their pleadings won for their clients more than a billion dollars in refunds. Uncle Andy and his companies shared to the extent of at least $7,000,000. Papers relating to the Standard Steel Car Company's request for an amortization allowance of more than $3,000,000 bore a notation: "This is a Mellon company." It got what it asked, but no one in the Treasury Department was able to say who penciled that cryptic phrase on the papers and no one had the faintest idea what it meant.

The tax relation between Secretary Mellon and Billionaire Mellon by no means exhausted the fields in which the Mellon fortune benefited from government action—or inaction. Harding had been enormously impressed by the range of his Secretary's interests and tried jocularly but vainly to discover their limit. Once when the Chinese Eastern Railway was being discussed at a Cabinet meeting, Harding had hopes. Gleefully he whispered to Daugherty:

"Now we've got him. Surely he wasn't in on this." And then in more courtly tones: "I don't suppose, Mr. Mellon, that you were interested in the Chinese Eastern Railway, were you?"

"Oh, yes, we had a million or a million and a half of the bonds."

"It's no use," Harding confessed. "He's the ubiquitous financier of the universe."

That being hardly an exaggeration, Mellon interests were appearing constantly before government departments, and it would have been strange if they had not received tender consideration. The Aluminum Company of America, enjoying one of the most perfect monopolies in modern business history, was in need only of protection, not concessions or subsidy. It shared in the refunding largesse of the Treasury, but in 1924 it faced a more dangerous threat than taxes. The Federal Trade Commission, filled with holdovers from the New Freedom, had at last published a report, called for by the Senate some years before, flatly accusing the company of violating a 1912 consent decree.

Daugherty's successor, Harlan Stone, agreed with the Commission that there was a case. In one ·Federal department the company was pleading for refunds because in its wartime zeal it had built, entirely to aid the government, more plant facilities than it could use for peacetime production. In another Federal department the same company was earnestly protesting that delay in supplying aluminum to independents was not part of a monopolistic plot to crush competition but due solely to the company's inability to produce in existing plants enough for all. A company that could get away with both these pleas at once obviously had something.

On Oct. 20, 1924, Stone announced that he proposed to find out what that something was. In January, 1925, he wrote that "the evidence submitted supports to a greater or less extent the above cited complaints" in the Trade Commission's report. He found that some of the violations of the consent decree were frequent and of long standing. He declared, therefore, that his department would continue the work begun by the Commission. But before this investigation could be fairly started, Mr. Stone was "kicked upstairs," as one critic put it, into the Supreme Court. Months later the Department of Justice under a less dynamic leadership absolved the company.

The whitewash was applied largely on the basis of work done by a clerk sent out in the role of investigator. He had training in neither law, accountancy nor economics, but he accomplished in days what experts said would have taken them weeks. His qualifications were so conspicuously those that only the Aluminum Company could admire that a Senate committee recommended hearings. Senator Reed of Pennsylvania, son of one of Mellon's old lawyers and recognized spokesman of the Treasury in the Upper House, led a hard struggle that averted the Senatorial attack and saved Aluminum by two votes.

But of course the fact that Andrew Mellon was Secretary of the Treasury had no bearing on the result.

When Gulf Oil needed help, the State Department responded. That Mellon company had bought a three-quarter interest in the Barco concession in Colombia in 1926 for $1,500,000. Gulf's final payment was made after the Colombian government had canceled the concession on the reasonable ground that in nine years none of the specified development work had been carried out. Secretary Kellogg, Hughes's successor, rushed to the defense. He asked Colombia to suspend its oil laws, demanded time for Gulf Oil to present its case. When Colombia insisted Gulf Oil had no case, the State Department assumed a threatening tone. That, too, failed, whereupon the department informed New York bankers, then enjoying an orgy of Latin-American loans, that Colombia had become a bad risk.

Short credit rations bludgeoned the little country into submission. A new administration was elected there, and when it too was refused loans far more soundly secured than many that met with Washington's benevolent approval, Gulf Oil was permitted to negotiate a new and satisfactory concession. Immediately the coffers of the National City Bank were opened. It was learned only later that the new President of Colombia had been assured at a meeting with the American Secretary of the Treasury that if the oil question could be settled, Colombia's credit would be much improved.

But of course the fact that Andrew Mellon was that Secretary of the Treasury had no bearing on the result.

Results anyway were what mattered, a philosophy that was repudiated only when they turned sour. However, judged by their own standards, the practitioners of Mellon's type of graft must be credited with contributing through the plunder they permitted and shared to the greatest era of prosperity the country ever knew as well as to the most disastrous crash.

XIX

THE NOBLE EXPERIMENT

1

"THE FUNNY THING ABOUT prohibition is the people behind it," said the puzzled Senator Penrose. "For years I have been bedeviled by the reformers, who are always accusing me of being somehow responsible for graft in public office. They are against graft. But now they are advocating something which will make all previous graft look like a beggar's tin cup before noon."

Penrose was talking about the identical phenomenon that Herbert Hoover called "a great social and economic experiment, noble in motive and far-reaching in purpose."

Senator and President were both right. In fact the very nobility of motive and extent of purpose helped to make the experiment a conglomeration of all the graft that ever was. Adopted in the hysteria of war, conducted to the accompaniment of fanatical controversy and abolished in a mood of desperation, it was chiefly remarkable for its deplorable effects upon public character. The repentant mood of the national hangover having lasted about as long as such moods generally do, the sovereign people proceeded in the most natural way in the world to bribe themselves to forget a praiseworthy impulse.

They had wanted to get rid of the evils of the liquor traffic. That these were principally inherent in the enormous profits that could be derived from uncontrolled selling of drink was a generally recognized fact. Logic would seem to have dictated the elimination, or at least curbing, of the

340

profit and imposition of strict control. Neither principle was popular. A war for freedom was going on—at least so men said—and profits were pretty sacred. There was something of genius in the proposal that, in theory, abolished drink rather than the evils thereof and left us with even less control over the liquor traffic than before, with even greater profits and with an ample supply of spirits.

The noble experiment actually proved nothing new about liquor one way or the other. But it did provide a laboratory in which graft could be studied under almost ideally scientific conditions and open to the public gaze in a manner that had never been true of the more furtive process by which a comparatively few land grabbers, transportation magnates, financiers, franchise snatchers and contractors influenced the course of government. Prohibition was a game at which the masses could play.

Every man (and every woman and child, too) who entered a speakeasy or bought a bottle from a bootlegger or visited a home where liquor was served knew that he was contributing, actively or tacitly, to the graft. Every one of them came up against the hard fact that lies at the basis of all political corruption. The government had something someone wanted and was not supposed to get. The only way to get it was by bribery in one form or another. Until prohibition, Americans could complacently argue that they, like Penrose's reformers, were against graft. Their sincerity may be gauged by calculating the number of thirsty individuals who wanted a drink and refrained from accepting one during the fourteen years of prohibition.

The chief item that government had for sale to its people was immunity from the operations of its own laws. There were such sidelines as liquor withdrawal permits, by which the bootleggers got their hands on existing stocks of liquor, and industrial alcohol licenses under which spirits could be made, and medicinal whisky. But the main contribution to the welfare of the thirsty was a benevolent hampering of law enforcement. The machinery for carrying out the intent of the Eighteenth Amendment was kept at a point ridiculously ineffective in stopping the flow of booze, although always adequate to the collection of graft.

This was an eminently wise arrangement. If wets and drys could not have blamed their troubles on grafters, they might have had to come to grips with each other. Corruption, as so often in the past, cushioned the shock and enabled the country to get on about its business. Before that was apparent, however, the most alarmed citizens were those skillful practitioners like Penrose who were by no means eager to find themselves the custodians of a nation's thirst.

"Politics and liquor apparently are as inseparable as beer and pretzels," was a discovery made by Mabel Walker Willebrandt only after she had been for some time Assistant Attorney General in charge of prohibition cases.

The Penroses had known it all their lives and had no wish to see the pleasant relationship outlawed. Conservatives to a man, the machine leaders distrusted the new graft. They were not hogs, and they were afraid of as much money as they could see coming in behind prohibition to disrupt their hitherto simply ordered lives. Foes of liquor believed this opposition to the great reform was inspired by a base desire to curry favor with the dregs of our noisome cities (so the drys were wont to refer to folks who drank anything but hard cider). The bosses were more practical than that. Prohibition gave drink an undue importance in politics, throwing out of balance the carefully adjusted organizations built up by years of work.

In practice, the fears of the timid politicians proved groundless. With millions of citizens looking upon graft as a necessity, and failing to be shocked by the sight at close range, a tolerance to all forms of corruption was speedily developed in the national conscience. It became a matter of mild boast like income tax dodging, getting a ticket for speeding "taken care of" or putting a poor relation on the public payroll. The Republican party in 1924 was very properly grateful to prohibition, for nothing else, not even Mellon's prosperity, could have induced the popular indifference to the scandals of the Harding administration. Voters now knew all about graft, and their chief reaction was a cheerful surprise that Fall got so little as $100,000 for Elk Hills. A $1,500-a-year dry agent could do as well as that.

Naturally the appetite for plunder was not confined to bootleggers and politicians. All sorts of private businesses adopted something from the technique of prohibition violation, and racketeering developed the robust proportions of a major industry thanks to the example set by bootlegging, King of Rackets. The terminology of the gunman and the modern pirate were absorbed into the language, and citizens spoke over their illegal tipple of "muscling in" and putting a fellow "on the spot," while children at play learned to speak out of the corners of their mouths in the harsh, flat tones said to be habitual with our better racketeers. It was all very colorful and entertaining and exciting and a damned nuisance; it added zest to the argument over prohibition.

Both parties to the debate, setting out in opposite directions, arrived at the same conclusion. Wets declared that the attempt to interfere with personal liberty, the folly of reforming morals by fiat and the intolerant fanaticism of confusing temperance with abstinence had debauched public servants and weakened all law. Drys retorted that the subterfuges of sots steeped in sin and alcohol, the flouting of the nation's sober sense, the encouragement of the underworld, had debauched public servants and weakened all law. Both sides owed (and never paid) a debt of gratitude to those who provided such a convenient scapegoat.

President Harding, whose genius lay in embodying the thoughts and feelings of more of his fellow countrymen than any other politician of his day, exemplified with an aptness that was beyond skill the contradictory phases of prohibition. Like millions of others, the President thought the experiment a fine thing for someone else. He was, therefore, prodigal of stern public pronouncements on the duty and necessity of enforcing the law. He had an unswerving dry record, legislatively speaking; he came from the Anti-Saloon League's home state, and his manly eloquence surged easily into overtones of indignation as he railed against men who drank.

"I do not see how any citizen who cherishes the protection of law in organized society can feel himself secure when he himself is the example for contempt of law," said Mr. Harding.

This was his last public statement on the subject, and perhaps he spoke from the heart, for that was the period when he had, in Hoover's phrase, "a dim realization" of what scandals prohibition and its by-products had brought upon his administration. Jess Smith, Daugherty's intimate, had been deep in abstruse dealings with big bootleggers in the capital. At "the little green house on K street," which gained fame as the haunt of the Ohio Gang's inner circle, Harding's own friend, Howard Mannington, and a few associates negotiated profitably with a newly illegal industry. But the President himself told a Congress that contained more dry votes than teetotalers:

"Let the men who are rending the moral fiber of the Republic through easy contempt for the prohibition law because they think it restricts their personal liberty remember that they set the example and breed a contempt for law which will ultimately destroy the Republic."

Mr. Harding's theories were as common as his practice. He was one of a vast though uncounted constituency that, as a matter of actual fact, did not shrink from endangering the public by example. Many flaunted their contempt more openly than the Chief Executive. He at least took his friends into a bedroom of the White House when they wanted a drink or, on formal occasions, had the presidential bootleg served in a smoking room upstairs rather than in the main reception apartments. This seemed perfectly natural in a city where any well-informed man could point out Senators and Representatives whose votes were at the disposal of the Anti-Saloon League, but whose legislative zeal was frequently stimulated by beverages of much more than the permitted one-half of one per cent. alcohol.

"Ours," as Mr. Harding so well said, "must be a law-abiding Republic and reverence and obedience must spring from the influential and the leaders among men, as well as obedience from the humbler citizen, else the temple will collapse."

2

The wing of the temple that housed prohibition was, on the President's own terms, doomed from the start. The Eighteenth Amendment went into theoretical effect on Jan. 16, 1920, and three days more than a month elapsed before the first arrests for corruption. Baltimore had the dubious honor of this première in a series of graft exposures so numerous that, as has been noted, only the President's Cabinet could compete on a percentage basis. The fact that it happened to be one-twelfth of the enforcement officers who were so unlucky as to get caught was actually turned to good advantage by their leaders.

"One out of twelve of the disciples went wrong," remarked the dry Senator Harreld of Oklahoma.

The serene if slightly blasphemous assumption—so infuriating to the wets—that prohibition was a holy crusade for Christian principles was one of the factors that made militant prohibitionists tolerant of graft. According to their theology, there were devils as well as angels. They did not doubt that they themselves were entitled to wings, so they rather welcomed the opposition of hellish foes upon whom failure could be blamed. As a Congressional committee, inquiring into enforcement with care not to uncover too much, was told:

"The blame is not on prohibition, but on the political conspiracy that has so largely filled the enforcement machinery with crooked and corrupt appointees who were selected to insure that the prohibition law could be violated with impunity for the profit of professional bootleggers and the venal politicians who are their silent, powerful partners."

During the first years of the noble experiment, the drys did not stress this point too strongly, for they knew that they themselves had smoothed the path for the "venal politicians." The clause exempting enforcement agents from civil service rules had been passed by dry votes in Congress. The lobbyists who cracked the whip over the legislators later explained that Congress insisted upon the exemption in return for passage of the Volstead Act, which implemented the prohibition amendment in accordance with the most arid interpretation.

"The plain fact is that the Congressmen wanted the plunder and you let them have it," retorted the Civil Service Reform League. "You bought the bill and paid for it, not with your own money but, far worse, with offices paid out of taxes levied upon the people."

The anguish felt because such jobs were given for political effect, as they have always been given when there is no restraint put upon the donors, was not shared by the Congressmen who had arranged for the patronage nor by the political machines behind the Congressmen. Senator Penrose, although one of the select minority who voted against the Eighteenth Amendment, had a good deal more to say about who got jobs in the new bureau than, say, Representative Volstead, author of the enforcement act. Furthermore, the Pennsylvanian was animated solely by care for his organization, and neither he nor his lieutenants saw any reason to withdraw support from a friend because he had changed from a saloon keeper to a speakeasy proprietor. As long as they could name the field men, the dispensers of patronage cared not who occupied the thankless, uncomfortable office of Prohibition Commissioner. Therefore the men in that post could be and were ardent drys, friends of the Anti-Saloon League, but each one, unless he chose to be blind, knew that most of his subordinates were tempted on one side by loyalty to the benefactor who got them their jobs and on the other by sheaves of currency such as have seldom been offered in graft. Commissioner Roy A. Haynes, explaining that under favorable but not altogether unknown conditions a state prohibition administrator on a salary of $6,000 a year could take in $1,000,000 a month in bribes, continued:

"Millions of dollars added to other millions are strewn carelessly across the pathway of those engaged in law enforcement. All or anything that human fancy can devise or desire is offered unhesitatingly. The reverberating chorus of corrupt dollars sounds day and night in the ears of all classes of employees from the highest officials down to the humblest clerk."

It was this siren song that was responsible for the condition found after ten years of prohibition by one of those commissions which Hoover thought could correct by written reports the abuses of a system more potent than paper. There had been at that time 17,972 appointments to the prohibition service and 1,604 dismissals for fraud, extortion and bribery. This was monstrous, but one is tempted to believe that the unusual feature was the moderation or cleverness of the majority.

Perhaps, in view of the temptations and the general public's approval of their graft, it is small wonder that even after civil service was applied to the prohibition agents in 1927, conditions remained about the same. Most of the current employees failed to pass the examination, but their better-educated successors were not more notoriously honest, nor more efficient. After four years of their presence in the bureau, Judge William S. Kenyon of Hoover's commission reported:

"Evidence before us by those accurately acquainted with the workings of prohibition in the great cities shows that in many of them the supposed enforcement of prohibition has been reeking with corruption."

The proportion of convinced drys in the bureau had been increased between 1920 and 1931, but $1,500 a year and prohibitionist principles did not suffice to hold them in line. One in twelve, anyway, fell for the thirty pieces of silver. In New York alone the speakeasy graft was estimated at $60,000,000 a year at a time when the Police Commissioner said there were 32,000 such establishments in the city. Of course this did not all go to the Federal agents, for they held no monopoly on prohibition bribes. Judge Kenyon spoke of the city with truth, but he might with equal veracity have extended his remarks to rural regions. Whole irregular armies of Federal, state, county and municipal officials filled their pockets, their bank accounts, safe deposit vaults, old socks and little tin boxes.

Dislike of the law added less to the prevalence of the graft than the profits to be gained. Bootleggers were more generous with their governmental henchmen than Doheny and Sinclair, than any Vanderbilt or Gould had ever been. Public servants were taken into liquor deals as partners; in franchise, land and other steals they were only the cheap help. Even the mighty Tweed had never made nearly as much as his more powerful patrons. Now a new era dawned for the grafters.

Major Haynes, for example, reported that one of his agents had been offered a retainer of $300,000 a week. This was the highest offer Haynes had ever heard of, and higher, too, than any recorded in other fields of corruption. But what made it truly unique was that it would have given the grafter a bigger profit than the tempter.

The beer barons involved in this particular case were proposing to produce 30,000 barrels a week and sell it for $23.50 a barrel. In addition to the prohibition agent's share, they were setting aside a weekly stipend of $60,000 for local officials. Thus the graft was to amount to $12 a barrel or more than half of the gross revenue of the syndicate. An irresistible appeal and a practical share-the-wealth idea.

3

Policemen who were hired to guard bootleggers from marauding hijackers, legislators who voted to uphold prohibition and consistently violated it, the myriad officeholders who conspired against enforcement, had Robin Hood's excuse. They were crooks, but they quenched the thirst of the poor, sometimes with wood alcohol.

How without graft were 100,000,000 people to get a drink? The only answer to that was repeal, and in the 'twenties even the wets despaired of that solution, for corruption seemed the simpler and more traditional way. Therefore they confined themselves to verbal disapproval of the officials who helped circumvent the obnoxious law, and the drys no more dared protest effectively against the graft of their minions than Croker had felt able to stop the petty thievery of Tammany underlings. But neither side was quite prepared for an outbreak of fiscal scandal in the very palladium of dry virtue, the Anti-Saloon League.

That organization, before putting over prohibition with a display of propaganda equaled only in the war, had managed to identify itself with religion, the sanctity of the home and purity in general. It had used the churches as a collection agency, and had been able to amass an average of $2,500,000 a year for its campaigns. Lawmakers were hired as lecturers and a uniquely efficient lobby maintained, but the propriety with which the League garnered and expended its millions was not questioned seriously until in

1924 there fell from grace one of the most stalwart warriors of all the dry host, William H. Anderson, Superintendent of the Anti-Saloon League in New York.

To a positively biblical talent for invective, this man added a more modern gift for organization. His opposition to rum was sincere enough; his fearlessness in championing his cause in a constituency that liked rum commanded some admiration, and his smoothly running machine made him an outstanding figure in the fight.

His history was ordinary for the time and place. A small town boy in Illinois, reared in a strictly moral atmosphere that accorded well with his own sentiments, he accepted without question the tenets of rural Methodism—that only the elect will be saved and that alcohol is the root of all evil. Firm in that simple faith, he prepared to drive reluctant New Yorkers along the path of arid righteousness.

Anderson charmed many, even foes, by his remarkable unlikeness to the prohibitionist of cartoon and legend. A bulky figure with black hair and mustache, full fresh face and comfortable double chin, he was of a generally cheerful, smiling cast of countenance, far from the usual impression of a sour preacher of gloom. Life had been kind to him and he knew as well as had Mrs. Blaine how good it was "to win and be on the strong side." He could afford to laugh and be happy, as his dearest dreams were written into the fundamental law of the land.

Only the most unregenerate could have dared suspect that such a man, so high in the councils of a moral party, so orthodox, so prolific of phrases applauded by every Anti-Saloon Leaguer and Christian Temperance Woman, could be caught out in the most minute variation from the line of severest rectitude. There was, therefore, a mighty stir in the ranks of the godly and the dry when a grand jury handed up an indictment accusing Superintendent Anderson of forgery. It was only third degree forgery, but the degree was not so greatly stressed then as later. The drys held it was unthinkable that a crime in any degree could be brought home to their leader. Ardent wets were content to point out that disrespect for law was not confined to them. Neither would let the facts speak for themselves, with the result that they became somewhat obscured in a cloud of argument and recrimination. Anderson's own theory that he was a martyr to his principles, victim of a base (alcoholic) plot to ruin him, gained headway, for the very violence of the attack upon him created a reaction in his favor.

One of the facts that got lost in the shuffle of debate was that the books of the League for the year 1920 had been falsified at Anderson's direction and this was the specific charge against him. He maintained that the inaccuracies were harmless, made to protect O. Bertsal Phillips, one of the League's high pressure solicitors, hired on a salary and commission basis. Phillips had agreed to divide evenly with Anderson all of his "take" in excess of $10,000 a year, and he was so successful in levying upon the well-to-do for the support of prohibition that the surplus was considerable. The Superintendent's share for 1920 amounted to $4,400.

Whatever may have been the merits of this arrangement according to any given system of ethics, there was no doubt that it was so far quite legal—one instance of the fact that our standards in private life are not equal to those we set for our public servants, since a government official would have been guilty of a fraud under similar circumstances. Nor was it in this case criminal even if Phillips told the truth when he said the agreement was forced upon him by Anderson as a condition for keeping his job.

Where the Superintendent overstepped legal limits was in causing the $4,400 to appear upon the League's books in Phillips's expense account. If this bit of jugglery had defrauded no one, there still would have been no crime, and it was proved that the only loser was the government, which got no income tax on the item. So eloquent a man as Anderson might easily have found an excuse for this peccadillo to appeal to the sympathy of his people had he not raised a less simple question. In his defense, he declared that a donation not otherwise accounted for had come from one "John T. King," and at the mention of that name the irreverent hooted gleefully, the godly hung their heads in shame and the impartial roared in anger.

The alien property case was then being brought against Daugherty and Colonel Miller, and the only John T. King anyone knew anything about was the late Connecticut politician who was being used as a scapegoat in that trial. Anderson's explanation was derided unmercifully, and a few students recalled with amusement the Crédit Mobilier defense of Schuyler Colfax, who had received a similar present from an unknown man conveniently dead and had been branded by his own party in Congress as a perjurer for saying so.

Observers of Anderson's trial thought that introduction of the name of King prejudiced the jury and led to the verdict of guilty. But the irrelevant point was not the basis for the Appellate Division's ruling on appeal that the evidence "warranted a finding by the jury that there was an entry in the corporation's books falsely made by defendant's direction with intent to defraud." The second highest court in the State pointed out in calmly reasoned opinion that criminal evasion of the income tax was plain from the Superintendent's own testimony.

Anderson was already in Sing Sing when this decision was handed down, and he stayed there for nine months. Released on parole, he found his usefulness to the dry cause ended, although other indictments against him were dismissed on the ground that he had been punished enough.

The astigmatism through which the incident was regarded, as well as the incident itself, was typical of the corrupting influence of prohibition. The noble experiment had proved this much, that even those who were most convinced of the nobility were not immune to the temptations.

As for Anderson, the adventure outside the law altered him surprisingly little. No longer able to exercise his talents in the Anti-Saloon League, he threw himself into a battle against Catholicism, organizing an "American Protestant Alliance" which was "conceived in prayer and suffering," he explained, during his residence up the river. Whether in prayer or otherwise, the crusader had learned to keep his books to himself. The noteworthy feature of the new venture was a rule that subscribers must make their contributions in the form of outright gifts to the treasurer. Thus, said Mr. Anderson, "the transaction is no affair of any wet, antiprohibition, snooping tool, whether public or private."

Even with this precaution, the crusade languished, although its leader was in some demand in those communities that still liked to hear the Pope denounced with old-fashioned vigor. The Alliance perished. Rum and Romanism both had let Anderson down as profitable foes, and he turned to what he doubtless considered a tilt against rebellion. His latest recorded activity was as an ardent supporter of the Liberty League.

The original hoot against Anderson was strong because the grafters who helped circumvent the dry law were more popular than the ones who attempted to enforce it. These last were only a small minority of the prohibition hosts, who showed by their steady refusal to vote sufficient funds for enforcement or proper safeguards to keep their agents honest that they recognized the uses of corruption.

In the light of prohibition experience, there could be no denying that corruption had its uses. And if drink was worth millions in bribes, perhaps railroads, electric power, successful wars, paved streets and the thousand fruits of illicit relations between government and private enterprise were no more dearly bought. After the popular tolerance of dry law graft, it was much easier to evaluate more justly the merits of bribery in other fields.

Of course graft is not the one known way in which it is

possible to get a cocktail. But a better one could be achieved only by overthrowing the whole prohibition system which made graft inevitable. After fourteen years, the people chose to abolish the noble experiment rather than put up any longer with its evils for the sake of its supposed benefits.

Similarly, graft is not the only way to develop the country and its industries. But a better one could be achieved through no other course than overthrowing the system that made graft inevitable. By and large, the people preferred peace and corruption to violence and revolution.

XX

RACKETS

1

Two cars rolled side by side; two guns barked and flashed redly in the dark of a June night in 1930; the crowd of Chicagoans on the corner of State and Quincy Streets scampered for shelter. Then brakes squealed, an exhaust roared and Police Lieutenant Barker, smarting from the indignity of seeing his own automobile the target of gangsters, stood in the roadway firing hopelessly at the retreating assailants. From the back of their machine a great cloud of smoke poured in a billowing screen that neatly blocked off the view. The battle was over, short and sharp like the cinema. But this was no scenario. The guns had been loaded and one non-combatant lay dead on the pavement while another clutched a wounded arm.

When Barker turned around, the cause of the shooting was gone. Witnesses had seen a short, stocky figure leap out of the Lieutenant's car, but no one could tell which way he went. Barker returned to his station to report, regretting the good-natured impulse that had prompted him to offer Jack Zuta a lift after questioning in the matter of a homicide. The detectives hadn't been able to pry any information out of the fellow, who was a nasty bit of work at any time, and now they would have to pick him up again for a probably futile investigation of this latest scrape.

But the intended victim was fleeing from greater perils than the police and managed to keep well hidden. It was a month before any officer of the law saw Jack Zuta again, and then they were called in to view his lifeless body, thoroughly riddled with bullets, lying on the floor of a Wisconsin summer resort dance hall. He had been innocently feeding nickels into an automatic piano when his killers entered, and the instrument was still grinding out its mechanically gay tune when they left.

Next day Chicago learned there had been another casualty in the latest "racket war" and there were the usual protests that such goings on disgraced civilization, the usual moral reflections on conditions that breed such acts of violence. But regrets for the lawlessness of Zuta's passing hardly dimmed the general satisfaction that another of the community's less desirable elements had been eliminated.

Complacence was justified. Jack Zuta in life had been so unfortunate as to look what he was—a pander, a gangster and a cheap politician. His swarthy skin was unnecessarily oily, his features had escaped being repulsive only by being insignificant. Yet there must have been some capacity for business in the man since he had survived in prosperity to the ripe age of forty in a trade whose occupational hazards are particularly numerous and fatal.

He had begun his career as a peddler in the Chicago slums, but he had the wit to embrace less arduous and more lucrative pursuits. His talents lay in the manipulation and terrorization of women, and he developed a small chain of bawdy houses that prospered sufficiently to merit the notice of men more dangerous than himself.

Prostitution in Chicago, as in other cosmopolitan centers, needed more protection than even well-paid police could give it. Men who had no direct interest in pimping marked out for themselves a share in the easy profits of the bordello, and sold at high prices immunity from the evils they were prepared to bring upon those who did not pay. Zuta himself had once attempted to resist, but not for long. His unofficial, would-be guardians sent envoys to beat his girls, stage brawls in his houses and threaten the proprietor. Zuta bought them off by making them his partners, and thus had the use of their thugs to repel the raids of other "protectors" and check the independence of his workers. He was quick to see the advantages of the system and, being a reasonable man, was soon a member in good standing of one of the most highly publicized gangs of the decade. That gave him so great a sense of security that he added gambling to the more primitive attractions of his establishments.

Purveyor to lust and the gaming instinct, Zuta was one of the Chicagoans who took enough interest in the government of his city to work at it. He belonged to the William Hale Thompson Republican Club, was a devoted follower of the patriot for whom the organization was named, contributed handsomely to campaign funds when Thompson ran for Mayor and rejoiced with the rest of his kind when his chief won. He was a busy factor in that feature of American urban life for which the term "racket" was coined, a different breed of underworld character than simple burglars, swindlers, pickpockets and gunmen.

From such bolder criminals Zuta differed in nothing so much as his habit of preserving business documents, a habit that resulted in some little stir after his death. His chief profession was one that normally discourages friendship, and servants of the people twisted uneasily as they tried to explain the relations which the murdered man's records revealed.

With perhaps pardonable pride, Zuta had saved a very friendly letter addressed to "Dear Jack" and subscribed "Your old pal" by one William Freeman, who was grateful for a loan. At the time of Zuta's death it did not lessen interest in the borrower to discover that he was Chief of Police of suburban Evanston, a city that holds itself rather pridefully aloof from the sinful, riotous iniquities of her neighbor on the south.

Equally embarrassing were Zuta's checks that had passed

through the bank accounts of two Chicago jurists, a former State Senator and an assistant state's attorney. They made clear why the pimp, gambling house keeper and bearer of a courtesy card from the Sheriff of Cook County was untroubled by the authorities who were supposed to make life unpleasant for his ilk. His racket was safe from everyone but other racketeers, and could be made so only by one process, the immemorial greasing of the machinery of government.

Police chiefs, magistrates and prosecutors were attracted to such slimy creatures as Zuta in part by the fact that the service racketeers bought seemed very slight, a mere nothing. Indeed, that was literally all they asked—nothing. They paid the grafters well to do nothing, see nothing, hear nothing. Officials who might have scorned to engage actively in the racket had no qualms about ignoring the existence of the Zutas in their towns except when they wished to borrow money. It was only necessary for policemen to look the other way, for district attorneys to refrain from seeking evidence and discourage complaints, for occupants of the bench to grant the delays which would tire out prosecuting witnesses. This might be done with so little effort that the grafters could overlook the sordidness of the business in which they were such very silent partners.

Although racket graft was the easiest to earn and the most difficult to trace, it had one weakness. Its results were of no public benefit. Therefore it failed to win the tolerance which other forms of corruption often enjoyed. At the same time it had a high publicity value, and any crusader against racketeers was assured of ample space in the newspapers. However, until these latter day muckrakers should materialize in public office, the guns that left Zuta lying beside the tinkly piano were the only law that could reach him, the weapon and the Nemesis of the racketeer.

2

Having attached themselves comfortably to the fat profits of bootlegging, gambling, prostitution and organized thievery, the racketeers turned their attention to more legitimate industries. They and their official partners discovered with pleasant surprise what any seventeenth century colonial governor had known, that honest trade yields greater dividends than the most prosperous piracies.

As this lesson was conned with increasing thoroughness through the 'twenties, the well informed in every city could point out with a proper display of civic pride the head of the laundry, the cleaning and dyeing, the restaurant, the taxicab or any one of a dozen other rackets. These mighty men were as much envied, respected and feared as Captains Tew and Shelley had been in the New York which Bellomont tried in vain to reform. However, the turnover in these modern potentates was rapid. Their huge incomes were a constant temptation to rivals, and the right to boss a given set of extortioners changed hands with the rapidity of the Erie Railroad in the days of Vanderbilt and Gould.

The methods were roughly, very roughly, the same—somewhat bloodier and therefore more decisive. The loser seldom remained alive to recoup his lost position by brilliant speculation. He departed this world after the manner of Zuta, but his funeral was of splendid proportions, worthy of royalty. Vast crowds lined the sidewalks to view the magnificent procession, the flamboyant piles of expensive flowers, the bullet-proof limousines of the dead man's colleagues, the distinguished mourning figures of bench, bar, finance and industry.

The amusement value of the racketeers almost warranted the billions they extorted, the individuals they ruined, the economic waste their crudely violent methods entailed. The whole world enjoyed the show, rocking with laughter at the inimitable comedians, weeping happy, sympathetic tears when the plot took a tragic turn, thrilling with excitement to the gaudier moments. Not without pride the followers of Antonio Lombardo, "King of the Underworld" in Chicago for a brief period in the middle 'twenties, pointed to the photograph of their chief among the city's prominent citizens of Italian birth who gathered on a January day in 1927 to greet the current Italian Ambassador. Lombardo survived the honor for more than a year.

While life lasted, Chicagoans of his type developed a ready technique in the establishment of new rackets. An industry that they could most thoroughly dominate would be one in which a host of small independent business men competed for the trade of an army of consumers. These proprietors should be served, if at all, by employees not too well organized. Racketeers did not care to test their strength against industrial powers such as steel or automobile makers, the Du Ponts or the Mellons. Nor did they entangle themselves in battle with unions of proven strength, the United Mine Workers or the railway brotherhoods. Rather they selected the puny hand laundries, cleaning and dyeing establishments, fish or poultry dealers, restaurant owners.

For each of these groups, and many more, a "protective" association would be formed. The racketeers with their armed followers—reincarnations of medieval robber barons and their retainers—fixed dues at whatever it seemed the traffic might bear. Prospective members who hesitated to join or enrolled tradesmen who fell behind in their payments were slugged and bombed, their places of business wrecked, their customers intimidated.

If the racket developed on approved modern lines, the heads of the protective association also organized the employees in the industry upon which they had fastened. If a union already existed, it was taken over by threats, promises or force. The racketeers thus collected dues from two sources and were in a position to levy extra tribute upon proprietors by wielding the strike weapon.

The only expense of operating the racket, aside from the routine costs of munitions and occasional high-priced funerals, was the share of the loot that found its way into the tin boxes of municipal officials. When Chicago finally wearied of its unsavory eminence in the world of rackets and organized a crusade against the modern buccaneers, the leaders of that fight speedily learned that theirs was a political as well as a commercial battle. Business men so prosaic as not to appreciate the farce staged by their underworld rivals formed a Crime Commission to arouse officialdom and citizenry to the need for action. Frank J. Loesch, who served as president of that body, was quick to discern the basis of graft that supported the racketeers. Seeing that the most powerful of his foes had begun (and continued) in bootlegging, he declared:

"Those organizations of murderers and arch criminals can only be destroyed when their bootleg liquor profits are taken from them."

But it was not quite as simple as that, for graft enabled them to survive repeal. Loesch found in studying the career of the most spectacular of the racketeers, "Scarface" Al Capone, that an intricate political fabric was woven around the nucleus of extortion. Capone, leading man of a thousand newspaper stories and honored by imitation on stage and screen, went to jail over so mild a matter as his income tax, and Loesch was permitted to glimpse something of the political forces that made the picturesque Italian immune to any save Federal prosecution.

Capone, boss, or perhaps only front man for a greater boss, over a prime array af gangsters, maintained two of his henchmen in the State Senate. One of these paragons of legislation was James B. Leonardo, the highlights of whose career were thus reported by Loesch:

"Senator Leonardo was convicted of conspiracy to murder, to kidnap and other crimes in 1928, was sentenced to pay a fine, according to the verdict of the jury, and paid that fine. He was subsequently tried on two kidnaping charges and escaped conviction, but the presiding judge sent several men to jail for contempt of court in seeking to bribe the juries trying those cases."

The other member of the Capone bloc in the Upper House was Daniel A. Seritella. He had held the office of City Sealer in Chicago, a post in which he had been of such service to racketeers that he was indicted. His attorney, a Capone lawyer, had his own claim to fame. He had been elected to Congress "by fraud so gross," said Loesch, "that the County Judge sent a number of the [election] judges and clerks committing the frauds to jail." The attempt to form a "Scarface" party in Congress was defeated when the House of Representatives unseated Counselor Granata.

Such visible political influence was really not necessary. In most cities it was enough that the powerful backing of the local boss could be mentioned in whispers by the racketeer to his victim. The obvious fact that the racket prospered without official hindrance emphasized the point sufficiently; there was no need for the grafters to wear labels. At the same time, the sort of work that the politician wanted done on election day by the organization of thugs and persuaders, and which was part of the price of protection, did not require formal endorsement or publicity. The alliance thrived better off the record.

3

Whisky, gin and beer were the liquids generally associated with racketeers, but the entrepreneurs of crime were equally alive to the possibilities of milder beverages. New York had been uncomfortably aware of such a thing as a milk racket for years before Tammany elevated James J. Walker to the Mayor's chair in succession to an amusingly incompetent former jurist and street car conductor. Walker's own administration was not destined to shine in the pure light of investigation, but when he took office in 1926 he appointed a Health Commissioner, Louis I. Harris, who was really interested in the problems of his office.

A good many busy physicians with large but not especially lucrative practices in crowded districts had been wondering why New York babies responded so poorly to milk as a remedy for dietary faults. Some of them seemed to thrive as well on pickles. Dr. Harris found the answer; milk had become a racket and adulteration provided the profit.

Rackets have czars, as do baseball and the moving pictures, and the autocrat of all the butter fats was one Harry Danziger, so secure in his power and protection that he was surprised into a confession when Dr. Harris put the screws on him. His racket added perhaps a cent a bottle to the price of milk, it removed the nourishing qualities and it was worth millions a year.

This kind of czar needs as much support as a Romanoff. Danziger, in addition to the operatives who upheld his claim to rule the racket, had the usual official allies, and the indictments named Thomas J. Clougher, Fred Kautzman and William H. Kehoe. Clougher, chief of this band, had achieved the purple himself. He had been called "Czar of the Health Department" and was in point of fact secretary to the Commissioner. Kautzman was superintendent of milk inspectors and Kehoe had been Assistant Corporation Counsel attached to the department.

The combination was a perfect racket setup, providing all the political influences that could be useful, and might have continued if Dr. Harris had not been able to enlist the active help of District Attorney John McGeehan of the Bronx. In New York's other four counties the crusade had inspired little assistance, for district attorneys as a rule prefer to leave any legal drive on rackets to special prosecutors. McGeehan, however, went after the "baby poisoners" with as much zeal as if they had been shoplifters, and the alarmed Danziger turned state's evidence.

The Czar had been paying Clougher $90,000 to $100,000 a year for permitting the sale of cream not approved through the Health Department. The fees for winking at other adulterations and violations were equally great, but the exact figure could never be determined. Clougher kept the secret of who shared the spoil even after sentence of from five to ten years had been imposed, and won the reward of silence. After two years, he was included in the first batch of pardons that Franklin D. Roosevelt issued as governor. Clemency, the executive explained, was "based in part on the very excellent recommendations which have come to me."

The attack on the milk racket featured the halcyon beginnings of the Walker administration. Exposure of another racket hastened the end of the popular Mayor's stay in office. It was a peculiar racket, too, unique in that it was operated by public officials themselves with a minimum of bloodshed.

The gang was composed of city policemen of the so-called vice squad, part of the ponderous machinery by which the law undertakes to suppress a profession that is said to be even older than racketeering. These particular racketeers knew better than the lawmakers, perhaps, the futility of their official mission. They therefore turned their attention to their own business and built up a steady trade in extorting money from innocent women they arrested on charges of soliciting. Their prey had to be innocent because prostitutes would not pay to avoid the shame of conviction, and besides they were organized and protected by far more imposing underworld figures than the little men of the vice squad dared attack.

As the racket was operated, a policeman would arrest the prospective victim after she had been accosted by a stool pigeon. This agent, the "unknown man" of police court parlance, never appeared as a witness lest someone grow suspicious of the number of times he was beset by women. The arresting officer did his lying for him, and the terrified prisoners never had a chance, since the tribunals charged with settling these cases seem everywhere to function on the assumption that womanhood is universally frail. The racketeers were able to collect from $250 to $1,200 a head as the price for beating the tight little system. Forty policemen, twenty-three lawyers, thirty-eight bondsmen, the stool pigeons and the prosecutor at Women's Court formed the personnel of the racket. Nor did the magistrates who sat in that court emerge unscathed from the inquiry.

Like other rackets, this one relied upon the reluctance of dupes to testify, a factor that was even more potent than in lines of business into which sexual morality did not enter. The less a woman had to fear from a public airing of her case, the more she was afraid of it. But the amateur psychologists of the vice squad guessed wrong just often enough to bring witnesses against them in the end.

One of their major mistakes was Mrs. Genevieve Potocki, a scrubwoman and therefore fair game for any cop, by the reasoning of Policemen William B. Lewis and Edgar P. McFarland. She had some small savings and was not unattractive in their eyes. So, comfortably confident that the oath of two sworn defenders of the city's hearths must outweigh that of any charlady the town could produce, they went at their arrest lustily and none too gently. They could hardly know—and probably would not have cared much—that Mrs. Potocki belonged to a mission maintained by Trinity Church, a multi-millionaire parish that can afford to look after its own. One of the mission's social workers called on Mrs. Potocki two days after the arrest, took one look at her and rushed her off to the hospital. The medical report read:

"Contusions and abrasions above and below the left eye and the left forehead; bruises on the left breast, possible teeth-marks above left breast; undeniable teeth-marks above right breast; finger-marks on arms, finger-marks on both thighs from knees to hips, bruises about lower body."

Lewis and McFarland went to Sing Sing for what the law delicately calls "attempted criminal assault."

That was a personal tragedy for them, but worse was to follow, a body blow at the whole racket. The error in judgment this time started out as a routine conspiracy against a rooming house keeper entrapped by one of the vice squad's most useful stool pigeons, the "unknown man" of countless convictions for soliciting and even more extortions. He was nicknamed, because of the country of his origin, "Chile" Mapocha Acuna, and the landlady he framed happened to be the wife of a compatriot who had recognized the "unknown man." As one Chileño to another, he offered Acuna the simple choice of going to court to tell the truth, "or else." The alternative was quite clear, and for the first time in his career Acuna took the stand. Against the evidence of the police, he established the woman's innocence, but the vice squad was annoyed. Stool pigeons should do as they are told. A few days later "Chile" was in custody on an airtight extortion charge.

He emerged from jail a year later, in 1931, to find the investigation of his old racket just getting under way. His own share in it was forever ended, and his honor cried for satisfaction. He offered his expert testimony, which was graphic, damning and convincing. The day that "Chile" stepped down from the stand and, touching his former partners on the shoulder, called them by name as racketeers, a horrified Police Commissioner suspended each of the twenty-eight so tapped.

That was the great moment of the long hearing. But the most dramatic incident of the investigation took place elsewhere. Vivian Gordon had promised to reveal exactly how she had been framed by the vice squad eight years earlier. Before she could return with her evidence, her murdered body was found thrust into the bushes beside a quiet uptown street, and her sixteen-year-old daughter committed suicide amidst the blare of resulting publicity. The policeman who had arrested the mother—and had in three years banked $35,000 more than his total salary for the period—was cruising during that February, 1931, in southern waters. The Gordon murder is still on the roster of unsolved crimes. Of course public employees who conduct a racket of their own are rare, and not very bright. It is easier for them to collect for keeping out of the way of more industrious operators. Grafters who take this precaution last longer, too, since racketeers are economically so inutile that their existence is comparatively fleeting. They fall from official grace, whereupon they are prosecuted, or they flourish so abundantly that a rival kills them. But their profits are so large that new figures constantly appear to take the places of the dead and the jailed. Shrewd politicians survive to serve several generations of those engaged in what may be termed the criminal aspects of public plunder.

XXI

AND OTHER RACKETS

1

P̞OWER! MEN HAVE STRUGGLED
for it with an intensity surpassing the love of woman, money
or salvation. It has meant many things in many ages, but
a new generation is increasingly conscious of the word as a
synonym for electricity. Communications, transportation,
the driving force of millions of machines, a host of comforts and luxuries, exist because electricity is power. Its
manifold benefactions meet us at every turn, and most of
us repay the genie with a seemly reverence. Yet most of us
are also aware that our god has feet of clay, an earthly corruption that the pioneers of a new science never foresaw.

Even wise old Ben Franklin, drawing lightning from the
sky with a toy, did not dream how greatly that innocent
experiment would contribute to the truth of his observation:

"There is no kind of dishonesty into which otherwise
good people more easily and frequently fall than that of
defrauding the government."

Otherwise good people were not less prominent in the
utility industries than elsewhere. As the illimitable realms
of electricity opened out before them, they saw only a few
frail bastions of law and government between them and realization of their dreams of Power. The graft that swept the
obstacles aside was a necessary part of the process by which
the good work was accomplished by private enterprise.

Franchises, water power sites, rights of way for transmis-
sion lines, assurances of monopolies, formed the basis for

marvels of expansion. To get them, the companies had to go into the business of government. The only alternative would have been for the government to go into business. The people who mattered and had the last word so much preferred graft that Samuel Seabury, a Republican jurist of integrity, scholarship and anything but revolutionary views, wrote as early as 1905 of the Consolidated Gas and New York Edison companies, his city's dominant power organizations:

"Their record has been one of extortion. Their privileges were conceived in fraud and political corruption and throughout their existence they have been a constant source of temptation to corrupt officials. Both of these corporations exist in violation of the law and both enjoy absolute monopolies in the necessaries of life. Both have violated the law of the State, both have made false reports to avoid the payment of their just taxes and both have entered into a close and friendly alliance with public officers whose duty required that they should protect the public from extortion."

These companies were not outstanding offenders. But they, like their fellows, were engaged in the struggle for Power, and success cannot be bound too tightly by scruple. The stake was imperial, and imperialistic methods commend themselves only to the users. A clear-sighted politician, Newton D. Baker, Wilson's Secretary of War, stated the issue years before he became an attorney for utilities that were opposing a great government project in the Tennessee Valley. In his earlier period, speaking of the nation's hydroelectric resources, he said:

"Whoever owns them in a large sense may be said to own the United States. If I were greedy for power over my fellow men, I would rather control Muscle Shoals than be continuously elected President of the United States."

To many plain folks nurtured on the legend that the occupant of the White House wields a power greater than that of kings and emperors, Baker's remarks seemed fantastically exaggerated. Utility promoters, if we may judge by their actions, agreed with him thoroughly.

The means by which they achieved and maintained eminence were many and devious, but they fell into a general pattern by which groups of men who contributed nothing to scientific development, technical operation or financing (in the old-fashioned sense of putting up money) acquired control of heat, light and power. Consolidation, merger, holding company and stock manipulation based on monopoly franchises made them great. Continual propaganda, incessant vigilance against the threat of public ownership, lobbying, political pressure and graft to prevent too stringent regulation kept some of them at the top of the heap.

While the engineers and inventors were creating their wonders for the service of mankind, the promoters were devising marvels of their own. They defied proverbs by eating their cake and having it too. And for good measure, they sold it for cash as well. It was layer cake, and the layers were disposed of one after another, but the seller always kept the topmost for his own, and that had all the frosting.

The art of accountancy and the variety of units assembled in one loosely held mass led to endless complications, but the pattern was relatively simple. The usual practice was for a promoter to get an operating utility, by actual purchase if need be. Suppose that for this Company A he paid $1,000,000. He would organize Company B, a holding company, to buy Company A's stock. Company B would issue $1,000,000 worth of bonds and preferred (non-voting) stock, which would go to the promoter in exchange for the stock of Company A. He would sell these bonds and preferred stock to the public, recouping his million but keeping B's common stock, say 100,000 shares with sole voting rights, in which would be vested absolute control of both companies.

Meanwhile he would have "revalued" Company A to a book worth of $2,000,000, the "write-up" being credited to the advantages of reorganization. (An Insull company once increased its paper value $8,000,000 simply "by resolution of the Board of Directors.") The business of Company A remaining the same, it would have to earn a profit on $2,000,-000 instead of half that, the "real" value, and the rates would be adjusted accordingly, thus making the promoter's common stock in Company B, which represented no investment or assets of any kind, worth something in the market.

The pyramid of reorganization need not stop there. At the height of their prosperity the two "top" Insull companies had six layers of subsidiaries underneath them, the whole tangle being composed of 248 firms. Even members of the Liberty League were unable to offer any valid excuse for this feature of the American system they liked so well, and one of them, Bainbridge Colby, referring to the Insull setup, asked:

"What possible explanation that squares with reason or good intent can be offered for such a masterpiece of designed confusion?"

The answer was profit and power, good reason if not good intent. Experience proved that despite an increasing web of government regulation, highly inflated values as a basis for rates producing "a fair return" on alleged investment would be approved. The "designed confusion" was the method of inflation that was most effective.

The connivance of public utility commissioners and legislatures in these write-ups, even if only passive, was one of the rules by which alone this game could be played. Their support was obtained by direct methods as well as by lobbying and a propaganda machine unequaled since the war. The length of a utility purse was famous among the politicians who were for sale, but the companies were not quite so gullible in their lavish generosity as the beneficiaries of their bounty supposed. Again Power accomplished its gastronomic feat with cake. The utilities poured out hundreds of thousands for lobbyists, retaining former Senators and the firms in which influential statesmen were partners as freely as if they were police court shysters. Millions went for newspaper publicity, lecturers, writers of school books; millions more to finance the campaigns of political allies.

The money was never missed. Every penny of it was charged to operating costs, met by the rates for service to householders and industrial consumers. As Managing Director Aylesworth of the National Electric Light Association said in addressing one of the subdivisions of his highly organized publicity service:

"Don't be afraid of the expense. The public pays the expenses."

Mr. Aylesworth gained quite a reputation as one of the miracle workers of the electrical field, perhaps in part because his first name was Merlin, and to many business men this notion of having the public pay for propaganda directed against public interest seemed as wonderful as the emergence of Excalibur from the lake had been to King Arthur. But the modern knights of the round table discussions in holding company directors rooms took the miraculous properties of the new weapon as a matter of course. The result was that most local governments were forbidden to build their own water and electric plants; few agencies of the sovereign people were privileged to enter into competition with the lords of Power.

Sometimes money can be beaten, usually after it has been flagrantly offensive. When in 1935 Congress voted a law to abolish the worst abuses of the holding company system, the firms most affected vainly offered millions—including the cost of a flood of forged telegrams to legislators—to defeat the measure. The Associated Gas and Electric Company alone spent about $700,000 and destroyed the records of that expenditure. But a Senate investigation of this lobby subjected Ursal Beach, head of the Associated Gas securities department, to the embarrassment of questioning by a mere stockholder, Senator Schwellenbach, who had bought into the company at $49 a share in the boom.

"What's the stock worth now?" he asked.

"About fifty cents," replied Beach.

The Senator refrained from pointing out that it was ostensibly in the interest of this 1 per cent. remnant of his investment that the holding companies were campaigning so vigorously. They had been pleading as usual that a lot of their stockholders were widows and orphans, but they did not attempt to explain the features of holding company control that cost these pitiful objects of managerial solicitude 99 per cent. of their stake, on which dividends had been passed for years, while the heads of Associated Gas, who were far from being the owners, made handsome profits in addition to their generous salaries. That point, after all, was not germane to the investigation of the imposing attempt to browbeat and otherwise influence Congress. So Schwellenbach contented himself with asking:

"Do you think that I, who paid $49 a share for my stock and have never collected a dividend and never had a chance to because Mr. Mange and Mr. Hopson [the heads of Associated Gas] grabbed it all, will get any good out of this campaign to defeat the bill?"

"Yes," said Beach stoutly, "I do."

"Oh, yeah!" retorted the Senator bitterly, and there was a note of the same bitterness in the laughter that swept the room.

2

Thorough airing of the holding company system revealed the close resemblance between distinguished citizens who presided over utility destinies and the Zutas, Lombardos and Danzigers. They had all imposed their leadership upon organizations that did business with many individuals, but the racketeers never captured anything quite so fat.

If Power had not been organized as a racket, it might have propped up the whole national financial structure when the general crash came, for it was the one great industry

whose revenues were but little affected. At the depth of the
depression in 1932, the country's annual electric bill was
only 11 per cent. less than at the height of the boom. Such
stability might well have served to rally the nation, but because regulation had broken down, because the grafters permitted irresponsible control, utility stocks were among the
most spectacular divers on the market. Associated Gas was
not the only one that shrank to 1 per cent. of its former
price. The corruption that enabled the promoters to carry
on their chicane without interference played its part in the
shrinkage.

Just as Al Capone had use for his own men in the political life of Illinois, so it was with Samuel Insull. The analogy
was close, even before both fell afoul of the law, Capone to
go to jail and Insull to escape to Greece, hiding in disguise,
fleeing from place to place and finally being returned to
win an acquittal and what some considered a vindication.

But before that unpleasantness, Insull was a big shot, bigger than Capone. He had even more to say about the operation of Chicago's eccentric municipal administration; he rose
to the peak of his power at the same time that the racketeers
were permitted to achieve their greatest prosperity; he rode
in a bullet-proof limousine as large and safe as theirs, and
in 1926 he wanted a United States Senator. His candidate
was Frank L. Smith, chairman of the Illinois Commerce
Commission, charged with the regulation of utilities within
the State. In Illinois that meant Insull, and Smith's conduct
in office had deserved well of the companies whose affairs
fell within the scope of his duty.

He was not too well known to the electorate, and his
opponent in the Republican primary not only held the
Senatorship but rejoiced in the name of William McKinley. However, money more than remedied the disparity of
natural handicaps, and Smith had a campaign fund of no
less than $175,000. Insull had contributed $125,000 of it in
cash. Smith won the nomination and went on to sweep the

election, although his chief backer, realizing that industry could no more afford to be partisan than in the days of Gould, protected himself with a bet on the long shot in the race. The Democratic candidate had only $18,000 to spend, plenty for the representative of a party doomed to defeat in the midst of the Coolidge prosperity, but $15,000 of it came from the broad-minded Insull.

Smith won a barren victory. The Upper House proved less cordial to him than the Lower had been to Capone's Representative. The utility Senator was not allowed even to take his seat, barred at the same time as Bill Vare of Pennsylvania and for the same reason—immodest display of campaign wealth.

The spirit of mutual sympathy and helpfulness existing between State Commissioner and utility magnate was a surprise to complacent citizens who assumed that government regulation really regulates. But in many states commissioners were hardly more than agents of utilities. They approved inflated rate bases, ignored reckless financing and frequently graduated into lucrative posts with private companies.

However "tainted with corruption and fraud" these relations might be—the phraseology is that of the Senate in holding Smith unfit to serve there—the rest of the community was similarly tarred. One of the lengthier inquiries conducted by the Federal Trade Commission produced volumes of testimony proving that newspaper publishers, college professors, women's club leaders and other righteous elements all over the country were as eager to sell themselves to the utilities as any legislator or commissioner.

The millions spent in molding opinion for the press, pulpit, school, platform and legislative hall were not entirely a cold-blooded investment dictated by unmitigated greed. Power carries responsibility and may even induce quite sincere delusions of grandeur. The men who wielded Power came easily to regard themselves, as Baker regarded them, above merely elected or appointed officials of the commonwealth, beyond crude considerations of majority rule, superior to vulgar masses who used electricity and owned utility stocks.

"It is just as much the business of the electric light and power industry to preserve republican institutions as it is for it to give its patrons service and to make profits for its share holders," said one spokesman.

The aim was laudable, no doubt, but what the industry meant by republican institutions appeared in a statement of Franklin Griffith, president of the Portland (Ore.) Electric Power Company:

"An attack upon the principles for which we stand is an attack upon the government itself."

Many public officials were won to the same point of view. In New York, H. Edmund Machold, Speaker of the Assembly and Republican State Chairman, was so much the slave of this doctrine that his successor in the party leadership complained:

"The trouble is not that Mr. Machold believes in the private ownership of public utilities but that he apparently believes in the private ownership of the State government."

Legislators who fell easy victims to the dogma of pyramided holding companies, fancy write-ups and reckless financing could also be convinced that the wide distribution of utility stocks constituted a form of public ownership. Profit, or rather talk of profit, was brushed aside. A Philadelphia utility man even worked out a theory that "in the utility business, in a sense, there are no profits." He proposed that this should be taught in colleges, although professorial ingenuity might have been taxed to reconcile the doctrine with the $100,000,000 Insull fortune and Mr. Hopson might have been very much alarmed if it proved true.

The Chicagoan was a refutation of the notion that investment has anything to do with ownership. The 100,000 or more shareholders in the 248 Insull companies had put up hundreds of millions but they could hardly be said to own the business. Insull interests apart from these anonymous subscribers held more than 60 per cent. of the two top holding companies. The theoretical owners of the rest of the empire had nothing to say about the corporate policies that finally toppled the whole structure into ruins—on paper, as it had been built up—with a loss estimated as high as $4,000,000,000 to stockholders.

The blessings of Insullation rested on the foundation of franchises obtained by the usual boodle methods. Yet it was often said in justification of these grabs that they did not cost the people anything. This was a theory that dated at least as far back as Mark Hanna. The great boss once refused a request to have a Cleveland street paved where it would increase the value of friend's property, and the man reminded Hanna how he had helped the leader of the party win franchises. Mrs. Hanna used to tell the story as illustrative of her husband's rigid integrity, and would conclude:

"Mr. H. answered that it did not cost the city a penny to grant him a franchise, but that it would cost $100,000 to pave this street."

The campaign against municipal power plants, extending over years and utilizing every known means of propaganda except sky-writing, was designed to protect similar franchises that had cost the taxpayers nothing, but were worth millions. J. B. Sheridan, one of the most active press agents of Power, who had informed his employers that it was his great ambition to put every municipal plant out of business, succeeded in enlisting all but one of Missouri's 600 dailies, he said. But what he really thought of private vs. public ownership after five years of successful service on behalf of private interests was contained in a letter to a friend in 1927.

"What can we do when the financiers will inflate, overcapitalize, sell securities based on blue sky and hot air, and rates must be kept up to pay returns on said blue sky and

hot air?" he asked rhetorically. . . . "I know places where I
believe a thirteen-cent top rate should be eight cents. . . .
I believe in private initiative, but I don't believe in sub-
sidizing it three or six cents per kilowatt-hour. . . .

"The bankers in the electrical industry do not appreciate
what a fat thing they have had in the past seven years. They
do not appreciate the enormous value of the monopoly feature. They do not appreciate that electric light and power
properties are not loaded dice to be employed in a craps
game in which investors and the public are injured."

But the game went on under the eyes of the benevolent
guardians of the law, who raked in some of the winnings
with one hand while the other shook a threatening club in
the faces of protesting losers. However, there were fewer
complaints about this than about the games played by the
racketeers, which were noisier, although the stakes were
smaller. Utility methods were therefore allowed to continue
despite the revelations of 1926, where a racket similarly exposed would have been crushed, at least temporarily.

3

The operations of Capone and Insull differed in another
important particular. Violence and the threat of violence
against individuals were at the foundation of the racketeer's
power. Smoother subtleties sufficed to erect the inflated edi-
fice of the Insull utilities. But other industries not usually
classed as rackets were as prodigal of bloodshed as any
gangster. The sponsors of industrial warfare were respectable
citizens with reputations to lose, so they needed even more
official protection than Scarface Al, and where their thugs
operated, the standard of government morality was something at which toughened Chicago racketeers shuddered.

Steel and coal, foundation of heavy industry, applied the
law of gun and club most relentlessly, although in the general scramble for government favor they did not ignore

milder corruption. The steel men were always ready to help revise a tariff upwards, and their support in Pennsylvania never failed the Penrose machine, whose founder had been an ironmaster. But steel and coal could be secure only behind a stronger bulwark than high duties.

Production in mill and mine was carried on by armies of strong illiterates whose vague aspirations could not be entirely deadened by unconscionably long hours, filthy living conditions and grinding poverty. To keep them quiet in their misery was no task for the squeamish. Arguing comfortably that less than twelve hours' work in twenty-four or more than bare subsistence pay would undermine the health and morals of their workmen, executives in well-appointed offices set themselves bravely to the ordeal of saving labor from unwholesome cravings.

As individuals the men were negligible. As a purposeful mass they could be formidable, and this was so obvious that they were drawn instinctively to organize. Force alone kept them apart, and force on a scale sufficient to coerce desperate thousands was hardly a practicable private enterprise. Therefore it was not enough for mine and mill owners to bribe or influence public officials. Municipal and county if not state governments had to be owned outright.

In some of the coal fields, the operators lost their grip on local administration, and the United Mine Workers came into being, forcing in long, dramatic and often bloody struggle some amelioration of their bitter lot. But other coal areas and all of steel held on grimly for years, clinging to the ideals of Baer and his Christian men of 1902. The squalor of their unlovely towns, peopled by a dirty, undernourished race, were the themes of horror stories unrivaled by the hottest inter-gang battles of the racketeers.

In the steel towns and the coal fields pretense of popular government ceased to exist. Sheriffs and their deputies, police, mayors and prosecutors were openly in the pay of the companies. The supposedly elementary rights of men to hold public meetings, trade where they liked and cast votes for candidates of their own choosing, not to mention organizing in unions, were crimes punishable by beating, blacklisting, exile and death.

Strikes flamed into civil wars and the hired armies of the employers, farcically sworn into the service of the people, battled enraged workers grimly seeking some few of the privileges guaranteed in documents most of them did not know existed. Miners, who had the power to arouse the public by interfering with heat and light far from the mines, sometimes won concessions. The steel workers, whose products were not consumers' goods and who had to rely on sympathy, which was of as much value to them as their constitutional rights, were beaten time after time. In every contest the force of local government, absolutely at the disposal of the mills, was the decisive factor.

Once in a while the frightfulness of steel drew national attention, as during the great strike after the war when the cry for a union and bearable living conditions ran out in blood among the slag heaps and dumps that the workers called their homes. The Coal and Iron Police earned their pay, and in Allegheny County, Pa., 5,000 deputy sheriffs were sworn in, paid by the mills, armed by the mills and turned loose upon refractory strikers. The Sheriff enrolled anyone the companies recommended, and the thugs of Pittsburgh reaped a harvest in the unfamiliar role of officers of the law.

Even in a world made callous by war, this seemed to call for a remedy, and nothing less than a Senate investigation was deemed adequate. The august Committee on Education and Labor, therefore, listened with some patience to inarticulate men struggling in a strange tongue to express their sense of injustice, their fantastic hopes that an industry swollen with the profits of mass slaughter might afford its workers homes in which it would be possible to keep clean, schools for their children, mills where human lives might be safeguarded as carefully as the machinery.

The Senators heard the frank revelations of civil officers that they served the mills rather than the people. They heard over and over the story of terrorization, beatings, shootings and the overshadowing menace of an arrogance that regarded steel workers as something lower than domestic animals, for pigs and cattle have intrinsic value and will die if not properly cared for. They heard descriptions of company towns where the beds were never empty, the tired men of one shift flopping wearily into the places of not quite so tired men rising for the day's toll. They heard this expert testimony from Judge Elbert H. Gary, the starched shirtfront of the United States Steel Corporation:

"None of these men, with very few exceptions, perform manual labor as I used to perform it on the farm, neither in hours nor in the actual physical exertion."

They heard the same witness admit that his shops had employed labor spies to fight the union. They heard that the hours at which Gary scoffed consisted of a twelve-hour day with a twenty-four-hour trick when the two shifts changed over. They heard Sheriff Haddock of Allegheny County protesting:

"The strikers make great complaint that they are denied their constitutional rights of free speech and free assemblage. But this has not been denied them except in strike zones," the only place it might do them some good.

No one could say the investigation had been scamped. The whole story was carefully transcribed and the decision solemnly recorded that the troubles were all caused by scheming fellows who perverted the perfection of American institutions to their own guilty aims. Not Judge Gary. Not Sheriff Haddock. Not the local administrations that took their pay and their orders from the steel companies. No, these men, the Committee on Education and Labor held, partook of the true American spirit. The real culprits were union organizers, workers, foreigners, radicals.

Amazing? Not really. For the committee had its own ideas about those sacred institutions for which most of its members had recently called upon the youth of the land to fight and bleed and die. Said Senator McKellar of Tennessee:

"The trouble is that we have got a very liberal provision in our Constitution about the freedom of the press and freedom of speech."

Some of the Senator's predecessors had not considered that provision "trouble." They had been inclined rather to regard it as a privilege and a duty, but of course they had never had the inestimable experience of hearing Judge Gary on the rights of man. McKellar, thus inspired, evolved a constructive plan for circumventing the troublesome provision. The gentleman from Tennessee left this passage in the record, a fragment from the examination of Lieutenant Donald C. Van Buren, a lawyer who had seen strike service as assistant to an intelligence officer:

McKellar: How would it do to pass a law punishing by imprisonment and fine every American citizen who belongs to one of these radical societies; and I mean by that the societies like the anarchists' societies and the I.W.W. societies, or who sends out literature of such societies, and have the punishment fixed so we can take care of them in this way: If they did not want to suffer the penalty, to give them the option of taking ten years and $5,000 fine or be sent to an island in the Philippine Archipelago, where they can carry out their peculiar bent of mind in a way that would be interesting to them only.

Van Buren: In other words establish a soviet on the island?

McKellar: If they wish. It occurs to me that it would be a very good plan. What do you think of it?

Van Buren: Excellent, sir.

Senator Smith: It might be all right if you could cut off

all means of communication between them and the rest of the islands.

McKellar: They would have to be under guard, of course.

Fascist dictatorships appear to be as ungrateful as republics. Research fails to disclose any acknowledgment by Mussolini (with his island pest centers) or Hitler (with his concentration camps) to McKellar of Tennessee, who had the idea long before Duce and Fuehrer were familiar headline words.

The incipient Fascism of 1919 failed to drive the Senator's countrymen into the nation-wide racket that is a totalitarian state, but the racketeering propensities in certain industries were strengthened by Federal and local participation in an artfully inflamed hysteria of red-baiting. Sheltered from interference by this screen, steel and coal continued to usurp government functions by means of the same ruthlessness with which Chicago gunmen imposed their own law and order upon those they "protected." Gunman and corporation executive alike relied upon the purchased inactivity of the grafters.

The report of the Senate Committee on Education and Labor proved the value (to the racketeers of big business) of that form of graft which consists of electing statesmen so committed to the economics of profit that they are not even aware of the facts when industries organized for gain degenerate into rackets.

XXII

THE OLD MODEL

1

A TAME TIGER WAS ON DIS-
play in New York in the time of the big boom. Tammany,
purged of its predatory instincts, its ferocity and its treachery—so men said—basked in an aura of purity. A benevolent
complacency induced by several years of indubitable world
ascendancy pervaded the whole nation and was evident in
a calm satisfaction with existing institutions. Envied and
respected for its power, assured and reassured of the superior
nobility of its ideals, confident that the national genius had
found the secret of perennial progress, the richest country
on the globe assumed a congratulatory arrogance which for
generations had been regarded as a monopoly of Englishmen.

A great and idealistic people would never knowingly tolerate corruption and inefficiency, so it was logical to suppose that the Hall's standard of honesty must be on a level
with that prevailing in the business community. Although
men who said this meant it for high praise, even flattery, it
was true. But then of course it always had been true. It was
why government was not always in the hands of men as
devoted to the public interest as Fourth of July orators
maintained.

Fitting representative of the new era in municipal politics was the Mayor who took office in January, 1926. James J.
Walker, young (but not as young as he looked), witty,
talented, friendly and gay, assumed with dapper insouciance
and light words the burden under which a succession of

384

dull executives had complained. Jimmy—for so he was known at home and abroad—cherished the political philosophy of the Italian Renaissance at its best. He believed government should be fun for both governed and governor.

He and the times, in his first term, were made for each other. The crescendo of illusory riches was the only adequate background for His Honor's pyrotechnical gifts. Drugged with a prosperity that was mistakenly supposed to be general as well as permanent, delighted New Yorkers were as heedless of the cost of his regime as of the price of bank stock or a new house with two-car garage. Tolerantly they forgave the city administration for being expensive so long as it was amusing, and for a time few cared that the rulers of the country's oldest political machine were only as scrupulous with other people's money as bankers.

More truly representative of the new Tammany than the talented Mayor was Thomas M. Farley, "Big Tom," Sheriff of New York County, the office that had been worth $100,000 to "Big Bill" Tweed. Farley, molded in the school of Croker, was leader of an influential district and for years had held jobs that were exceedingly important in the political routine of the city but did not attract the searchlight of publicity. As early as 1925, when he was County Clerk, Big Tom had been able to save $34,824 in a year. Since his salary and only ostensible source of income amounted to $6,500, this was a notable example of thrift, but Farley never boasted of his financial skill.

His political club was one of the busier centers of New York's unofficial government. Here patronage was dispensed, favors at city expense passed out, instruction in citizenship provided for voters and an assorted service in jobs (municipal and otherwise), advice, charity and comfort maintained for the use of Farley constituents. It was, in short, a typical Tammany club, devoted to shrewd politics whether in the guise of benevolence or corruption. It was also, according to complaints, a place where cards and other games were played for money, but for years justice had turned only her blindfolded eyes in that direction.

However, one of the gestures of the new Tammany was a Police Commissioner, George V. McLaughlin, who was as serious as Dr. Harris about his job. He elevated to Deputy Chief Inspector a Captain whose efficiency and intelligent interest in departmental funds had hitherto stood in the way of his advancement. This honest cop was Lewis Valentine, a man of no known politics, afflicted with such exaggerated political astigmatism that he raided Tammany clubs as if they had been establishments of friendless gamblers.

Among the premises thus invaded were those presided over by Farley, Register James McQuade of Kings County and Alderman Peter McGuinness of Brooklyn. Big Tom accepted the attendant publicity with outward serenity, but some of his fellow victims were betrayed into unseemly rage. The Alderman was heard to predict, neither darkly nor in a low voice, that McLaughlin and his place wouldn't know each other long. But then The McGuinness, as this representative of the new Tammany liked to be known, had suffered the indignity of arrest.

His feelings were salved no doubt by the remarkable accuracy of his prophecy, and into the Commissioner's job stepped the Mayor's former law partner, Joseph A. Warren. He encouraged Valentine to continue his quixotic tilting, and soon Warren too was writing letters of resignation. His first composition was rejected on purely literary grounds (without, however, implying any lack of merit); the second, offering ill health as the reason for retirement, was accepted and published. Just at this time popular curiosity had been aroused by the murder of one of the city's best known gamblers, Arnold Rothstein. Police failure to arrest his murderer was an opportune screen for whatever other reasons Farley, McQuade and The McGuinness might have been able to discern for Warren's resignation.

The extent to which the new Tammany differed from the

old was never seen to better advantage than in the choice of the administration's third police commissioner. The people had laughed at "Red Mike" Hylan, Walker's predecessor; they laughed with Jimmy. Only a desire to keep the fun going could have guided the appointment of Grover Whalen, who had made a niche for himself in the gallery of useful public servants by wearing a flower in his coat lapel and being the first American to greet many visiting celebrities.

His burlesque overshadowed for a time the polished performance of Jimmy himself. The populace roared with laughter as the new Commissioner reduced metropolitan traffic to an even more hopeless snarl than it had been, wore his boutonniere with exaggerated aplomb at conferences with hardened cops and elaborated absurd pronunciamentos for the public prints. It was easy to forget what he was there for, but the clown of the Walker regime knew his business had a serious side.

Whalen took office on Dec. 18, 1928. At eight o'clock on the morning of Dec. 20th, the uneasy thousands of New York's "Finest," lined up in their station houses, were hearing the order that reduced Lewis Valentine from deputy chief inspector to his civil service rank of captain with an assignment to a remote district known as a depository for those officers of the law who were in disgrace with their superiors.

2

While the honest cop was rusticating in his semi-suburban retreat, Farley, McQuade and McGuinness pursued careers that would make sheriffs of all of them; Jimmy got himself re-elected; Tammany continued to bask in the glamor of having its morals compared politely with those of business.

Unfortunately business seemed bent on proving itself no better than Tammany. Permanent prosperity collapsed in October, 1929, with a crash that left a good many highly respected financiers and industrialists exposed to popular bitterness with no other protection than their own sorry records.

The legend of a new Tammany was one of the minor bits of wreckage. The local politicians shared the ruin of their partners in trade, and few of either class saved anything but money. That they could cling so stubbornly to this was an added cause for resentment. The people, betrayed in their fond hopes of a perpetual boom, were no longer in any mood to relish the humor of the Walker administration. Savagely they were counting the cost at last, and as paper profits, savings, jobs, security and homes were swept into the rubbish heap of the depression, the victims raised an increasingly angry cry for an accounting.

The economic blast that tore some of the decorous drapery from the not very pretty framework of high finance and speculation revealed that the curtain had shrouded grafting public officials as well as recklessly greedy masters of money. A banking department head who took bribes to allow an insolvent financial institution to remain open, judges who used the bench for stock promotion schemes, a former Fire Department veterinary whose fees for representing private clients before the Bureau of Standards totaled $2,000,000, these and a host of others were dragged into the light of day—and some of them were later dragged back to the seclusion of prison cells.

Through it all Farley and McQuade stood up stoutly for the principles of the new Tammany. Others might run for the cover of "I decline to answer on the ground that it might tend to incriminate me" or go to jail or resign in haste. But Farley and McQuade were made of sterner stuff, ready to play to the end their roles of highly paid buffoons.

Big Tom cheerfully acknowledged that his only source of income was his salary and about $25,000 in commissions on real estate deals. He agreed with equal readiness that in six years he had banked $300,000 more than the total of salary and commissions, and that at the end of that period he was "worth" $250,000. To citizens who had already traveled two years away from the boom's peak at the time of this admission, it seemed to call for explanation, and the big fellow blandly offered one. Smiling and confident, he faced former Judge Seabury, a much-feared interrogator of corrupt officials, with this result:

Q.—On your salary of $6,500 a year [as County Clerk] in 1925, will you tell the committee where you could have gotten $34,824?
A.—Moneys that I saved.
Q.—Where did you keep the moneys that you saved?
A.—In a safe-deposit box in the house, at home.
Q.—And, Sheriff, was that box a tin box or a wooden box?
A.—A tin box.
Q.—What is the most money that you ever put in that tin box?
A.—I had as much as $100,000 in it. . . .
Q.—Well, then, we come to 1928. That year you deposited $58,177.75. Where did you get that money, Sheriff?
A.—That was moneys the same way.
Q.—It came from—?
A.—The good box I had.
Q.—Kind of a magic box, Sheriff?
A.—It was a wonderful box.

Big Tom was by no means the first to offer the explanation of such a receptacle as the source of mysterious wealth, but he made the story all his own. Farley's magic box took rank with the marvelous rings, chests and lamps of mythology.

It could hardly be said, however, that McQuade was outdone as a raconteur. Not for him the impudent and implausible use of the supernatural. He relied on sob stuff for his appeal, and if the audience chose to laugh instead of weep, he could not be blamed for the lamentable taste of a cynical age. McQuade was called upon to explain the amount of $500,000 that had passed through his bank account. Some people thought it a lot of money in 1931, but to McQuade it was just a headache. For, said he, it all traced back to the failure of a brokerage house operated by his brothers.

"After they liquidate," he mourned from the witness stand, "the thirty-four McQuades are on my back, I being the only breadwinner, so to speak, and after that it was necessary to keep life in their body, sustenance, to go out and borrow."

Despite the eccentricities of the McQuade grammar, the sympathy of his hearers might have been aroused more deeply but for one McQuade who was not getting his sustenance from the politician. This one was being boarded and lodged at public expense following his conviction as a bucket shop operator.

"After they paid up all they could," went on the witness, skipping tactfully over that criminal case, "I took over their responsibilities. It was not necessary; I felt it my duty, being that they were my flesh and blood, part and parcel of me, to help them. I am getting along in fairly good shape, when my mother, Lord ha' mercy on her, in 1925 dropped dead. I am going along nicely when my brother, Lord ha' mercy on him, in 1926 or 1927 dropped dead. But doing nicely when I have two other brothers, and when my brother died he willed me his family, which I am still taking care of, thank God. Two other brothers, who have been very sick, and are sick, so much so that when your committee notified me, I was waiting for one of them to die.

"They have twenty-four children that I am trying to keep fed, clothed and educated, which means that I must borrow money. The extra money that you see in this year, or any year from that year on, has been money that I borrowed —not ashamed of it—if the Lord lets me live, I intend to pay it all."

Any satisfaction McQuade's creditors may have derived

from this last phrase must have been short-lived. Their anxiety can only be imagined—they have never been identified—when the witness added that although he had borrowed from a great many friends, he couldn't remember the name of a single one and had no paper of any kind to show who they were.

Dick Croker or George Washington Plunkitt would have seen nothing out of the way in these stories, but they would have been sincerely shocked by the unsympathetic way in which they were received. Even Sheriff Grant's notions of his duties as godfather to Flossie Croker had aroused nothing like the ridicule that greeted Farley and McQuade, and Big Tom was removed from office while his fellow comedian led the thirty-four starving McQuades into oblivion.

The lightning of punishment struck in its usual capricious fashion among the others of the new Tammany. Walker, forced to resign in disgrace, took shelter in Europe and returned only to face that complete finish to a promising political career which seems to be the destiny of all New York Mayors. Whalen, on the other hand, retiring into commercial sinecures where his publicity value was appreciated, actually heard himself mentioned as a possible Mayoral candidate in 1937. Some occupants of the bench went to jail; others resigned hurriedly; others faced trial on charges; still others, whose names had been involved as deeply, remained in the courts to pass judgment on their fellow sinners.

That judgment was merciful on the whole, and it should have been. With millions of their countrymen pursuing easy money in blind stubbornness, the followers of Croker and Murphy could hardly be blamed for joining the scramble. Their graft reached excessive proportions just at the same time that all other forms of gain were being fantastically expanded. It was only after they had begun mournfully to count the cost that New Yorkers realized Tammany, for all its professions of reform, had not changed its stripes.

3

Another delusion of progress was harder a-dying. This was the theory, proclaimed by Senator Henry Cabot Lodge, that the combination of graft, stock juggling, corporation looting and general politico-financial chicanery lumped under the heading of "transportation abuses" had gone forever.

The automobile, carrying its millions without benefit of land grants, subsidies or purchased Congressmen, was the shining example. Certainly the new industry did not pause in its rush to greatness to corrupt governments. There was, however, no need to leap to the conclusion that capitalists and politicians had suddenly been converted to a higher probity. Graft kept away from the motor car maker's door because it was unnecessary; the gentleman got what he wanted without it.

In every period of our history, we have seen that graft rose when the economic development of the country ran counter to the aspirations of the masses; corruption fell to a minimum when the popular voice favored the aims of capitalist progress. Approval of exactly the sort of assistance the automobile industry desired was so nearly unanimous as to eliminate bribery. The clever fellows who devised mass production of cars were prepared to pay the grafters for just one thing—hard-surfaced roads and plenty of them. In other countries they built highways at their own expense to stimulate the use of their products. In the United States they were spared any cost in this connection. Farmers, merchants, workmen and excursionists, city folks wanting to visit the country and country people yearning for a trip to the city forced every State, county and town to build all the roads it could afford.

The automobile manufacturers made their money from the sale of cars and were willing to leave the unprofitable operation of highways to the public. If the railway builders had been interested only in selling equipment rather than in the carrying trade, they would have been as honest as any automobile man in the world. The graft involved in actual road construction and buying rights of way ought to have convinced even Senator Lodge that the old "abuses" yield to an economic, not a moral, cure.

Those who learned the lesson of the motor car imperfectly were instructed all over again by an even newer form of transportation. Airways, like railways, had to make their profits as common carriers. Once again the conflict between public interest and private gain was sharp, and once again it was settled in the traditional fashion.

The war lifted aviation from the class of toy or experiment into the realms of practical business. But even Colonel Deeds and his colleagues were slow to perceive the immediate potentialities of the airplane, so the first air mail in 1918 was a Federal enterprise. Publicly owned and operated air lines, however, smacked of the Red Terror that haunted the dreams of such men as Attorney General Palmer in the post-war reaction. The post office, for the encouragement of private initiative and the development of science, therefore soon issued contracts to private plane owners to carry mail at so much per pound per mile.

The first companies engaged in this traffic were small, managed and controlled by practical aviation men interested solely in their own business. A good many of them were reprehensibly bent on improving their equipment, but that did not divert them from posting to themselves old telephone books and chunks of lead when legitimate air mail was light. None of them understood the art of modern financing by which they might have puffed their holdings into great paper fortunes. They carried passengers along with the mail and telephone books, talked of a future when millions in a hurry might safely travel by air, devised better planes, mapped landing fields and supposed they were creating a transportation system.

They had made a good deal of technical progress and very little money when in May, 1927, a refreshingly inarticulate mechanic named Charles Augustus Lindbergh piloted a plane from New York to Paris. Incomprehensibly the world went mad; the young flyer catapulted into a dizzying fame that upset all his previous plans for a modest barnstorming tour, testimonials and serial rights to his own story—and aviation had become big business.

Only then did the financial geniuses awake to the fact that they were in danger of losing something. Once again the name of Deeds was heard in connection with aviation. The Pennsylvania Railroad, a Vanderbilt, representatives of the most important financing houses, stepped condescendingly into the picture and prepared to take over direction of the new industry. They knew they were on the right track when a Mellon-controlled aviation company appeared in Pittsburgh. Where Uncle Andy led, it was safe to follow.

To these newcomers it was at once apparent that Lindbergh's flight in itself would not make air travel sufficiently profitable for them. Fares, freight rates and the sale of planes could not offer a basis for the fat executive salaries, bonuses and stock issues by which they were attracted. Naturally they turned to the usual fount for assurance of profit. Subsidy, a word that had been lisped appealingly by a long succession of infant industries, was heard again.

While the new companies were printing stock certificates and electing imposing boards of directors, disdaining the unpretentious little oufits that merely flew the mail, the man predestined for their service was rising to the strategic position that would enable him to steer aviation history into the course taken by canals and railways. Walter F. Brown had been Republican boss of Toledo and although he had worked for Harding had not shared the opprobrium of the Ohio Gang. As a local machine leader of talent and experience, he had been eminently qualified to preside over a Committee of Reorganization of the Executive Departments of the Government. This task, carried on during the Coolidge administration to the satisfaction of his fellow bosses, led Brown in the fall of 1927 into the Department of Commerce as Assistant Secretary.

There he was at once struck by the presidential availability of his chief, Herbert Hoover, an outstanding promoter who was widely publicized as a great engineer, savior of the Belgian people and organizer of wartime food economy. In 1928 the prospect of a rich man entering the White House did not seem as politically ridiculous as usual, and Brown threw himself into the task of directing the Hoover boom. It was a walkover, and Brown collected the Postmaster Generalship, traditional reward for successful campaign managers. Since his party had been snugly in power for eight years, there was little opportunity for a redistribution of jobs; he was able to turn his attention almost at once to aviation.

There were in the field only three large combines whose financial structure showed evidence of the expert touch, and they were sadly lacking in mail contracts. Foremost of these was the Transcontinental Air Transport Company, the T.A.T. of popular speech. Its board boasted Colonel Henry Breckenridge, Lindbergh's backer, as well as William H. Vanderbilt and three members of the great financing house of Hayden, Stone & Co. It was swathed, too, in the glory of Lindbergh himself, who accepted a salary and $25,000 worth of stock. Later the Pennsylvania Railroad bought in. Perhaps even more important to the Postmaster General was the company of his Cabinet colleague, the Secretary of the Treasury. Aviation Corporation's board was graced by a Mellon and by Uncle Andy's son-in-law. Last of the big three was United Aircraft & Transport, a holding company that owned the United Air Lines and manufacturing plants. Colonel Deeds was chairman of the executive committee; his son, Charles, was treasurer, and the directing genius was

Frederick B. Rentschler, brother of the president of the National City Bank of New York.

Brown's authority to deal with what he considered a rather muddled situation was not very broad. After fruitless efforts to make it stretch, he appealed to Congress for nothing less than power to arrange contracts and fix rates by direct negotiation with the operators and without competitive bids. Congress refused; even in the year of the big boom it was not ready to throw away all anti-graft safeguards. But in the closing days of the 1929 session, it passed a law containing this sentence:

"The Postmaster General in establishing air routes under this act, when in his judgment the public interest will be promoted thereby, may make any extensions or consolidations of routes which are now or may hereafter be established."

In May, 1930, Brown was ready to take advantage of this. He summoned a meeting in Washington, and invited only those companies that had contracts or upon whom official favor was to smile. To this "spoils conference," as it was irreverently called, the Boss of Toledo explained that he wished to avoid competitive bids, that he had authority to extend existing contracts almost indefinitely into unserved territory and desired that some of this gravy in the form of subletting should be passed on to the big three, the only companies represented that did not have contracts to extend. He then withdrew, expressing the hope that his guests would parcel out the country by agreement, and he left another of Hoover's former assistant secretaries, William P. Mac-Cracken, to preside.

Only Brown's presence, with his assumption of autocratic power, could have controlled that conference. As soon as the restraint was removed, every operator claimed everything in sight for himself. Brown's assurance that he could make the tail of a small existing contract wag the dog of vast new territory was not altogether convincing, but operators demanded, as one of them said, "all the lines I could think of that might connect with our line," even though they did not think it was legal.

The attempt to distribute the spoil amicably failed, and the Postmaster General set about eliminating competition by eliminating the competing companies. Small lines were advised, threatened or cajoled into selling out to the big three, whose influence was felt more strongly every day. The independents might offer to fly the mail at a lower rate, but that was not enough. The pioneers of the industry—Lindbergh's old employers among them—were out in the cold.

Nor were the small operators alone in their misery. Their plight was shared by one of the largest in the game, Western Air Express. This outfit had a thriving network of successful routes in the West and among its backers were some of President Hoover's wealthy friends, so its head, Harris Hanshue, expected no interference from Hoover's campaign manager. He was too sanguine. Abruptly Brown informed him that Western Air Express "must" submerge itself in bigger interests. There would be no mail subsidy unless the company agreed to consolidate with T.A.T. and give a minority holding to Pittsburgh Aviation Industries, a subsidiary of Mellon's Aviation Corporation. Hanshue was decidedly unwilling. Neither T.A.T. nor Uncle Andy had anything to offer his company in the way of enlarged traffic or better service. But when he telephoned his California backers, they told him not to do anything that might embarrass Mr. Hoover, whose prestige was already dimming.

The merger went through and T.A.T. became T.W.A., still "the Lindbergh Line" and so well intrenched that when it asked 97½ per cent. of the postage in return for carrying transcontinental mail, it got the contract, although a group of independents offered to do the job for 64 per cent. The loss to the government would have been $8,000,

ooo for the life of the contract on one flight a day, but
since T.W.A. averaged more trips, the cost was correspond-
ingly greater.

4

In Brown's defense, it was said that he subsidized a new
industry of great value to the country. Actually he subsidized
a choice assortment of stock jobbers, financiers and promoters. Between 1930 and the end of the Hoover administration on March 4, 1933, the government paid nearly $80,000,-
000 for flying the mail. Half of it was subsidy. Furthermore
Brown had allocated the routes so admirably that 90 per
cent. of the entire sum went to three companies—T.W.A.,
United and Aviation Corporation.

The $40,000,000 subsidy may have provided some of the
funds for the amazing development of passenger craft in
those years, but it was more certainly the basis for fortunes
that seemed to defy economic laws. While the rest of the
industrial world was sinking into depression, the big aviation firms never noticed any lag from the glorious booming
'twenties.

Rentschler, to take a brilliant example of the men who
fattened on the subsidy, drew more than $1,500,000 in sal-
ary, bonus and directors' fees from United Aircraft in six
years, but that was a small part of his gain. In the early days
of the company he had made a grand investment of $253
in its stock. He sold a block of it for $9,514,869 but what he
had left had been worth $26,000,000 in the boom and was
quoted in January, 1934, at $2,100,000. Young Charles Deeds
paralleled Rentschler's achievement. His original investment
had been $40, but his profits pyramided so rapidly that
he was able to sell part of his holdings for $1,060,314.90.
The remnant was valued later in the depression at $450,000.

These profits to insiders in an infant industry that professed to rely upon government subsidy for mere existence
were not unprecedented. Nor were the means, political and

otherwise, by which they were achieved. But for once, public indignation was not appeased by the suggestion that a more business-like administration of public affairs would fix everything. Business methods had lost their charm as the most impressive reputations in America were dissipated in the gales of bitter merriment that accompanied revelation of the chase for profits in 1929.

A method used by the House of Morgan, for instance, had been gifts to public men in the form of permission to subscribe to new stock issues at ten points or so below the market. The beneficiaries were distinguished by their influence in both political parties as well as by their attachment to the system under which Morgan's bank thrived. They included even a Charles Francis Adams, who had been Coolidge's Secretary of the Navy, and Coolidge himself. There was also Charles D. Hilles, Republican leader of New York, and that Machold whose belief in private ownership of state government had been so useful to the larger utilities. The Democrats included Baker, Senator McAdoo, John J. Raskob, chairman of the National Committee when Hoover defeated Al Smith, and William Woodin, who was to be Franklin Roosevelt's first Secretary of the Treasury. Like Oakes Ames and Dick Croker, these statesmen saw no reason for refraining from profitable stock deals.

Publicity given to this Morgan preferred list eased the situation of Boss Brown, who not many years earlier would have borne the onus of his aircraft dealings in as solitary shame as Boss Tweed had endured the Ring exposures. But when the details of his administration were spread before a Senatorial Committee after he had retired in Hoover's wake, the former Postmaster General suffered little more in reputation than his industrial colleagues. In the end it was MacCracken, chairman of the "spoils conference," who went to jail, and he only for contempt of the Senate in trying to plead a lawyer's professional immunity as a reason for not testifying.

Without the aid of his testimony, the air mail contracts were canceled on Feb. 9, 1934, by a politician of infinitely greater astuteness than poor Brown. James A. Farley was to Franklin Roosevelt what Brown had been to Hoover and earned the same reward, the Postmaster Generalship. He had been a little delayed in getting around to the air mail. There were a delightful number of post office jobs exempt from civil service, and the filling of these took time. But when the Senate committee's publicity reached its peak, Farley acted promptly. He prepared a new system of letting contracts, in which competition figured to a degree that no doubt horrified his predecessor. In May the companies discovered that they could do the government's work for $7,700,238. The cost for the same service under Brown's contracts had been $19,400,264.

A professional politician who saves the taxpayers $12,000,-000 and gets on every front page in the country while doing it can reasonably expect to make a magnificent splash as a true servant of the people. But in the interval between canceling the old contracts and letting the new, Farley had permitted the army to fly the mail. The weather was atrocious; the military aviators, with no passengers to worry about and eager to show their ability, pressed their luck too hard; they lacked, too, the best equipment for commercial flying, and eleven of them were killed.

Those eleven young lives cheated Farley of a minor triumph, but he did not attempt to enforce his meed of acclaim as a lesser man might have done. He bore whatever disappointment he may have felt with a more than stoic, a smiling, fortitude. Jim Farley was gunning for bigger political game than mere praise as an efficient Postmaster General.

XXIII

THE NEW DEAL

1

The new administration of which Farley was an ornament wrought many wonders, and not the least of these was a chapter in the history of graft. In the first fine frenzy of enthusiasm for loftier aspirations, this achievement was overlooked as the people, betrayed by a too ready trust in slogans, prepared to redeem themselves by marching with renewed confidence beneath political banners emblazoned with the magic words "New Deal."

Many of those who in 1933 hailed the dawn of a braver, better world could recall without greatly taxing their memories how Theodore Roosevelt's New Nationalism had been displaced by Wilson's New Freedom. They had seen both lost in Coolidge's New Prosperity as it faded into Hoover's New Era, and the taste of that was still bitter in their mouths. "New Deal" had a less Utopian sound, indicating nothing more revolutionary than a redistribution of old cards. Although millions watched breathlessly to see where the aces would fall, the political shuffle was not too keenly remarked, even when the riffling was done by the expert fingers of Jim Farley. He, acknowledged dispenser of patronage, was using very old cards indeed. So old that Martin Van Buren could have handled them familiarly and recognized every mark on the back.

The Washington that waited for Farley was oddly reminiscent of the crude young capital into which Jackson's campaign manager had brought the spoils system. The Postmaster General was besieged by a pitiful army of hopeful but, for the most part entirely unfit applicants for jobs. In November, 1932, nearly 23,000,000 voters cast their ballots for Franklin D. Roosevelt, and next March half that number of citizens were out of work.

At first it seemed that the 115,000 Federal posts unprotected by civil service would afford ample scope for rewarding electoral merit. Before the administration took office, it was plain that ten times the number would have been inadequate. To old line party workers were added desperate millions whose only hope of outriding the economic storm was to scramble into public employ.

Fortunately Jim Farley was equipped to handle even such a confused tragedy as confronted him. Forty-five years old, of unusual height and bulk, with his blue eyes gleaming brightly in his bald, pink head, he commanded a cheerfulness of manner that was the first requisite for the task of discrimination, selection and rebuff. He also possessed a remarkable talent for political organization, the combination of his proven ability as a salesman with geniality, courage, firmness and understanding of all men's aims. He was fully capable of subordinating his own immediate desires to a more distant goal, and his experience had taught him to be judiciously lavish.

His chief public office up to this time had been chairmanship of New York's Boxing Commission, and his distribution of free passes had foreshadowed his eminence as a dealer in political patronage. Commissioner Farley's generosity with the Annie Oakleys had once wrung from the most noted of fight promoters, Tex Rickard, a murmur that he would rather keep the passes to sell and let Big Jim give away the rest of the arena. But never a free ticket was wasted.

Farley's gregarious instinct, a genuine liking even for unlovely types, had made him a devotee of politics ever since as a lad of eight he had whooped and hollered for Bryan in the gaudy campaign of '96. He had been a town committeeman in Rockland County—Big Jim was no city feller—before he was old enough to vote. As a star salesman he had seen much of his country, but his true field was not found until he set up as a contractor in New York, the traditional occupation for a political boss.

In 1920 his services were rewarded with the office of Port Warden, a job of which few New Yorkers had ever heard and which was later abolished. It was Farley's duty at $5,000 a year to inspect all galleons, caravels, frigates and other such craft that might come sailing into New York harbor out of the remote past. This left ample leisure to pursue a political rather than a nautical education, and when he joined the Boxing Commission in 1924 he was admirably fitted to deal with the prime assortment of racketeers, hoodlums, bandits, social and business leaders, sportsmen and politicians who make up the "fight game." His success with these people was evidence that he would not fail when his activities were translated to the national field.

Not since Van Buren's talents had been placed without reserve at the disposal of the picturesque personality of Jackson had a candidate and campaign manager so thoroughly complemented each other as Roosevelt and Farley. Politics were almost all they had in common, but enough to cement a reciprocal, enduring loyalty. It was one of the reasons they were in Washington in March, 1933, Roosevelt to soothe a nation stricken with panic and Farley to attempt the miracle of satisfying the insatiable job hunters.

Those earlier New Yorkers, Clinton and Van Buren, would have been proud of Big Jim. No one in the New Deal showed so well the progress of a century. Van Buren's largesse had of necessity been indiscriminate. There was nothing haphazard about Farley. His patronage mill was a perfectly balanced piece of machinery that produced Federal employees with the efficient speed of an automobile assembly line.

Elaborate card-indexing systems, a corps of political clearance aides in strategic departments and the Postmaster General's own phenomenal memory for men reduced the problem of its lowest dimensions, which yet remained formidable. Farley had to handle forty-eight state machines, innumerable local bosses, Senators, Representatives, high Federal officials. Most jobs were apportioned to State organizations, with local subdivisions left to get their gravy from the State bowl.

Congressional applicants for patronage were checked against a file containing the record of how each Senator and Representative voted on New Deal legislation. But that was not the sole test. Jobs for folks at home could be used to win over opponents as well as to reward supporters, and some of the latter complained that "no" votes paid better political dividends.

The new deal to the general run of government workers was no more than the bureaucracy had learned to expect when the party in power changed. Each outgoing administration tried to keep its spoilsmen in office by transferring some of them to the civil service by executive order, and Hoover was no exception. But they can be transferred back again by another executive order—Harding had done it to some of Wilson's appointees—and Roosevelt was at least that close to the Ohio Gang. In 1932 the total of Federal employees was 583,000, of whom 467,000 were under civil service. In 1935, with a multiplication of government functions, there were 770,000 on the Federal payroll, but only 455,000 were under civil service. Three years later the new servants were being brought under the rules as the administration took steps to "freeze" its own appointees into office for keeps. Another 100,000 were added to civil service.

So far as graft is based on patronage—and the foundation of political machines is just that—the Roosevelt "reforms" had succeeded in fixing the system more firmly in American government.

2

The feat of pouring a couple of hundred thousand extra jobs into the public trough would have sufficed to make the reputation of most administrations, but the New Deal was so prolific of achievements that this one was almost lost in the shuffle, and men spoke of the "Roosevelt Revolution." Now revolution is the transfer of power from one class to another, and by that definition the most clearly revolutionary aspect of the New Deal was its graft.

From the moment Samuel Argall landed in Virginia, corrupt politicians had been perverting public office to the uses of private enterprise. They had in so doing helped to confer immense benefits upon their country and they had earned for themselves much unmerited contempt as well as some small share in the spoil. Plunder cemented the ideals of our political philosophers, exercised modifying influence upon the formation of governmental machinery, lent incentive to territorial and industrial expansion. Land grabbers, manufacturers, mine owners, transportation promoters, utility operators and financiers had been the direct beneficiaries of all the important graft of 300 years. They were the class who wielded the power of corruption.

The Roosevelt revolution in graft consisted quite simply of transferring this age-old system of subsidy to other classes of the population. Federal largesse, once almost the exclusive possession of speculators and franchise snatchers, was suddenly bestowed upon farmers and unemployed factory hands.

Of course this was in line with sound public policy— it was as important to the general welfare to keep farmers on the land and workers from starving as it had been to open up the country with railroads. Furthermore the payment of agricultural benefits and distribution of relief carried out the most upright principles of honest graft. Never before in the history of the country had billions been spent with so little chiseling, and on a class that politicians had always treated like the weather, something to talk about but not do anything about.

It is more than coincidence that the number of persons supposed to be in need of relief in 1933 was 22,000,000 and that even in the best of times, according to figures of the International Chamber of Commerce before the crash, there were 22,000,000 persons living at less than a decent subsistence level. That these millions of private citizens should have been invited to the trough where hundreds once fed seemed to forward to that extent the coming of the millennium.

Measured by what the depressed 22,000,000 were able to buy with their relief checks, this was not much. Compared with the misery, fear and peril of outright starvation from which they were rescued, the progress was sufficiently notable that Jim Farley's prediction of forty-six states for Roosevelt in 1936 was uncannily accurate. There was some justification for the bitter campaign references to the $4,880,000,000 relief appropriation of that year as "Roosevelt's five billion dollar campaign fund."

While the part that this and the inimitable Farley organization played in the electoral victory could easily be exaggerated, making the triumph appear nothing more than a mandate for more and wider distribution of graft, the effect upon local and state machines was profound. As the great program of public works took shape, political bosses in widely scattered sections of the country found the chief props of their power were being kicked from under them. They no longer monopolized either jobs or practical charity.

In Kansas City Tom Prendergast, who with Mayor Frank Hague of Jersey City represented the last of the Dick Croker school of political boss, saw his secure hold on the masses sadly loosened. "We feed 'em and we vote 'em," he had once explained the basis of his rule, but now the government fed 'em, gave some of 'em jobs and let 'em vote as they pleased. Of course they would have been crazy to vote for anybody but Roosevelt, which hardly helped Prendergast. He was a Democrat but not a New Deal Democrat, so his henchmen were sent to jail for mere election frauds, and it was with difficulty that he kept a semblance of control over his domain. Real power he had already lost.

His Eastern prototype, Hague, survived in undiminished strength because he had taken pains to let no opposition survive in his bailiwick to be nursed into greatness by Federal pap. In Jersey City, despite one of the most expensive governments ever known for a place of that size, there was no reform party and when Mayor Hague said, "I am the law," he stood uncontradicted except by "foreigners," that is, non-residents of Jersey City. Furthermore as vice chairman of the Democratic National Committee, of which Farley was chairman, he got his share of Federal patronage. Big Jim never smashed a machine he could use.

The Tammany sachems, who had once regarded the Fuehrer of Jersey City as a fairly small potato, came to envy his lot. The new deal that the Hall got from the Roosevelt administration was a sorry hand to play; the revolution in graft deprived the old organization of its onetime advantages. In the beginning Farley, determined to break boss rule when he could not bend it to his service, tried to smash Tammany with the sledge hammer of patronage. Wilson and Cleveland had failed in similar attempts, and the Hall, yielding the Mayoralty and a few other city offices to fusion candidates in 1933 after the Walker scandals, remained confident that it would regain its grip, as it always had in the past.

Two new factors upset this calculation. One was a Mayor, Fiorello La Guardia, who could play the game of practical politics as astutely as any grafter. The other was the New Deal. By 1937 Farley had ringed Tammany with rival machines in the boroughs outside Manhattan, which had never been securely held for the Hall, but the real revolution was caused by the New Deal program of subsidy and relief. Its share for New York had to be expended with the co opera tion of the fusion regime, and Tammany's monopoly on the gratitude of the poor was broken. They looked now to public works and home relief, voting with enthusiasm for Roosevelt and La Guardia. The Mayor had no trouble at all in ending the tradition that New York could never stand an anti-Tammanyite for two terms.

The New Deal in its revolutionary redistribution of the benefits of honest graft had created a reform organization even more efficient than the old, unregenerate model, a political machine as strange and incomprehensible to party hacks as Watt's steam engine had been to the English weavers whose independence it doomed.

3

This revolution was all to the good, but in effecting it the New Deal left in the old hands far more extensive powers than it took away, and these could work a counter-revolution. All that the old line grafters needed was to gain control of the administration of relief and public works. This was so promptly realized that it inspired persistent propaganda for the return of these services to local organs of government.

No one seriously interested in the efficiency and honesty of the relief system could suppose that the unemployed and the destitute, not to mention the taxpayer, would be helped by taking the machinery for spending billions out of the hands of unbribable Federal administrators. The billions would then have to be fingered by the Horner and Kelly machines in Illinois, the professional Democrats and Tories of the South, the Hagues and Prendergasts, the comic opera state legislatures like that of New York where the claims of faction, sect and section tangled endlessly in futile, expensive gestures.

From such puerile assaults the New Deal would have been safe if the "Roosevelt Revolution" had really permitted power to revolve anywhere except in the region of honest graft. But Roosevelt was no more a revolutionary than Farley, and he proposed to move toward a better world by the slow process of reform rather than the risky and violent course of revolution. There is no doubt that he could have chosen either in those early months of 1933 when the New Era was prostrate in its ruins and discredited leaders had abdicated in business as in politics. Industry clamored for a dictator and the bewildered masses were ready to accept anything that promised to restore the pleasant custom of three meals a day and a bed to sleep in. Roosevelt chose reform, and that in its very nature is at best a gradual elimination of abuses, resisted by the few who stand to lose by it and condemned by the impatient many who demand speedier solution of their troubles.

The program offered was ambitious enough to require energies usually reserved for war or revolution and usually modified in practice by realistic grafters. Capitalism was to be purged of all error while retaining every prosperous feature; the Coolidge boom would return, reinforced by a greater share of the benefits for millions who had hitherto been excluded from them; investors were to be freed from the perils of speculation; agriculture was to be restored to its proper place in the national scheme; industry would be reanimated with the hope of profits; labor would enjoy the security of decent wages and social insurance.

To do all this was going to involve some contradictions, but consistency is often a virtue of small minds and in politics it is expected to yield to expediency. It is also expected that corruption will supply the lubricant that keeps the clashing gears of governmental machinery from tearing themselves to pieces.

Graft alone could have reconciled the New Deal's eloquent concern for the forgotten man with its equally fervent desire to promote the recovery of business. But among the formulators of policy there was no graft, and even those great capitalists like the Du Ponts and Vincent Astor who had contributed to the first Roosevelt campaign funds could not control the operation of cherished New Deal measures which had the overwhelming support of the electorate and yet retarded the recovery of capitalist economy along the only proven lines.

Early in the depression the much maligned Hoover saw the problem and obeyed the rules courageously and in the face of considerable pressure. He did nothing. Essentially the great smash conformed to the pattern of a dozen previous panics, each of which had caught the country unaware and each of which was considered unique in its time. The accumulation of profit had grown apace until it overbalanced the other factors in the national income, whereupon they all toppled over together. Accumulation and reinvestments had piled up an enormous productive capacity which had to be operated at a profit, which had to be reinvested in further productive values, which swelled profits still further . . . and so on until the bubble burst.

In this particular instance, the process had been going on with such intensity that the topheavy accumulation—the long term debt of the country—had nearly doubled in eight years, from 75 billions in 1921 to 135 billions in 1929. Earnings quite failed to keep pace, and by 1932 one dollar out of every five of the national income went to pay interest on this load. But still it grew. What could a man like Andrew Mellon do with the twenty-odd million dollars that made up his gross income of 1931? Only put most of it back to earn more.

It is very exhilarating for a nation to ascend this financial spiral. When the car reaches the top, flies off into space and begins plunging back to earth, exhilaration gives way to terror. But according to the classic laws of capitalism there is nothing to do about it except wait for the crash, hope that the car won't be completely destroyed, and start up again. That is what Hoover saw, but he found that there are other scientific laws besides those of economics. One is the law of falling bodies, which decrees that the higher the starting point the greater the velocity of the fall and the harder the bump at the end. In none of our other panics had we to fall from such a height, and as the pace quickened, the great engineer was infected with the fear that had already stampeded the rest of the country. He began to wonder whether the capitalist system could survive the jolt, and whether it might not be possible to throw out a parachute to slacken the downward rush.

These thoughts led him to depart from his policy of doing nothing. The Reconstruction Finance Corporation was formed to lend money to hard-pressed industrialists and financiers. Although in New York a state banking official had gone to jail for permitting a bank to falsify the assets on its books, the Hoover administration allowed all banks to do the same thing by writing up bonds they held to a theoretical "fair value" rather than actual market worth.

Such measures were quite powerless to check the plunge into the depths of the depression. But the New Deal opened a parachute so effective that many people thought it was a balloon. The inexorable deflation, by which excessive accumulation was being squeezed out of the financial fabric, was reversed. At first glance it seemed that the theory of laissez faire economics had been exploded, that a planned profit economy had been substituted for the old wasteful system.

That was when men spoke of the "Roosevelt Revolution," but the misnomer became apparent when the supposedly most revolutionary of New Deal measures, the NRA, brought back to Washington the dollar-a-year men of wartime. The

NRA, under the misleadingly liberal slogan of "self-government in industry," was the broadest delegation of public power to private interests that the country had ever seen. The whole regulation of business, including price fixing, was turned over to organized groups of the very men whose leadership had been so bitterly discredited.

Both Hoover and Roosevelt would probably have disclaimed with heat the notion that NRA owed its inspiration to the great engineer. Yet it was his policy as Secretary of Commerce and President that built up the trade associations which NRA adopted as the co-ordinating factor in industry. Freeing them from anti-trust law restrictions, which many of them had been formed to circumvent, the New Deal bade them reconcile the innate contradictions between profit to their clients, high wages for their labor and service to the public. By May, 1935, when the Supreme Court decided unanimously that this sort of government of industry, by industry, for industry, was not the one set up by the Founding Fathers and had better perish from the earth, the men who had attempted to operate it were already passing to each other the blame for failure.

The need for a little graft to bridge the gap between what the politicians told the people they wanted and what the pursuit of profit demanded became more obvious. The country was still being assured that security, jobs and protection of farms and homes and savings were the aims of good government. But the leaders of capitalism, recovered from panic fears that their system could not survive the operation of its own economic laws, were impatient to carry the deflation to its logical conclusion so that the cycle of accumulation might begin again.

It was at this point that they separated from the New Deal because they saw that its billions for relief, public works and farm subsidy, which they now for the first time labeled a form of graft, preserved the conditions which caused the crisis. The masters of capital were ready to cut loose from the parachute. They would emerge from the resulting crash with more control than ever over the nation's resources, since the holdings of many small entrepreneurs would be squeezed into their hands.

In any case the cold logic of classical laissez faire theory dictated stern measures against any "planned economy." So far the plans had not proved dangerous, for they were directed to a gradual approach toward the goal which the masters of industry wished to reach quickly. But what if the enthusiastic planners should hit on a scheme to abolish profit? The men who live on profit were constantly voicing their fear of this prospect.

Corruption was the logical, traditional form for resistance to such perils. The leaders of the New Deal should have been persuaded to identify their interests with those of finance capital without dropping the pretense of loyalty to the will of the people. Roosevelt and his most trusted advisers, however, thought they knew better than the Du Ponts and Morgans where the true interest of finance capital lay. But Roosevelt was not the first President who thought he could run the country independently and there was a tried and true specific against such presumption. The men of much property turned to politicians who shared the older view of the American System.

Congress had always been more amenable to influence than the executive. Individually its members lived less in the spotlight of publicity, and it was possible for many of them to campaign with fervor as New Dealers in 1936 and vote with the old guard in 1937. In dozens of constituencies the campaign contributors who had once financed staunch Republicans of the New Era now enabled Democrats to go vote hunting in unaccustomed style. Successful candidates proved not ungrateful when they arrived in Washington, where the usual difficulties of a second term President were confronting Roosevelt. Legislators who had needed his indorsement for 1936 could ignore him afterwards because by 1940 they would be attached to a rising star.

When Roosevelt proposed in 1938 to go a little beyond Boss Brown in reorganization of government bureaus to prevent overlapping, confusion and waste, he allowed the spoilsmen to be seen at their best. The bill was in essential features one that had been sought by Republican Presidents and approved by all sorts of high-minded, non-partisan civic organizations. It would have promoted efficiency; it might have saved money; it would certainly have put out of reach a large slice of patronage which had come to be regarded as a vested Congressional right.

Amid a torrent of irrelevant criticism and abuse and with almost no reference to the measure's actual merits and defects, it was buried. Congress saved its graft, and in doing so was applauded by most of the press and virtually all of the leading industrialists. Patronage, the foes of the New Deal hoped, would divide executive and legislature so irreparably that the President's objectives would be lost.

Despite the sudden willingness of many Congressmen to vote in accordance with the conscience of their campaign contributors, the most deflationary measures could not be put through until the Roosevelt revolution in graft could be upset by a counter-revolution. Subsidy to farmers, relief for the unemployed and projects for local improvements at Federal expense were not to be tossed aside lightly by any politician in need of a vote. The millions were pressing for government aid with the same force as the capitalists, and both insisted they asked no more than their rights. Both, according to their interpretations of our system of government, were correct.

It was the old story of the nation having something to give away, and after 300 years of political progress it was no longer a foregone conclusion that the biggest bribes would decide who got it. The potential threat of mass action if not the development of a sense of justice made the struggle one between two schools of graft—the graft of votes and the graft of profits.

4

The New Deal's theory that the policy of giving, which had been found so nourishing by corporations, might also be fit for human beings brought nearer by the amount of relief and benefit payments the equal distribution of government favors. In some remote, impossibly Utopian future these may be passed out in exactly even portions to all the people. When that happens we won't call it corruption any more; the history of graft will be finished.

Meanwhile that history was made a good deal more intelligible to those who had once called gráft a dirty business and dismissed it at that. A basis for a discriminating attitude had been growing ever since the war, preparing us for the "Roosevelt Revolution." A nation that had been obliged to quench its thirst for fourteen years with the aid of bribery had also accustomed itself to the idea of chiseling on income tax returns and "fixing" traffic violations. Familiarity opened the way to a better understanding of the problem, which is one of economics rather than morality. In the feudal era, which America escaped, the taking of interest had been a sin, graft the legitimate perquisite of a public job. The growth of trade made the banker respectable and the bought official a crook.

Ever since the days of Argall, the newer idea had clashed with the remnants of the feudal theory of perquisites in office. Attempts to harmonize the two, although effecting improvements in public ethics, had been based on the fallacy that economic difficulties are susceptible of a purely political solution. For 300 years commerce, agriculture and industry stubbornly refused to fit themselves into a preconceived governmental pattern. They were always more likely to mold government to their own purposes, corruptly if it could not be done in a cheaper way.

As a nation, the United Stated started with the elimination of some grafts that had been hallowed by British tradition. The open sale of jobs, embezzlement of government funds, the piracies of the Bloomsbury Gang, had been well within the prevailing code for peers and gentlemen. The Revolution deprived these lordly practices of moral sanction.

These and later reforms, however, were direct blows at the sacredness of private property. The perquisites of office ceased to be owned by the individual as he owned a farm or factory. Therefore, every attempt to curb graft was resisted by those interests that denied the power of the people as represented by government to control the operation of private enterprise. Throughout our history, the masters of capital have regarded any attack on property rights as far more revolutionary than attacks on human rights—"men owning property should do what they like with it," J. P. Morgan used to insist. For that reason the denial of human rights, which is Fascism, has seemed more tolerable to such men than the denial of profit, which is Communism.

For the most part graft was the weapon that the Morgans used to enforce their claim. Graft thus became the handmaiden of profits, the indispensable persuader that reconciled the people's servants to a more exclusive policy than the general welfare. Ethical taboos were of no avail in checking the traffic. Samuel Argall's one unwavering supporter was Warwick, who wanted government license for his buccaneers; the land grabbers were the steady friends of every grafting governor; the railway looters were constant allies of the party of the largest grants and subsidies; Tammany never had stronger backers than Thomas Fortune Ryan and William C. Whitney, the franchise snatchers.

These men reconciled through graft the innate antagonism between government, whose theoretical aim is the development and protection of the national resources for everybody, and our system of private enterprise, whose purpose is to turn those resources to individual profit. Reformers who have sought to abolish the graft without abolishing the system that makes it inevitable have earned the just contempt of practical men. Statesmen who have improved on the older, cruder methods of corruption have earned the gratitude of the country.

Graft in moderation has always been tolerated as readily as any other form of gain. Only in those fields such as prostitution and racketeering where profit itself has been frowned upon as anti-social is government support of private enterprise condemned altogether. The corruption that protects this dishonest or dirty graft has grown less, and periodic housecleanings have taught most of us the remedy for it. It can be curbed if not eliminated by vigilance, publicity and careful guarding of the civil service from spoilsmen. That would leave only the normal cussedness of human nature to contend with in these departments.

Honest or subtle graft is not so platitudinously disposed of, for it is to public life what profit is to private enterprise. Both are essential to our economic system. The great advances in the American standard of political honesty have been limited by the needs of capitalism, and the graft that faithfully serves industry and trade has aroused no mass resentment. Webster's services to New England mills and banks, Douglas's work for the Illinois Central, are examples of the modest graft that brings no popular wrath to visit the practitioner. The progress they fostered was generally admired and the profits not so great as to arouse uncontrollable envy.

That sort of graft is recognized as actually corrupt only when the beneficiaries amass gains of such proportions that they warrant attack. The excessive size of the fortunes wrested from privileges bestowed by the government rather than the method of obtaining the privileges led to criticism

of Huntington's Central Pacific loot, Penrose's tariff mongering or Mellon's tax manipulation. Yet it ought to be plain
that the degree of corruption cannot be controlled very
strictly as long as the form of corruption is sanctioned. The
only safeguard against abuse is the individual's good taste
and restraint, a most unsatisfactory bulwark.

The true solution of the problem is to overthrow the
economy of profit for one of use. Meanwhile the alertness or
indifference of the bulk of the population will decide
whether the graft we tolerate leads in the direction of greater
private concentration of industrial wealth or preserves some
slight economic independence for the average citizen. At the
end of the first road lies Fascist regimentation in the interest
of big business, which will then have acquired the complete
domination of government that is the aim of all important
graft. The second road has no end; it is the treadmill by
which we maintain the status quo in graft as in industrial organization until the evils of the system force us to detour into
a third road—Revolution.

BIBLIOGRAPHY

BIBLIOGRAPHY

Newspapers and news letters of the times covered in this book have been consulted for light on the contemporary scene. The principal authorities for the facts contained in the narrative, however, are listed below:

Adams, Charles Francis, Jr., *An Autobiography*.
Adams, Charles Francis, Jr., and Henry, *Chapters of Erie*.
Adams, Henry, *The Education of Henry Adams*.
Adams, James Truslow, *The Founding of New England*.
—— *Provincial Society*.
—— *Revolutionary New England*.
Adams, John, *Works*.
Adams, John Quincy, *Diary*.
Alvord, Clarence W., *The Mississippi Valley in British Politics*.
American State Papers, Public Lands Series.
Beard, Charles A., *An Economic Interpretation of the Constitution*.
—— *Economic Origins of Jeffersonian Democracy*.
Beard, Charles A., and Mary R., *The Rise of American Civilization*.
Beer, George L., *British Colonial Policy*.
Beer, Thomas, *Hanna*.
Biddle, Nicholas, *Correspondence*.
Blaine, Mrs. James G., *Letters*.
Boettiger, John, *Jake Lingle*.
Boutwell, George S., *Reminiscences of Sixty Years*.
Bowers, Claude G., *Jefferson and Hamilton*.
—— *The Tragic Era*.
Brown, Alexander, *The Genesis of the United States*.
Calendar of Colonial State Papers.
Calendar of Virginia State Papers.
Chambers, Walter, *Samuel Seabury*.
Colden, Cadwallader, *Papers*.
Congressional Globe.
Congressional Record.
Corey, Lewis, *The House of Morgan*.
Craven, Wesley W., *Dissolution of the Virginia Company*.
Croly, Herbert, *Marcus Alonzo Hanna*.

Daugherty, Harry M., and Thomas Dixon, *The Inside Story of the Harding Tragedy.*
Davenport, Walter, *Power and Glory.*
Depew, Chauncey, *My Memories of Eighty Years.*
Dewey, Davis R., *Financial History of the United States.*
Dictionary of American Biography.
Documents Relating to the Colonial History of the State of New York.
Donaldson, Thomas, *The Public Domain.*
Dunn, A. W., *From Harrison to Harding.*
Force, Peter, *Tracts.*
Foulke, W. D., *Fighting the Spoilsmen.*
Franklin, Benjamin, *Writings.*
Gruening, Ernest, *The Public Pays.*
Hallgren, Mauritz A., *The Gay Reformer.*
Hamilton, Alexander, *Works.*
Haney, Lewis, *A Congressional History of Railroads to 1850.*
Hansl, Proctor W., *Years of Plunder.*
Hart, Albert Bushnell, *American History Told by Contemporaries.*
Haskins, Charles H., *The Yazoo Land Companies.*
Haynes, Roy A., *Prohibition Inside Out.*
Howe, Frederic C., *The Confessions of a Reformer.*
Hughes, Charles Evans, *Report on Aircraft Inquiry.*
Jackson, Andrew, *Correspondence.*
James, Marquis, *Andrew Jackson.*
Jefferson, Thomas, *Writings.*
Josephson, Matthew, *The Politicos.*
—— *The Robber Barons.*
Kingsbury, Susan Myra (editor), *The Records of the Virginia Company of London.*
Lindley, Ernest K., *Half Way with Roosevelt.*
Lindsey, Ben, *The Beast and the Jungle.*
Lynch, Denis T., *Boss Tweed.*
—— *An Epoch and a Man, Martin Van Buren and His Times.*
Lundberg, Ferdinand, *America's Sixty Families.*
Maclay, William, *Journal.*
McClure, Alexander K., *Abraham Lincoln and Men of War-Time.*
—— *Old Time Notes of Pennsylvania.*
McConaughy, John, *Who Rules America?*
Maryland Archives.
Merz, Charles, *The Dry Decade.*
Millis, Walter, *The Martial Spirit.*
Myers, Gustavus, *History of Great American Fortunes.*
—— *History of Public Franchises in New York City.*

Myers, Gustavus, *History of Tammany Hall.*
Nevins, Allen, *Hamilton Fish.*
New York City, *Report of Special Committee of the Board of Aldermen Appointed to Investigate the "Ring" Frauds.*
New York State (Assembly), *Erie Railway Investigation* (1873).
—— *Mazet Investigation* (1900).
New York State (Senate), *Fassett Investigation* (1890).
——*Lexow Investigation* (1895).
New York State (Joint Legislative Committee), *Seabury Investigations* (1931-32).
North Carolina, *Colonial Records.*
Oberholtzer, Ellis P., *Jay Cooke.*
O'Connor, Harvey, *Mellon's Millions.*
Pennsylvania (House of Representatives), *Report of Select Committee on Alleged Frauds in Election of United States Senator* (Simon Cameron, 1863).
Platt, Thomas C., *Autobiography.*
Polk, James K., *Diary.*
Pringle, Henry, *Theodore Roosevelt.*
—— *Big Frogs.*
Ramsay, M. L., *Pyramids of Power.*
Sakolski, A. M., *The Great American Land Bubble.*
Scott, William R., *The Constitution and Finance of English, Scottish and Irish Joint Stock Companies to 1720.*
Smyth of Nibley Papers.
Steffens, Lincoln, *Autobiography.*
Stolberg, Benjamin, and Warren Jay Vinton, *The Economic Consequences of the New Deal.*
Sullivan, Mark, *Our Times.*
Sumner, William G., *The Financier and the Finances of the American Revolution.*
Symmes, John C., *Correspondence.*
United States
    Board of Tax Appeals, *A. W. Mellon vs. Commissioner of Internal Revenue.*
    Federal Trade Commission, *Report on the Electric Power and Gas Utilities Inquiry.*
    General Land Office, *Annual Reports of Commissioners.*
    National Commission on Law Observance and Law Enforcement, *Report on the Enforcement of the Prohibition Laws.*
    Pacific Railway Commission, *Report* (1887).
    Testimony Taken by.

War Industries Board, *Final Report of the Chairman.*
Minutes.
United States House of Representatives
  Investigation of Defalcations of Samuel Swartwout and Others (25th Congress).
  Report of Committee on Public Lands (30th Congress).
  Investigation of Government Contracts, Civil War (37th Congress).
  Gold Panic Investigation (41st Congress).
  Report Concerning Frauds and Wrongs Committed Against the Indians (42d Congress).
  Report of the Poland Committee on Crédit Mobilier (42d Congress).
  Report of the Wilson Committee on Crédit Mobilier (42d Congress).
  Report on Expenditures in the War Department, World War (66th Congress).
United States Senate
  Trial of Samuel Chase (1805).
  Report of Committee on Public Lands (23d Congress).
  Trial of William W. Belknap (44th Congress).
  Report of Commission to Investigate Conduct of the War Department in the War with Spain (56th Congress).
  Investigation of the War Department, World War (65th Congress).
  Steel Strike Investigation (66th Congress).
  Investigation of the Veterans Bureau (67th Congress).
  Investigation of the Attorney General (68th Congress).
  Teapot Dome Investigation (68th Congress).
  Investigation of the Bureau of Internal Revenue (69th Congress).
  Report on Senatorial Campaign Expenditures (69th Congress).
  Hearings on Oil Leases (70th Congress).
  Mexican Land Grants in California (71st Congress).
  Hearings on Stock Exchange Practices (72d and 73d Congresses).
  Air Mail Investigation (73d Congress).
  Munitions Investigation (73d and 74th Congresses).
  Lobbying Investigation (74th Congress).
Washington, George, *Writings.*
Werner, M. R., *Privileged Characters.*
—— *Tammany Hall.*
Wharton, Francis, *State Trials of the United States During the Administrations of Washington and Adams.*
Wharton, Samuel, *Case of William Trent and Other Traders.*
—— *Plain Facts.*
Willebrandt, Mabel W., *The Inside of Prohibition.*
Wolcott, Oliver, *Memoirs of the Administration of Washington and John Adams.*

INDEX

INDEX